THE IDEA OF CATHOLICISM

*An Introduction to the Thought
and Worship of the Church*

**Edited by Walter J. Burghardt, S. J.
and William F. Lynch, S. J.**

Greenwich Editions published by Meridian Books, Inc.

The editors were assisted in the preparation of this volume by the following:

Joseph A. Galdon, S.J.
John W. Healey, S.J.
Joseph G. Murray, S.J.
John S. Nelson, S.J.
Joseph L. Roche, S.J.
Edward V. Stevens, S.J.

IMPRIMI POTEST:
John M. Daley, S.J.
Provincial, Maryland Province, Society of Jesus
November 5, 1959

NIHIL OBSTAT:

Edward A. Cerny, S.S.
Censor, Archdiocese of Baltimore
January 11, 1960

IMPRIMATUR:

✠ Francis P. Keough, D.D.
Archbishop of Baltimore
January 12, 1960

The Imprimi potest, Nihil obstat, *and* Imprimatur *are official declarations that a book or pamphlet is free of doctrinal or moral error. No implication is contained therein that those who have granted the* Imprimi potest, Nihil obstat, *and* Imprimatur *agree with the contents, opinions or statements expressed.*

Greenwich Editions Original
First published 1960 by Meridian Books, Inc.

First printing 1960

Library of Congress Catalog Card Number: 60-6768

Manufactured in the United States of America

Typography and design by Bob Melson

Contents

Preface

The purpose of this book is to provide the serious student of Catholicism, be he Catholic or non-Catholic, with those materials which will put him in basic and solid contact with the theology and prayer of the Church.

There are many anthologies that serve a useful purpose in this direction. But we prefer to think that we have not composed an anthology. Rather, we have allowed the theologians of Europe and the United States, each of them skilled in a special way, to write a book for us; we have helped them, so to speak, in tying their separate competencies together and in unifying their separate images within a total painting. It is a painting of the total image of Catholicism, the parts not chosen at random but all set and related within the central and master ideas that unify them. We have ourselves chosen the master ideas and central patterns, though of course they were lying in wait for us. Within their illuminating power we have kept asking the editorial question: Who can competently explain the parts? In each and all we have held in mind the needs and the researches of the

serious man of books. After all, there can be a book on Catholicism
for every man.

Thus, the first part of the book presents the developmental structure
of the whole of Catholic theology, within such limits as any one book
can reach. As for the second part, we hope that it is a valuable extension and a useful novelty in the plans that have gone into any
similar study. We asked ourselves the further question: What documents, what basic useful materials, apart from all thinking out of
things, would the serious student of the Church want to have at hand
for ready use and consultation? We answered: the great creeds of the
Church; the text of the Mass; the liturgy of the sacraments; her central
prayers; the basic documents that throw light on the ascetical and
spiritual treasures of Catholicism; and some taste of the relationship
of the Church to the pressing, sometimes agonizing problems of our
contemporary world. The second half of our volume is an attempt to
form a little library of essential things.

So much, then, by way of preface for our two major divisions. But
what can a brief preface say about the plan, the theological structure,
of the first half of this book? One book gives so little space for the
accomplishment of so great a task as the constructing of The Idea of
Catholicism. And a few pages is so much less than that. But, no matter how lightly, let us sketch what we have tried to do.

The idea and the reality of Christ is the foundation stone on which
we build and the link by which we tie together all our chapters. But
before our writers enter upon the fulness of that reality, from the
Christic form of the whole created universe to the Christic form of
the inward life of the individual soul, they begin by placing us all,
believers or unbelievers, Catholic or non-Catholic, in the presence of
"the religious problem," in all its simplicity, in all its nakedness, as
it touches every heart in its most honest moments.

Once a man recognizes the religious problem in his own life, he
is in a position to see Catholicism for what it is: a transcendent act
of God in history and an answer to man's religious longings. For, as
all our remaining writers will indicate, Catholicism is unique. But it
is unique, not in the sense that Christ and the Church are just so
many more special interesting developments of the religious sense
and religious history. This book wishes to say that these two things,
Christ and the Church, *are* religion; they are not parts of it but
dominate it and define it as God sees it. They either cancel out every
other form or bring it to perfect fruition. The Idea of Christ is not
another idea of God; He is *the* Idea of God, the eternal Logos and
Son. This is the scandal which St. Paul preached to that scientific
intelligence which loves all ideas and is willing to accept Christ as
another idea—but there is no other Word. The first of all the Christic
chapters has been written by the Editors, in order that this single
frame for the whole book might be the more easily projected and
summarized.

For in one form or other Christ occupies and possesses all that is to come. And when we say "in one form or other," we mean exactly that; for He has many forms and shapes. He is looked forward to and slowly reached by all the forms of the religious story of the human race as it is told in the Old Testament and as it is told here in an analytic way by Fr. Charlier. He is not only the single, historical Son of Mary, born two thousand years ago, true God and true Man. He also has a historical life and form which goes beyond the single life which ended on Calvary. He takes on a great social form, for He is the Church, which is His Mystical Body. He has a sacramental existence in the Eucharist. He has a "touch" for us, and that touch is found in the sacraments. He has a mother, and He has a vicar in the papacy. And finally, and in a way most relevant of all for us, He has a life and a form in the very inward life and form of our own souls. Already from all eternity He was and is the one Form and Logos from which every form and substance, every art and science, has been derived; but now, in the Christian scheme, He *is* all those things and processes. Logos incarnate, He is indeed all in all. And it is all these forms that are described and analyzed for us by different theologians in practically every page of this work.

If, then, the book is to make easy and unified reading, it is recommended that the reader keep his mind and eye on Christ. For He has been sent by God. He stands midway between the eternal life of the Trinity and that eternal life which will be given to us and which will consist in the possession of the inward recesses of the Trinitarian life. Until that day He is for all of us the Mediator, standing in-between. His vocation is to give life to all things in-between. The vocation of this book is to show how that is so.

Part

Part 1

The Perennial Sense of Religion

The Meaning of God
Emmanuel Cardinal Suhard

Belief in One God
John Henry Newman

The Master Idea of Christian Morality
Bernard Häring, C.SS.R.

PREFACE

The religious sense is present in every man. At some time or other the religious problem must be faced by all. No matter how much we try to hide or disguise this powerful depth and need in the soul, it is there, doing its work and demanding to be filled.

In this first section we listen to the majestic description of this "sense of God" as it was written for war-torn France by the remarkable Cardinal Suhard. Then the mind of Cardinal Newman, possibly the greatest Catholic mind of the last hundred years, applies all its marvelous sensitivity to an exploration of the human feelings and the human conscience as these things are affected by the question of God. And finally Fr. Häring carries us through a thoughtful analysis of the perennial problem of the moral life, raising it to its proper height and dignity, where morality is not a mere code of action but a law of life which places us in personal contact with the living God. We thought it would be helpful if these chapters were read before the reader turned to an examination of the Catholic Idea in its pure form. They will do much to prevent the reading of the subsequent chapters out of a spirit of mere scientific curiosity and will ensure that Catholicism be seen as the unique thing that it really is for the religious sense and for religious history.

Emmanuel Cardinal Suhard

The Meaning of God

THE ABSENCE OF GOD

The contemporary world has been often defined as the age of the machine in which everything is relative; but the civilization of the present day can be defined more accurately by a feature which marks it off from any civilization which has preceded it. It is an age without God.

This absence of God causes contempt today among the most diverse kinds of men. It is not an evil on the surface of life; nor is it a geographical absence, as though God were missing from certain regions only. It is a chronic and universal absence, at one and the same time a fact and a deliberate intention. God is absent, banished, expelled from the very heart of life. Society has closed up on that exclusion and the resulting emptiness, a desert without God, is a void from which it is dying.

It would take a book, not merely a letter, if we were to try to enumerate all the forms of contemporary atheism. It is enough to realize this if we look at the posters in the streets, the pictures in magazines, the headlines in the press, the publicity given to certain films and novels. Nor could we hope to carry out such an analysis in a few pages, as much qualification would be needed.

We are concerned more with making Catholics realize this absence of God acutely and even painfully than with enumerating its different aspects. We must escape the slow movement of asphyxiation, and the need is urgent, by one of indignation. "God is absent from the towns, the countryside, laws . . . manners . . . art. He is absent even from the life of religion in the sense that those who still wish to be His friends do not need His presence." [1]

This last assertion may cause surprise. But need we be surprised if this universal atheism affects Christians themselves? Because they have to breathe that atmosphere they are in the end impregnated by it. The subtle poison is drawn in through all the senses, the deadly peril being that it does not kill its victims but immunizes them against itself. Thus we do not have to go far to find the godless. They are found at every step. A large number of baptized Christians, while they are not genuine atheists, in practice live and act like atheists. . . .

In any case everything comes back to the central question: do we possess the meaning of God? In other words, do the paganizing surroundings imperceptibly color us? Have we kept the notion of God sufficiently high and sufficiently pure? We are engaged in the temporal —is our engagement sufficiently situated in the perspectives of the faith?—for without them our reforms would be neither legitimate nor successful. Does the meaning of man eclipse in us the meaning of God? Is God for us always God?

The first danger concerns the very notion of God. The accent is put on everything that brings Him near to man: God as Father rather than God as Master. He is "Our Father," but on earth rather than "in heaven," a good God rather than the Sovereign Judge. Of the Word of God we have especially retained the adjective "Incarnate," and Christ has become the Friend, the Confidant, the Elder Brother, the model of life for multitudes of souls. But His Sacred Humanity, which was wholly referred and absolutely faithful to the Father, the Lord who grafts us upon the intimate life of the love of the three persons— all that takes the second place. Our age has fortunately rediscovered the extraordinary brotherly character of the Son of Man but misses the mystery of the Son of God. We regard the coming of God into the world as a prodigious event and point to His action in history as at once directing it and giving it meaning. But not to see beyond that role, to forget that God has raised man towards Himself, comes near to making God a means for the service of the world rather than a Being sufficient to Himself apart from us. In short, we keep the

●

[1] Léon Bloy.

immanence of God [2] and are in danger of forgetting His transcendence.

What is happening? Without our realizing it the great systems of philosophy and the great currents in the modern world with which our intelligence and sensibilities are entangled, inevitably exercise a contagious influence and penetrate the very bases of our faith. All the time "the meaning of man" tends to take the place in us of "the meaning of God."

Scientific discovery is directing everything towards technical achievement and the domination of material forces, and in the battle against all forms of enslavement *homo faber* expels *homo sapiens* and any form of disinterested contemplation. At the same time as man's power over things increases so also do his liberty and his autonomy. Man has the knowledge and the power; he is self-sufficient and has become his own center of interest. The majority of the modern tendencies in philosophy lead to atheistic humanism; and this is an abuse. In former days the attacks of heresy were directed against a dogma; during the last century they envisaged all dogmas. But at the same time a certain deism was still tolerated. Today the denial is the most radical of all, for the besetting sin of the modern age, as it was in the Old Testament, is idolatry, the idolatry of man.

This conclusion clearly applies to the atheist; it applies also in a lesser but more subtle degree to the children of light themselves, for whom concentration upon man threatens to become a fatal poison. It consists in a reversal of values, in grafting God on man and not man on God. "What interests us is not God as He is in Himself, but man, the world and its explanation, an answer to which must be found. Once the explanation has been given there is no need to look further. . . . We have ceased to be aware of God in Himself but only of God in us, that is of ourselves in our relation with God." [3] Everything is done as though God were at the service of man, as though He had a part to fulfil in relation to man, namely, the perfecting of the individual or of society.

Such a reversal of viewpoints, if it were once accepted, would destroy all religion. It would also contradict the whole of Scripture as well as the tradition of the Fathers and the Doctors of the Church. God made to our size, God in this human form, would cease to be God. . . .

The problem . . . raises the whole question of humanism as well as the whole question of God. How much room does the meaning of God leave for the meaning of man? What rights does the kingdom of God leave for the city of man?

●

[2] Even though this word was recently disputed, we must use it in the meaning given to it in contemporary writing and in connection with the ideas of St. Thomas, expressed for instance in the title he gives to question 8 of "The Existence of God in All Things."

[3] H. Paissac, "L'Athéisme des chrétiens," *Vie spirituelle: Supplément.* May 15, 1947.

At one extreme are those for whom they leave nothing. This world of ours must not only not be pursued for itself but we must not try to make it better or transform it. It is corrupt beyond redemption, an evil world, a closed system, the plaything of the dialectics of history and of technical change, and thus it admits of no "conversion." The world and grace are two different planes which call for divorce and not for reconciliation. The duty of the Christian is not to shape events or structures but to witness to the transcendence and the eternity of God, even to scandal.

This theoretical position is really based on two facts. Its followers point first of all to the many deviations we have just mentioned in the religious life of the present day and conclude that humanism has failed spiritually: it is an obstacle between the soul and God. To attempt to put God into the world is a hopeless task, the eternal temptation of making heaven on earth, the sin of idolatry. There is one way only of escaping from it, namely, to return to a transcendental outlook and to find asylum unconditionally in the mystery of a sovereign and absolute Being compared with whom any interest taken in the things of this world is necessarily missing the point and procrastination.

In the present distress of the world is not this precisely what is revealed by the unconquerable instinct impelling man to seek outside himself the achievements larger than himself which he needs? With the unbeliever this instinct emerges in obscure substitutes for God, entities touchingly and defiantly deified such as Fraternity, Progress, Peace, Humanity—all of them impersonal substitutes for the God they do not know and think they do not seek. Next, how can we explain the extraordinary fascination now obvious among many Catholics for some Eastern religions except because they find in them a sense of the absolute and of divine contemplation which Western Christianity, too geared to natural methods, does not, they think, give them to the same degree? . . .

Against this exalted idealism and a supernatural position which looks elsewhere, the upholders of immanence bring forward the great fact of the Incarnation. If God has sent His Son into the world and made Him the model of the perfect man, He intended thereby to show us the road to follow, namely, that we must reach God through man, through the holy humanity the Word assumed. If He shed his blood on earth, how is it possible short of blasphemy not to maintain that He did so except to redeem it? Ought not the efforts of the disciple of Christ be efforts in the world, in order to complete the redemption done by its Head?

Even those, however, who have chosen to engage themselves in the temporal (and we remind you here, without repeating the reasons we have already given, that this is a pressing duty for every Christian) are anxious. For they know only too well that those attempting to complete creation—to "increase and possess the earth"—and to organize the world to the image of the kingdom of heaven are in danger of becoming so enamored of their task that they may forget the other city which it ought to mirror and towards which it should lead. A degradation of values is thus caused whereby what is specifically Christian loses its savor and disappears. The spirit of the apostolate can become proselytism or recruitment, charity can become philanthropy or party comradeship, hope merely trust in the indefinite possibility of progress; faith in man deprives man of that in him which makes his genuine nobility, namely, that he is incapable of completing himself except by going beyond the possibilities within him and by embracing vistas larger than his own. . . .

Only the theology of God, by showing that these two unilateral conceptions are complementary, will make their reconciliation possible, and only it will enable us to save the meaning of man by returning to the meaning of God.

THE TRUE GOD

What are the sources from which we draw a proper knowledge of God? The Church formally says there are two, the first being reason, which proves to us that God exists and can moreover tell us something authentic about His nature although in a very summary fashion. The Vatican Council enlarges on this double power and duty of the human mind. "Whoever says that the one and only true God, our Creator and Lord, cannot be known with certainty by the natural light of the human reason by means of created things, let him be anathema."[4]

But in reality and by right such meager knowledge yields place to an infinitely deeper and warmer knowledge, that of revelation. "God," says Pascal, "speaks of God," but man does not. It is therefore in the Bible that Christians will find what God teaches about Himself, as well as in tradition, in the writings of the magisterium and the Doctors of the Church, which form the complementary and living source of faith.

It need scarcely be said that in these pages it is not our intention to recall or even to sketch a treatise on God. Our purpose is to take some of these inspired texts and show that in them God appears constantly and at the same time in two aspects which are apparently contradictory: He is sometimes transcendent and apart, at others present to man and immanent in the world.

We advise all who feel hemmed in by a closed and stifling world to open the Old and the New Testaments. They will there find vistas which will liberate them, and the excellent food of the only true God.

The first element when we meet God will be that of mystery. God is the Inaccessible, and He is inaccessible for all. "No one has seen

●

[4] Denz. 1806.

20

God," says St. John (Jn 1:18); and even for those to whom God gives
Himself to be known He remains the hidden God. "Show me thy
face, that I may know thee," asked Moses, only to receive the categorical answer: "Thou canst not see my face: for man shall not see
me and live" (Ex 33:13, 20). No illusion is therefore possible: God
remains the incomprehensible, and the human mind possesses no key
which can unlock His secret. All that the human mind at its best can
experience is fear and consternation at the impenetrable mystery. Of
God man knows that he does not understand Him, and that all he
sees of Him is His shadow falling on the things of this world: He
remains inaccessible, in His intimate reality, to the eyes of the spirit.
"Verily thou are a hidden God" (Is 45:15). "We realize how majestic
the nature of God is," says St. Gregory of Nyssa, "not by understanding it but because it cannot be proved by any demonstration or
grasped by our intellectual powers," [5] and St. Augustine insists just
as much: "God is not what you imagine or what you think you understand. If you understand you have failed." St. Thomas in his turn does
not try to feed our pretensions or our flippancy.[6] God is darkness. To
know God is to realize that we do not know Him.

This conclusion does not mean, as some philosophers maintain, that
God cannot be known by reason; it merely makes clear that the
created mind is too small to encompass and seize the Infinite Being.
God is utterly beyond any ability of ours. Christian philosophy tells
us that there are two ways of reaching him. The first and royal road
consists in saying of God all that we know of created perfection and
developing this to an infinite degree, and by extension to the nth
degree to try and gain some idea of a perfection that is infinite and
uncreated. We arrive at it by the principle of causality and analogy;
and our knowledge of God is thus neither a myth, nor false, nor
exhaustive; it is meager and relative.

But the mind has a second road to God, the way of negation, the
opposite of the first. In order to be certain that we do not contradict
the Infinite, by bringing Him within our categories, we deny of Him all
that we affirm of ourselves, and we define Him by all that we ourselves
are not.[7] The philosophers and the theologians, but especially the
great spiritual writers, thus sought to know God by denying any
common measure between His being and the world. "All the being
of creatures is nothing when compared with the infinite being of God.
. . . Not one of them comes even close to God, or has any likeness to
His being.[8] "There is not merely a difference of degree but of essence:
I am who am, thou art who art not," our Lord said to St. Catherine

●

[5] St. Gregory of Nyssa, *In Cant. hom.* 12.
[6] Cf. *In Boet. de Trinitate*, q. 1, a. 2, ad 1m; *Expositio super Dionysium de divinis nominibus*, c. 7, lect. 4.
[7] Cf. St. Thomas, *C. gent.* 1, 30.
[8] St. John of the Cross, *Ascent of Mt. Carmel* 1, 6.

of Siena. "Every created thing considered in itself is nothingness";[9] and St. John of the Cross goes even further: "the beauty, the grace, and the attractiveness of creatures, when compared in their entirety with the beauty of God, are utterly ugly and horrible."

These phrases and many another are not rhetorical developments, nor are they condemnations of the work of our Creator; their whole aim is to isolate for us the absolute transcendence of God.

At the very moment God allows Himself to be known to us, He remains separate, quite other from us. Between His immaculate pureness and man, infirm, weakened and sordid, the gulf cannot be bridged: "Come not nigh hither; put off the shoes from thy feet," God ordered Moses from the burning bush (Ex 3:5), for He is "the Holy One of Israel" (Is 1:4). Respect and trembling are the sentiments which are least adapted to recognize His mystery.[10] Adoration is the inescapable condition always, even in heaven: "Holy, holy, holy is the Lord God, the Almighty" (Ap 5:8). Faced with God, the children of Adam know they are radically impure and are thereby unworthy to continue in life. God has no equal: "To whom then have you likened God? Or what image will you make for Him?" He has Himself asked (Is 40:18).

He is for this reason the sovereign Lord: "I am the Lord, and there is none else: there is no God besides me" (Is 45:5; 43:13; etc.), the Living God, self-sufficing, in no way bound to explain Himself to us, to whom must go all obedience and all homage: "I am the Lord thy God, mighty, jealous" (Ex 20:5).

He is the master and free: His revelation erupts into the life of man and disturbs our established institutions. Abraham had to leave Ur of the Chaldees, Moses to lead his people through the desert in spite of his attempt to avoid the task, for God's interests take first place over ours. He has His plan, and His ways are beyond our scrutiny, He is the master of time and of history; He manipulates both as He wishes: "for my thoughts are not your thoughts; nor your ways my ways" (Is 60:8). This mastery of God over the development of the world is beyond the ability of man to grasp, for we look upon the events of time as we would wish them to be.

What is true of the Old Testament is true also of the New. "Mosaic and prophetic revelation was not destroyed, it was consummated in the gospel. The affirmation that God is one, that He is the sole Lord and loved above everything created, was to be as sacred to the Christian as much as and even more than it has been to the Jew." [11] Our Lord did not cease to point to the infinite majesty of His Father: "Why dost thou call me good? None is good, except God only" (Mk 10:18).

●

[9] St. Thomas, *Sum. theol.* 1-2, q. 109, a. 2, ad 2m.
[10] Yahweh was "feared" by Isaac: Gn 31:53; Jacob "trembled": Gn 28:16; cf. for the same meaning Heb 10:34.
[11] Jules Lebreton, S.J., *Lumen Christi: La doctrine spirituelle du Nouveau Testament* (14th ed.; Paris: Beauchesne, 1948) p. 5.

His sovereignty was without division: "You are not to claim the title of Rabbi; you have but one Master, and you are all brethren alike. Nor are you to call any man on earth father; you have but one Father, and He is in heaven" (Mt 23:7-8). Our Lord mystified His contemporaries as much as Yahweh had mystified their ancestors: Israel expected a victorious Messiah and the Son of Man told them of the ruin of Jerusalem and of the Cross. The mystery of God's ways remains inscrutable to man: there also God is apart from man.[12]

Having reached this stage in his researches, it seems that the Christian has no need to choose; his road seems inexorably laid down: to divorce himself from the world and take refuge in transcendence, with the two consequences which are inevitable in relation to actual life, the end of humanism and the end of history. How should humanism be other than blasphemy when every created value is worthless and there is not merely an abyss but a contrast between the High God and the worthless dust we are? [13] How can any interest taken in this fleeting life be other than madness if our last end be considered, and an inexcusable frivolity with the eternal? How can man's attempt to constitute a human order not escape the charge of idolatry—that sin which more than any other calls down the anger of Yahweh? Since God is the great one apart, since He is not "immanent" in His creature, the latter cannot as such situate itself outside Him without being against him. Whatever we do, the "meaning of man" goes directly against the "meaning of God," and the meaning of God is precisely the greatest lesson and the constant reminder of the whole of the Bible.

The same is true of history. Since God seems to despise "our ways" and bothers with them merely in order to upset the normal course of events by disconcerting interventions, we can no longer talk of the developments in time or of the progress of society and of human institutions. God does not act from within but from without, in a completely external way. He does not arrive from this side of things but from the other. An "eschatological" direction must therefore take the place of the views of history. Our Saviour did not teach us to say

●

[12] The teaching of the Church is no less clear: "The Holy, Catholic, Apostolic, and Roman Church believes and confesses that there is one only true and living God, Creator and Lord of heaven and earth, all-powerful, eternal, immense, incomprehensible, infinite in intelligence, in will, and in every perfection, who, being a unique spiritual substance by nature, absolutely simple and unchangeable, must be declared distinct from the world in fact and by essence, happy in Himself and by Himself, and lifted above all that is and can be conceived outside of Him." Vatican Council, constitution *Dei Filius,* chap. 1.

[13] St. John of the Cross says so: "All the wisdom in the world and all human cleverness compared with the infinite wisdom of God is sheer and extreme ignorance. All the riches of the world and the glory of creation, compared with the wealth of God, are extreme and abject poverty." *Ascent of Mount Carmel* 1, 6.

"Our Father who are in our hearts" but "Our Father who art in heaven," and it is there and not here that we must look for Him and find Him in pure faith and contempt of the world.

But is this notion of God complete? He is apart. But is He not also the everywhere present? Scripture and tradition with equal certainty show this second aspect of God. He wished also to be God with us, a God who gives Himself.

The revelation of this began in the Old Testament with the idea of an alliance, which lays down from the beginning and with growing clearness that God is not only a mystery of infinity but a mystery of love. He calls Israel, then all the nations, to community with Him, first in the imperfect reconciliation made by the first "testament," then in the pardon and the intimate union of the new alliance in Jesus Christ. What else do the prophets proclaim if not the rigorous and tender love of "the God of Israel"? [14] Because if God seems to deny or upset history, this is not the contempt or the cruel game of a despot, but a tireless appeal to us to enlarge our vision.

He intervenes from without in order to transfigure us from within. Abraham had to leave his own country, but it was in order that he might become the father of those who believe; Moses had to obey even against his own will, but it was in order to save a people; St. Paul was thrown to the ground on the Damascus road, but it was in order to become the apostle of the Gentiles. God uses men and events to fulfil his plan of salvation. Can we say that He does not lead history? Will anyone say that the God Apart is not also everywhere present?

But this presence of God in its turn is merely a particular case of a more universal fact and intention, that God, by the fact of their creation, should be present in all creatures. "In Him we live, move, and have our being," says St. Paul (Acts 17:28). In some splendid pages of the *Summa,* St. Thomas takes up this statement of "God existing in things." [15] "As long as a thing has being, God must be present in it. . . . It is a necessary conclusion from this that God is in all things and in an intimate way." [16]

What reason teaches on this matter is exactly what is taught by Scripture: not pantheism, not the God of Aristotle wholly apart from

●

[14] Cf. Is 43:4; 49:10; cf. also the words of Jeremiah in the office of the Sacred Heart.
[15] *Sum. theol.* 1, q. 8, a. 1.
[16] A.-M. Sertillanges, O.P., *Dieu ou rien?*, pp. 87-88: "Our very being bathes in the being of God, who is the being of our being, if such an expression may be allowed; and there is immanence. . . . On the other hand, St. Thomas again says: 'God is incomparably lifted above every form of being,' and there is His transcendence. What isolates God and makes Him 'the Holy One' is the unique plenitude of God. . . . This plenitude is also the reason why nothing can subsist except in Him, a conceptual relationship we express by the term 'immanence' or more currently by 'God being present in all things.'"

a world He does not know. "The God of the Christians," writes Pope Pius XII, "is not an empty phrase . . . or an abstract idea decked out by thinkers. He transcends all that is, and everything that exists owes its existence to Him. . . . Millions of men can hurry through the streets . . . absorbed by their affairs . . . without ever thinking of God. Yet it is He who keeps them in existence." [17]

What, then, must we say of God's presence by grace in the soul, a presence which is not merely that of God the Creator immanent in His creature, but the intimacy of the three divine persons shared with us? "We will come and make our dwelling there" (Jn 14:23). The last word has been spoken, the very mystery made open to us: "God," says St. John, "is love." At once the double chasm is bridged; God's sovereignty is now seen to be love, seeking its own glory by communicating itself. God in Himself and God given to us are one, the Holy God is also Emmanuel, God with us. If we forget that gigantic reality—which is also certain—we lose sight of the meaning of God and fall into a Manichean conception of the relations between God and the world.

Transcendence and immanence are thus the two notions which the theology of God reveals to us and tells us never to separate. God is simple; but our minds are so made for understanding the world that they cannot imagine what the infinite is except by its relations with the finite, within or without, immanent or transcendent. A believer may try hard to convince himself of the shortcomings of his intelligence when confronted with the Absolute, and of the truth these two aspects simultaneously contain; but all he can do to express these opposites is to set them down side by side. The danger thereupon is great of retaining only one of the two terms: of seeing God only as opposite from the world, with the conclusion going with it that he must have nothing to do with the fatal and corrupt dialectic of this life; or on the contrary, of not seeing God except in the world and in life, with the danger of divinizing one or the other. In each case the result is secularism: God in the world or the world in God, each being the end of two distinct processes.

Those who hold uncontaminated transcendence do indeed see the majesty of God but they at once contradict it and injure it by limiting it; for they withdraw it from creation, mistake the rule of providence over the world, and are quite blind to the fact of Incarnation. At once, quite naturally, they tend in practice to isolation, to faith without works, to contemplation without the apostolate, to the Church deprived of her features in time. That attitude of refusal is the same which, according to the period and the problem, is called Quietism, Pessimism, or Jansenism.

On the other side, those who uphold an exclusive immanence forget

●

[17] Pius XII, in radio message to the United States Catechetical Congress; *Documentation catholique*, Dec. 8, 1946.

the infinity of God. Their wish to put God everywhere ends in with-drawing Him from everything; for what remains of a God who is present only in the world, a God who has ceased to be present to Himself, a God who is no longer God? What meaning is there in an immanence which is the immanence of no one or of nothing? Incar-nation presupposes being, and in the same way immanence postulates continuing existence and continuing self-sufficiency. It has been pointed out that the wish to humanize God in order to make Him closer to man is an error; God is close only if He is the High God; and far from denying transcendence, immanence all the time supposes it. Without it the world, far from being intelligible, is absurd, inexplicable, or guilty: inexplicable because it has no object, absurd because it has no reason for being, guilty because it sets itself up in competition with "Him apart from whom there is no God" (Is 45:5). We can indeed get rid of the problem by confusing God with the world, and at once the result is pantheism.

We once more find that the truth lies in uniting and harmonizing these two symmetrical statements. The God of Israel has the right to be called "the true God" because, combining all perfections, He is both pure spirit and creator, of whom it can be said "True praise of thee is silence," and "All ye works of the Lord, bless the Lord" (Dn 3:57). The problem is not solved by an abstract formula; the solution itself is alive and is found in a person, the Word of God. He is revealed to us by the Incarnation, "taking the nature of a slave" (Phil 2:7), come among men, at the same time the equal of the Father by His nature as God. The God of the philosophers is thus outstripped in grandeur, and that of the philanthropists in nearness to man. The Lord we adore is not a compromise of two extremes, but the completing of both in the mystery of His Person. Here again, and especially here, everything is unified and made perfect in love. Every-thing is explained by Him on condition that this statement is at once clarified. The expression "synthesis" and "unity" in God of the two words making up transcendence-immanence is capable of being wrongly understood and of giving the impression that they are on the same plane, that they are two complementary perfections inherent in the essence of God. It is quite clear that this is not true. Immanence is understood only of God's presence to created beings. Created be-ings, however, are not necessary beings; creation is the consequence of a free act in God, is not part of His nature, and adds nothing to Him.[18] God continues independently of the world with His infinite perfections. The brief analysis just made from the Bible and theology

●

[18] It has been pointed out that St. Albert the Great, in an obviously expanded sense, calls the world "an accident of God," meaning by this that the world is not essential to God but that He is essential to it, as substance is essential to accident and is part of the definition of accident. Cf. Sertil-langes, *op. cit.*, p. 87.

applies to a state of fact only, to a reality which is, but might not have been, or might have been different.

All the perspectives which the meaning of an incarnate God causes to faith and humanism are admissible only in the hypothesis of the economy of salvation, which revelation presents to us as a fact. To forget that, to forget that God created the world freely and out of love, and that He also saved it by the same means by becoming incarnate out of love, would be to lose the meaning of man and the meaning of God.

Both are bound up together, not by their depending upon each other, for God suffices to Himself, and immanence and Incarnation on His side are love absolutely and freely given; but in the sense that in its definition humanism is entirely dependent on the idea of God.

If God is only immanent, the consequence is pagan humanism; man is enclosed within himself, a prisoner in the world, and forever incapable of going beyond himself.

If God is only transcendent, the world loses all meaning, ceases to be related to the mind and the heart, becomes night and sin; man becomes a prey to an unappeasable disquiet.

But if God is "He who is," a high God as well as a near God, everything is different, and humanism is provided with two foundations.

The first comes from the fact of creation. To pledge oneself to action in the world is justified, because everything being upheld by the presence of God in everything, bears the imprint of the Creator. That presence and likeness exist more deeply in man, since in virtue of his spiritual nature he has been created to the image of God. But God is present in things not merely to preserve them in existence; by pure love He decided to become incarnate in the person of His Son. This second degree of immanence draws God closer to man, and thereby the world and mankind are consecrated.

Thus by divine adoption in Christ man assumes an infinitely higher likeness to God, for God places in him by His grace His living imprint.

By this double title—man as citizen of this earth and son of God—the whole Christian humanism is founded, and with that our temporal and supernatural engagement is entirely justified. On the one hand, man can and ought to root himself in the world, following the example of its Head; and that is a reason for his nobility. On the other hand, he is called to go infinitely beyond his own nature, and he already shares in the kingdom of heaven: *Conversatio nostra in coelis est:* our true home is in heaven (Phil 3:20).

The humanism of the Christian is thus founded in its whole extent, since it comes from the only lasting origin, that is, from God. The conclusion is crucial, and it does not appear as a new problem, but as the only solution for the theoretical and practical lack of certainty dividing Christians in the problem of their attitude towards the world. It is not a question, it need hardly be said, of exhausting here or even setting out the scheme of the vast problem of humanism. Others are busy in this matter, philosophers, theologians, and saints, for it is one of the most urgent problems of our day. We cannot emphasize enough how urgent and fruitful such an examination is if it remains closely faithful to itself and docile to the suggestions of the Church's magisterium. Our only object, in the same spirit in which we write our pastoral letter, *Growth or Decline?*, and in order to enrich from within the lines of action we then gave you, is to show that the meaning of God can alone safeguard the primacy of the spiritual and make legitimate and efficacious a wholehearted engagement in the temporal.

THE RETURN TO GOD

We are now able, in no arbitrary fashion, to see the ways this return to God must take; it is urgent and indispensable if the hesitations of Christians committed to action are to be resolved. . . . We must go to the root of the trouble, that is, the weakening of belief; as we pointed out at the beginning, this is the feature found in all contemporary errors. Many who believe are convinced they have the faith. In fact the God they honor is often a God created or modified by themselves. They do not accept; they choose, they do not receive, revelation; they elaborate a rational divinity, a dangerous counterfeit, a product of their own guilty errors.[19] God, we have seen, in mystery, and His infinite Being, escapes our grasp. The Absolute does not become known to us as the conclusion to a syllogism or as a clear and distinct idea. We shall only reach him by faith. That knowledge is certain knowledge because it is enlightened by love; but it will always remain obscure. The infinite is beyond our human experience; and the ineffable reality of a Trinitarian God is larger than any gesture or intuition we can make.

Must we therefore refuse to use our reason?

The whole effort made by theology is a standing witness to the contrary. Its rational elaboration does not start with man; it starts with revelation and stands on the authority of God. We do not therefore deduce God from history or from man, we receive Him as what He is, prodigious and free, as the Reality without answer or precedent.

The world and human life in this perspective are explained. "I am the First and the Last" (Is 48:12). "I am Alpha, I am Omega, the beginning of all things and their end" (Ap 1:8).

It is not He who is at our service but we who ought to gravitate towards Him as our life-giving end. This straightforward reversal of

●

[19] Pius XII, *Divini Redemptoris*: "Above all beings there is the unique Being, God. . . . It is not man's belief in God which makes God exist; it is because God exists that all men, if they do not deliberately close their eyes to the truth, believe in Him and address their prayers to Him."

direction eliminates any anthropomorphism from religious life and centers it truly on God by a surrender of self which is both respectful and disinterested. Where before we were sensitive to our rights, we become receptive to the idea that we have duties to God. . . .

The return to God must show itself most clearly by prayer.

We do indeed pray today, but we pray far too much for ourselves. Perhaps we also pray far too much for others, and then our prayer for them is spoilt by interest or takes the place of thanksgiving and praise. We must become conscious again of the grandeur and splendor of God, annihilate ourselves before His majesty, humbly recognize our sinfulness before His countenance, dedicate all things to His exclusive love.

An effort needs to be made to restore the sense of the sacred, the progressive weakening of which has been pointed out by many competent judges, to the external manifestations of religious life. In our Father in heaven we are tempted to see merely an easy-natured providence, and in His eternal Son a companion like ourselves. Let us therefore restore to the center of our own lives that "fear of God" and respect for actions and feelings which, far from harming the descent and intimate presence of love in the soul, on the contrary fittingly translate how deeply conscious we are of our smallness.

The liturgical revival which can be seen so successfully at work today will then produce all its fruits and will not be jeopardized by the obsession, lawful in intention but sometimes clumsy in procedure, of adapting it to modern society. The liturgy will undoubtedly be able to carry further all the values which uplift life, and harmonize the linguistic, aesthetic, and community methods which are clearly necessary if we are to draw all men into a truly Catholic worship. There is no question of returning to the pernicious individualism which dried up so many generations; we must continue more than ever to promote a community worship. But we must not be afraid to bring silence into it, a silence which is not the collective dumbness of individual worshipers but a community silence which unites all as brothers and lifts the soul to God.

This collective prayer which is so productive of good ought, however, to be always accompanied by or rather express a more profound and more secret intercourse with God. All prayer is not on the same plane. The best prayer is the prayer of which our Lord said: "When thou art praying, go into thy inner room and shut the door upon thyself, and so pray to thy Father in secret" (Mt 6:6). A disciple of Christ should be capable deliberately and alone of paying homage to God by shutting himself off from the world and forgetting himself in prayer. . . .

Contemplation contains two realities, each of which is different. The first, that of the contemplative separated from the world, is directed to keeping ever present and fresh the dialogue which united Christ to the Father in His long hours of prayer. The contemplative, indispensable to the Church, is dedicated by his state to witness to the transcendence of God. The duty of the Christian is to understand the contemplative; and that of the contemplative is to remain faithful to his mission.

But in ordinary language contemplation also means a reality more readily accessible; and it is to this form of it that we invite you. It is not necessary to be a theologian or a great mystic to reach it; it is enough to enter into oneself and approach God as a present and living person. It therefore consists above all in an effort of *direction:* instead of turning our prayer towards things and men, it is enough to turn it towards God.

The essence of contemplation is to make God our object, to place ourselves face to face with Him, to direct ourselves towards Him, as a river runs to the sea instead of wasting its waters in the sand or harmfully spreading them beyond its banks. When we look at God, who has no equal, all we need do is let the soul admire and be uplifted by His grandeur and His beauty. It is enough to let the soul sing and to tell God that we thank Him for all His goodness, to offer Him our work, our joy, our sorrow, and above all ourselves. The essential thing is to become humble before Him and to open ourselves to Him, letting Him invade the soul with His strength and gentleness. Contemplation is thus not a matter of human ingenuity; we make ourselves over without holding back, like children and time after time, to that inner grace ceaselessly at work upon us and uninterruptedly calling us to turn ourselves to God. . . .

The Christian is asked not to destroy or belittle the world but to assume it and sanctify it in order to offer it as a homage to God. It is in this that real incarnation resides, in the strength of God invading humanity in order to lift it up and bring it within the sphere of the life of God; and an understanding of His transcendence illuminates this incarnation and gives to it significance and meaning. For creation itself is from Him, and the element which constitutes creation is that it is a reflection and image of Him. Far from despising a work as valuable as this, the Christian understands creation because he sees it with the eyes of God and loves it dearly. He makes no gesture of refusal, utters no scarcely veiled regret for the attractiveness of human values—it is more a matter of his unconcealed joy sweeping him onwards to the triumphant plenitude of the infinity of God. No humanism can be complete without faith, for it alone enables us to view the world from the standpoint of God; and we owe to this theological virtue, which in some way assimilates us to God's own knowledge, that we can see the created world with the eyes of its Creator.[20]

We at once see on what conditions human endeavor is made possible and legitimate; it is not a question of how much, or of where, but of the spirit. Everything must be assumed in order that everything

●

[20] Cf. St. Thomas, *In Boet. de Trinitate*, q. 3, a. 1.

may be offered, and the movement of incarnation must be made to emerge in consecration; thereby we restore to God the universe He has entrusted to us and at once stamp this world with the sacred sign that it is meant to be ordered to Him.

We find that Christ Himself perfectly expressed this consecration in His prayer after the Last Supper: "I am not asking that thou shouldst take them out of the world, but that thou shouldst keep them clear of what is evil. . . . Keep them holy, then, through the truth. . . . Thou hast sent me into the world on thy errand, and I have sent them into the world on my errand; and I dedicate myself for their sakes, that they too may be dedicated through the truth" (Jn 17:15-19).

The feature which saves Christian humanism and differentiates it from atheistic humanism is the object towards which we try to direct it. In atheistic humanism everything is made for man and stops at man; Christian humanism, on the contrary, is theocentric: everything goes towards God, everything is for God.

Editor's Note.—From THE CHURCH TODAY: THE COLLECTED WRITINGS OF EMMANUEL CARDINAL SUHARD (Chicago: Fides, 1953) *pp. 173-211.*

John Henry Newman

Belief in One God

There is one God, such and such in nature and attributes.
I say "such and such," for, unless I explain what I mean by "one God,"
I use words which may mean anything or nothing. I may mean a mere
anima mundi; or an initial principle which once was in action and
now is not; or collective humanity. I speak then of the God of the
theist and of the Christian: a God who is numerically one, who is
personal; the Author, Sustainer, and Finisher of all things, the life of
law and order, the Moral Governor; one who is supreme and sole; like
Himself, unlike all things besides Himself which all are but His creatures; distinct from, independent of them all; one who is self-existing,
absolutely infinite, who has ever been and ever will be, to whom
nothing is past or future; who is all perfection, and the fulness and
archetype of every possible excellence, the Truth Itself, Wisdom, Love,
Justice, Holiness; one who is all-powerful, all-knowing, omnipresent,
incomprehensible. These are some of the distinctive prerogatives
which I ascribe unconditionally and unreservedly to the great Being
whom I call God.
   This being what theists mean when they speak of God, their assent

to this truth admits without difficulty of being what I have called a notional assent. It is an assent following upon acts of inference, and other purely intellectual exercises; and it is an assent to a large development of predicates, correlative to each other, or at least intimately connected together, drawn out as if on paper, as we might map a country which we had never seen, or construct mathematical tables, or master the methods of discovery of Newton or Davy, without being geographers, mathematicians, or chemists ourselves.

So far is clear; but the question follows, Can I attain to any more vivid assent to the Being of a God, than that which is given merely to notions of the intellect? Can I enter with a personal knowledge into the circle of truths which make up that great thought? Can I rise to what I have called an imaginative apprehension of it? Can I believe as if I saw? Since such a high assent requires a present experience or memory of the fact, at first sight it would seem as if the answer must be in the negative; for how can I assent as if I saw, unless I have seen? But no one in this life can see God. Yet I conceive a real assent is possible, and I proceed to show how.

When it is said that we cannot see God, this is undeniable; but still in what sense have we a discernment of His creatures, of the individual beings which surround us? The evidence which we have of their presence lies in the phenomena which address our senses, and our warrant for taking these for evidence is our instinctive certitude that they are evidence. By the law of our nature we associate those sensible phenomena or impressions with certain units, individuals, substances, whatever they are to be called, which are outside and out of the reach of sense, and we picture them to ourselves in those phenomena. The phenomena are as if pictures; but at the same time they give us no exact measure or character of the unknown things beyond them; for who will say there is any uniformity between the impressions which two of us would respectively have of some third thing, supposing one of us had only the sense of touch, and the other only the sense of hearing? Therefore, when we speak of our having a picture of the things which are perceived through the senses, we mean a certain representation, true as far as it goes, but not adequate.

And so of those intellectual and moral objects which are brought home to us through our senses: that they exist, we know by instinct; that they are such and such, we apprehend from the impressions which they leave upon our minds. Thus the life and writings of Cicero or Dr. Johnson, of St. Jerome or St. Chrysotom, leave upon us certain impressions of the intellectual and moral character of each of them, *sui generis,* and unmistakable. We take up a passage of Chrysostom or a passage of Jerome; there is no possibility of confusing the one with the other; in each case we see the man in his language. And so of any great man whom we may have known: that he is not a mere impression on our senses, but a real being, we know by instinct; that he is such and such, we know by the matter or quality of that impression.

Now certainly the thought of God, as theists entertain it, is not gained by an instinctive association of His presence with any sensible phenomena; but the office which the senses directly fulfil as regards creation, that devolves indirectly on certain of our mental phenomena as regards the Creator. Those phenomena are found in the sense of moral obligation. As from a multitude of instinctive perception, acting in particular instances, of something beyond the senses, we generalize the notion of an external world, and then picture that world in and according to those particular phenomena from which we started, so from the perceptive power which identifies the intimations of conscience with the reverberations or echoes (so to say) of an external admonition, we proceed on to the notion of a Supreme Ruler and Judge, and then again we image Him and His attributes in those recurring intimations, out of which, as mental phenomena, our recognition of His existence was originally gained. And, if the impressions which His creatures make on us through our senses oblige us to regard those creatures as *sui generis* respectively, it is not wonderful that the notices, which He indirectly gives us through our conscience, of His own nature are such as to make us understand that He is like Himself and like nothing else.

I have already said I am not proposing here to prove the Being of a God; yet I have found it impossible to avoid saying where I look for the proof of it. For I am looking for that proof in the same quarter as that from which I would commence a proof of His attributes and character—by the same means as those by which I show how we apprehend Him, not merely as a notion, but as a reality. The last indeed of these three investigations alone concerns me here, but I cannot altogether exclude the two former from my consideration. However, I repeat, what I am directly aiming at is to explain how we gain an image of God and give a real assent to the proposition that He exists. And next, in order to do this, of course I must start from some first principle; and that first principle, which I assume and shall not attempt to prove, is that which I should also use as a foundation in those other two inquiries, viz., that we have by nature a conscience.

I assume, then, that conscience has a legitimate place among our mental acts; as really so, as the action of memory, of reasoning, of imagination, or as the sense of the beautiful; that, as there are objects which, when presented to the mind, cause it to feel grief, regret, joy, or desire, so there are things which excite in us approbation or blame, and which we in consequence call right or wrong; and which, experienced in ourselves, kindle in us that specific sense of pleasure or pain, which goes by the name of a good or bad conscience. This being taken for granted, I shall attempt to show that in this special feeling, which follows on the commission of what we call right or wrong, lie the materials for the real apprehension of a Divine Sovereign and Judge.

The feeling of conscience (being, I repeat, a certain keen sensibility,

pleasant or painful—self-approval and hope, or compunction and fear
—attendant on certain of our actions, which in consequence we call
right or wrong) is twofold: it is a moral sense and a sense of duty;
a judgment of the reason and a magisterial dictate. Of course its act
is indivisible; still it has these two aspects, distinct from each other,
and admitting of a separate consideration. Though I lost my sense of
the obligation which I lie under to abstain from acts of dishonesty,
I should not in consequence lose my sense that such actions were an
outrage offered to my moral nature. Again, though I lost my sense
of their moral deformity, I should not therefore lose my sense that they
were forbidden to me. Thus conscience has both a critical and a
judicial office, and though its promptings, in the breasts of the
millions of human beings to whom it is given, are not in all cases
correct, that does not necessarily interfere with the force of its testimony and of its sanction: its testimony that there is a right and a
wrong, and its sanction to that testimony conveyed in the feelings
which attend on right or wrong conduct. Here I have to speak of
conscience in the latter point of view, not as supplying us, by means
of its various acts, with the elements of morals, such as may be developed by the intellect into an ethical code, but simply as the dictate of an authoritative monitor bearing upon the details of conduct
as they come before us, and complete in its several acts, one by one.

Let us then thus consider conscience, not as a rule of right conduct,
but as a sanction of right conduct. This is its primary and most authoritative aspect; it is the ordinary sense of the word. Half the world
would be puzzled to know what was meant by the moral sense; but
every one knows what is meant by a good or bad conscience. Conscience is ever forcing on us by threats and by promises that we must
follow the right and avoid the wrong; so far it is one and the same
in the mind of every one, whatever be its particular errors in particular
minds as to the acts which it orders to be done or to be avoided; and
in this respect it corresponds to our perception of the beautiful and
deformed. As we have naturally a sense of the beautiful and graceful
in nature and art, though tastes proverbially differ, so we have a
sense of duty and obligation, whether we all associate it with the
same certain actions in particular or not. Here, however, taste and
conscience part company: for the sense of beautifulness, as indeed
the moral sense, has no special relations to persons, but contemplates
objects in themselves; conscience, on the other hand, is concerned with
persons primarily, and with actions mainly as viewed in their doers,
or rather with self alone and one's own actions, and with others only
indirectly and as if in association with self. And further, taste is its
own evidence, appealing to nothing beyond its own sense of the
beautiful or the ugly, and enjoying the specimens of the beautiful
simply for their own sake; but conscience does not repose on itself,
but vaguely reaches forward to something beyond self, and dimly
discerns a sanction higher than self for its decisions, as is evidenced in

that keen sense of obligation and responsibility which informs them. And hence it is that we are accustomed to speak of conscience as a voice, a term which we should never think of applying to the sense of the beautiful; and moreover a voice, or the echo of a voice, imperative and constraining, like no other dictate in the whole of our experience.

And again, in consequence of this prerogative of dictating and commanding, which is of its essence, conscience has an intimate bearing on our affections and emotions, leading us to reverence and awe, hope and fear, especially fear, a feeling which is foreign for the most part, not only to taste, but even to the moral sense, except in consequence of accidental associations. No fear is felt by anyone who recognizes that his conduct has not been beautiful, though he may be mortified at himself, if perhaps he has thereby forfeited some advantage; but, if he has been betrayed into any kind of immorality, he has a lively sense of responsibility and guilt, though the act be no offence against society; of distress and apprehension, even though it may be of present service to him; of compunction and regret, though in itself it be most pleasurable; of confusion of face, though it may have no witnesses. These various perturbations of mind which are characteristic of a bad conscience, and may be very considerable—self-reproach, poignant shame, haunting remorse, chill dismay at the prospect of the future— and their contraries, when the conscience is good, as real though less forcible, self-approval, inward peace, lightness of heart, and the like— these emotions constitute a specific difference between conscience and our other intellectual senses—common sense, good sense, sense of expedience, taste, sense of honour, and the like—as indeed they would also constitute between conscience and the moral sense, supposing these two were not aspects of one and the same feeling, exercised upon one and the same subject matter.

So much for the characteristic phenomena which conscience presents, nor is it difficult to determine what they imply. I refer once more to our sense of the beautiful. This sense is attended by an intellectual enjoyment, and is free from whatever is of the nature of emotion, except in one case, viz., when it is excited by personal objects; then it is that the tranquil feeling of admiration is exchanged for the excitement of affection and passion. Conscience too, considered as a moral sense, an intellectual sentiment, is a sense of admiration and disgust, of approbation and blame: but it is something more than a moral sense; it is always what the sense of the beautiful is only in certain cases; it is always emotional. No wonder then that it always implies what that sense only sometimes implies; that it always involves the recognition of a living object towards which it is directed. Inanimate things cannot stir our affections; these are correlative with persons. If, as is the case, we feel responsibility, are ashamed, are frightened, at transgressing the voice of conscience, this implies that there is one to whom we are responsible, before whom we are ashamed, whose claims upon us we fear. If, on doing wrong, we feel the same tearful, broken-hearted sorrow which overwhelms us on hurting a mother; if, on doing right, we enjoy the same sunny serenity of mind, the same soothing, satisfactory delight which follows on our receiving praise from a father, we certainly have within us the image of some person to whom our love and veneration look, in whose smile we find our happiness, for whom we yearn, towards whom we direct our pleadings, in whose anger we are troubled and waste away. These feelings in us are such as require for their exciting cause an intelligent being: we are not affectionate towards a stone, nor do we feel shame before a horse or a dog; we have no remorse or compunction on breaking mere human law: yet, so it is, conscience excites all these painful emotions, confusion, foreboding, self-condemnation; and on the other hand it sheds upon us a deep peace, a sense of security, a resignation, and a hope, which there is no sensible, no earthly object to elicit. "The wicked flees, when no one pursueth"; then why does he flee? Whence his terror? Who is it that he sees in solitude, in darkness, in the hidden chambers of his heart? If the cause of these emotions does not belong to this visible world, the object to which his perception is directed must be supernatural and divine; and thus the phenomena of conscience, as a dictate, avail to impress the imagination with the picture of a Supreme Governor, a Judge, holy, just, powerful, all-seeing, retributive, and is the creative principle of religion, as the moral sense is the principle of ethics.

And let me here refer again to the fact, to which I have already drawn attention, that this instinct of the mind recognizing an external Master in the dictate of conscience, and imaging the thought of Him in the definite impressions which conscience creates, is parallel to that other law of, not only human, but of brute nature, by which the presence of unseen individual beings is discerned under the shifting shapes and colours of the visible world. Is it by sense, or by reason, that brutes understand the real unities, material and spiritual, which are signified by the lights and shadows, the brilliant ever-changing kaleidoscope, as it may be called, which plays upon their retina? Not by reason, for they have not reason; not by sense, because they are transcending sense; therefore it is an instinct. This faculty on the part of brutes, unless we were used to it, would strike us as a great mystery. It is one peculiarity of animal natures to be susceptible of phenomena through the channels of sense; it is another to have in those sensible phenomena a perception of the individuals to which this or that group of them belongs. This perception of individual things, amid the maze of shapes and colors which meets their sight, is given to brutes in large measures, and that apparently from the moment of their birth. It is by no mere physical instinct, such as that which leads him to his mother for milk, that the new-dropped lamb recognizes each of his fellow lambkins as a whole, consisting of many parts bound up in one, and, before he is an hour old, makes experience of his and their rival individualities. And much more distinctly do the horse and dog recognize even the personality of their master. How are we to explain this apprehension of things, which are one and individual, in the midst of a world of pluralities and transmutations, whether in the instance of brutes or again of children? But until we account for the knowledge which an infant has of his mother or his nurse, what reason have we to take exception at the doctrine, as strange and difficult, that in the dictate of conscience, without previous experiences or analogical reasoning, he is able gradually to perceive the voice, or the echoes of the voice, of a Master, living, personal, and sovereign?

I grant, of course, that we cannot assign a date, ever so early, before which he had learned nothing at all, and formed no mental associations, from the words and conduct of those who have the care of him. But still, if a child of five or six years old, when reason is at length fully awake, has already mastered and appropriated thoughts and beliefs, in consequence of their teaching, in such sort as to be able to handle and apply them familiarly, according to the occasion, as principles of intellectual action, those beliefs at the very least must be singularly congenial to his mind, if not connatural with its initial action. And that such a spontaneous reception of religious truths is common with children, I shall take for granted, till I am convinced that I am wrong in so doing. The child keenly understands that there is a difference between right and wrong; and when he has done what he believes to be wrong, he is conscious that he is offending one to whom he is amenable, whom he does not see, who sees him. His mind reaches forward with a strong presentiment to the thought of a Moral Governor, sovereign over him, mindful, and just. It comes to him like an impulse of nature to entertain it.

It is my wish to take an ordinary child, but still one who is safe from influences destructive of his religious instincts. Supposing he has offended his parents, he will all alone and without effort, as if it were the most natural of acts, place himself in the presence of God, and beg of Him to set him right with them. Let us consider how much is contained in this simple act. First, it involves the impression on his mind of an unseen Being with whom he is in immediate relation, and that relation so familiar that he can address Him whenever he himself chooses; next, of one whose good will towards him he is assured of, and can take for granted—nay, who loves him better, and is nearer to him, than his parents; further, of one who can hear him, wherever he happens to be, and who can read his thoughts, for his prayer need not be vocal; lastly, of one who can effect a critical change in the state of feeling of others towards him. That is, we shall not be wrong in holding that this child has in his mind the image of an invisible Being, who exercises a particular providence among us, who is present everywhere, who is heart-reading, heart-changing, ever-accessible, open to impetration. What a strong and intimate vision of God must he have already attained, if, as I have supposed, an ordinary trouble of mind has the spontaneous effect of leading him for consolation and aid to an invisible personal Power!

Moreover, this image brought before his mental vision is the image of one who by implicit threat and promise commands certain things which he, the same child coincidently, by the same act of his mind, approves; which receive the adhesion of his moral sense and judgment, as right and good. It is the image of one who is good, inasmuch as enjoining and enforcing what is right and good, and who, in consequence, not only excites in the child hope and fear—nay (it may be added), gratitude towards Him, as giving a law and maintaining it by reward and punishment—but kindles in him love towards Him, as giving him a good law, and therefore as being good Himself, for it is the property of goodness to kindle love, or rather the very object of love is goodness; and all those distinct elements of the moral law, which the typical child, whom I am supposing, more or less consciously loves and approves—truth, purity, justice, kindness, and the like—are but shapes and aspects of goodness. And having in his degree a sensibility towards them all, for the sake of them all he is moved to love the Lawgiver, who enjoins them upon him. And, as he can contemplate these qualities and their manifestations under the common name of goodness, he is prepared to think of them as indivisible, correlative, supplementary of each other in one and the same personality, so that there is no aspect of goodness which God is not; and that the more, because the notion of a perfection embracing all possible excellences, both moral and intellectual, is especially congenial to the mind, and there are in fact intellectual attributes, as well as moral, included in the child's image of God, as above represented.

Such is the apprehension which even a child may have of his sovereign Lawgiver and Judge; which is possible in the case of children, because, at least, some children possess it, whether others possess it or no; and which, when it is found in children, is found to act promptly and keenly, by reason of the paucity of their ideas. It is an image of the good God, good in Himself, good relatively to the child, with whatever incompleteness; an image, before it has been reflected on, and before it is recognized by him as a notion. Though he cannot explain or define the word "God," when told to use it, his acts show that to him it is far more than a word. He listens, indeed, with wonder and interest to fables or tales; he has a dim, shadowy sense of what he hears about persons and matters of this world; but he has that within him which actually vibrates, responds, and gives a deep meaning to the lessons of his first teachers about the will and the providence of God.

How far this initial religious knowledge comes from without, and how far from within, how much is natural, how much implies a special divine aid which is above nature, we have no means of determining, nor is it necessary for my present purpose to determine. I am not engaged in tracing the image of God in the mind of a child or a man to its first origins, but showing that he can become possessed of such an image, over and above all mere notions of God, and in what that image consists. Whether its elements, latent in the mind, would ever be elicited without extrinsic help is very doubtful; but whatever be the actual history of the first formation of the divine image within us, so far at least is certain, that, by informations external to ourselves, as time goes on, it admits of being strengthened and improved. It is certain too that whether it grows brighter and stronger, or, on the other hand, is dimmed, distorted, or obliterated, depends on each of us individually, and on his circumstances. It is more than probable that, in the event, from neglect, from the temptations of life, from bad companions, or from the urgency of secular occupations, the light of the soul will fade away and die out. Men transgress their sense of duty and gradually lose those sentiments of shame and fear, the natural supplements of transgression, which, as I have said, are the witnesses of the unseen Judge. And, even were it deemed impossible that those who had in their first youth a genuine apprehension of Him could ever utterly lose it, yet that apprehension may become almost undistinguishable from an inferential acceptance of the great truth, or may dwindle into a mere notion of their intellect. On the contrary, the image of God, if duly cherished, may expand, deepen, and be completed, with the growth of their powers and in the course of life, under the varied lessons, within and without them, which are brought home to them concerning that same God, one and personal, by means of education, social intercourse, experience, and literature.

To a mind thus carefully formed upon the basis of its natural conscience, the world, both of nature and of man, does but give back a reflection of those truths about the one Living God which have been familiar to it from childhood. Good and evil meet us daily as we pass through life, and there are those who think it philosophical to act towards the manifestations of each with some sort of impartiality, as if evil had as much right to be there as good, or even a better, as having more striking triumphs and a broader jurisdiction. And because the course of things is determined by fixed laws, they consider that those laws preclude the present agency of the Creator in the carrying out of particular issues. It is otherwise with the theology of a religious imagination. It has a living hold on truths which are really to be found in the world, though they are not upon the surface. It is able to pronounce by anticipation what it takes a long argument to prove—that good is the rule, and evil the exception. It is able to assume that, uniform as are the laws of nature, they are consistent with a particular providence. It interprets what it sees around it by this previous inward teaching, as the true key of that maze of vast complicated disorder; and thus it gains a more and more consistent and luminous vision of God from the most unpromising materials. Thus conscience is a connecting principle between the creature and his Creator, and the firmest hold of theological truths is gained by habits of personal religion. When men begin all their works with the thought of God, acting for His sake, and to fulfil His will, when they ask His blessing on themselves and their life, pray to Him for the objects they desire, and see Him in the event, whether it be according to their prayers or not, they will find everything that happens tend to confirm them in the truths about Him which live in their imagination, varied and unearthly as those truths may be. Then they are brought into His presence as that of a living Person, and are able to hold converse with Him, and that with a directness and simplicity, with a confidence and intimacy, *mutatis mutandis,* which we use towards an earthly superior; so that it is doubtful whether we realize the company of our fellow men with greater keenness than these favoured minds are able to contemplate and adore the unseen, incomprehensible Creator.

This vivid apprehension of religious objects, on which I have been enlarging, is independent of the written records of revelation; it does not require any knowledge of Scripture, nor of the history or the teaching of the Catholic Church. It is independent of books. But if so much may be traced out in the twilight of natural religion, it is obvious how great an addition of fulness and exactness is made to our mental image of the divine personality and attributes by the light of Christianity. And, indeed, to give us a clear and sufficient object for our faith is one main purpose of the supernatural dispensations of religion. This purpose is carried out in the written Word, with an effectiveness which inspiration alone could secure, first, by the histories which form so large a portion of the Old Testament, and scarcely less impressively in the prophetical system, as it is gradually unfolded and perfected in the writings of those who were its ministers and spokesmen. And as the exercise of the affections strengthens our apprehension of the object of them, it is impossible to exaggerate the influence exerted on the religious imagination by a book of devotions so sublime, so penetrating, so full of deep instruction as the Psalter, to say nothing of other portions of the Hagiographa. And then as regards the New Testament: the Gospels, from their subject, contain a manifestation of the divine nature, so special as to make it appear from the contrast as if nothing were known of God when they are unknown. Lastly, the Apostolic Epistles, the long history of the Church, with its fresh and fresh exhibitions of divine agency, the lives of the saints, and the reasonings, internal collisions, and decisions of the theological School, form an extended comment on the words and works of our Lord.

I think I need not say more in illustration of the subject which I proposed for consideration in this section. I have wished to trace the process by which the mind arrives, not only at a notional, but at an imaginative or real assent to the doctrine that there is one God, that is, an assent made with an apprehension, not only of what the words of the proposition mean, but of the object denoted by them. Without a proposition or thesis there can be no assent, no belief, at all—any more than there can be an inference without a conclusion. The proposition that there is one personal and present God may be held in either way: either as a theological truth, or as a religious fact or reality. The notion and the reality assented to are represented by one and the same proposition, but serve as distinct interpretations of it. When the proposition is apprehended for the purposes of proof, analysis, comparison, and the like intellectual exercises, it is used as the expression of a notion; when for the purposes of devotion, it is the image of a reality. Theology, properly and directly, deals with notional apprehension; religion with imaginative.

Here we have the solution of the common mistake of supposing that there is a contrariety and antagonism between a dogmatic creed and vital religion. People urge that salvation consists, not in believing the propositions that there is a God, that there is a Saviour, that our Lord is God, that there is a Trinity, but in believing in God, in a Saviour, in a Sanctifier; and they object that such propositions are but a formal and human medium destroying all true reception of the Gospel, and making religion a matter of words or of logic, instead of its having its seat in the heart. They are right so far as this, that men can and sometimes do rest in the propositions themselves as expressing intellectual notions; they are wrong when they maintain that men need do so or always do so. The propositions may and must be used, and can easily be used, as the expression of facts, not notions, and they are necessary to the mind in the same way that language is ever necessary for denoting facts, both for ourselves as individuals and for our intercourse with others. Again, they are useful in their dogmatic aspect as ascertaining and making clear for us the truths on which the religious imagination has to rest. Knowledge must ever precede the exercise of the affections. We feel gratitude and love, we feel indignation and dislike, when we have the informations actually put before us which are to kindle those several emotions. We love our parents, as our parents, when we know them to be our parents; we must know concerning God, before we can feel love, fear, hope, or trust towards Him. Devotion must have its objects; those objects, as being supernatural, when not represented to our senses by material symbols, must be set before the mind in propositions. The formula, which embodies a dogma for the theologian, readily suggests an object for the worshiper. It seems a truism to say, yet it is all that I have been saying, that in religion the imagination and affections should always be under the control of reason. Theology may stand as a substantive science, though it may be without the life of religion; but religion cannot maintain its ground at all without theology. Sentiment, whether imaginative or emotional, falls back upon the intellect for its stay, when sense cannot be called into exercise; and it is in this way that devotion falls back upon dogma.

Editors' Note—From THE GRAMMAR OF ASSENT (Image Books; Garden City, N.Y.: Doubleday, 1955) *pp. 95-109.*

Bernard Häring, C.SS.R.

The Master Idea
of Christian Morality

Christ's moral code is *religious* in its very essence. To express it another way, Christian morality should in structure correspond to
religion. Indeed, this is true of all genuine morality, morality which
sees man as a creature made in the image of God. This chapter will
develop the parallel structure of religion and morality in the following
stages.

First, if religion is considered phenomenologically, i.e., not as a
doctrinal system but rather as something lived, as religious life, we
will see that its structure is essentially a dialogue between persons.
Secondly, having established the dialogic structure of religion, we
will have a criterion by which to evaluate the most widespread moral
systems as well as the key ideas of Christian morality, such as salvation of the soul, law, etc. In this way we will try to determine which
key idea or category best expresses the structure proper to a *religious
morality*. The category of "response-responsibility" will be shown to
do this best. In the light of this category we can then situate in its
proper place the fundamental idea of salvation. Finally we will show
how *morality based on the imitation of Jesus Christ* most perfectly

fulfils all the requirements of a "response-morality," and at the same time includes and sanctifies in itself all the other traditional moral categories.

As matters now stand, religion seems to be the motivating force of morality. Yet the terms "moral" and "religious" are not interchangeable. They are not even necessarily linked together. A certain morality still seems possible where religious feeling has lost all vitality. There even exist moral systems which are deliberately nonreligious. All the duties, norms, and laws of these systems find their complete explanation and full flowering in the "I" of man without any reference to God.

It is a subtle snare that morality can draw its rationale from this source even though it claims to be and wants to be religious! But in this case it is religious only from the outside and extrinsically. For such a morality, religion is a mere superstructure, or better, a veneer on a moral code which remains essentially human.

A genuinely religious morality, however, should in structure correspond exactly to the structure of religion: it should have the very form of religion. For religion—and we must plumb the depths of this —appears as a dialogue: it is a response to the divine Word.

THE IDEA OF RELIGION:
RESPONSE TO THE DIVINE WORD

For the Christian, religion is infinitely more than a feeling, a need, an experience. It is a communion with the living God. In themselves, neither concern for one's soul, nor one's inner life, nor even the glory and grandeur of God constitute religion. Genuine religion exists only when the Word of God and the response of man meet. It is this mutual converse of God and man (St. Augustine's "Deus et anima") that best expresses the essence of religion.

"God and the soul." Religion can be said to rest on two solid pillars: personal God and created person. Two themes are essential to it: God in the glory of His love and man in the grace of God. Only when two beings really take each other seriously can there be true personal relations. God in His glory takes man seriously. He speaks to him. This makes religion possible. And the superabundant treasure and unspeakable mystery of the true religion is that God has taken man seriously enough to sacrifice His only-begotten Son.

God requires in return that man take Him, the Most Holy One, seriously. For God respects this role He has given man. Religion requires two poles infinitely apart. If this essential difference is obliterated and if the infinite distance is so suppressed that man forgets the holiness of God, then the essence of religion is destroyed. Where there is no meeting with the "Holy One," there is no longer any genuine religion.

Similarly, if the human pole is no longer taken seriously—though this fault be on the part of man—there is no longer any communion of persons, no longer any religion. From the moment that the soul truly meets God, it enters the brilliance of infinite holiness and takes on value, a value closely linked with this divine communion. In the presence of the Most Holy God the soul is not only totally absorbed in adoration, she also recognizes with astonishment the look of the divine love upon her. God is the salvation of the soul. All the great dogmas of creation, of Incarnation, and of redemption have a parallel theme: the glory of God, the salvation of the soul. When we sing, "Who for us men and for our salvation came down from heaven," we are bursting into a joyous hymn of praise for our participation in the loving glory of our God. God reveals to us His glory by humbling Himself in love (*agapē*); He reveals His holiness by accomplishing our salvation.

"God and the soul." The mystery of communion between God and the soul speaking to one another both terrifies and enraptures us. It is ultimately the very mystery of the eternal Word of God. We are created in and through this Word, and in His image we are capable of speaking in our turn. In Christ, the *Verbum* made flesh, incarnate Word, God comes to us: He literally speaks the Word to us. We have to welcome it and give back a favorable response.

His personal Word is the foundation of our capacity for dialogue with God in the intimacy of an "I-Thou" relationship. From this sole fact, all the words which He addresses to us—whether through our reason by natural revelation or by supernatural revelation properly so called—take on an unheard-of brilliance and solemnity: God speaks to us because He wishes to be in one society with us and this desire is rooted ultimately in the mystery of the Trinitarian society. Each one of our responses concerns this union with Him and hastens or compromises the achieving of His image in us.

This throws some light on the fundamental role of prayer as an essential expression of religion. To pray is to make oneself an attentive, respectful listener; it is an attempt to give a response to God, however stammering it be. Religion lives by prayer because there cannot be any personal bond (*religio*) with God without His holy Word, His *Verbum*, and the power that He gives us to answer It. In the *Verbum*, the personal Word of the Father, prayer has its source; in Word and response, it is achieved. The more deeply the religious man penetrates the Word which God addresses to Him, the better his entire life develops into an all-embracing response; and the stronger his bond with God, which is religion, the more clearly he reveals the divine likeness.

When our person and our own salvation no longer have meaning except in the light of God's loving will, when our anxiety for salvation is no longer anything but the response (inspired by divine love) to the theme composed by God Himself telling of our elevation to His beatitude—only when our dealings with God have reached these depths, only then are we fully religious.

The apex of Christian personalism, therefore, is not the cult of one's own personality, but the "divine Word—human response" relationships which are established between the God of holiness and the soul receiving its salvation. It is completely different from a closed system revolving about the Ego. Rather it is openness and availability for the response of love. In a word, there is no true personalism except in communion with God. The human person can be understood only by beginning with his likeness to God. And the more a man maintains with God a relationship of Word and response, the more he grows aware of his own personality: he exists in the image of God.

"God and the soul." Do not interpret this formula, "God and the soul," in an individualistic sense. Kierkegaard and many others who followed him erred in thinking that religious life uproots the soul from the community and sets it alone before God. To be sure, God's beckoning call signifies for us liberation from the anonymous masses. God calls us personally by our name. Summoned before Him we find ourselves; but we find our neighbor also.

Religion, since it is communion with God, is by that very fact the foundation of every true human community. Personal communion among men is also achieved by a dialogue of love. What is the source of this power to reach my neighbor in the very depths of his Ego by a loving word? It is the Word of love which God first speaks to me that actuates this word in me. Thus I am inspired in turn to make a response of love. This communion with God makes me aware of my personality, which consists in being "capable of uttering a word in the image of God"; and this communion fulfils that capability. At the same time it makes me aware of my essentially social nature. For this reason, religious life—if its essential dynamism is not contradicted—necessarily leads us into relationships of charity with our brothers.

Doubtless, idle words hinder our communion with God. But when we respond to the Word which God speaks to us, we are joined directly with our neighbor: our response joins us in a Word! In this Word, in whom God has made all things (Jn 1:3), i.e., in Christ, the *Verbum* made flesh, we are in communion with the Father. But "to be in Christ" necessarily means to be united to all His members, the "Body of Christ," all those whom Christ calls and forms into His "convocation," His Church. Therefore, it belongs to the essence of the religious life to place ourselves in a community of speaking the Word with men, since it is a life in Christ, eternal Word made man.

CHRISTIAN MORALITY:
"MORALITY OF RESPONSE-RESPONSIBILITY"

It is our religious relationship to God that must totally and absolutely nourish our moral life in Christ. Christian morality cannot be satisfied with seeing in religion its external sanction; it must let itself be absorbed by religion. Accordingly, the more clearly morality corresponds to the religious structure we have just considered, the more it will allow itself to be intimately shaped by an attitude of religious dialogue and the healthier it will be. Now we have a criterion by which we can measure the value and importance of the concepts currently considered to be fundamental in morality.

Perfection of Oneself and Salvation of the Soul

Although genuine moral life is based essentially on religion, some moral systems have been constructed whose primary orientation is not religious. At least, they do not consider the personal encounter with God as their basis.

We can dismiss immediately those scientific ethical systems and moral attitudes which sacrifice the human person to the collectivity or to some impersonal end. Such conceptions can hardly be the foundation of a morality which will be taken seriously; rather, they undermine morality. We need consider only the systems in which the value of the human person is recognized. What are their characteristics? First of all, they emphasize the imperative duty of man to fulfil and perfect himself. Aristotle, the Stoics, Kant, Schleiermacher (to name only a few) make man and his grandeur both the foundation and the proper end of ethics. While they may not deny the existence of a personal God, they do not understand the human person and morality in terms of God. These systems to a certain extent still safeguard the seriousness of morality, because they situate man in an encircling web of values and laws and require that he place himself freely in this web. But as his ultimate purpose and last end, man strives only to achieve his own flowering. "The man of worth never forgets his value. He never loses himself in things that are inferior to him." For him the supreme values are his soul and the preservation and development of his personal dignity. Man is at the center of all these ethical systems. His moral task is designated as the perfecting of himself.

When religion encounters such a moral attitude, it further enhances the value of the soul by introducing it to a higher world. Religious language no longer speaks of perfecting oneself, but of saving one's soul. From this point of view, the Hindu religions of salvation could be distinguished from the Stoic morality of self-perfection. But in reality, those too are only the extension into the religious order of the man-centered ethics. Man must eventually come to think in a "personal" way. Where God is not considered as a person, or where, in any case, a communion with Him is not sought, necessarily the person of man becomes the center of the moral system. And this happens even when salvation is conceived to be a dissolution of the personal, for example in Hindu pantheism. Nirvana is thought to be either the positive beatitude of the surviving soul or its extinction and its vanishing. In either case, at the center of all the asceticism and all the virtuous effort there is only man and the salvation of his soul. But salvation of the soul in the Christian sense is something completely different. It is neither a happy solitude nor a happy insertion into an impersonal being, but rather a society of love with the living God. Neither the Aristotelian nor the Stoic concept of self-perfection can be introduced formally and on the same level into an authentically Christian ethics. In other words, concern for saving one's soul should no longer be understood simply in terms of Stoic self-perfection. Personal community with God does not allow the human soul to make itself the center of morality.

The only way the human person can understand himself in a religious perspective is in terms of his personal bond with God. As it works out, at least in the beginning of religious awakening, the case is usually otherwise. The man whose religious effort has up to this point consisted in perfecting himself is very likely to think of religion as a superior means of self-fulfilment and salvation. Since he will not immediately see or look for what is primary in religion, namely, the community of love with God, he looks more to the advancement and safeguarding of his salvation which follows from religion. In so far as he consciously or unconsciously maintains such an attitude, he closes off from himself the best and deepest approach to God. He does not understand the keystone of religion, the holiness of God, which is not the "means" for anything. He does not rightly appreciate that communion in love which beatifies once it is sought for itself.

Someone will object: Naturally the glory of God and loving adoration of Him are at the center of *religious* relations; *moral* aspiration, on the contrary, concerns man and his salvation! But is not moral aspiration concerned also and especially with obeying God, dwelling in His love, and realizing the coming of His kingdom?

The genuineness of religious life runs the greatest danger when all relationship with God and all service of Him is seen primarily from the viewpoint of the profit man draws from it. Even when this danger is bypassed in directly religious activities, a perilous dichotomy remains as a shadow over his hopes of success: on the one hand, prayer and participation in sacrifice have their meaning in communion with God, while on the other hand, the moral life, remaining extrinsic to these, has man and his salvation as its final goal. Thus religious life and moral life are separated from one another, and the man-centered moral way of acting communicates more and more of its human orientation to the religious attitude.

The effort of the nonreligious man to fulfil himself is not without value. These efforts provide a positive basis as long as the religious question remains open. But once the religious orientation has been adopted, this effort retains value only on condition that it be "baptized." If this effort is to enter truly into the realm of the sacred, it must be placed at the service of the sacred.

In conclusion, morality and religion should be centered in communion with God. And this communion should be the characteristic mark of Christian morality in its scientific presentation and in preaching. Unfortunately, both of these, especially from the time of the Enlightenment, have more often continued the Aristotelian emphasis on self-perfection than the emphasis of the gospel on the sovereignty of God.

Commandment and Law

Commandment and law are and should remain the central concepts of Christian moral teaching. Since "commandment" is a totally religious concept, the preaching of the commandments is essentially God-centered. They are the response in our dialogue with God. God Himself promulgated the commandments on Sinai only after proclaiming the double theme of religion, namely, His sovereign glory and His revelation of love: "I am the Lord, thy God; I brought thee out of Egypt, the house of servitude" (Ex 20:2). God's commandments are the words (Decalogue = ten words) which divine love speaks to us. They open with the great commandment of charity. And their observance, rightly understood, is an obedient response of love; in a word, obedient love.

Like the commandments, the nature of law is completely religious, and therefore obedience to law is our response in a God-directed dialogue. Even granting that the concept of "natural law" (which expresses the order of creation) is borrowed from the moral philosophy of the Stoics, still Christian morality, stimulated especially by St. Augustine, has purified it of all impersonalism and fatalism. In St. Augustine's understanding, law expresses the holy essence and will of God. It is the very intimate call which God addresses to each human heart.

Responsibility

By now it should be clear that if we give full value to the concepts of "salvation," "commandment," and "law," in no one of them will we find the central idea of Catholic morality. The key to this morality, it seems to us, lies in the concept of "responsibility," understood in its religious sense.

Since morality should adopt the structure of religion and since religion is essentially a dialogue which sets up between God and man a personal relationship of call and response, evidently responsibility becomes for us the foundation of morality. Man has to answer to God for his behavior. He is responsible before God.

Nevertheless, our moral relationship with God, understood in a religious sense, is not precisely the same as the religious relationship in itself. Our moral relationship has its own specific nature, namely, responsibility.

The strictly religious life is a response to the Word of God. Through His Word, the eternal *Verbum*, our God and Creator stoops to us. Through Christ, the divine Word made man, we are in communion with God.

If we are to understand the theological virtues in the light of this dialogue, we will come to see that faith, hope, and charity not only turn man toward God, but also assure man that God is turned toward him in His truth, His promises, and His love. Just as we cannot see God face to face except in His Word, so it is only in Christ, *in Christo*, that we can work out our response and only through Christ that we can enter into communion with God.

The practice of the virtue of religion now becomes our response to the glory of God the Creator as revealed to us through His Word (Jn 1), and our response to the glory of God the Redeemer as it reaches us through Christ, the Church, and the sacraments. We can distinguish between the virtue of religion and the theological virtues, because, unlike the latter, the virtue of religion includes an exterior action. For this virtue is entirely directed toward faith, hope, and charity, and is unintelligible when this orientation toward God is lacking. Religion is related to the other moral virtues as well, because these virtues which regulate the daily conduct of our life are themselves integral parts of the virtue of religion. In fact, it is through the practice of religion that the service of God will find its place in both our public and private lives. For in this virtue, all things, whatever be the circumstances surrounding them in time and space, can be properly ordered to the glory of God.

The moral life is a responsibility before God. The virtue of religion differs more radically from the other moral virtues than it does from the theological virtues. By their very definition, the other moral virtues do not have God as their object. (Here we are speaking phenomenologically, not ontologically.) They are never an immediate response to Him. Of themselves they are concerned with the working out of the order of creation. They deal with created persons, values, and goods. From this point of view, they do not merit the name of "response," nor consequently the name of "responsibility" in the full sense of the word. For a response supposes a person to whom one responds. Only to the degree that moral virtues through the mediation of created goods are related back to God do they take on the value of response-responsibility in a dialogue. Actually, even in the order of creation the believer hears the call of God his Creator and Lord. In created reality the child of God hears the Word of his Father. Thus the responsibility of the Christian becomes a filial response, since the three theological virtues support this dialogue between "the Word of God" and "the response of man."

The word "responsibility" seems the most apt way to express this permeation of morality by religion. At the same time this word helps us keep the distinction between them. We are responsible for something or someone, i.e., "responsibility is not a direct response to God but a response through created goods." Let us explain this distinction.

Religious acts consider God directly and respond to Him. Moral acts look to the fulfilment of the order of creation. Moral acts become a response of man to his Creator only to the degree that he shows in these acts a serious concern for earthly duties and created values.

At the very heart of *religious* acts is an *adoring love* of God. But *moral* choices are dictated by an attitude of loving obedience to God, a "yes" to His will. However, these decisions are more than a facile and general "yes" or "no" to the will of God. They must be a personal search for the proper and fitting response to the Creator. Here lies the risk of that response. Assuredly the moral commitment presupposes that one has made himself constantly and humbly attentive to the will of God, his Creator and Father. But from the number of possible choices offered to him, often a man realizes this commitment only in hesitant or bold choices. For in such choices a man sees his response in the context of his particular situation.

This responsibility before God does not free us from taking into account human authority. For whether we obey or disobey this authority, in either case we have to shoulder the responsibility, though in different ways. In our search for the divine will we cannot scorn the helps given by God, namely, the authority of the community or of a wise counselor. Nonetheless, obedience and consultation should not become excuses for avoiding responsibility. Rather they should be the necessary means which we use in doing what we can to come to a fully responsible decision. Naturally an act of disobedience more than any other must be severely tested to be sure of an unselfish motive and carefully evaluated to determine its consequences for the community. Without such a clear examination, one can never take the responsibility for disobedience. Our responsibility to the community already has particular importance when there is question of *obeying* human authority; this responsibility must be even more firmly underscored when there is question of justifiable disobedience.

The moral act is not only a responsibility before God in which we commit ourselves to a particular attractive value; it is always, to a greater or lesser degree, a responsibility before our neighbor in the natural or supernatural community of men. Our moral lives and religious attitudes shine out for all to see. Nothing that we say or do or think is without its importance for the rest of men. Our actions, words, and thoughts affect our brothers by raising or lowering their own moral life and religious commitment. The doctrine of the Mystical Body of Christ highlights this truth for us. In our communion with God in the Word, we exist in Christ. This can only mean that we exist and act in communion with all the members of the Mystical Body.

In every moral decision, and especially in an act which endangers his moral integrity, a man realizes that his response involves his existence and salvation. Hence every moral situation involves obligation. When a man finds himself in a position in which he has to respond to the Most Holy God, no longer is he free from obligation. In a moral act a person must answer for himself. The general judgment at the end of time will reveal the response that each man will make before God.

This aspect of responsibility evidently also applies to the religious act. In placing such an act, man knows that his salvation is linked with the proper response that he gives to the Word of the Most Holy God. For this reason, it should be unnecessary to emphasize that religious acts belong to the domain of moral theology and partake of moral responsibility.

Responsibility and Personal Salvation

Though we have not made self-perfection, nor even the salvation of one's soul, the key idea of Christian morality, preferring rather the idea of responsibility, still we should not overlook the privileged place that personal salvation holds in this responsibility. Our own salvation outranks all the impersonal values for which we are responsible. Granting that it should not be higher in the scale of values than the kingdom of God and the salvation of our neighbor, the fact remains that we are more responsible for our own salvation than for the salvation of others. Responsibility for ourselves takes precedence over coresponsibility for our neighbor, because we have immediate control over our own will alone. Since responsibility and free will are intimately related, we have to answer most for that which most depends on our liberty. Therefore we can and must be concerned about our salvation. Accordingly, many of our actions (e.g., voluntary discipline and ascetical practice) must be directed to this end. Viewed in this way, even concern for passing goods will find a rightful place, though not the most exalted. But we would seriously err if we subordinated coresponsibility for our neighbor's salvation and the kingdom of God to our own salvation. Since these values are not in themselves inferior to the value of our own salvation, we should not act as if they were, but we should carefully co-ordinate each of them with our own salvation. Finally, God stands at the center of all of these values. It is in our communion of love with *Him* and our responsibility before *Him* that all fits into place.

In this way we acquire a hierarchy of values in Christian morality.

It might seem at first sight that here concern for perfection and the salvation of the soul are not given the prominence they have in present-day preaching. But the contrary is true. Viewed in the light of its true central perspective, the essence of our salvation and its urgency are seen all the more profoundly. Yet we must not forget one thing. The religious-moral man realizes himself by degrees in continuous growth. The "I" must be more and more concerned with the genuine order of things. Progress consists precisely in this, according to the great spiritual masters. From the very beginning the soul should have a very clear idea of that order, but of course always using the motives which will be most efficacious to its stage of growth at any given time. And so, when a priest is dealing with souls distant from God or still at the beginning of their progress toward God, it would be most improper for him not to speak of the intimate desire for beatitude and of the legitimate interest a man has for salvation. It should be clear by now that thirst for happiness and morality are two different things, but nevertheless they do go together. For not only is desire for beatitude the great ally of moral duty, but often it is the only voice which still penetrates to the depths of sin's abyss. Or better, it is the last echo of the divine invitation to submission and love.

Both in our preaching and in our personal struggle for morality we should consider from the beginning the final goal of each: the full return of man to his God. But each must be assisted too by whatever in the concrete are the most efficacious motives. Certainly the call to save one's soul should not be regarded as an invitation to an egoistic and egocentric attitude. Rather it is a call for response to God and responsibility before God in all the breadth and depth of true moral behavior. It should be clear nonetheless that in the soul closed off by sin the one narrow crack through which God's light can still penetrate is the legitimate self-interest of that soul together with the uneasiness it has about its salvation. Still it is just as true that for us pilgrims here below no love is so perfect that we can neglect joining it with an innate desire for beatitude. The unrest of the soul is not yet the love of God. Rather it is the spring which keeps the soul stretched out toward this love. The same God who leads us to love by holy fear and hope has implanted this force in us. Self-perfection and happiness are a moral goal, but not the final goal. It is true that legitimate interest in personal salvation remains the fulcrum which will lift a soul from self-deceptive perdition and raise it toward God, its sole true center. But it is a delusion to confuse the base of operations with the goal. "Save your soul!" This cry awakens the soul, but not yet to the full message.

CONCLUSION:

A MORALITY OF RESPONSIBILITY IN CHRIST

Needless to say, moral theology, and especially moral preaching, do not have to limit themselves to philosophic analyses of the word "responsibility." Their object is essentially the rich and living content of the history of salvation and our communion of love with God in Christ. Yet precisely the requirements established by our analyses are found more than satisfied in a morality centered on union with Christ. In fact, a morality centered on the kingdom and on the imitation of Christ not only realizes the essentials of religion and communion with God, but it contains the requirements of morality and responsibility before God.

Word and response. Our union of grace with Christ is the foundation of our imitation of Christ. Conversely, the life of imitation is the proof, in love and obedience, of our existential union with Christ. This is another way of saying that we are joined to the Word of Christ, that we enter into dialogue with Him by His grace. Through the gift of His love Christ unites us to Himself. In love we join ourselves to His Person of Word made flesh. In obedience we join ourselves to His eloquent example and to every word that came from His lips. Further, the disciple must "actively" receive the Word of the Master and in each given age fulfil it as a personal response. For each is to follow the example of Christ according to the individual gifts for which he is responsible.

Social responsibility. To be in Christ is to come to share His kingdom. And immediately we are responsible to a community! It is impossible to be a member of the Body of Christ without an awareness of being united to all the members, of being responsible to all the redeemed and compelled to put all one's personal abilities at the service of the kingdom.

Commandment and law play their part in this kingdom, but no longer are they impersonal forces intervening between God and the soul. They are the living words which Christ speaks to us, the ever-new invitations of the grace of Christ. They are what makes each one responsible for carrying out His great commandment, in the measure of grace which He has given to each. They are completely above the minimal level of the commandments given at Sinai, infinitely superior to the natural law.

Salvation. For a disciple of Christ the natural value of self-perfection and the supernatural value of the soul's salvation are not by themselves the key values. Rather, it is when he is committed to the following of Christ that these values are best realized. For the Christian the following of Christ will not be simply a means of saving his soul. In the light of one's love for the Saviour, the soul's salvation suddenly takes on a new importance. In the beginning the disciple might consider the promises of the Master rather than His unbounded love. But in following Christ he learns little by little to love himself in a new way, beginning with the love the Master has for him. His salvation enters into the light of the kingdom of God and His loving glory.

Christian morality, therefore, is not centered on man, nor yet on a God who is alien to the world. And only in Christ does our moral life take on the value of a response to God, because Christ is the Word by which the Father seeks us and calls us. Our loving commitment to the following of Christ makes our lives an echo, an image, and a sharing in the Trinitarian life. Our lives become an eternal colloquy of Word and response of love.

This commitment to the following of Christ is possible to us because He, the Word of God, is the key to our resemblance to God, and because His redemption has bestowed it upon us. Our imitation fulfils it in us and makes it manifest. One cannot discuss an image without being led to the original. Thus moral theology must in everything relate the Christian life to the Word-model, in whom and through whom man in the image of God can live and make response.

Editors' Note.—From LA LOI DU CHRIST (Tournai, Belgium: Desclée, 1956) *pp. 29-46;* translated for this volume by J. Nelson, s.j., and E. Stevens, s.j.

The Catholic Idea

The Catholic Idea
William F. Lynch, s.j.

PREFACE

Our first formal chapter on the nature of Catholicism tries to strike at the crux of the difference between every form of the purely scientific or mathematical or rationalizing intelligence and the kind of thinking and believing that goes on in the revelation of Christ.

It is the general mark of the scientific and rational intelligence that it reduces all the particular forms of existence to the status of sources or examples of ideas and abstractions. If applied to religious history, this would mean that Christ is only an example, no matter how lofty, of the religious sense. He could be fitted into a pattern, ultimately on an equal plane with Apollo or Buddha. The important thing would be the idea of "religion."

But Christ and the Church reverse this whole order of thinking and are therefore a scandal to the rational mind. Christ, the single historical man, is the religious reality, its center and finality. Ideas, abstractions, religious affectivity have value only as they explain or elaborate on Him. The Idea of Religion does not give shape to Him; He gives religious shape to everything in this world. We shall see that in a very special way He gives shape to the Church. Christ is the Idea of Catholicism.

William F. Lynch, s.j.

The Catholic Idea

I

Catholicism begins at that point where religion has always been born, at the point of the sense of God, the need, the longing, the reaching for Him, the union with Him. And if one were to ask how Catholicism differs from this universal search of the heart, wherever it has been found in history, it would surely not be here; for God and man have been permanently there, from the eternity of the one and the creation of the other. These two, God and man, these two persons, are the permanent terms of the religious relationship, which is and must be a completely personal relationship, though it need not be purely individual or private. *Ego dilecto, dilectus meus mihi.* "I to my beloved, my beloved unto me." It has always been, and always will be, as simple as this.

St. Augustine has said it: "My heart is not content, O God, until it rest in Thee." Magdalene has said it in one word: *Rabboni,* "Master." Thomas the Apostle has said "My Lord and my God." And St. Peter simply: "Thou knowest that I love thee." But how permanent and personal this relationship is, is perhaps best put by St. Paul. For he tells us that on that day when all need of theology and seeing with faith "as in a glass darkly" has vanished, and when there is no more need of hope because that which the heart desires has been reached, then this love of the person for the Person shall remain:

"*The time will come when we shall outgrow prophecy, when speaking with tongues will come to an end, when knowledge will be swept away; we shall never have finished with charity. Our knowledge, our prophecy, are only glimpses of the truth; and these glimpses will be swept away when the time of fulfilment comes. . . . At present, we are looking at a confused reflection in a mirror; then, we shall see face to face; now, I have only glimpses of knowledge; then, I shall recognize God as He has recognized me. Meanwhile, faith, hope and charity persist, all three; but the greatest of them all is charity*" (1 Cor 13:8-13; Knox).

What happens uniquely in Catholicism, and according to the electing will of God, is that two other terms have been added to complicate (the Catholic would say, to intensify) this relation between the human and the divine person. These two new things are Christ and the Church. Of them the rest of this book shall, of course, have much to say. But before we turn back to look at the underlying tie between man and God, let it suffice at this early moment to speak briefly now of Christ and the Church.

To many these two new things seem, at least on the surface, only to disturb the wonder, the majesty, the purity of the soul's bond with its Maker. This new pair of terms appears suddenly out of history; they are both covered with all the reality and blood and dust of the past. Therefore they are a scandal to the mathematical intelligence of our time, whose gifts have nothing to do with the handling of blood and dust, or with a Christ who was born at an unpredictable year, or with a Church claiming to be without spot or wrinkle but covered on the outside with all the grimeful reality of the reader and the writer; they are also a scandal to every devotee of pure and unpolluted religion, that is to say to all those forms of it, whether they be Indian or Protestant or Judaic, which cannot tolerate the invasion of the glorious concept of religion by history, by men, by sacraments, by salt, fish, water, by bread and wine and priests. It is exactly this scandal that has been predicted and declared from the beginning: "What we preach is Christ crucified: to the Jews a discouragement, to the Gentiles mere folly."

These two historical facts are, therefore, the content, the glory, and the problem of Catholicism. But actually it is not altogether true to say simply that they introduce two historical novelties into the great relationship of God and man. What they rather do is this: Up to the moment in which they appear, the finite and the infinite confront each other, intimately indeed and with love, but yet they keep their place of altogether separate existence. Man is man and God is God, *Deus absconditus,* the hidden God, and who shall be like unto Him, *quis similis Dei?* But something has intervened, a great mystery indeed, to break down the fright at this gap and this distance. In Christ God and man meet and are one person, and the Church claims resolutely, scandalously, to be Christ Himself. Instead, therefore, of the first two majestic terms having been multiplied with disturbing confusion into four, the mystery is that in a more profound sense than has ever been made possible before by even the greatest religious loves of man, the four terms all make but one. Of God we can say, *Verbum caro factum est*, "The word was made flesh"; of man we can say, you shall be gods. "For as the Lord took a body and became man, so we men, being assumed by the flesh of the Word, are by Him made divine and heirs of eternal life" (St. Athanasius).

II

But where one problem has been solved by Christ and the Church (they do not create four terms, they do not confuse that enormous goal of the religious instinct which is union with God, but simplify it), yet another and more intense problem, the true stumbling block, has been set up for the man of our day who is challenged anew to believe. He can be comfortable and perhaps even entertained by the religious challenge of India, of the nothing before the All. This kind of mysticism is superb but finally not hard for the mind to take, especially at a time when man threatens to become less than nothing. But that the mind should have lifted up its head, in the forms of Christ and the Church, and in the shape of the altogether definite *this* Man born at no other time than *then*, and *this* Church with *these* disconcerting men, full of the actualities of their virtues and weaknesses, and both laying claim to divinity—this is the shock and the rub for the purely orderly or the purely mystical mind.

Yet if Christ or the Church lower their claims, lower the level of the new mystery, or lower the new challenge to belief, they would become unimportant, nondisturbing, there would be no place for this book and all books like it. But the purpose of this book—with the help of many good men—is to try to indicate, without qualification and without narrowness, the unabated Idea of Catholicism. Anything else would be a deception and a passing moment of consolation for the heart that seeks only beauty or the mind that seeks only interest and stimulation. Beauty there is, and intellectual stimulation. But first and underneath these, there must be the true challenge and scandal of the Church—enormous and new—the scandal of her challenge that in herself she ties together the mind of man ("What is man that thou art mindful of him?") and the inner life of God ("Who dwelleth in light inaccessible") in an indissoluble way ("The gates of hell shall not prevail against it"), and all this not despite but in the midst of its suspect humanity ("Thou art all fair, O my love, and there is not a spot in thee").

The same structure, therefore the same problem, occurs for the mind in both Christ and the Church. It is the structure of ugliness and eternal beauty, not the second on the outside of the first, but the two tightly interpenetrating each other. Of Christ Isaiah said predictingly: "There is no beauty in him, nor comeliness; and we have seen him, and there was no sightliness, that we should be desirous of him: despised, and the most abject of men, a man of sorrows, and acquainted with infirmity; and his look was as it were hidden and despised, where-upon we esteemed him not. . . . We have thought him as it were a leper, and as one struck by God and afflicted" (Is 53:2-4; Douay). Yet the same Christ is described in the following way in the Canticle of Canticles:

> My lover is radiant and ruddy;
> he stands out among thousands.
> His head is pure gold;
> his locks are palm fronds,
> black as the raven.
> His eyes are like doves
> beside running waters,
> His teeth would seem bathed in milk,
> and are set like jewels.
> His cheeks are like beds of spice
> with ripening aromatic herbs.
> His lips are red blossoms;
> they drip choice myrrh.
>
> His arms are rods of gold
> adorned with chrysolites.
> His body is a work of ivory
> covered with sapphires.
> His legs are columns of marble
> resting on golden bases.
> His stature is like the trees on Lebanon,
> imposing as the cedars.
> His mouth is sweetness itself;
> he is all delight.
> Such is my lover, and such my friend,
> O daughters of Jerusalem. *[Ct 5:10-16; Confraternity]*

The same interpenetration of scandal and glory is in the Church. There would be no shock for the mind if these two things were not one, if she were only a suffering and modest servant of the Lord, waiting, despite her sins, for the coming of her glory. For these sins, for all human hesitations about her ugliness, for that mind in her which shocks the meticulous or the pure mystic, let the following from George Bernard Shaw stand as expressive symbol:

"In Italy, for instance, churches are used in such a way that priceless

*pictures become smeared with filthy tallowsoot, and have sometimes
to be rescued by the temporal power and placed in national galleries.
But worse than this are the innumerable daily services which disturb
the truly religious visitor. If these were decently and intelligently
conducted by genuine mystics to whom the mass was no mere rite or
miracle, but a real communion, the celebrants might reasonably claim
a place in the church as their share of the common human right to its
use. But the average Italian priest, personally uncleanly, and with
chronic catarrh of the nose and throat, produced and maintained by
sleeping and living in frowsy, ill-ventilated rooms, punctuating his
gabbled Latin only by expectorative hawking, and making the decent
guest sicken and shiver every time the horrible splash of spitten mucus
echoes along the vaulting from the marble steps of the altar: this un-
seemly wretch should be seized and put out, bell, book, candle, and
all, until he learns to behave himself."*

But for her beauty, in the midst of the hawking, and her claim to be
one with the Son of God, forgiving sins, and intending to encompass
all the flesh of the human race in His flesh, one person all of us with
Him in God, let us return to the Canticle of Canticles. There Christ
speaks to her as His beloved, that which He has made with His blood,
not merely with His beauty:

> Ah, you are beautiful, my beloved,
>   ah, you are beautiful!
> Your eyes are doves
>   behind your veil.
> Your hair is like a flock of goats
>   streaming down the mountains of Galaad.
> Your teeth are like a flock of ewes to be shorn,
>   which come up from the washing,
> All of them big with twins,
>   none of them thin and barren.
> Your lips are like a scarlet strand;
>   your mouth is lovely.
> Your cheek is like a half-pomegranate
>   behind your veil.
>
> Your neck is like David's tower
>   girt with battlements;
> A thousand bucklers hang upon it,
>   all the shields of valiant men.
> Your breasts are like twin fawns,
>   the young of a gazelle
>   that browse among the lilies.
> Until the day breathes cool and the shadows lengthen,
>   I will go to the mountain of myrrh,
>   to the hill of incense.

> You are beautiful, my beloved,
> and there is no blemish in you. . . .
> You are an enclosed garden, my sister, my bride,
> an enclosed garden, a fountain sealed. *[Ct 4:1-7, 12;*
> *Confraternity]*

There is none of us who would not at times desire an easier fact to be offered to the mind and the will. Either we love to run away from reality into a dream, or we desire finally to return from the dream to the things we know better, our own human things. But here the interlocking gives no escape, no alternate choices. No beauty in Him or it, and all beauty in both. We resort to invisible churches, churches for the saints alone, or one without flesh and blood. We warn it to keep within the sanctuary where, we say, it belongs. Or we command it to be flesh and blood and nothing else, or command it to become purely American, in the poorest sense of that word. But the Word become flesh, and flesh at its center divinized; the race made Christ, and Christ the race—this is indeed a challenge to the mind and imagination, that both remain thus open to God's possibilities and free elections. Yet the Church is by many called a closed system, a narrow servitude for the mind. This book says the reverse, that only the free, only the truly open mind, will elect it and believe. Only let us understand that it often takes time and patience to open and free the mind.

III

The same can be said for the sense of God, and belief in Him. It is fashionable these days to say that He is irrelevant, that His relevancy to our situation must be established. Even if men believed, how then would this change our situation? As though He were but a name and a word that, believed in or not believed in, changes nothing. As though perpetually it is our situation, *our* situation, that must be fitted, explained, improved by God.

Whereas the truth is that He will not abide our "situations" or our temporary or limited descriptions of ourselves. He demands that we be open and free, so that He may enter into us. The God of St. Paul refuses to be challenged but challenges us. The position of unbelief can be truly sincere at any age of man, whether he be six or sixty, provided there is a movement in the soul, even unconsciously, toward belief. For that combination of spiritual events which includes man's inner struggle through many darknesses and God's grace, which is given when He knowingly wills, can contain many indeterminates so far as age and personal history are concerned.

But unbelief can also stand in the position that we do not need God and that He is irrelevant. Then it is being used as a defense— a defense which is declaring that neither this present "I" nor this present situation requires God. As though He will allow us to stand in the "me" we have chosen or the situation we have fixed for ourselves. The God of St. Paul is altogether otherwise. He would not abide that situation which the Jews had created for themselves by saying: if we have the external law, if we observe it, we have our God. ("How is it that you are going back to those old schoolboy tasks of yours, so abject, so ineffectual, eager to begin your drudgery all over again? You have begun to observe special days and months, special seasons and years. I am anxious over you; has all the labor I have spent on you been useless?") Where human wisdom and its fair forms had become not only the only way to Him but had in a way become Himself and the final thing, He will bore deeper still into us and into the declaration of what He is ("I will confound the wisdom of wise men"). If prudence is the measure, He will go beyond it ("I will disappoint the calculations of the prudent"). We of today are tempted, openly or subtly, to ask: Is God as great as our knowledge or our suffering? Does religion belong to the surge of our minds or our nerves, both today undoubtedly enormous? But God is so relevant to both that His only insistence is to push the process further. God is so relevant to both our knowledge and our suffering that His only insistence is to push them even beyond themselves, so that, without losing anything, they come to rest in Him. How, then, shall He, in the very act of respecting these two things, force their majestic logic and meaning beyond themselves to Him?

IV

We will not understand Christ, or perhaps even be interested in Him, until we begin to sense that He has been offered as the answer to that question. He does not mean something different, He does not go in a different direction, from that which we wish. He wishes to deepen the process of knowledge. The God of St. Paul has established His Son among us to do exactly this, *to lead us to total consciousness.* But for this it is necessary to drive us below and above the wisdom of our categories, our tentative shining knowledge, below every conceivable brilliance and experience, down into the depths of being itself, into a union not unobservant of observance and clear knowledge, but deeper still than these. This is done by what St. Paul daringly calls "folly."

"When God showed us His wisdom, the world, with all its wisdom, could not find its way to God; and now God would use a foolish thing, our preaching, to save those who will believe in it. Here are the Jews asking for signs and wonders, here are the Greeks intent on their philosophy; but what we preach is Christ crucified; to the Jews, a discouragement; to the Gentiles, mere folly; but to us who have been called, Jew and Gentile alike, Christ the power of God, Christ the wisdom of God. So much wiser than men is God's foolishness; so much

stronger than men is God's weakness. . . . God has chosen what the world holds foolish, so as to abash the wise, God has chosen what the world holds weak, so as to abash the strong. God has chosen what the world holds base and contemptible, nay, has chosen what is nothing, so as to bring to nothing what is now in being . . ." (1 Cor 1:21-28; Knox).

On the surface this is simply a process of destruction, inimical finally to our highest modern purposes. But one must read further in St. Paul, and further into the Christ of St. Paul, to discover that his thought always goes in pairs: folly and wisdom, death and resurrection. One dies to a limit to rise to a new hope. Modern psychiatry would tell us the same thing in its clinical, evidential way; one dies to infantilisms to rise into a greater reality. Resurrection through death. The process is long but not endless. The pairs are united in Christ, the man of ugliness and beauty; they exist in final, concentrated form in His passion and resurrection, though these two things are repeated many times, ascendingly, through the stages of human life. It leads toward a "secret," the crown of all our hopes and work, whether ancient or modern, by a folly driving not only, and without shame, into the midst of our human mud, but by the same stroke and by the same man (*per Christum dominum nostrum*) into the face of God: "What we make known is the wisdom of God, kept hidden till now; so, before the ages, God had decreed, reserving glory for us (none of the rulers of this world could read His secret, or they would not have crucified Him to whom all glory belongs)." So we read of "things no eye has seen, no ear has heard, no human heart conceived, the welcome God has prepared for those who love Him."

The major function of a book on Catholicism is to say that this and so much else which can be said of Christ can be said of the Catholic Church. Scandal this may be, but on no lesser plane can the discussion be pitched. For Christ and nothing else is the Idea of Catholicism.

Editors' Note.—This essay was written specifically for inclusion in this volume. It has not appeared in print elsewhere.

The Bible and History

The Word of God
Célestin Charlier, O.S.B.

PREFACE

There is nothing as important to man as history. For what else is history but everything that has happened or will happen or is happening to the human race. It is also the twenty-four hours of our everyday life. On the surface, especially today, it is formless, bewildering, or frightening. It would be wonderful if at its center it had a shape, and if that shape were Christ.

From the very beginning of human history there is a specific thing called religious history, given, controlled, and dominated by the special action of God. Its center, toward which a formed set of early events leads and out of which all later patterns grow, is Christ, the Son of God and Son of Man.

This religious history is never without patterns of clarity, always repeating themselves on higher and higher planes and in such a way as to give hope for the future to those who know its past. Some of these patterns are: always the election of persons and places by God, the making of divine covenants with man, the constant exaltation of the human community as center of religion, the conquest of sin, the grant of mercy. All are perfectly realized in the pattern of the life of Christ. They emerge with power and clarity in these scholarly pages of Fr. Charlier as he sums up the central themes of the Old and the New Testament.

Célestin Charlier, o.s.b.

The Word of God

HUMAN AND DIVINE

The profoundly human character of the Bible is obvious enough to anyone who reads it. The divine character can be seen only through the eyes of faith. Now faith does not come from man but from heaven: it is God giving Himself. We cannot grasp God of our own free will unless He first bestows Himself. We do not, therefore, intend to prove that the Bible is divine. It is part of our faith to believe that it is so, because we believe in the Church of Christ which gives us the Bible from God. We do not look to the Bible to justify our belief in Christ and His Church; other than in Christ God does not give Himself to us, and without Christ the Bible is deprived of its divine element. It is only because Christ has left it for a witness of Him that we put our trust in it.

All the same, we must not imagine that faith is a thing apart, unrelated to human experience. The truth known by faith and the truth known from reason or experience are both elements which go to the making of the one divine truth. Faith can never be a product of human reasoning or intuition, but if it is to be true faith it must be fully reasonable and capable of enriching the human soul. Without this interaction of one sphere on the other there is no faith. There may be illuminism or rationalism, but in either case we stay on the purely human level.

Nowhere is this more clearly shown than in the Bible. To the unbeliever the Bible is no more than a collection of unrelated books of unequal merit. The humanity of the Bible blinds his eyes to anything else. To the believer, its profound logic convinces him more and more that this strange book bears the stamp of God's hand. Those people whose faith was shaken some fifty years ago by the difficulties of the Bible were not clear in their minds about this relationship between faith and reason. If they had read Pascal they would have had a deeper understanding of their mutual interaction. Mere scientific and technical weapons will never allow a man to penetrate to the divine citadel hidden behind its human outworks; in fact, they will only lead him astray. Only a spirit of burning faith and submission will enable him to turn those scientific and technical weapons to good account, and let him realize that the blemishes and surface inequalities are indications of a latent strength. Only a Christian, armed equally with divine faith, intellectual honesty, and a willingness to look at the Bible as a whole, will be able to see its profound unity and divine direction.

Yet faith must not be appealed to indiscriminately. It is the easiest thing in the world to represent an opinion or a prejudice as a dogma of faith. Many an obvious fact has been sacrificed to this sort of "faith." Intellectual honesty and common sense go for nothing if a man is really determined to stick to the "truth" he is familiar with. How can faith do anything but slumber in such an atmosphere? It is bound to become weak and unable to face reality. Real faith is fearless. It is confident that there can be no quarrel between God's right hand and His left. It knows that contradictions are only apparent and are occasioned by a human weakness which has either obscured the divine element or misunderstood the human.

Faith like this will reach the very heart of the Bible. It will not vacillate on the fringe of signs and wonders, but will make straight for the heart of the matter, which is God's over-all action. Rather than risk getting lost in a maze of detail, it will seek to find the broad trends which flow smooth and unbroken beneath the ripples of human fortune. If it does happen to meet an extraordinary manifestation of God's power, it will treat it as a climax in the rhythm, a sort of "shock" given in moments of crisis, emphasizing a movement which was already present in principle.

In this light the Christian will see that the Bible with its two Testaments, distinct but complementary, is the key to the divine plan. Out of the raw material of humanity the Spirit fashions the Word of God. The Bible cannot give faith, but the open mind cannot fail to see in it the hand of God. It is not the source of our faith in Christ, but it is the Church's surest guide to that faith. It does not create faith, but it does dispose the soul to receive faith, since without Christ the Bible is a puzzle. Furthermore, without the Bible in its context, which is the Church, we would have no knowledge of Christ under the human aspect in which the Son of God became incarnate.

THE BIBLE'S CONVERGENT THEMES

Before all else in this search after the true meaning of the Bible, we must accept the texture of the cloth into which the Word of God has been woven. It is made up of a number of threads tightly laced together. These threads are the doctrinal themes which run the whole length of Israel's history. Supported one by the other in a hierarchy of mutual dependence, they gradually converge and become identified with a single central theme—the incarnate Word. Each theme is a pre-incarnation of this Word, outlining its individual aspects and effectively preparing for its final revelation.

It will not be possible to mark the development of all these themes, for they are numerous and deftly interwoven. Often they are entwined with minor themes which serve to underline a particular aspect. It is equally difficult to range them in precise order of importance, because even that varies according to time and circumstance in Israel's history. The nearer they come to their common realization in Christ, the more difficult it is to separate them. All that we can do here is to pick out those that seem to form the warp on which the complex unity of revelation has been woven.

First among these is the *theme of election*. It appears in a number of guises, but whether it is social or individual, whether it is miraculous birth or an unlooked-for victory, a reversal of human precedence, a free gift, or a minor theme like that of the "faithful remnant," it always emphasizes the primacy of the divine initiative and the absolute sovereignty of God over the affairs of men. From the call of Abraham to the magnificent statement of Christian predestination in the opening verses of the Epistle to the Ephesians, this is the burden of God's plan. It rings out in the episode of Esau and Jacob, in the story of Joseph, in the passage through the Red Sea, in the conquests of Joshua and the Judges, in the choice of David and the rejection of Saul, in the preservation of Judah from the fate of the ten tribes of Israel, in the wondrous return from the ruin of Exile, in the unexpected triumph of the Maccabees. It gives significance to the birth of John the Baptist, to the conversion of St. Paul, and to the phenomenal growth of a movement which had its humble beginnings among a handful of Galileans.

Throughout, God's strength is shown in weakness, in the exaltation of the lowly and the humbling of the mighty, in the triumph of life over death. Throughout, outlines are being sketched of one who was to take flesh from a Virgin and be born the Son of God, the archetype of all those who are predestined, whose humility and abandonment to the Father lifts them up to the right hand of God. Throughout is prefigured His Mystical Body, embracing all those on whom He has freely bestowed His Spirit and Life. The theme of divine election begins with the account of creation in Genesis and achieves its fulfilment in the song of the blessed in the Apocalypse. Without doubt, this gift of God is the most profound, the most revolutionary, and the most distinctly divine theme in the Bible. From it stem all other themes.

Another fundamental theme is that of *covenant*, flowing directly from the idea of divine gift or testament implicit in the theme of election. This is not a covenant in any ordinary sense. If it involves a sort of bilateral contract, it is only because the divine initiative demands a response. God's gift is entirely free. It puts Him under no obligation to man. Yet those who receive it are necessarily bound by certain obligations, and this interchange forges between God and His people a bond so close that there is communion between them. The elect shares in the holiness of God: he is a man apart. For His part God binds Himself to ensure happiness, on condition that He is acknowledged as the highest good.

It is a legal covenant insofar as it implies conditions for both parties. But its truest terms are bonds of love. It is already present in its first beginnings in the patriarchal religion, where God is looked upon as the Father of the clan (a concept which forms part of the religion of the people from whom Abraham came). With Moses and Sinai it assumes a more formal aspect, though the intimacy of individual piety is not altogether forgotten. After the Exile, so much emphasis is placed on the remoteness of God that the element of love seems at first to be compromised. But both themes are needed if they are to be harmonized in the revelation of the Father in the Son, under the new law of the Spirit.

Together the two themes of election and covenant give rise to a third. The recipients of God's favors are set apart: they are *God's people*, stamped with His seal. The religious exclusiveness which made Yahweh the private possession of Israel and Israel the heritage of Yahweh may surprise and trouble us. Yet the very transcendence of Christianity, this religion of revelation and superhuman life, is the product of the tension in the apparent contradiction of the *exclusiveness* of a God who is *one*. Yahweh is the God of Israel, but He is the only God and all the world is His. He chooses Israel, but only that through her He may assert His claims over all mankind. The people of Israel are, like the Church of Christ, a theocracy. They were very keenly aware of their mission to the world. It is the explanation of their intransigence, and the cause of the invincible dynamism which they have handed on to the Church, the new Israel of God. From the tribes wandering out of Egypt for the conquest of the Promised Land to the kingdom of David pushing out its national frontiers, from the postexilic community awaiting a miraculous victory to the eschatological kingdom of Christ established through the preaching of the Church, always there is this theme of God's chosen people, the divine leaven which must transform the whole world.

These three themes, election, covenant, and the people of God, form the basic trilogy which underlies the whole unfolding of revelation. But as a cycle it is not closed. In its themes of covenant and conquest there is room for development: covenant implies the co-operation of man, and in his conquests man is liable to suffer setbacks. Thus a new cycle opens out of the first, in the *theme of sin*. Sin in the Bible does not mean the scar left on the integrity of arrogant human nature, as it does in the pagan conception of morality. Sin is a defection of loyalty to the covenant, a rejection of God's love and God's gift. By sin man breaks away from the charmed circle of God and is thrown back on himself and his own nothingness. It may assume many forms: in Eden it is a blow struck for independence, in the desert it is the apostasy of the idolaters, with Saul it is a failure to observe the prescribed ritual, during the period of the Prophets it is moral corruption, after the Exile it is the pride of the ritualist or the self-sufficiency of the materialist, in the time of Christ it is the rejection of the Messiah, among the Pauline converts it is blasphemy against the Spirit. Whatever shape it takes, it is always a breaking of the covenant of love and a rejection of God's courtship.

It involves the necessity for *punishment*. This too varies with the aspect of the sin. The almost arbitrary and unaccountable vengeance of God is expressed at the height of Israel's victory in terms of temporal misfortune and national catastrophe. At this stage there seems to be no connection at all with what we conceive to be the primary effect of sin, namely, the loss of God. After the Exile a deeper understanding of the interior life and the personal implications of the problem of evil brought new light to the question of temporal retribution. For Job, human suffering is not inevitably the result of sin. In the book of Wisdom the punishment begins to be regarded as something immanent—the eternal loss of God.

In Christ the theme reaches its perfect expression. It is He who finally revealed the depth of the void left in man by such a loss. Those who were inspired to interpret His message did no more than clarify this revelation. For St. John, the gift of eternal life means accepting the Father in His Son; for St. Paul, sin is the utter emptiness of the man who has cut himself off from the Spirit of Christ. Thus the Bible grafts the problems of evil and pain and death on to the theme of punishment, whether it be personal punishment or social, moral or material, spiritual or eschatological. Always the problem is set against the background of God, always it emphasizes man's absolute need of God. No other book has so pointedly depicted in "existentialist" terms the confusion of man without God.

In the depths of his nothingness, there is one course left open to man, the acknowledgment of his guilt. The very nothingness to which he is reduced impresses upon him the knowledge that this is all he has. And so the *theme of repentance* is of cardinal importance in the development of the plan of redemption. It is the fallen soul's only way back to God. It may be motivated by contrition or merely by self-interest. Sometimes it is the poignant experience of the disasters which follow his breach of the covenant; sometimes it is the misery of the man who knows he cannot escape God's wrath; sometimes it is the melting of a sinner's heart before the infinite love of the Father in His Son. The one theme embraces such apparent diversities as the moralizing book of Judges, the weary disillusionment of Ecclesiastes, and the passionate appeal for love in the Song of Songs. From all of them comes the same cry of man's acknowledged nothingness, a cry which is echoed in the New Testament by Mary's Magnificat and the vibrant doxologies of Christian thanksgiving. This confession of need with its awareness that all men are "under the bondage of sin" (Gal 3:22) completes the sin-cycle and introduces the cycle of redemption.

The God of Scripture hears the cry of man's distress. If He is a jealous God and one who punishes harshly, it is because He is a loving Father. The *theme of mercy* is the pivot around which all other biblical themes revolve. It is an echo, a poised overtone of the election theme, a new and richer development of it. A gift is twice-blest if it has already once been refused. In Scripture God "repents," He relents, there is no limit to His love. He has pity and is moved with compassion for His well-beloved. He swears He will not harm mankind again, He mourns for His trampled vineyard, and He weeps over the holy city which has rejected Him. From the infinite treasury of His divine pity He reveals His breathtaking plan, determined from all eternity in "the hidden purpose of His will" (Eph 1:9). From Paradise lost to the first Christmas night, He reasserts His promise in ever more glowing terms. Noah, Abraham, Moses, David, the Prophets, John the Baptist, these are all its witnesses, the forerunners to the angels' song, "Glory to God in high heaven, and peace on earth to men that are God's friends." The whole Bible is the detailed publication of the "good news" which reaches its climax in the Gospel.

This mercy of God is not an empty word. It is infallible and efficacious. The Word of God does not return to Him until it has accomplished its task (Is 55:11). God's pity is translated into action and His promise is made flesh. To bring His people out from the bondage of Egypt He raises up Moses, a leader for His people, strengthened with the power of His Spirit and commissioned to make with His people a covenant of blood. Joshua conquers the "Land" in His name. Each of the Judges is an incarnation of God's desire to rescue Israel from the plight to which her sins have reduced her. The long line of divine mediators, the instruments of Yahweh in the founding and restoration of His kingdom, culminates in David, a second Moses. Henceforth God's captain is a King Messiah, the Anointed of

Yahweh's own Spirit. It is David who gives direction to the *theme of messianic salvation*. Before him Israel had always looked for a second Moses. Now Judah would look for a second David to be both King and Prophet. The darker the gathering clouds in the political sky before the Exile, the more eagerly did the Prophets turn their eyes to the day of wrath when the Messiah would eventually appear as the hoped-for Saviour. When that hope became dimmed in the pallid Restoration after the Exile, Daniel looked to heaven to see the Son of Man coming on the clouds in a victory which was to be the consummation of all things.

As these glorious messianic traits are more precisely developed, so are they unexpectedly modified. Persecuted like David, like Jeremiah hated by God's enemies, like the Psalmist the victim of wicked men, like Job the innocent in the power of Satan, so the Servant of Yahweh will suffer for His people, their guilt imputed to Him. He will be the new Paschal Lamb, led to the slaughter. The salvation of His people will not be won by force but by the shedding of His blood. He will give them God's life at the price of His death. He will carry them along in His triumphal glory, but only when He Himself has drained the cup of the divine anger. The poignant songs of the Servant of Yahweh are a symposium prefiguring those of St. Paul and St. John on the mystery of Christ. Jesus, Son of David and Son of God, unites and synthesizes in His own person all the characteristics of the long-awaited Mediator. He is the expression of God's love, the firstborn of His beloved children, the scapegoat for God's anger over His sinful people, the supreme lawgiver of the new covenant in His blood. He is the harbinger of new life by His victory over death, through sanctification in the Spirit of God.

The cycle of redemption is not completely achieved by the work of Christ. He is the mediator, joined with His Father, but joined too with those whom He has redeemed in His blood. Therefore He is the firstborn of the new race of God's people, and His victory is not communicated to His own except by their sharing in His death. This brings us to the "in-between" theme or the *theme of the desert*. It completes the third cycle and opens on to the fourth. Noah's ark must wander for forty days on the bitter waves; forty years of pilgrimage separate the Red Sea from the entry into the Promised Land; before he is king in Jerusalem David must go to earth in the hill country of Judah; before he receives his commission to anoint the kings Elijah must fast forty days in the desert of Negeb; the Exile is a painful confinement for the eventual rebirth of God's people. Christ Himself finally inaugurated His own mission with forty days of lenten fast and so hallowed the custom He gave to His Church. In the symbolism of the Apocalypse (12:6) He consigns the woman in childbirth to the desert for three and a half years (half of the perfect seven) so that she can escape the persecution of the dragon and bring forth her Son to triumph.

The desert theme gives point to the *theme of life through death*. This paradox is truly the fundamental principle which gives biblical morality its supernatural quality and distinguishes it from the so-called "natural" morality of paganism. Judged by worldly wisdom, the morality of the cross is folly. There is no promise of happiness but only of future suffering, death, and perhaps martyrdom. It is a divine promise that biblical morality offers the Christian, God's wisdom that it prepares him for, and the Spirit of sonship that it breathes. For entrance fee into this world of God's fulness, a man has nothing to offer save his own nothingness and the confession of his misery. Christian morality is a morality of death to the old so that the new man may be born. It is only to babes that the Father reveals the splendor of His Son, only to those who are parched that He gives the water of life. With set purpose Christ turns upside down the world's accepted design for happiness (Mt 5:3-12) and smashes the proud code of human perfection. The justification preached by a humanism of good works is not pleasing to God. Man was created to be satisfied not with himself but with God.

The humble whom Christ calls "blessed" are those whom the Psalms have called the "poor" and whom St. Paul will call believers, the true sons of Abraham. The faith which brings salvation is the passionate surrender of that nothingness which is all a soul has to give when it is faced with God's own gift of His Son. To believe in the Son of God is to die to one's own self-sufficiency, to make over the whole heart to the call of the Spirit's love. Thus the life of a Christian here on earth is a constant battle, where the forces of the world are straining to check his escape into the joy of the Spirit. The Christian suffers Christ's own agony, completing in his body what is lacking in the passion of Christ. In the Church he is in the world, but not of the world. It is here that he goes to earth to be transformed from death to the life which was won on the first Easter morning. The Church is in the desert, waiting for the harvest to ripen, waiting for the Body of Christ to achieve that absorption of death by life which was begun by Christ, and which will not be complete until all men belong to Him as He belongs to God.

This brings us to the last cycle in the fulness of revelation, the *cycle of accomplishment*. To every advance in the realization of the messianic hope there corresponds a qualifying disillusionment and *partial setback*. Abraham was not to know his numerous posterity, Moses was not to see the Promised Land. Joshua's conquest was not the fondly imagined military rout, David saw portents of ruin in the civil war of his own lifetime. Judah was confident of resisting Assyria, but like Israel she was led into exile. The Restoration saw little of the grandeurs promised by Isaiah. Even before it finally collapsed under Pompey, the triumph of the Maccabees was compromised by the successors of the early heroes. Finally Christ Himself was put to death. . . . Where was the end to this insistent rhythm of failure and success, of defeat and victory? With Easter morning the disciples thought that it had reached its climax, but instead of the glorious Parousia they were given the consoling Spirit. There was to be no victory in fire and thunder, but only a slow and painful conquest in teaching and blood. Their kingdom turned out to be a Church. *Disillusion* is the very first theme in this cycle of accomplishment.

But disillusion is only an aspect of death to the world. Out of that death God's people are to be reborn to God's life. Each failure is a prelude to the rebirth of a stronger and more vibrant hope. The Bible is constantly looking beyond what is, to the wider scope of what will be. With Christ that scope becomes present, it is begun. Yet it too lacks completion: Christ's victory has not yet realized its accomplishment. The *theme of hope* is the Bible's expression of the believer's last resort, the living synthesis of his faith and love, of his death and life, of his need for salvation and his thirst for the kingdom of God.

The kingdom of God is begun, the seed has been sown and it grows. But there are tares among the wheat. The combat between good and evil, between Christ and the devil, between light and darkness, this is not the supreme battle. That has still to be fought when all these preliminaries are done. The serpent in the Garden, Pharaoh and Assyria, false brethren of Moab and Edom, Philistines uncircumcised, Balak and Mesha, Gog and Magog, Antiochus Epiphanes and Herod the Great, these are just names, incarnations of Antichrist, personifications of the "man of sin," agents of the "mystery of iniquity" (2 Th 2:7). Before the end comes, Satan will all but prevail and apostasy will be widespread, until the Son of Man appears in all majesty to destroy the enemy with the breath of His mouth. Resurrection and judgment will follow to set the final seal on the kingdom and restore all things in the harmony of divine fulness.

So the doctrinal themes of the Bible come back full circle to their starting point. From the eternity in which mankind's election is first planned, they carry us through the vision of *eternal life*. In the very first pages of Genesis, the Bible portrays the memory of this vision: God in the Garden of Eden talking with man in the cool of evening. It is with the same thought that the Book closes in the Apocalypse: a picture of the heavenly Jerusalem. If the earthly Paradise was only a nostalgic memory of a home that was lost, and the Promised Land only a narrow strip in the Middle East, they yet expressed a yearning for the place where God has pitched His tent. It was Christ Himself who showed the significance of these images when He gave to His own kingdom the titles of "Land" and "Paradise" (Mt 5:5; Lk 23:43). If the kingdom is prefigured in a way which is human and inadequate— the clan of Israel, the twelve tribes, the kingdom of David, the religious community of the Restoration after exile, even the Church which rules the earth—the reader of the Bible knows that they are but pale reflections of that everlasting glory which the Father has destined for His elect, through the life-giving Spirit of His Son.

We conclude this section with a theme which is outside the scope of those we have dealt with. It will serve as a frame to contain them: the *theme of thanksgiving*. This is the form in which the Bible most happily expresses the over-all view of salvation. Here the organic unity of all the themes is underlined. Whether it is expressed in a simple formula of praise like "Blessed be God," or more fully as in some parts of the Psalms, always there is an attempt to draw a picture of God's great "mercies" in the three or four successive movements which correspond to the cycles we have described. First, there is the statement of praise. This is followed by a description of some favor, pictured as one aspect of salvation. Thirdly, this favor is connected with a promise made in the past, and so becomes part of God's hidden and eternal design. Finally, the purpose and effects of the favor point to the last times, of which these present times are a presage.

There are classical examples of such doxologies to be found in both Testaments. Some comprise a single short stanza, like Christ's song of thanksgiving in Mt 11:25-27 and the Nunc Dimittis. Others, like the Magnificat, the Benedictus, and especially the opening of the Epistle to the Ephesians, repeat the theme time and again with continual variation on the original four movements. These are perhaps the most perfect examples of the circular movement which characterizes the poetry of the Bible. When the first Christian liturgies came to express their own thanksgiving in the "eucharistic act" (the climax until Christ comes again of God's eternal mercy incarnate in His Son), they found here a ready-made and natural framework.

THE GRADUAL TRANSPOSITION

OF THE BIBLICAL THEMES

The Organic Development of Revelation

The doctrinal themes of the Bible can all be reduced to a few closely-knit cycles, each leading to the next, each incomplete without the next. An outline of these themes in their mutual relationships should resemble a series of concentric circles and illustrate both their organic unity and their living complexity. To see revelation thus in its entirety is to see a perfect blueprint of the eternal plan of God. Yet it has its dangers. Such a view is so rich that we are liable in our fascination to be unaware of its dynamic progression.

In fact, such an outline must of its nature be abstract, and its value can only be relative. The fact that we have caught it poised in the order of logic must not blind us to its movement in the order of time. Revelation is necessarily bound up with its development at any given moment in history, and the concentric circles of the different biblical themes open out historically into a spiral. The explanation of the themes given above was a bird's-eye view. It showed the inner structure, the fixed woof across which the shuttle travels. What we must do now is to give this view a third dimension, to see it in its side elevation. In this way we will see its gradual unfolding. The four cycles and the dozen or so themes which we have singled out are present in embryo from the beginning of revelation, just as all the organs of man are present in a fetus. If we pluck revelation from the perspective of history in which God wished it to grow and develop, if we level out all the different themes and forget their dimension in time, we will pervert the full sense of revelation. Our contact with the eternal is made at some point in time, and we cannot think of it except in that context. There is indeed a similarity of proportion between the different human expressions of the divine thought (they are related to each other by analogy), but they retain their essential differences. There is a world of difference, for example, between Yahweh's covenant with a roving band of bedouins bent on the conquest of land they covet, and the transcendental design in which the Spirit of Christ sanctifies the union between the Father and His elect, and bestows on them the eternal life of the Son.

All the same, the similarity between the different expressions is not merely superficial. The realities they represent are cognate, and one is the flowering of the seed contained in the other. Though it is something less than identity, there is more than mere analogy between the covenant of Sinai and the covenant ratified in the Spirit by the risen Christ, between the crossing of the Red Sea and Christian baptism, between Abraham's race and the royal race of the elect. Between these realities there is a living unity, which progresses but is constant, which is able to effect change without itself changing, which can operate on different levels without losing its irresistible and unifying dynamism. The external similarities are simply the spontaneous manifestations of this dynamism. They are the confining shell, the kerbs which define the road. To rip up the kerbstones and set them side by side to show their similarities is to lose both the confines of the road and its direction. The Bible is like a reel of film which shows the different forms assumed by a living tradition through the ages. To cut this film in order to rearrange the sequence of its frames is to take all meaning out of it and destroy the possibility of it ever being screened. *The Bible will have meaning only if its sequence is preserved and its upward movement understood.* This cannot be done without the living Spirit which continues to breathe this tradition in the Church.

It is difficult to know which to admire most, the constancy of the themes or the rich variety of the ways in which God has taught them. It is of the utmost importance to mark this divine technique as one stage succeeds another. With infinite tact God molds His approach to suit prevailing needs. He will fasten on disillusionment to raise men's hopes to a higher level; He will turn a material failure into a spiritual victory; He will try every expedient that a Father's love for His child can fashion. The rationalist's microscope will discover here nothing that is not human; the eyes of faith alone will see beneath the surface the guiding hand of God, weaving this mass of humanity into the unity of His plan. It is not a heavy hand—more often than not it is imperceptible and almost furtive. But it is always there, interlacing the divine thread into every section of the human pattern, showing itself occasionally to impart a twist to the direction or stimulate a new beginning. Generally the movement is scarcely noticeable except as a gradual upward trend. Now and again, when a hidden snag has fouled the work, a sudden acceleration of pace is a sure sign that the divine hand is there. When the work of revelation is eventually viewed as a whole, it is seen to fall into a number of clear-cut stages. In each the same basic pattern may be recognized, sublimated and transposed as one stage leads to another. In each transposition it is possible to see the human element at work, but under the direction of God's firm hand. It is this hand alone which can explain the unwavering continuity of the movement and the overwhelming transcendence of its final achievement.

St. Paul divided the two thousand years of revelation's development into three main periods. We could do worse than follow his example and mark the progress towards Christianity in three stages: the *cycle of the Promises,* the *cycle of the Law,* and the *cycle of the Spirit.* Alternatively, we could lay emphasis on the historical, geographical, and spiritual aspect of these stages by calling them *patriarchal, national,* and *universal.* Or again, if we wish to mark the development in the concept of the God who is the pivot of this evolution, we could see them as the cycles of the *God of the clan, absolute monotheism,* and the *revelation of the Father.* Finally, by underlining the unique influence of God's Word on the human founders of these three stages, we could call our three cycles *Abraham, Moses,* and *Christ.* The name is not important. What is important is that we realize the length of the road between the stages and the unswerving unity of its direction. In the last two stages especially, we should take notice of a number of secondary themes which define more closely this direction.

The Cycle of the Promises

Abraham is well named the father of those who believe. If there was a rudimentary revelation made before his time, the patriarchal traditions are the only evidence we have of it. Some historians are inclined to believe that the prehistoric religion of the Semitic peoples had a monotheistic bias. This may well be: they were all of nomadic race, and the constant use by the whole group of the name *El* to designate the Divinity may be an indication of a common monotheism. The crowded pantheon of Babylon was a later development, and in any case more symbolic and imaginative than real. Even so, the possible existence of an ancestral monotheism which may have survived to Abraham's time does not in any way detract from him. His Babylonian background was one of polytheism and his own clan most likely paid cult to the moon gods of Haran. His sudden determination to break with his clan and its gods may have been made under pressure of historical circumstances. Even so, they were subordinate to a religious experience which was the real cause of the break, for which the world will ever stand in his debt. This was the first of those divine "shocks." Abraham retired to the desert under the spell of the mysterious call, a call which was to take hold of him and dominate the rest of his life. In this call he became aware of his vocation. He was to be the chief of an autonomous clan; the fact that it was called into being by a new and unknown God would ever be the mark of its uniqueness. That is all there is. But in that little is contained the germ of the fulness of revelation.

The Patriarchs were not theologians or metaphysicians. They were simply sheiks of the steppe land, occupied with their flocks and fully intent (as was all mankind in the dawn of history) on ensuring the power and growth of their clan. We see their numbers growing but making no great mark on the naturalistic polytheism of the Corridor. Now and again the Experience is repeated, sometimes brutally, sometimes graciously, but always insistently. Those who suffer the Experience are possessed, for it is a shock which has no parallel in the petty religions of their neighbors. But the first feeling of terror is followed by a more reasoned calm. The shock has rocked the foundations of their religious ideas, but they still keep to the old religious forms, and they try a little clumsily to make these old forms contain their new emotion. Thus Jacob erects a *menhir,* and Abraham is prepared to sacrifice his only son. But these are surface things. Beneath is the forceful grip of a new and mysterious God who has captured their imaginations and established a new claim in their hearts. They express their feelings in the only way they know, and see themselves as the children of a *divine Father.* When the shock of the first impact has passed, their childlike candor reasserts itself in the sly and self-interested familiarity engendered of this new relationship. Whatever profit there is in being adopted by this rather disturbing God, it must be turned to the account of the clan. It is a down-to-earth sort of religion, with little or no appreciation of the transcendence of God. Yet this same infant candor which babbles to the God-Father about the good of the clan is more than the germ which will later develop into the formidable covenant of Sinai. Already it has the flavor of that filial piety which will mark the feelings of the true sons of Abraham for God, their Father.

The Cycle of Mosaic Law

The promises of the nameless God were fulfilled in Egypt. The Israelite clan had become a great people there. The God of their fathers had not fared so well: a demoralizing slavery had almost destroyed their national identity and religious personality. The Experience had ceased to grip their souls. The smooth waters of the Nile had washed away the clinging sand of the desert, and the heavy hand of Pharaoh had speeded the work of time. Then, suddenly, the shock came again. Moses had fled into the desert and there, before the burning bush, he found once more the faith of his fathers.

This second manifestation of God's design is not just a return to the past; it bears the hallmark of a new departure. The God of their fathers at last speaks out His name. The name of Yahweh, "He who is" or "He who causes to be," is not a metaphysical abstraction. It is a name which distinguishes Him from the impotent gods of other nations. This is the God *who is*, as opposed to those others *who are not*. This is the living God who causes all things to be. And this God has chosen the race of Israel for His own people. Until now, they had been only separated groups without a bond of unity; but now Yahweh would snatch them out of Egypt and lead them into the desert, and there, in the crucible where their ancestors were fashioned, He would weld them together by giving them a leader, a law, a religion, a God, and a destiny. The covenant of Sinai was a strange and unprecedented contract. The God of their fathers bound himself to be to this tribe of nomads what Kamosh was to Moab and Marduk to Babylon. For the Israelite, Yahweh was an exclusive possession, and yet also (though less articulately) a God who had sovereign rights over all the earth, the living God who is and who created all things. Israel's stupendous destiny stems from this belief. In the matrix of this tiny people, hemmed in both geographically and mentally, there lay hidden an intuition with infinite possibilities. The history of this people is the gradual opening of the matrix under the pressure of divine force.

At first the achievements were modest enough. All that these wild bedouins expected from their formidable and strange God, whose claims they hardly understood, was immediate military success. His power was like the elements: He was Yahweh of armies, the warrior God with lightning in His hand. The burning faith which energized their dynamic power was tribute enough to His transcendence. All other gods were dead. This was the living God who must conquer His land, and Israel was certain of victory. Canaan must fall into their hungry hands like a cluster of ripe grapes. Yahweh would bring His people back to Canaan, where He had first revealed Himself in the promise made to the Patriarchs that they would one day share this land which was His home. The cycle of Egypt had closed with the crossing of the Red Sea; the cycle of the desert closes on the banks of the Jordan, with the coveted paradise in sight.

But just as the rescue from Egypt was followed by the despair of the desert wanderings, so too the victories of Joshua were succeeded by the long and disappointing period of the Judges. Quite clearly Yahweh was not like other gods. His jealousy had already kept them wandering in the dry southern steppes. Now He again deserts His people: alone they must grapple with the difficulties of a slow campaign of infiltration. He had undeniably proved Himself to be a God of war and occasionally would raise up a captain to "wage the wars of Yahweh." But why did He not now rise up and with one fell blow smash these peoples on whom He had pronounced His anathema? Why must He be so fastidious, why the moral demands? The Baals of Canaan were easier to please and had a better understanding of flocks and herds than the rough warrior-God Yahweh. What harm could there be in consulting them in this new and settled life which they must learn to live? Hardly had the little band of invaders become united before they were in danger of crumbling before the sensual gods they had vanquished. At the end of this period they are back to where they were under the Egyptian oppression. The Philistines have them by the throat, for all the allegiance their fathers swore to Yahweh. Even the ark, the symbol of their covenant and conquest, the memorial of their second resurrection, even that had fallen into the hands of the uncircumcised.

The Cycle of Royal Law

This was the depth of despair for which Yahweh had waited. Now He would return a third time to show His people the dazzling prospect of an even more wonderful salvation. Backed by the new prophetic movement, David not only crushes the power of the Philistines but leads Israel under her king and her God to a state of political, social, and geographical significance beyond her wildest dreaming. In His Anointed One, Yahweh inaugurates the kingdom of God already inherent in the terms of the commitment made at Sinai and in the promise given to the fathers. The national aggrandizement was based on what was in essence a religious conquest. Israel's faith in Yahweh has been tried and has become deeper, purer, and wider. Henceforth, Israel is sure that Yahweh alone is the living and omnipotent God. Henceforth she is open in admitting that boundless ambition which has been her secret hope since Sinai. Yahweh would no longer be content to defend His own against enemy peoples and strange gods: He would now carry the fight to them, destroy those false gods, and subdue their followers. Through Israel the whole world must be dominated and serve the kingship which is Yahweh's by right.

David's reign marks a climax in Israel's religious development. Two salient interventions of God have so far given it direction: the call of Abraham and the revelation of the name Yahweh. Yet in spite of the progress that has been made David's faith is still the faith of Abraham. Both are bounded by the confines of this world; for both, salvation is thought of in terms of man's temporal happiness; both are primarily social and national in outlook.

If Israel's faith during this period is something less than monotheism, it is something more than monolatry. Yahweh is more than one among many gods, to satisfy the material and political hopes of His people. He is totally unlike the blind tyrannical gods of other nations. He is a living God, who searches the reins and hearts of those He wants to possess. From Sinai onwards, Israel's religious outlook has a moral, personal, and interior bias. There is only one God; His name is Yahweh and His will is binding.

The conclusions reached in these first stages mark a revolution in religion. They contain a seed that has the power to grow into the most supernatural of revelations. The one and only moral God will not be satisfied with outward observance. His object is the very soul of man: He will go to the very fibre of man's being and be his beginning and last end. He breaks the barriers which divide the human from the divine and tears down the iron curtain of a "natural" religion, to establish between God and man the mystery of Father-hood which Abraham had glimpsed, which the covenant of Moses had consecrated, and which was the mainspring of David's unclouded love for his God. All this is inherent in the faith of Israel on the eve of the great prophetic movement.

Inherent, but not obvious. The ordinary man was still thinking in terms of a national and earthly kingdom. The cult of Yahweh is merely the highest expression of the political life of the nation. He is expected to vouchsafe human bounty to the nation as such. Whatever He may demand by way of moral injunctions and ritualistic pre-scriptions are simply His conditions for granting salvation. There is no intrinsic connection between the two. Yahweh is the desire of all hearts because He brings earthly bliss. It will need some catastrophe to swing the balance between the two axioms of their traditional faith. Only in this way will the more fundamental axiom win the day and the other sink back into its proper context. Prophetism marks the third intervention of God: its precise purpose was to achieve this swing of the balance.

The Cycle of Prophetic Law

The Prophets up to the time of the Exile seem at first to revert to a merely national messianism, to be reformers conserving the work of the past. In fact, even the triumph of Yahweh in the time of David could not escape the downward trend to decadence, and Solomon's glory was thin enough covering for the impending ruin. If the nation had risen to great heights, it had further to fall. After the Schism the apostasy in both kingdoms was almost absolute, and the first impression given by the Prophets is that they were men who had arrived too late to prevent the apostasy and could only refer the realization of the disappointed dream to a remoter future. In point of fact, however, the Prophets belonged to the future as much as to the past. Not that they were innovators—salvation was still thought of on a national and earthly level, to be achieved by religious reform. But insofar as they championed this reform, they were forced to delve deeper than ever before into the real significance of the cove-nant which had dictated earlier conceptions of salvation. In this way the glory that was Yahweh emerged from the twilight of polytheism.

His moral requirements outgrew the ritual which had clothed them, and His political horizon reached to the ends of the earth. Salvation assumed a personal aspect, in answer to the tormented cry wrung from the heart of a people oppressed by sinners. In His love, Yahweh would make Israel His bride, with the nations for her dowry.

Thus these apparent survivors of a past generation became pioneers of the future. Incapable of understanding the new language they spoke, Israel and Judah went the accustomed way of infidelity. Then came the momentous disaster. Moses had staved it off once by his timely intervention. David, too, had managed to postpone it. But the slavery of Egypt and the oppression in the time of the Judges were as nothing compared with this. Yahweh's people were simply wiped off the political map, once for all. Never again, not even under the Maccabees, would the Jewish people have even a semblance of freedom and independence. They should have disappeared altogether, like the ten tribes of the northern kingdom. Yahweh Himself had been conquered in the defeat of His people, and by rights His name should have been obliterated in the destruction of a nation whose only purpose was to perpetuate His name.

And yet the seed which the Prophets had sown bore fruit in the land of exile. For the fourth time the dawn of salvation was to break, this time for the "Remnant" which germinated there in penance and the spirit of hope. Freed from the confines of its national and ritual framework, its faith was slowly refashioned and purified. Shorn of its national and earthly ties, religion went deeper and its perspectives became wider. Salvation was no longer national but personal; the things of the world made way for the things of the spirit; a narrow exclusivism gave way to a world-wide proselytism. Above all, there was a deepening of the concept of God. The name of Yahweh with its nationalistic connotation gave place to the almost too transcendent "God of heaven." The Exile marked a profound stage in the history of God's people. They were no longer a nation but a religious community: here a national cult was transformed into a spiritual force.

The Cycle of Priestly Law

Important though this metamorphosis was, we must not exaggerate it. The old nationalistic hopes were to endure for a long time yet. Even up to the fall of Jerusalem in A.D. 70 they would be for the ordinary people the most natural expression of that infinite happiness which is the inspiration of all religion. It was the fortune of history which gave these aspirations a new shape. The meager results of the Restoration from exile sowed disillusionment in their hearts. Even the successes of the Maccabees were soon a bitter memory of what might have been but for the enslaving hand of Rome. Hers was a rod that no human Messiah could break. So it is to the clouds of heaven that they look for their messianic deliverance, and they live

for the day when the cataclysm promised by their apocalyptic literature will create a new Israel and establish her dominion over the
world.

This messianic hope, transformed though it was into an eschatological one, was no longer the only source of the Jewish community's
religious energy. For the very first time the people are governed by
priests. Under them, religion becomes a cult, and all the main themes
of the past begin to shift on to a moral and juridical plane. The teaching of the Prophets in particular is taken up and made more precise.
The idea of God's transcendence is pushed to its furthest limits, and
the moral aspect of the covenant is the only one that receives recognition. In fact, the theme of the covenant becomes the pivot on which
all Jewish thought turns, and the narrow confines of the community
give it a new look: it becomes more rigid and polished, more legalistic and juridical. Whereas prophecy was a dynamic movement which
looked forward, the cult of the Law looked back to the past. Where
the interior religion of the Prophets made them hope for an actual
historical Messiah to fulfil their ideal, the spirituality of the votaries
of the Law was achieved and consummated by the letter of the law
and its fulfilment. The covenant becomes more of a contract than a
testament. So compelling is the concept of God's transcendence that
eventually all relationship with Him is inconceivable, apart from
the purely external one flowing from this contract. No longer does
God give Himself to men; He simply exacts their obedience and
worship.

This conception is not without its splendor. The chosen people
are the priests of God, whose office is to proclaim His transcendence
and order His praise in all righteousness. The theme of accomplishment and eternal life is enriched by this new revelation. However,
the conception contrasts too violently with the wretchedness of human
misery for it to be sufficient. What is worse, it tends to upset the
delicate balance of the whole of revelation on the very eve of the
Christian era. In seeking to base the covenant on moral perfection
rather than on the free choice of God, and by setting God at an incommunicable distance from His people, this outlook threatened
to split asunder the two basic aspects of salvation which revelation
had constantly tried to bring together. In such an outlook, man with
his free will has no absolute need of divine grace, and with his inner
perfection he can look God in the face. In place of a religion where
wretchedness called forth mercy, where nothingness gave birth to free
election, where the cry from a child's heart stirred the love of a
Father, there is substituted a natural and watertight religion, where
man has nothing to offer God but his own self-sufficiency, and nothing to hope for but what he has earned.

The cult of the Law was bound to be at loggerheads with reality.
It was inconsistent with man's weakness in giving him no support
save a code of rules. It was incompatible with God's goodness in

making the existence of evil incomprehensible. In fact, the "just" man did not inevitably receive his reward: not infrequently it was the sinner who prospered. Such a cult of the Law could never suppress that yearning for consummation and new life which was at the root of all messianic expectation. The yearning remained, and it was deeper than ever; the mere fact that all hope of political power was now gone and that the Law itself assumed a moral aspect only shifted its emphasis from an earthly and social level to a personal and spiritual one. The book of Job first showed the utter bankruptcy of the kind of law and covenant which automatically rewards man's perfection with God's happiness. Ecclesiastes went further, showing from experience that the very opposite is true: a soul filled with every human bliss could still be empty and famished. These "sages" of the postexilic period remained true to the real current of prophetic revelation. While they enlarged its moral import and applied it to the problem of personal salvation, they still managed to preserve the prophetic conviction of man's inadequacy and to insist on the need for a justice which came entirely from a merciful God. By admitting their own inability ever to achieve it, they underlined the traditional hope all the more.

Final Bearings

Thus the old religion of Israel had reached the threshold of Christianity in three distinct forms: the down-to-earth messianism of the ordinary people, the religion of the Law, and the ideal of the sapiential books. So clear-cut had these three become that they sometimes seemed to delineate three separate sects. The mass of the people were fired with hopes of national sovereignty. The ruling classes took refuge behind a religion which they claimed to be definitively closed, the Sadducees smiling at the popular illusions, and the Pharisees expecting nothing of the Messiah except his endorsement of the Law. Even the immortality promised by the last inspired books was seen only as a confirmation of their belief that revelation was to reach its perfection in the eternal cult of the Law. Certainty of an afterlife had done no more than take away their hope of receiving anything on this earth.

It was the third, the sapiential school of thought that inspired the final surge of revelation, the greatest and most revolutionary yet. The triumph of the Maccabees had increased the anxiety and dissatisfaction of men like Job and Ecclesiastes. They were bewildered by the pointless sacrifice of men who had not lived to enjoy the fruit of their work. It was the Greek hope of a life after death that gave the eventual answer to these soul-searchings. Ben Sirach had already pointed to the solid foundations for such a belief; the book of Wisdom asserted it with God's own authority, and with a boldness and precision which left no room for doubt. In this new hope of immortal life was contained a conception that was to upset all previous ideas.

The author of Wisdom appealed to it, drawing revolutionary conclusions as if they were self-evident. In making eternal life the end-term of personal salvation, of the last judgment, and of man's happiness, he brought together the two parallel streams in which the old yearnings of Israel had bypassed legalistic orthodoxy and survived. Eschatological and interior, national and personal, earthbound and moral, historical and sapiential, these aspects were for the first time fused together. Unfortunately, this reconciliation in eternity left the present life empty, and this happiness with God still required a name.

To sum up then: On the eve of the birth of Christ, revelation had reached such a stage of maturity that it seemed to the more responsible elements among the Jews to have reached its term. And yet some vital thing was wanting. This happiness, whether it was given or promised or only hoped for, still had to be given a name. Official Judaism looked for it in the satisfaction of legal fulfilment; the ordinary people awaited it in the Conqueror who was to vanquish the Romans; the sages turned to the unknown beyond. If this prodigious growth of Abraham's faith was to be given some unity, if this three-fold harvest was to be gathered together, nothing less was demanded than the revelation of this happiness in person. God must name Himself.

THE CHRISTIAN TRANSPOSITION
OF THE BIBLICAL THEMES

The Problem of Christ

So far we have tried to disentangle the themes which constitute biblical revelation. We have traced them in broad outline from the beginning to the period immediately preceding the Christian era. Enough has been said to allow the reader to assess the revolution occasioned by the appearance of Christ.

In a study like this, it is as important to underline the continuity of the two Testaments as it is to mark the differences brought about by the new leaven which is Christ. Anyone who has grasped the logical and upward trend of revelation will be able to appreciate the place occupied in the scheme by the fact of Christianity. Jesus of Nazareth is not only the term of the evolution; He so transcends it that its whole perspective is changed. He is not only the building's keystone; He is, in His own words, the "cornerstone."

A merely human appraisal of the beginnings of Christianity will always boggle at this duality. Judeo-Christians of all time have looked upon Christ as no more than the fruit of Judaism at its best. By contrast, the Marcionites have always made of Him a revolutionary pure and simple, whose aim was to give the deathblow to a Judaism already on the point of death. Either He is put into an eschatological and social framework, and His scope restricted to the achieving of

Israel's old hope for a definitive kingdom, though on a higher level; or else only the moral content of His teaching is recognized, and He takes His place in the line of the ancient Prophets, an artist with a talent for communicating an intimate experience of God.

In point of fact, Christ did present Himself both as the national Davidic Messiah of the Jews and as the supreme Prophet of renewal in the Spirit. His teaching embraces both streams of Israel's divided hope. At one and the same time He claims to be God's wonder-working messenger to His people Israel, and also the ideal of personal intimacy with the Father, the model for all men of good will. He is the answer to those who yearned for a Messiah and to those whose hearts were heavy with dissatisfaction. He finds only one insurmountable barrier, the self-sufficiency of Pharisaism, which will not admit any need for hope and finds no room for one who claims to be the answer to all hopes. All the same, He is careful not to add fuel to the feverish expectations of the mob, and He paints His picture of the eschatological kingdom in colors striking enough to deceive even the "liberal Protestants" of His day. He puts Himself at the very center of the two streams, messianic and sapiential, so that He can the more happily embrace both and transform them in His own person.

The New Fact

In its immense simplicity, the message of Christ simply put a name to the expectation of Israel. It is His own name—the Son of God—and He died rather than renounce it. This unprecedented claim sums up all that was new in His teaching, and in its light everything else is changed. Happiness, or "salvation" as the Jews called it, does not consist in the triumph of Israel, nor in human perfection, not even in immortal life. It is identified with *God Himself*. The covenant is no longer concerned with a promised land or a mere earthly paradise; it is a divine betrothal, a gift greater than the numerous posterity of Abraham, a favor more wondrous than the rescue from Egypt, an election more radical even than that of David or Solomon. It is God Himself that Christ brings to a humanity waiting in the emptiness to which sin has consigned it, a God who, like a loving Father, bends down and begs men to open their empty hearts so that He may fill them with His fulness.

Christ alone can reveal this Fatherhood, for He alone is the true Son of God. But this sonship is to be shared by those who accept in Christ the witness of the Son of God and so discover the Fatherhood of God for themselves. For Christ is both the messenger and the message of God, and the bond that ties His disciples to Him ties them also to the Father. He is strictly the Gift of God to men: when God gives men His Son, He gives them Himself as a Father and thereby accepts them as His children, asking only that they open body and soul, mind and heart, to receive the fulness of His gift.

In short, Christ unites in Himself all the themes of past revelation *and thereby transposes them*. He answers the anxious cry of the masses for a Messiah who will found an earthly kingdom by bringing a heavenly kingdom into their midst. He meets the self-sufficiency of the Pharisees by showing them the deep void which can only be filled by the Father's love. The personal dissatisfaction of the sage He answers with His revelation of God's vast plan for a renewed Israel. He is indeed the promised Messiah, though His kingdom is from within—in the world but not of the world. To those who receive Him He brings a gift from God, and that gift is Himself, for He is the Messiah-Son of God, whose mission is to show forth His divine sonship as testimony to God's Fatherhood. He has come to give to the world the life of the Father, which He shares by right, as the pledge of a new covenant, to which man is asked to contribute only his nothingness and commit it into the hands of God.

The Indispensable Setback

There is nothing in the above outline of Christ's doctrine which cannot be gathered from an objective study of the oldest Gospel traditions, even if no account were taken of the miracles. But those who first heard Christ did not grasp the full significance of this doctrine. They colored it with their own prejudices and preconceived ideas. Nor was Christ under any illusion about that. As He approached the end of His ministry, He foretold in ever clearer terms that there would be a fatal setback. He had set Himself to co-ordinate in His person all the traditional themes and to raise them to a supraterrestrial level. It would have been remarkable if such a programme had not led to misunderstanding and provoked conflict with commonly accepted views.

Those who saw this most clearly were the Jewish theologians. Their own instinct of self-preservation made them realize the revolutionary character of this seemingly traditional doctrine. If such a Messiah-Son of God should ever find His way into the already completed edifice of Jewry's official religion, even if it was only through a side door, then the whole structure was in danger of being blown sky-high. How could the barred and bolted framework of Judaism contain a Messiah whom the earth itself could not contain? What would become of established traditions under the influence of such an unknown quantity? Born conservatives that they were, the Jewish theologians were not going to take chances. He must be put to death. It took longer for the ordinary people to reject Him. Charmed by His miracles and His forthright approach, they found His preaching ambiguous and harmless enough. It was only when they decided that this gentle Messiah was an idealist incapable of striking a hammer blow for freedom that they, too, lost interest and dropped Him. Even those who were attracted more by His personality than by His sublime wisdom were amazed that He did not clear away all misunderstanding by a dazzling manifestation of His apocalyptic glory. The disciples themselves understood little of their Master, except that He had looked into their hearts and left a mark which would remain always.

So the inevitable catastrophe came. It had to come to shatter the illusions which had dogged this people from the beginning, from the racial ideal to the escape from Egypt, from the Promised Land to the Messianic kingdom, from the Restoration after exile to the justification of the Law. The oppression of Pharaoh did not shatter it, nor did the arid desert, nor the Philistine invasion. Deportation, exile, suffering, oppression, the promise of immortality even, none of these had destroyed it. What was needed was something that would pluck the illusion out by the roots. Man must learn once for all that his happiness does not lie *in himself*, that heaven is not to be found on earth, that God cannot be called upon to vouchsafe a perfection that is exclusively human. Christ must die, in order to reverse the scale of values established by the mummified laws of a paralyzed Judaism. An unbridgeable chasm must be driven between man and the mirage of a happiness of which he himself was the center. Man must himself be split in two, take a blind leap to the sublime level of the divine Fatherhood, without ever ceasing to plumb the sickening depths of his own nothingness. Man must learn to see death and suffering, evil and sin, as the springboard for this twofold leap. Christ must die and show up the emptiness of the earthbound hope for a closed moral perfection or for material goods, and the futility of an ideal which would make man a god or make God the unknowable mystery. Christ must die, if the Jewish masses were to die to their earthly messianism, if official Judaism was to be shaken out of its false security, if His own disciples were to be rescued from their intoxication. Judaism must die to whatever was perishable in the Promises and inadequate in the Law. Christ's death must kill the yearning born of the Promises and the hope based on the Law, in order that the letter should die and the spirit live. The ambiguity which made the Promise its own fulfilment and the Law an end in itself must be shattered. Shadow must give way to reality, and the fair copy replace the rough draft. The earthly setback must become the pledge of a heavenly success. The human matrix must be cracked to reveal its divine content. Christ must tear Himself away from the earth and so open the way to the Father. "Christ must suffer and die and so enter into His glory" (Lk 24:26).

Renewal in the Spirit

The death of Christ is incomplete without His resurrection. Good Friday is the annihilation of all that was only human: it is Easter Sunday that begins the work of re-creation. For the disciples, the death of their Master would always be regarded as a catastrophe beyond imagining and the death blow to their illusions. It is not until Easter morning that a new faith is born and that they discover a new world. If Christ is truly risen, then the enterprise is not doomed. It needs only to be taken up again, though on a higher and wider level than before. Hardly have they had a chance to glimpse this new world before it comes on them like a mighty wind, in the wake of a Christ ascending to heaven. The Spirit descends on the little band. There is no room now for hesitation. The very vitality of Christ, which had so captivated them before His death, is now surging through their veins. The glorious life which He now lived was being poured out on them. His mission from the Father had been precisely to share this new life with them, as a new gift of Himself and a new mode of His presence among them. The Spirit filled them now, as the principle of an otherworldly covenant and the giver of heavenly life. Through the Spirit, Christ bestowed on man the privileges of His own divine sonship. The Spirit was the very life of Jesus, the Son of God sitting at the right hand of the Father.

It is impossible to overemphasize the effect that this experience of the heavenly vitality of the risen Christ exercised on the infant growth of Christianity. Admittedly it was not an altogether unknown experience. Throughout its long history, Israel had known the Breath of God as the irresistible power behind His Word. When the Word commanded creation, already the Spirit of God stirred over the waters (Gn 1:1). It was the Breath of God which dried up the waters of the Flood (Gn 8:1) and divided the Red Sea to provide a passage for the chosen people (Ex 14:21). It was His fire that surrounded Sinai when God proclaimed His law (Ex 19:15 f.), His strength that filled all those through whom the divine Promises were effected. In the Prophets, especially, it was He who gave a supernatural light and life, His Breath that energized the Word of God they proclaimed. But in the person of Christ the disciples had touched this vital power of God at its very source. No one else could have said with such truth "The Spirit of the Lord is upon me." The new Moses had published the terms of the new covenant. The son of David had been anointed God's Messiah from the womb of His mother, proclaimed Son of God at His baptism, and crowned as such from the moment of His resurrection by the sanctification of the Spirit. The Prophets had only been given the Spirit to speak of this Prophet. He knew the Father before ever Abraham was. This greater than Solomon had received the fulness of the Spirit. He had been singled out by the voice of the Father and the descending dove as the one in whom the Father was well pleased and on whom the Spirit rested.

Now, it seemed, the roles were to be reversed. Up to this the Spirit had been the symbol of God's incommunicability and the mainspring of His holiness. If the disciples had seen Christ as the Son of God, it was because they saw the fulness of God's Spirit in Him. But now it was no longer the Spirit who pointed to Christ, but Christ who communicated the Spirit. It was no longer Christ who pointed back to the Spirit, but the Spirit who pointed forward to the hidden glory that was Christ's. It was no longer the Spirit who consecrated Christ as Son of God, but the Son of God who at His Father's right hand freely bestowed the Spirit. Pentecost had indeed turned the world upside down. The disciples found themselves suddenly transported from earth to heaven, lifted up by the Spirit into the incommunicable world of God, taken up in the risen Christ to the very center of this new world.

To the Spirit, then, must be attributed the vast misunderstanding between Judaism and Christ. The Spirit alone, through Christ, was responsible for the friction from which the Church emerged. It was the Spirit who compelled His Anointed One to be untrue to the fossilized letter of the Law. It is the same Spirit who will now gradually make the disciples realize that by His death and resurrection Christ was faithful to the deepest meaning of Israel's revelation. If Christians today do not understand their faith, it is not because they have forgotten Christ, but because they have forgotten the meaning of Christ, which is the Spirit.

The Final Illusion: Kingdom or Church

At Pentecost the disciples learned only the bare essentials of this meaning of Christ. Although they were in contact with the divine through the person of Christ, their minds were still burdened by the cramping framework of a moribund Judaism. Far from making a clean break from this framework, they clung to it and tried to remodel it along new lines. The old illusions had died with Christ, but this new Spirit of Christ seemed to lend them a new lease of life. And indeed the unfolding of revelation was not completed at Christ's death, or even at Pentecost; it would not be completed until the last of the apostles died. Until then the Spirit of Christ must work through Judaism like a leaven, must put new life into those old limbs and bring them to their full stature.

The New Testament writings bear witness to the fact that the first disciples took time to realize the change that the new Spirit was going to introduce into their traditional ideas. Only very slowly did the Spirit bring about that evolution of ideas which enabled the disciples to adjust their minds to the new outlook and draw the line at the end of the verbal incarnation of the Word Incarnate. They had accepted Christ as Israel's true Messiah. His death taught them that He had not come to deliver Judaism from the yoke of Rome, and His resurrection that His messianic rule had indeed begun but that it was an entirely spiritual one, the final flowering of Israel's prerogatives. The coming of the Spirit had convinced them that all things were now accomplished. In the little group of Christ's followers the kingdom was established on earth in all its heavenly reality. The end could not be far off. Christ would soon return, to consecrate by His presence the triumph of His reborn people.

So the illusion came back for the last time. The first generation of Christians thought that the Spirit was the key to the kingdom, the whisper before the storm of the Parousia. They were not entirely wrong. But the Spirit was no more concerned with earthly achievement than was Christ. Neither of Them came to set up a heaven on earth, but to lift up earth to heaven. It was not enough that Christ Himself should die: the sons of the kingdom would have to die too. The life of the Spirit could be made manifest only in the death of all flesh, the kingdom achieved only in the Church. The final combat was joined between life and death: the kingdom itself must die if it was to yield its hundredfold.

Growing Pains: St. Paul and Judeo-Christianity

The first delusion that had to die was that of nationalism. In its attempts to get the Jews to accept the Promises, the little community met with failure and bitter opposition. All the hatred that had been vented on Christ was now turned in its direction, and there seemed to be little or no future for this tiny offshoot of Judaism. It fed on a hope that grew weaker as the looked-for miracle failed to materialize. By all human reckoning it could not survive for long. There was little point in being heir to the promised kingdom if the kingdom had no subjects. This was the moment for which the Spirit had been waiting. Out of this death He forged a new life, totally unexpected and tremendous in scope. It was almost by chance that the pagan masses came rushing headlong to inherit the kingdom which the rightful heirs had abdicated.

The movement first started in Jerusalem. Peter had baptized Cornelius the Roman centurion and Philip the Ethiopian eunuch. The Spirit had come down on the Samaritans and declared clean the Gentile food that no Jew would touch. But all this was insignificant compared with the revolution brought by St. Paul. For him, the surrender to the goad of Christ on the Damascus road meant the renunciation of his whole past. Cured of the blindness of Pharisaism, the scales fell from his eyes and he saw the dazzling vision of the mystery of Christ. He had not known, as the other disciples had, the slow development from the baptism of Christ to the day of Pentecost, from illusion to reality, a development which still held them in the clutches of Jewish preferment. For St. Paul the issues were clearer: his conversion was a complete break. Either Christ was a Jewish impostor, in which case all His claims must be denounced, or else He was the Son of God, who could not be the exclusive property of a restricted group. Paul envisaged the conquest of the world, and Jerusalem, dumb with astonishment, agreed that the Spirit was on his side.

This numerical emancipation was not enough. Before things could be finally settled, there would have to be a spiritual emancipation too. Liberation from Judaism meant nothing unless there was a liberation from the Law as well. Considerable anxiety was felt among some sections of the Jerusalem community over this open invitation to the "lame and halt" to come and fill the places left empty by those who had refused the feast. As they had seen at Antioch, Gentile conversions inevitably threw convert Jews and pagans together. Jewish law forbade such contacts. The Jew, indoctrinated from early childhood, felt almost a physical revulsion against such proximity. Was he expected now to deny all that he had been taught? The Judaizers at Jerusalem maintained that it was for the pagans to submit to the Law and adopt circumcision. Clearly principles were here at stake: the whole meaning of the Christian revolution was being questioned.

Judeo-Christianity was Pharisaism's last effort to absorb the Church of Christ back into Judaism by cutting her off from the Spirit that was her inspiration. If a baptized pagan must first be circumcised before he could consort with a baptized Jew, then baptism in the name of Jesus was not the passport to the kingdom. It meant that sanctification by the Spirit was of no avail without the Law, and Christ was no more than the Law's complement. Salvation was achieved by the Law and its observance, and man was back where he started. Instead of the free outpouring of divine life into the empty soul of man, there is only the old juxtaposition of the two parallel perfections which never meet—that of the just man and that of God. The whole metamorphosis involved by Christ's death and resurrection, and the incorporation of man into that risen life through the Spirit, that was the point in question.

In his piercing wisdom, St. Paul saw the danger. His was the task of weaning the infant Church from the dried-up breasts of Judaism and imparting to her a consciousness of her own dynamism. In no uncertain manner he cut away the parasite growths of outworn ideas and revealed the deep intuition which the first disciples had drawn from their faith in Christ. Christ was not the servant of the Law but its Master; not its fruit but its meaning. He was not only the keystone of the old covenant, but also the cornerstone of the new; not only the Jewish Messiah but also the universal Lord. His kingdom was not the privilege of one people, but the Mystical Body in which Jew and Gentile have their place and receive the Spirit of sonship freely bestowed by the Father. All mankind, Jew and Gentile alike, stand in need of this justification—the Gentile caught in the abyss of his moral indigence and the Jew chained in the prison of his legal arrogance. It was not only from Judaism that Christ freed man by His death, it was from the whole law of sin which Judaism symbolized even while it denounced it. Christ's death undermined both Jewish righteousness and Gentile corruption, to lay hold of the very root of man's insufficiency, wring from him the admission of his nothingness, and open to him through the resurrection the way to heaven and that free justification in the Spirit of the Son who makes him cry out, "Abba, Father."

Henceforth salvation is not achieved by the works of the Law, but by faith in Christ (the Epistle to the Romans is full of the theme).

This means, first of all, that Christianity and not Judaism is the way of salvation. It means further that salvation is a personal and interior attitude of abandonment to God in Christ, and not the automatic privilege of those who observe the Law. In the last analysis, it means that the very adhesion of the believer to the salvation achieved by the Son of God is the free gift of new life, whereby he becomes, through the sanctification of the Spirit, a child of God.

Growing Pains: St. Paul and Hellenism

While St. Paul was still occupied with the Judeo-Christian problem, his attention was being drawn in another direction. Before he had even begun to marshal the doctrinal justification for his work among the Gentiles, he had organized the people into independent "assemblies" or churches to take the place of the synagogues which were now closed to them. Here he had spent much effort in trying to translate the Jewish message of Christ into concepts which would be understood by the Greek mind. But at the very moment when he had finally settled the emancipation of the churches from Judaism, he found that he must apply his own brake to the movement. One of the churches had gone too far, and the great teacher of Christian freedom had to insist that the pure spirit of Israel must be preserved in the Church.

To bring about the complete emancipation of the Christian movement, St. Paul had selected words, images, ideas, and themes which were more sympathetic to the Greek mind. In this way he tried to overcome the obvious difficulty which the Greeks felt when they were faced with the Jewish vocabulary of words and ideas in which the Gospel was written. As we have already seen, the primitive Christian faith had grown naturally out of the national hopes and the religious themes inherited from the Jews. These would not mean very much to the Greeks. Their inheritance was one of a hope for immortality, for a new life to be found by rites of initiation. The inspired genius of St. Paul saw what could be achieved if the finest elements of both these religious currents were combined and boldly sublimated to a new level. The Greeks would understand the mystery of Christ if it was presented to them as a "wisdom" of divine life. The Christian fact would be accepted by them if he could show them that it alone held the true "mystery" of death and life. Moreover, the simple religious rites which the first Christians had brought with them from Judaism to express their new faith would translate immediately, without adaptation, to become the rites of initiation into the salvation of the risen Christ. With magnificent skill and tact St. Paul was able to change a thoroughly Jewish movement into a universal and Hellenistic religion, without losing anything of the essence of primitive Christianity.

Such a transformation was not without its dangers. Would the convert pagans press the adoption of forms so far as to alter the content of the Christian message? Since they were dispensed from initiation into Judaism, would they think that they were also free to throw over the fundamental religious values of Israel which remained as the foundation stone of Christianity? In other words, would this process of the Hellenization of Christianity threaten to cut Christianity away from its origins and make it an easy prey for the prevalent syncretism? These were the dangers which had troubled the minds of the Judeo-Christians and prompted their conservatism. It would be sheer folly, in their view, to bring straight into the Christian fold pagans who could not overnight shake off their legacy of idolatry and immorality. The decisions of the Council of Jerusalem in the year 49 (Acts 15) had given some support to these fears; the Corinthian crisis was to show how well founded they were.

St. Paul accused the Corinthians, first of all, of moral indifference: the case of incest and the question of idol-offerings were evidence of it. Such indifference was not only the legacy of their former paganism, it sought to justify itself in the very teaching of Paul, and in his proclamation of the Christian's emancipation from the Law and the man-made conventions of religion. So far removed was this interpretation from the true tenor of St. Paul's thought, and so obviously indebted to Greek philosophy, that the Apostle came down on it with all his vigor and denounced the "wisdom" that had inspired it. What had these pagans done but idolize "wisdom" as the Jews had idolized the Law?

Worse still, such moral indifference was based on a misconception of Christ's mission that was reminiscent of the Greek "mysteries." The whole religious yearning of the Corinthians seemed to be satisfied with the "experience" of salvation which they received from the rites of Christian initiation. It was to soothe the worries of the first Christians over the delay of the Parousia that St. Paul had gone out of his way to emphasize the "spiritual" reality of the kingdom. What the Corinthians had done was to exaggerate this to the extent of losing sight of the essentially dynamic and moral aspect of Christianity.

To those Jews who wished to prolong the economy of the Law, St. Paul had preached the scandal of the Cross, which dealt the death-blow to hopes of Jewish nationalism. To the Greeks who now, with typical optimism, made Christ a salvation-myth, he preached the foolishness of the Cross and its lesson of the Christian ideal of suffering and self-immolation. It is this context of sin, suffering, and hope that puts the "mystery" of Christ solidly in the tradition of Jewish thought. The kingdom is not yet realized, except in faith (it is a variation on the theme of Romans and Galatians). It will be manifested in glory, but not until it has followed Christ dead and risen. It will reach its full stature, but not until "death is absorbed by life" and the day of the Parousia dawns.

Growing Pains: St. Paul and Christian Anxiety

The Judeo-Christian crisis and its Corinthian correlative were not the only factors which gave St. Paul this wide view of Christianity that embraced both the New Testament and the Old. There were other factors to influence him, and of these the most important was the inner development of Christianity itself. The Judeo-Christianity which he was fighting outside had taken an even subtler form inside the Christian communities themselves. The specter was still there, finding an unlooked-for ally among the Greek converts, with their yearning for that tangible earthly happiness which he had condemned in the Corinthians.

For the elite Judaism had meant the cult of the Law, but for the ordinary folk it had always meant the expectation of a Messiah. Christ had supplanted the Law, but surely His title of Messiah still remained. Surely Messianism was the very soul of Christianity. For the apostles and for St. Paul himself, the burning desire to see the kingdom established for all time was the mainspring of their dynamism in the Spirit. And yet it had not happened, and any hope of it happening grew fainter as the ideal frontiers of the kingdom were extended further and further in the Gentile mission. Christian faith was troubled. If Christ was the definitive Messiah, why was salvation delayed? Had there not been disillusionment enough—the long desert journey, the failure to subdue Canaan, the divided Monarchy, the Restoration that misfired? Were these now to be crowned by a disappointment more cruel still, that of a kingdom which was given only to be taken away again? Was not the bitter blow of Good Friday disillusionment enough? How could it be said that faith in Christ had saved His followers if it brought them nothing but hatred from Jew and Gentile alike? Faithful but perplexed, the Thessalonians became impatient. The Corinthians gave up hope altogether and fell back on their Greek "wisdom": the delay and Paul's explanation of Christian freedom meant that the kingdom was a Greek mystery, amoral, outside time, a mere serviceable pledge of immortality. The two attitudes were radically distinct. The first, typically Jewish, aggravated the all too earthly yearning for external salvation; the second, typically Greek, did away with the need and hope of salvation by making it no more than a spiritual pledge already given. Both had this much in common (and they always will have until the Parousia), that they made salvation something entirely human—an earthly crown which can be fondled and enjoyed. In St. Paul's words, both are "unspiritual." Both imprison man in the very way that the Law had done.

St. Paul himself had known the pangs of this evolution. In the Captivity Epistles he made the synthesis of ideas which were still unresolved in Romans, Galatians, and 1 and 2 Corinthians. His final solution lies no longer in Christ, but in the Spirit of Christ, and it is from the intimate experience of that Spirit that his synthesis springs. Those who wait impatiently for the Parousia Paul counters with a parousia of Christ already established in the Spirit. Those who have given up all hope of Christ's second coming he counters with the unspeakable groanings of the Spirit laboring in a new creation in Christ. To both he shows the essential mystery of the Church, the new halfway stage of the "desert," where the people of God, the new Israel, are slowly transformed from the "flesh of sin" into the glory of the risen Christ. He emphasizes the utter necessity of this struggle between death and life, as a perpetuation of Christ's own death and resurrection, where evil and suffering serve as the catalysts essential for the Christian's spiritualization in Christ. He paints a bold picture of the unfathomable designs of the Father, begun in eternal predestination, slowly unfolded and transposed through the ages, and reaching their achievement in Christ and their full flowering in the Spirit. The whole human race and its fortunes are held in a complex rhythm of evolution. Already the last phase has uttered its birth cry, but it has not yet reached its full stature.

Having announced the death of Jewish exclusivism, the death of the Law's humanism, and the death of the Greek idea of happiness, St. Paul now proclaims the death of the kingdom in the Church, until such time as the Church shall be absorbed in the victory of the kingdom.

The Hostility of the "World" and the Johannine Synthesis

At this point, revelation had reached such a degree of fulness in form and thought that its completion was imminent. In fact, the Johannine writings, the last of the inspired Book, make no new advance but only a final review of precision, force, and harmony.

The fall of Jerusalem was the signal for the last convulsive kick of Judeo-Christianity. The Church had spread so widely, throughout Asia especially, that Christians found themselves far more involved in the civil life of pagans than they had originally intended. What was worse, the fall of the Holy City had not brought the return of Christ that His words had led them to expect, and they were left to face the gathering storm of paganism alone. St. John met their growing anxiety with the solution which St. Paul had offered, although his presentation is distinctly his own. He gives the Christian mystery the atmosphere of peace and certainty that Paul's genius lacked and fixes his vision far above the shifting horizons of this earth. Not without reason has he been called an eagle: he hovers without apparent effort, his eye fixed on the divine Sun. Not that he has no feeling for men: he is no metaphysician or dreamer. He can scale these heights only because he has measured the depths of his own heart and has reached far beyond the void of his own nothingness to discover the Word of God which sets him free.

His first thought is to look back at what has gone before. To those who stand hesitating at the crossroads he gives a warning: they must not go back. It is the whole purpose of the fourth Gospel to render impossible, once for all, any such return to Judaism. By the end of the first century Christianity had reached a much fuller appreciation of its own meaning. In the light of this, and with his own astonishing power, John applies his mind to the life of Christ and recognizes it for the revolution it was. He picks out precisely the elements in this history which give promise of the way Christianity would go after the resurrection. He delves deeply into the essence of Christ's thought underlying the ambiguity of expression forced upon Him by the mentality of His hearers. He singles out its message of eternal life in this world, gained by dying through faith in the Son of God. He offers that life to the Christians in Asia, in answer to their fears of the mounting persecution and their frustrated hopes of the Parousia.

In this sense, the aim of the fourth Gospel is to allow the meaning of Christ's life to shine in its true light. The first catechesis, found in Mark, Luke, and Matthew, had given a detailed account of the outward facts of Christ's life. Time was needed for the true import of that life to appear. At first sight, St. John's Gospel seems far removed from the picture given by the Synoptics, but a closer study reveals that he has remained as true to the picture as he has penetrated deep beneath it. Not only is it an authentic interpretation of the basic facts of Christianity, it is also the key to the Synoptics. In his Christ, the Son of God, St. John shows the hidden meaning of the Scriptures as they are recapitulated in the person of the Word Incarnate. The old covenant had one purpose—to support the new; the new covenant has one meaning—to transform the old in the Spirit. The final balance is struck between the Jewish revelation and the Christian revolution. Between them he establishes a unique rhythm of types and fulfilment. Grace answers grace, and the believer learns to die to justification by Law and to be born again in the glory of the Father.

John stands between the past and the future, synthesizing the one and looking towards the other. Having cut off all possibility of a return to Judaism, he now faces the persecution of paganism, in the Apocalypse. The Church has been newly born from the womb of its Virgin Mother, but it still has to learn from her how to walk the hard way of the desert before it can reach the fulness of maturity in Christ. It is a pity that the Apocalypse has so often been regarded as a secret code containing details of the whole of Church history. In fact, the only prophecy that it makes is that there will always be persecution until the final triumph. It is much more than a cipher—it is a prolongation throughout time of that rhythm of God's plan which was conceived in eternity and gradually woven into the very material of this world through the double incarnation, verbal and personal, of the Son of God. The entire history of all ages in the framework of the Father's plan—that is the theme of the Apocalypse. The Father's merciful design has not been cut short, nor is His love in any way exclusive. Christ is infinitely more than the climax of God's plans—

He is the beginning of a new cycle of redemption which penetrates heaven itself. Revelation is born; it must now grow. Redemption is achieved; it must now be applied. Christ is dead and risen from the dead, His death and resurrection have still to be fulfilled in His Church. The Parousia of the Lamb, slain but triumphant, is not, in the Apocalypse, something still to be achieved in the far future: it is *here and now, within us.* It begins and comes unceasingly, as new life is born out of death, and as the world's persecution blossoms into the liberation of the Spirit. How is it that we have been able to lose the meaning of this book, which is the only one that was ever written directly for us? Standing as it does between the two comings of Christ, its message is one of consolation and hope to a Church that will reach its glory through suffering. This book should be for us a most powerful encouragement to await with patience the fulfilment of God's eternal designs.

Thus the Apocalypse sets its seal on the Bible's message. It is the last "revelation." The long unfolding of man's yearning and God's answer comes to an end in the mystery of life in the Spirit. In one sense the Apocalypse is the least eschatological of all the books of the Bible, since it spells the end of the tormenting delusion which God was able to use to such effect throughout Israel's long history. Henceforth the Christian knows that he can expect nothing but suffering and death from without. He knows that within him this death will be exactly balanced by the life of the Spirit flowing to him from the throne of the triumphant Lamb. The ultimate victory over the forces of evil will come, to establish the harmonious completion on earth of the work begun at the creation. But already the victory of the Christ-life is announced in the death of the Christian. Already it raises him from earth to heaven.

CHRIST THE FOCAL POINT OF THE SCRIPTURES

In the light of what has been said, the reader will at least know what to look for when he reads the Bible. If he concentrates too much on detail, he will rarely feel the touch of God's hand; he will even risk losing himself altogether in a welter of secondary causes behind which God is hidden. Revelation and the supernatural are rarely obvious in the Bible. It is frequently possible to explain things by natural agencies and causes. What the reader must look for is rather the constant, sure, and irresistible movement of the whole towards one end, irrespective of human conditions. It is here that the hand of God is most surely in command. Every nation has a history of success and failure, but no nation has a history like this one, where success and failure alike conspire to produce a living and complex upward movement towards a single end. The call of Abraham can be explained by natural causes. So can the Exodus from Egypt, the Conquest, the success of David, Israel's survival after exile, even the "miracle" by which neither Persia nor Greece nor Rome were able to absorb this nation. What cannot be so explained is how all these events gradually and surely led this tiny, materialist, and dull-minded people to the conclusion that the God of Abraham was the supreme Creator of all things. What passes understanding is that a people as hardhearted as this could pin their hope on an unbelievable manifestation of love and see that hope realized in such splendor that their hearts could not contain it.

All the lines of this history converge. All the Bible's themes, whether we consider them horizontally or vertically, logically or historically, at rest or in motion, all meet at a single point. We might well compare the Bible to one of those elegant turrets which decorate the great towers of our cathedrals. They are really spiral staircases, where each step fans out from a slender central column which is itself made up of the angle end of the successive steps. The whole turret is built on the base of this central column, and the roof is the fan vaulting which springs from its top and keys the outer walls. Every full circle of the spiral is a repetition of the last. The same number of equidistant steps lead from one floor to the next, and so to the top. The cycles of doctrinal themes in the Bible are rather like these winding steps. One leads into the next with a similarity of construction which argues to the constancy of the part they have to play. On different levels, each depends for its support and function on the basic central column which gives cohesion and vital direction to the whole. This central column is *Christ.*

Christ is the focal point of the Scriptures on an *historical* level first of all. He is the fan vaulting which concludes the spiral. If we are to understand the Bible, we must before all else be absolutely clear about the line of direction of every single event and idea it contains. They have no meaning except insofar as they effectively prepare the way for the supreme event in this history—the Incarnation of the Word and the revelation of His message. From this point of view, the call of Abraham and the revolt of the Maccabees are of equal value. The only difference is that one is at the beginning and the other near the end of a succession of events which produced a background on earth against which the Son of God could be revealed. Man could never have assimilated that revelation if it had appeared out of the blue, divorced from this movement through time. It needed a favorable historical context (a people, a religious tradition, and a place in the economy of that tradition) and a favorable psychological climate (a faith inexorably directed towards a future revelation, a religious fervor, and above all a yearning). These were the components which God so slowly collected together when He determined to set apart the people of Israel in this particular corner of the Mediterranean to prepare a humble cradle for His Son.

Christ is not only the term of an historical sequence. He is there in germ at each of its stages, in the first as in the last. As the evolution advances, so His features become more and more precise. He is therefore the *logical* focal point of the Scriptures. At whatever stage they are considered, the various doctrinal themes are all centered on the idea of a divine and freely bestowed salvation, realized by an envoy sent from God. Basically, each theme is only one aspect of this single theme, whose potentialities are not fully brought to act except in Christ. His foreshadowing in the Bible is not, therefore, merely a subjective one; He is prefigured on the objective plane of reality (whether potential or actual). Only rarely were its writers, the Prophets included, even implicitly aware of the person of Christ. It was not important that they should be. His presence in the Bible transcends the consciousness of men. God Himself infused it into the profound logic of events and ideas, and into the living flesh of His people.

Christ is consequently the focal point of the Scriptures on the even deeper and altogether supernatural level of *revelation*. The Bible contains both revealed truths and truths attainable by the unaided use of reason. But there is only one Truth, living and revealed, and that is the incarnate Word. Reflection on the concept of supernatural revelation will show that God can reveal nothing which is not His Son. God, alone and in Himself, is beyond the attainments of created reason. Outside God there are many truths which man has not attained, but none that he could not attain. In this sense truth is natural to man, it is within his scope. God alone lies outside that scope, and everything else insofar as it is rooted in God. He alone bestows Himself freely. The natural knowledge that we have of God brings God into our minds, but it does not place us in God as He is, in all His ineffable reality. If we are to know God in that way (and our whole being cries out for it, since He made us for Himself), then God must give us the knowledge He has of Himself. This Knowledge of God, subsistent and personal, the eternal Word, is His Son. The eternal design of God from Paradise lost to the Parousia, the entire plan of salvation to which He invites us, consists precisely in this revelation of Himself in His Son. Thus, when God reveals "something" in the Bible, that something can only be His Son, reduced to human and halting symbols. That something can only be a logical and historical preparation for the revelation of His Son in person, in the flesh.

So we come to the final level: Christ is the focal point of the Scriptures as the *Incarnation of the Word*. If God is to give Himself to man, He must come to man's level, the level of fallen nature. When man wrenched himself from God's grasp, he had nothing but himself to fall back on. From that time onward he knew only himself, and whatever else he knew beneath him only led him back to himself. If God would now take a hold on him again, He must stoop down to man's fallen level and there offer His hand. The divine Word must be spoken in sounds that the human ear can hear; the divine

Light must shine in a way that the human eye can see. The Bible is the Word of God become audible, Christ is the Word of God become visible. Whether its function is to be heard or to enlighten, God has only one Word, and He speaks it only to give it. The pre-incarnation of His Word in the Bible is the prelude to the Incarnation of the Word in the womb of the Virgin Mary. "This is eternal Life, that they may know thee, the Father, and Him whom thou hast sent, Jesus Christ" (Jn 17:3).

Editors' Note.—From THE CHRISTIAN APPROACH TO THE BIBLE, translated by Hubert J. Richards and Brendan Peters (Westminster, Md.: Newman, 1958) *pp. 159-205.*

Christ

Christ Our Brother
Karl Adam

"Recapitulation" in Christ
Edward Leen, C.S.SP.

A More Excellent Way
Alban Goodier, S.J.

PREFACE

The central fact of human history and the central mystery of Christianity is that there have been two Adams, two founders and fathers of the human race.

There was the first and old Adam, whose existence and whose plight and sin and pain we do not today have to prove. The proof is in our hearts and in our contemporary history. This Adam is indeed in our hearts, so deeply that it made Ezechiel cry out the deep cry of man that is still both personal and communal: "In those days the hand of the Lord was upon me and brought me forth in the spirit of the Lord, and set me down in a plain that was full of bones . . . and He said to me: Son of man, dost thou think that these bones shall live?" This is surely our great question today. Only the ostrich with his head in the sand would not repeat that question for our time.

But there has been a new Adam who has rebuilt the race, making of it "a new creature" . . . "For He is our peace" . . . a "new man" . . . "Ye dry bones, hear the word of the Lord . . . Behold I will send spirit into you and you shall live . . . and you shall know that I am the Lord."

The following chapters by Karl Adam, Edward Leen, and Archbishop Goodier are studies of this new Adam, Jesus Christ, true God and true man, and of the way in which all things human are reestablished in Him. Our book has reached its center. It is good not to leave it too quickly. The saints and the theologians keep returning to it. All that follows, the Church, the Eucharist, the other sacraments, Mary, Peter, the inner life of our souls, will only be an elaboration in many forms of this mystery of Christ.

Karl Adam

Christ Our Brother

It is Christmas Eve and the bells are ringing to Midnight Mass. The night is dark, but the church is ablaze with lights, and full of quietly happy folk. The mystery of Bethlehem is renewed upon the altar, and the cry goes forth: "Christ is born to us. Come, let us adore!"

And, amid this pageantry, what am I? I am a solitary being among other such solitaries, cut off by an unbridgeable chasm from every other personality. Hence I obtain my tremendous certainty that I am not another. I am I. I am a world of my own. A mere bundle of forces? No. The lord of those forces? No, but one who ought to be the lord of those forces, and so one who is not their lord. I am one who has a war within him, I am a self at war with itself, a self that knows no peace. Above me the stars move in their regular courses, and they know whither they are going. Or rather, they do not know, but are simply moved on their way. Whither? I do not know; nobody knows. What is the meaning of that starry world above? I do not know. It is some sort of phantasm. And nature around me, lying asleep under thick snow—is that there for me? No, the flowers will wake again in the spring, even when I am no longer there, even when there is no more any man there. Even nature that surrounds me is a phantasm. I am alone. All that I can call my own is my restlessness and inner conflict, my desire to know and my ignorance, my consciousness of duty and my impotence. In my being a thousand lines cross. They all lead beyond me, far away into space, reaching out like the naked boughs of that tree there, by the church. Whither am I going? Whence have I come? All that I know is that yesterday I was not, and tomorrow I shall have ceased to be. What am I but a failing flame, a falling wave, a dying note?

Then comes the cry from the altar: "A Child is born to us and a Son is given to us. . . ." The Child in the manger is not like any other child, for He is God the everlasting, the all-wise, all-good, almighty; He is God the ineffable, mysterious, awful, wonderful. And has God become a Child? Is the Infinite wrapped in swaddling clothes? Is the Ineffable a Jewish boy, Jesus of Nazareth? Never has mouth uttered so bold an assertion. No, it is not merely bold; it is extravagance, it is blasphemy.

And yet, if it be true? If there be a God, can I argue with Him and prescribe to Him what He may or may not do? Are not my thoughts as dust before the thoughts of God? Is not all my experience a vain thing when God appears? Therefore I cannot say that it is nonsense or blasphemy to assert that God has become man. I cannot say it, because He who becomes man is God. In His thought and will are infinite possibilities, including the possibility of Bethlehem. And why should not God reveal Himself as a Child, if He reveals Himself at all? That He reveals Himself at all is the marvel, not that He reveals Himself in the form of a Child. Supposing God has determined to take our human nature—and who can forbid Him? —how else should He do it but by being born as we are born, yet from a virgin's womb? And supposing God has determined to become incarnate and thereby redeem the whole of mankind, both high and low—and who will forbid this comprehensive purpose?—could He have won the hearts of the children of men any better than by the lowliness and poverty of Bethlehem? Are not poverty and lowliness the natural vesture for the Divinity on earth? The purple and silk of an imperial cradle would have obscured the majesty of His divinity. How wonderful, then, this Christian mystery of God's condescension to the Virgin's womb! How admirable His birth in a manger! These mysteries of the Christian faith harmonize exactly with what we should expect in God's profoundest revelation of Himself.

Therefore I am not puzzled by the Child of Bethlehem, by the manger, by the swaddling clothes. It must have been so, granted God's will to come to us. But did He will to come to us? Did the Infinite, who controls the vast universe, will to come to the tiny and insignificant planet that is called earth? Did the All-Holy and Perfect will to come to our sin? Did the Eternal will to enter time, when Augustus was Emperor of Rome and Cyrinus Governor of Syria? All understanding fails us and there is an end to our reasoning. Here is the great mystery, the miracle. And here is belief and unbelief. "God so loved the world as to give His only-begotten Son": such is the gospel of Christmas. That is what we have to believe of God, that He loves us up to the surrender of His only-begotten Son. Surely a bold, audacious, extravagant faith! He who holds this faith believes firmly these several articles: first, that there is a living, personal God; secondly, that this God has a Son; thirdly—highest and most daring of all—that this God, blessed in His Son, stoops to our mortal clay, nay even loves it, and that so greatly that revealing the depths of His infinite love He arrays His own Son in that same clay, so that thus clad He may redeem us.

Is such a faith, which mingles God with our mortality and makes our clay divine, a true faith, or is it not rather a travesty of faith and an insult to God? Is it not a monument of selfishness and pride? We answer that this talk of the Incarnation of the Son of God would indeed be the veriest pride and presumption, were it mere human talk. Were that so, it would be hard to find words severe enough to censure it, or to reject it with adequate indignation. But what if it is God's saying? Supposing God does really love us to such an extent that He gives us Himself in His Son. Am I so to insist on my unworthiness, and so to exaggerate my duty of reverence, that in spite of all I put away the manger, saying: "Depart from me, O Lord, for I am a sinful man"? And what is this, under the rags of my poverty, but a nauseous pride? And what is my reverence but a puerile perversity? When God holds out His gift to me, and that His greatest gift, and that His only Son, what else should my soul do but look up to Him from the abyss of its unworthiness, and, ravished by His love, answer in all humbleness and trust: "Behold, the handmaid of the Lord; be it done unto me according to thy word"? Or else I am a contemner of His gifts, and one who would presume to dictate to God what He should do and what He should leave undone. Oh, how narrow and warped are our human judgments! Shall we never cease to make ourselves the measure of all things, even of the divine? But our unbelief goes deeper still, for it attacks the very nature of the living God in His essential attribute of generous, self-giving love. For that is what we deny when we deny Bethlehem. For the love of God is nowhere manifested with such radiant purity and such overwhelming force as in the mystery of Christmas, when all the fulness of the Godhead dwells corporally in human form. . . .

Certainly, according to revelation, Christ is the Second Person of the Blessed Trinity and true God. As the Creed says, He is God of God and Light of Light. But He is also true Man, consubstantial not only with the Father, but also with us. Jesus has a purely human consciousness, a purely human will, a purely human emotional life. He is a complete man. So unimpaired is this human nature of His that its union with the divine Word is founded only upon the unity of the (divine) Person and implies no destruction of itself. The mystery of the Incarnation does not necessarily entail any communication of the divine nature or attributes to the humanity of Christ. On the contrary, that humanity persists, even after its union with the Word of God, in its specifically human quality. The Second Person of the Blessed Trinity, the Word of God, contributes nothing to the human nature that implies any enrichment of the human nature as such. What is contributed is simply the Person. Without here investigating in detail the character of this personal union, we may nevertheless say this much: that it involves such an intimate and essential conjunction of the human nature with the divine Word that this nature belongs essentially to the divine Word, that it is His humanity, and that the divine Word can say, "I am this man."

And therein lies the mystery and the miracle of Christ. It is not that a human nature was taken up into the Divinity, but that the Divinity became a full and perfect man. It is not the ascent of the human to the divine, but the condescension of the divine to the human. It is not that flesh became God, but that God became flesh. Such is the mystery, the miracle, the stupendous prodigy. And hence the thrill and the joy of those words: "And the Word was made flesh." Can we utter them without thankfulness and joy? "He emptied Himself, taking the form of a servant, being made in the likeness of men, and in habit found as a man."

Why is the Incarnation the fundamental and decisive thing? Because it was the first manifestation and the literal bodying forth of God's will to redeem mankind. There is no conceivable form of redemption in which God's love could have revealed itself so visibly, so forcibly, so effectively as in the Incarnation. So visibly: for what is more visible than flesh and blood, more visible than the Child in the manger, than the Crucified, than the risen Christ? So forcibly: for what more could God have done than give us His only-begotten Son? And so effectively: for when God became Man, the redemption was no longer a mere announcement of glad tidings of future joy; it was already a present joy and a resplendent reality. We had a new Man in our midst, one who might with pure heart cry "Abba, Father," and to whom there came the heavenly answer: "Thou art my beloved Son." The many thousand generations of mankind, separated from God in their first parent, were again at this one point united to God, and so firmly and essentially united with Him that there shall never again be separation. In this one Man the whole of humanity was raised from out of its nothingness and worthlessness, and given a positive being and a genuine worth. And since this elevation of mankind was a fundamental and a real elevation, therefore were we made a genuine and a real unity in Him. He is our new foundation, our new origin, our new root. We are related to Him as the branches are to the vine. He is the Head of the Body, and we are the members. There is really now no longer any individual or isolated man, for we are all members of Christ and He is our Head. As there is but one Head, so is there but one Body.

And that is the central point of the glad tidings of the gospel. The vital fact is not that God dwelt bodily among us and that we can see the glory of God in the face of Christ Jesus, but that this God is our Brother, that He is of one blood with us, that He is the Head of our Body. Of course, the divinity is an essential element in the picture of Christ. If Christ were not true God, then the infinite gulf between God and the creature would not be bridged in the Person of Jesus. That was the point of the fierce struggle with the Arians. That struggle drew its energy and fervor from this very conviction, that if Christ be not Himself true God, He cannot raise us to God and give us to share in the divine life. But this divine element is not the only element in the picture of Jesus; nor is it even the prominent element, during the time of this world. Rather it is the golden background, from which His human activity stands out and from which it draws its secret strength and redeeming power. It is the element of peace and repose. But contrasting with that quiet setting is a thrilling fact: this Divinity appearing in our human form. Incredible though it may seem, we have among us a man who is God; in His Person all mankind is formed into a unity and bound to God; and we all through Him have access to God. For that is the deepest meaning of Christ to us, that we go through Him to the Father. The vital fact for us and for our world is not that He as the Incarnate God is entitled to the adoration of men, but that as the New Man He makes all who would be saved members of His Body and as King of God's new people leads them to His Father. Parallel with the eschatological contrast between this world and the next, between seedtime and harvest, there is a Christological contrast between the Man Christ Jesus here and the Triune God there, between the kingship of the Incarnate here and the rule of the pure Godhead there. There is a deep meaning in the statement that the history of Christianity is the history of the becoming, unfolding, and realization of the Man Christ Jesus. In the doctrinal, priestly, and pastoral functions of the Church the glorified Christ prosecutes His Messianic work. In that same Church He builds Himself His Body. As St. Paul says, the Church is His fulness. Through her He becomes whole and complete. For as long as His Father wills that this world shall endure, for so long is Christ unfinished and incomplete. He is still ever at His work, still constantly acting as our Mediator. Continually, in all places and at all times, He is completing Himself in ever new members, until according to God's unsearchable decision the Last Judgment shall come and the new era be inaugurated. Then end the eschatological and Christological contrasts of which we have spoken. The time of Christ's becoming and ripening, the time of His redemptive, mediatorial, high-priestly activity terminates; and the time of the Triune God begins. Then will He as the Head of the Body, as the King of the new Israel, lead His people to His Father and resign His authority to the Triune God: "And when all things shall be subdued unto Him, then the Son also Himself shall be subject unto Him that put all things under Him, that God may be all in all. . . ."

Editors' Note.—From CHRIST OUR BROTHER, translated by Justin McCann, O.S.B. (New York: Macmillan, 1935) *pp. 176-81, 59-65.*

Edward Leen, C.S.SP.

"Recapitulation" in Christ

"That He might make known unto us the mystery of His will, . . . in the dispensation of the fulness of times, to re-establish all things in Christ" (Eph 1:9-10).

The Sacrifice of Calvary was the supreme act of the religion of Jesus Christ. Because of that and because of the consequences that issue from it, it is the culminating point in the destinies of mankind. All that precedes it converges on it and derives its significance from it. What follows from it is but the evolution of what it contains in germ. It is a sign of contradiction and a source of salvation. If the history of man from the beginning to the end of time were likened to a lofty mountain, Golgotha would be the summit of that mountain. World events prior to it would be an ascending slope. World events following it would be a gradual incline falling away from that towering eminence. This is an idea familiar to every Christian from his infancy. He is aware that, were it not for the crucifixion, his life and that of others would be robbed of hope.

That the cross alone unbars heaven to us and makes happiness attainable is, in itself, sufficient reason for considering the passion and death of the Saviour as an event of supreme and unique importance for the human race. Salvation is the one thing absolutely necessary; hence, what happens in this world has value and significance only in so far as it bears on the salvation of souls. Events are good or evil according as they promote or frustrate the attainment of heaven. It is not, however, only in reference to what is to be that the cross has significance. A full understanding of it carries our vision right into the heart of the mysteries that surround actual human life. "The Cross," writes Newman, "has put its clear value upon everything which we see. It has given a meaning to the various shifting courses, the trials, the temptations, the sufferings of this earthly state. . . . In the Cross and Him who hung upon it all things meet: all things subserve it, all things need it. It is their center and interpretation." [1] Until one has, in some measure, probed the depths of the mystery of the cross and glimpsed there the plan of God's marvelous designs, radiant with wisdom, goodness, and mercy, one can but imperfectly grasp the full Christian philosophy of life.

It would be difficult to overestimate the extent of the change that would be wrought in the outlook of the average Christian were he to pass from the mere knowledge of the fact of his redemption through the cross to an intelligent grasp of the mode according to which that redemption was worked out. That vision, in a blinding flash of light, burst upon the soul of St. Paul. What he beheld, he reveals in terms rendered lyrical by his enthusiasm. "Blessed be the God and Father of our Lord Jesus Christ, who hath blessed us with spiritual blessings in heavenly places in Christ. . . . Who hath predestinated us unto the adoption of children through Jesus Christ unto Himself according to the purpose of His will . . . in the dispensation of the fulness of times, to reestablish all things in Christ that are in heaven and on earth in Him" (Eph 1:3-10). In these last words the Apostle enunciates what, for him, is the great central theme of Christianity: "the wondrous mystery hidden from ages and generations." He strains language to express what he feels to be inexpressible, because it is so far beyond human thought and human imaginings.

Redemption was a word familiar enough in a world where slavery entered into the very frame of the social fabric. But human experience furnished no adequate analogy to supply a term to convey the exalted, yet sublimely tender, manner in which God brought mankind out of the slavery of sin into the freedom of grace. The word "re-establish," which is the Douay translation of St. Paul's term in the text above quoted, gives a very feeble rendering of the Apostle's meaning. It must be confessed that the locution invented by the Apostle is practically untranslatable. This is necessarily so, for it expresses something unparalleled and incapable of being paralleled in created experience.

●

[1] John Henry Newman, *Parochial and Plain Sermons* 6: Sermon on "The Cross of Christ."

The Vulgate term "instaurare" gives the result of the accomplishment of God's mysterious designs but does not describe the mode of that accomplishment. The idea that, in the mind of St. Paul, is struggling to find expression is not merely that Christ restored order in creation out of the chaos created by the Fall. Nor is it that Jesus summarizes or synthesizes all creation in Himself. His thought is much more profound. It is that God, in order to reward Christ for having laid down His life to expiate the sins of humanity, made Him to be a new Head for humanity. Humanity supernaturally slain, or, to use a metaphor, decapitated by the disobedience of Adam, is "recapitated" or "reheaded" by the obedience of Christ.[2] The Saviour is Himself the new vital and vitalizing Head of the body of mankind, through whose veins flows the vivifying life blood of sanctifying grace. What is the import of the mystery revealed in this strange word?

To understand it, the parallel between Eden and Golgotha must be closely studied. The garden of delight and the hill of shame both witnessed a radiant dawn for humanity. In Eden that dawn was clear and cloudless. On Calvary it was tinged with red. The first dawn did not grow to its promise of a glorious noon. Its day ended in the darkness of eclipse. The second advances from brightness to brightness, and its sun will never know a setting. Of it will be verified the words: "Thy sun shall go down no more, and thy moon shall not decrease" (Is 60:20). As Eden witnessed the birth of humanity and was the cradle of its brief life, so Calvary in its turn sees a birth of humanity which is a rebirth. The cross is the cradle of the "new creature." The convulsions and throes which nature underwent at the death of the Son of God symbolized the birth throes of the newborn humanity. Many sensitive souls are shocked by the attachment of the attribute "good" to that dark day on which Christ suffered so shameful and so cruel a death. The adjective "bitter" might seem more appropriate. Yet the term which has sprung from Christian instincts is perfectly apt. In spite of the material darkness which blotted out the heavens, that Friday saw a glorious dawn. It was good, as was that day good in which Adam issued forth from the creative hands of God, not only in the full perfection of humanity, but pulsating with the divine vigor of a supernatural life. To the vision of St. Paul the horrors of Calvary dissolve and its bloodstained slopes become transfigured. He sees God at work, with a working which recalled the sixth day of creation. On that sixth day He made man to the divine resemblance with the words: "Let us make man to our own image and likeness" (Gn 1:26). On the sixth day of the week He re-created man and fashioned him

●

[2] E. Mersch, S.J., in his work, *Le corps mystique du Christ* 1, 152, points out that though the Greek verb ἀνακεφαλαιώσασθαι employed by St. Paul is etymologically derived from a term κεφάλαιον, meaning head in the sense of summary or completion, yet the context demands the notion of κεφαλή or head simply. The word κεφαλή or head occurs frequently throughout this Epistle to the Ephesians.

afresh to His own image and likeness, but in a still more marvelous way. He did it by casting man into the mold of the humanity of the Son of God. "For whom He foreknew, He also predestinated to be made conformable to the image of His Son" (Rom 8:29). In Eden there was a creation. On Calvary there was a re-creation. Through Christ's death humanity came to life. "And Christ died for all: that they also who live may not now live to themselves but unto Him who died for them and rose again. . . . If then any be *in Christ a new creature* [i.e., a being created afresh], the old things are passed away. Behold all things are made new" (2 Cor 5:15-17).

The first creation was a work of great power and goodness, in that God took humanity and, infusing into it a breath of His own life, made it, by sanctifying grace, His adopted child and heir to His riches. The second creation was a work not only of power and goodness: it was also one of incomprehensible magnanimity and surpassing mercy. Of a surety the Lord's "tender mercies surpass all his works" (Ps 144:9). Man had traversed God's designs for his happiness. He had rejected the Creator's divine gifts and forfeited the great preternatural privileges bestowed on him. He had proved himself ungrateful, senseless, and rebellious. He had plunged himself in ruin. Adam had made the earth a valley of death, strewn with the scattered members of humanity, supernaturally dead. It would have been much had God confined Himself to giving back the supernatural life which had been forfeited. He did more. He gave much more than was bestowed in the first instance. He restored more than had been lost and at an incredible cost to Himself. He loved man so extravagantly "as to give His only-begotten Son, that whosoever believeth in Him may not perish but may have life everlasting" (Jn 3:16). When sin was destroyed through the awful holocaust of the Son of God, the floods of divine grace, pent up in the Sacred Humanity, were free to pour themselves forth over all mankind. "But now in Christ Jesus, you who were afar off are made nigh by the blood of Christ. For He is our peace, who hath made both one, and breaking down the middle wall of partition, the enmities in His flesh . . . that He might make the two in Himself into *one new man*, making peace, and might reconcile both to God in one body by the cross, killing the enmities in Himself" (Eph 2:13-16).

The death throes of Christ were the birth throes of the "new man" of whom St. Paul speaks. The all-merciful God and Father of Jesus came into the valley of death, to the hill "of the skull," and breathing on the lifeless and scattered limbs of humanity, He revivified them and refashioned them into a living organic unit, animated by the same supernatural life. Under God's breath there arises a "new man" (2 Cor 5:17), the Mystical Body of Christ. It was not only Jesus came forth from the tomb in the garden, it was humanity reborn, revivified, "reheaded," in Him. On Holy Saturday in the morning office, Holy Church used to instruct her catechumens in the great mystery of rebirth, which they themselves were about to undergo in the waters of baptism. In the seventh prophecy the inspired seer relates: "In those days the hand of the Lord was upon me and brought me forth in the spirit of the Lord, and set me down in the midst of a plain that was full of bones—and there were very many up the face of the plain and they were exceedingly dry. And He said to me: Son of man, dost thou think these bones shall live? And I answered: O Lord God, thou knowest. And He said to me: Prophesy concerning these bones and say to them: Ye dry bones, hear the word of the Lord. Thus saith the Lord God to these bones: *Behold I will send spirit into you and you shall live* . . . and you shall know that I am the Lord. And I prophesied as He had commanded me; and as I prophesied there was a voice and behold a commotion, and the bones came together each one to its joint . . . but there was no spirit in them. And He said to me: Prophesy to the spirit; prophesy, O son of man, and say to the spirit: Thus saith the Lord God: *Come, spirit,* from the four winds, and *blow upon those slain* and let them live again. And I prophesied as He had commanded me, and the spirit came into them and they lived, and they stood upon their feet, an exceeding great army. And He said to me: Son of man, all these bones are the house of Israel" (Ez 37:1-11).

In this splendid allegory is set forth what was wrought by the redeeming death of Christ. The valley is an image of the world strewn with the bones of dead humanity, slain by the crime of Adam. Through the merits of the Sacrifice of Christ came the spirit into the wide spaces of death. The Fathers of the Church, using a striking figure, speak of the Mystical Body as having sprung from the open side of the Saviour on the cross. This expresses that the re-creation of humanity through the formation of the Mystical Body was the reward of Christ's obedience unto death. "If He shall lay down His life for sin, He shall see a long-lived seed" (Is 53:10).[3]

God, in creating, had planned to secure his glory through the deification of rational creatures. Deification consists in the knowledge and love of God, in that knowledge and that love which constituted God's own life and happiness. From the clear knowledge of God, praise pours forth spontaneously. This is the very definition of glory —*clara notitia cum laude*—undimmed knowledge issuing in praise.

●

[3] Cf. the following pages from F. Prat, S.J., *La théologie de saint Paul* 1, 266: St. Paul says "we are immersed in the death of Christ, that is, in the dying Christ. In truth, we become associated with Christ and are formed to be His members at the exact moment when He becomes Saviour. This moment coincides with the moment of the death of Christ. Thereafter all becomes common between us and Jesus. We are crucified with Him, buried with Him, raised from death with Him. We share His death and His new life, His glory, His reign, His inheritance. This is a union that defies expression. It is likened by St. Paul to the process of grafting, which commingles two lives, until they become undistinguishable and the life of the graft is lost in the life of the living tree."

The glory of God was meant to be coincident with the happiness of man. God's purpose was checked by the revolt of the first head of mankind. But the divine purpose remained unchanged and was forwarded on its way to fulfilment by the obedience unto death of the second Head of mankind. "Christ Jesus . . . humbled Himself becoming obedient unto death, even unto the death of the cross. For which cause God also hath exalted Him and given Him a name which is above all names" (Phil 2:8-9). The reward given to Christ for His heroic obedience was His being constituted the new life-giving Head of the race. . . . He merited that humanity should be re-created in Him, or, to give the full force of the term used by St. Paul, to which reference has already been made, Christ merited that humanity should be "reheaded" in Him. For humanity to be headed once more is equivalent to its being constituted a body—that is, a living body. For a dead body is but a body in appearance. It is an aggregate of elements amidst which reigns no unity. It is not an organism. As regards supernatural life, such was humanity as a result of Adam's sin. If the scattered members of dead humanity be given a head by a merciful intervention of God, it means they once more become one living thing, in which the different members are held together by, and share in, a common life. Mankind recovers organic unity through Christ. This is the mystery which St. Paul felt he had a special mission to reveal to men. "Let us," he writes, "grow up in Him who is the Head, even Christ: from whom the whole body, being compacted and fitly jointed together, by what every joint supplieth, according to the operation in the measure of every part, maketh increase of the body unto the edifying of itself in charity" (Eph 4:15-16). This position as Head of the Mystical Body which was to come into being through this very Headship, with all the consequent glorification for Himself and His members, was the splendid perspective that, set before the mental gaze of Jesus, strengthened Him to sustain the cross. "Who having joy set before Him, endured the cross, despising the shame, and now sitteth at the right hand of the throne of God" (Heb 12:2).

The members of the Mystical Body are called to share the same glorification as the Head. This is in virtue of their union with Him. They reach that glory by the same path. The Apostle bids them find courage to face the hardships of this path through "looking on Jesus, the Author and Finisher of faith" (*ibid.*). The good pleasure of God was to resupernaturalize the human race by forming it into a Mystical Body through Jesus Christ, its Head and the source of its life. This good pleasure of God was to Jesus, because of the love He bore His heavenly Father, as a law. Out of regard for it He braved His passion. The Church was the reward God held out for that great trial. Christ not only loved His Father, He also "loved the Church and delivered Himself for it, that He might sanctify it, cleansing it by the laver of water in the word of life, that He might present it to Himself a glorious Church, not having spot or wrinkle, or any such thing, but that it should be holy and without blemish" (Eph 5:25-27).

Many Christians, contrasting the condition that was theirs in the first creation in Adam with the condition that is actually theirs in their re-creation in Christ, judge themselves to be at a serious disadvantage. The loss of integrity, science, and immortality that had been enjoyed by the first Adam, casts, for them, a dark shadow on their restoration in Christ. At times forgetful of their huge indebtedness to God, they permit themselves to be querulous with Him and to consider that He was unduly exacting, and ungenerous in the terms of peace He granted to fallen humanity. This is an extremely superficial view of things and betrays a lamentable want of understanding of the "great mystery" of Christianity. It is not possible for us to explore all the reasons why the preternatural gifts were not given back with the supernatural in the rehabilitation of mankind.[4] But from the knowledge of God's heart that is gained through revelation it can be safely asserted that the reasons that moved God in this matter regard man's interests. They certainly did not spring from any narrowness on the part of God or any reluctance to grant unreserved pardon. He who in the interests of man's salvation did not hesitate to surrender His own divine Son to death, is certainly prepared to bestow on redeemed men, with limitless generosity, whatever in the order of divine wisdom is possible. That is, in order to procure man's eternal welfare, He gives all that in the nature of things is possible. St. Paul writes: "He that spared not even His own Son, but delivered Him up for us all, how hath He not, with Him, given us all things" (Rom 8:32).

The reasons why redeemed man is shorn of the preternatural gifts are certainly bound up with those for which the all-wise God decreed the passion as the mode of redemption. There was a mysterious moral necessity for the sufferings and death of the Son of Man, as He Himself revealed to His disciples on the evening of the resurrection. "*Ought* not Christ," He said to them, "to have suffered these things and so to enter into His glory?" (Lk 24:26).[5] The members must, perforce, share the passibility of the Head. It would be an utter incongruity, were this not so. As it was fitting, in accordance with the plan of God's wisdom, that He should reach His glory through pain, so it is fitting that His members should tread the same path in order to be glorified along with Him. "The Spirit Himself giveth testimony to our spirit that we are the sons of God, and if sons, heirs also: heirs indeed of God, and joint heirs with Christ; *yet so*, if we suffer with

●

[4] St. Thomas amongst other reasons gives the following: Man's perfection and happiness essentially consists in his love for God. Hence our heavenly Father willed that baptism should restore grace "unaccompanied by the preternatural gifts, lest man should be moved to desire baptism through self-regarding love of integrity and immortality rather than through a real desire of God." *Sum. theol.* 3, q. 69, a. 3.
[5] Cf. St. Thomas, *Sum. theol.* 3, q. 46, a. 1.

Him, that we may also be glorified with Him" (Rom 8:16-17). St. Thomas writes in this connection: "The satisfactions of Christ have their effect in us *inasmuch as* we are incorporated with Him, as members with their Head. But the members must be conformable to the Head. And just as Christ had grace in His soul, whilst at the same time having a body subject to mortality, and had therefore to attain the glory of immortality through the passion, so we, who are His members, are indeed freed from all the obligations as regards chastisement, by Christ's passion. But this is in *such wise* that we first receive the spirit of adoption of children (which destines us to everlasting glory) whilst still having a body subject to mortality and suffering. It is only later, when we shall have been conformed to the sufferings of Christ, that we are conducted to a glorious immortality." [6] Did we possess the preternatural gifts, this fellowship with Christ, in His human experience, would not be possible for us.

Hence the mystery of our redeemed state is intimately bound up with the mystery of the Mystical Body. These disabilities under which redeemed mankind labors are not due to any vindictiveness on the part of God nor any desire to make the human race smart for its great betrayal. The truth is that, in spite of these disabilities, the status of those redeemed in Christ is incomparably superior to that status that would have been theirs, were they children of an unfallen Adam. To be "graced" in a sinless Christ confers a far greater dignity than to be graced in a sinless Adam. To be united supernaturally with Christ's humanity is a much more royal privilege than to be united supernaturally with Adam's humanity. Adam, even when raised by grace to be the adopted child of God, was not united "personally" with God. He remained, even in his eminence, a human person. The humanity of Christ is substantially united to the Word of God. And we return to God's favor by being mystically incorporated in the Sacred Humanity which is so intimately united to the Godhead. It is through being one with the humanity of Christ that we effect contact with the divinity—a contact of faith and love.[7]

●

[6] *Sum. theol.* 3, q. 49, a. 3, ad 3m.
[7] Cf. the following from the *Ecrits spirituels* of the Venerable Libermann, C.S.Sp., p. 51: "The Word assumed the Sacred Humanity to render to the Father the duties of the creature. He thereby attached an infinite value to these duties. God henceforth sees all human nature as forming one with His Son. This manifests that the nature of man is raised to a more eminent dignity, since the sins of man have been atoned for, than it enjoyed prior to the Fall. Before Adam fell, man did not have such intimate relations with the Creator as he has now. His union with God was less perfect then than now, because since the redemption he in a certain measure, by his union with the Sacred Humanity of Jesus, Head of the Mystical Body, is brought into the economy of the hypostatic union. In the days of innocence God's communications of Himself to His creatures were limited. Now God imparts His spirit without measure. Formerly the glory rendered by man to God was finite, now it is infinite. In the first days sanctity was a pure gift of God, now it is something merited by Christ, the Head of the race.

United with the Sacred Humanity, we participate in all its privileges and graces. To the Sacred Humanity itself all these privileges and graces come from the Word, to whom the human nature of Christ is hypostatically united. The luster and distinction of the divinity of the Word are shed in us when we are made one with Christ. St. Thomas states that in somewhat the same way as the merits of a person in grace belong to that person, so the merits of Christ belong to Him and to His members. Christ's graces become ours when we are bound to Him by faith and love. "Christ," he says, "received grace not only in His individual capacity, but also as Head of the Church, so that grace should stream from Him to His members. For that reason, the [meritorious] actions of Jesus have the same relation to Him and to His members that the actions of an ordinary individual have to that individual himself." [8] It is the realization of this mysterious truth that provokes the cry, so daring and so paradoxical, that bursts from the lips of the Mystical Spouse of Christ on the morning of Holy Saturday: "Truly fortunate is the sin which procured for us a Redeemer, so great and of so exalted a nature." We are of more noble birth when born of Jesus Christ than we would have been, even were we able to trace our lineage to a sinless Adam. To be stamped with the image of a divine Christ is a title to glory far more exalted than the glory due to us were we to bear the image of a purely human head, even though a sinless one. When God pardoned, He pardoned magnificently. So far was He from being grudging in His concessions to submissive humanity, He loaded it with favors. He gave with a divine generosity. He did not content Himself with restoring what had been forfeited, He added superabundantly to His first gifts. God's incredible magnanimity brought it about that man, instead of losing all by the Fall, can profit exceedingly by it, if only he is willing to utilize all that has been won for him and placed at his disposal by the great Sacrifice of Jesus on the cross. It is no wonder that the Church exclaims: "O felix culpa, *quae talem ac tantum meruit habere redemptorem.*" Of this exclamation St. Paul's words in his Epistle to the Romans are an apt commentary: "For if by one man's offense death reigned through one, much more they who receive abundance of grace, and of the gift, and of justice, shall reign in life through one Jesus Christ" (Rom 5:17).

●
_____

In the beginning man was a servant, and the divine adoption extended to him was of a very restricted kind; now he is a child of God, having Christ for his elder Brother."
[8] *Sum. theol.* 3, q. 48, a. 1.

Editors' Note.—From THE TRUE VINE AND ITS BRANCHES (New York: Kenedy, 1938) *pp. 31-47.*

Alban Goodier, S.J.

A More Excellent Way

I

It is important for us to bear always in mind that we learn our Lord as He was, and therefore as He is, wholly from the Gospels. Other Lives of Him, other writings, books of meditation and the like, may help us to interpret Him; they may give us the fruit of the discoveries of others; but in the end even the most inspired and the most living of these must be referred back to the Gospels; if their picture differs from that given by Matthew, Mark, Luke, and John, then, however beautiful and fascinating and elevating it may be, it is not Jesus Christ, but some fine fancy of an artist's imagination. On this account, whatever else one may read and study—Lives of Christ, works on the spiritual life, mystical books, the letters and other writings of saints, great biographies, inspiriting histories, records of martyrs, subtlest theology, annals of the Church, poetry the most sublime— all, it may be, written to enlarge and deepen our concept of our Lord —still one can never lay aside the constant reading of the Gospel, the constant following of Him through their pages who alone, and in them alone, is set before us infallibly as the Way, the Truth, and the Life.

And, in fact, in them we have enough; not, it is true, enough to satisfy our human curiosity, for we are keen, almost beyond endurance, to know everything that can be known, even to the most trivial detail, about this "most beautiful among the sons of men"; but enough to form a perfect picture, nay more, enough to bring up before us a living reality, the study of which will occupy us all our lives, will occupy all men all their lives, and even at the end the mine will not be exhausted.

Let us but look for Him there, allowing other books to help us as they may, but not making them our final source, and we shall find Him for ourselves. We shall find this Man, Jesus, stamped from the beginning with a strange directness and clarity of vision, which nothing can ever divert, or draw aside, or make to falter; He could meet His mother's tears with a direct reply: "Did you not know that I must be about my Father's business?"; the remonstrance of John the Baptist, the first of saints, with the check: "Suffer it to be so; for so it becometh us to fulfil all justice"; to the end there is never any confusion, any doubtful understanding; He walks through life and death knowing always what would be.

We shall find Him next, as a natural concomitant to this, always clear, and firm, and decisive in His judgments, speaking always "as one having authority," always so that His enemies were forced to exclaim: "Never has any man spoken as this man speaks"; unhesitating, true, no matter what the circumstances against Him, no matter how men heckled Him, how they tried "to catch him in his speech," no matter what tact He was at times compelled to employ.

We shall find Him unerring in His estimates of men; He is never deceived or drawn away by a surface impression, never yields unduly, or against His better judgment, to occasion, never confounds evil with misfortune, but distinguishes truth from falsehood, real evil from real good, the canker at the root of human life from the mere withered branches, the "things that are for the real peace" of men as opposed to make-believe forms; He discriminates between reality and truth in all alike, whether in the heart of a disciple or in that of an enemy, in the saint or in the sinner, in the believer or the pagan, the conventionally good, those who pass muster among men, or the outcast criminal.

This stamp of utter, unerring certainty and of absolute trustworthiness because of certainty, is the first trait we discover. Alongside of this we shall find Him the tenderest of hearts, a father, a mother, a brother, a sister, a true and not a patronizing or condescending friend, the exact equal of each and all, with an individual understanding and sympathy for every heart that opens out before Him, yet never does He confuse one with another, never does He weary of one in preference for another, much less exclude one for the sake of another, never is the love or interest of anyone diminished because He has love for so many. On the other hand, never is He weak, or overindulgent, or soft, or too blinded by affection to see the evil or the limitations of His beloved. He gives love lavishly and to all who will have it, even the most debarred from human love, yet none would call Him languid or sentimental; He wins love from those who are conquered by His presence, because He is so true, so strong, so selfless in purpose, so single-minded, so unable to deceive. Men might call Him by bad names; they might accuse Him of other evil deeds; they might say that He worked by Beelzebub, that He was possessed, that He was an impostor, that He blasphemed; they could never say, though He loved so much and showed it, though His love went out to the most loathsome and abhorred so that some took scandal, that this His love was ever other than understanding, and true, and generous, and enduring, and uplifting, and in itself perfect.

Again, we shall find Him ever constant. He has a definite work to do, a definite life to live and death to die—that is written on every page of the record, in His journeys, in His teaching, in His attitude to men, as much as it is constantly and repeatedly expressed in His words—and never for a moment does He swerve in its accomplishment. Failure may depress Him, but He does not despond; opposition may alter His plan, but it does not slacken His effort; malice does not embitter Him; deceit, falsehood, trickery, deliberate misconstruction of His words or actions, desertion, treacherous friends, faithless or weak-kneed companions, fruitlessness of all He may do, even deliberate rejection—none of these things can lessen His endeavor, make His hand tremble, or the feet on the mountains falter. None of these things can alter Him; always and everywhere, from beginning to end, He is the same; He seems to give no thought to consequences, or fruits, or reward; whatever the results, He has a work to do, and the doing of the work is all that He considers; He labors, not looking for reward; toils, not demanding rest; steadily He walks through life to His goal, "giving testimony of the truth," "speaking as one having authority," always "going about doing good," to all alike, deserving and undeserving, friend and enemy, alien and ally, who will deign to accept from Him the blessing He strews along His path as He goes.

With these three, His absolute truth of understanding, His boundless, tender heart, His constancy in action, we shall find Him, as a necessary consequence, looking out on men with infinitely tender eyes. Never a human being comes within His horizon, but He looks through it with the eyes, of accurate judgment it may be, but indefinitely tempered by love; with intimate understanding He interprets it, with the welcome of friendship He receives it; there is not a good thought thinkable about it, not a good interpretation possible to put upon its wayward deeds, but that thought and that interpretation will have found a place in His mind. While others find reason justly to condemn, He will find reason to save; while justice puts a limit to the time of repentance, and permits the law to run its course, He will wait till the very last moment, and in the end will rescue. He does not compel men; He has too much regard for them to drive. He offers them Himself and awaits the issue; when they look wistfully He invites them to draw near; once or twice only does He make the first step, usually He leaves that to them; but when they do come near, when they do let Him see that they want Him, then His eyes glisten, and His heart expands, and His hand opens, and there is interest, and sympathy, and longing in every look and gesture; He was never so near seeming foolish as when some pleading soul showed that it believed and responded, and the key was thus applied to the floodgates of His bursting affection.

These are four main lines that go behind the portrait of Him "that cometh from Edom, with dyed garments from Bosra, this beautiful one in His robe, walking in the greatness of His strength," as the four Gospels consistently describe Him. This is He who, when the Evangelist himself endeavors to depict Him in the abstract, can only be summed up in the words of the prophet: "The bruised reed He shall not break, and smoking flax He shall not extinguish"; yet whom that same prophet also called "Wonderful, Counselor, God the Mighty, the Father of the world to come, the Prince of peace." We see Him clearly enough before us, and we know we are not mistaken; this Man of firm, unflinching manner, yet with not a shadow of hardness; grave in His looks, inspiring silence, yet with it something that attracts; an eye that looks out to long distances, yet not a soul feels itself passed over; glistening as through tears, yet strong as the eye of an eagle; a lip that trembles as the lip of a quivering maiden, yet so firm set that the weakest has courage from its strength. We see Him wrapt in deep thought, speaking words that set the wisest pondering, yet withal in such simplicity that the children understand Him; looking out beyond the limit of life, yet not a flower in the field, or a bird of the air, or an outcast cripple on the roadside is forgotten; with a toiler's hand, and brain, and heart, and ambition consumed with eagerness for labor, yet ever ready to yield up His task when His companionship is needed; consumed with zeal for His Father's house, with zeal for truth and justice, yet patient and pitiful even as He smites, gentle as the gentlest mother.

All this we see and much more: the love of loneliness, though "His delights are to be with the children of men"; the love of prayer, though He cannot tear Himself from the crowd, not even to take food; the love of peace, though His days are one long warfare; the love, seen in His every outside behavior, to be one with all men, though He could not keep from them that which prompted them to make Him their king. But it is useless to carry on the portrayal; we go on and on, the fascination grows, at each new step we see more and more, for He is utterly transparent; and yet at every point at which we stop we feel that we have said nothing. The Evangelists knew Him better than we, and they did not venture to describe Him. They were content to let Him walk through their narrative, preaching the kingdom, healing the sick, having compassion on the multitude, or retiring into the mountain to pray, knowing well that in so doing He would not be lost amid the details; His personality would be too great for that; they knew they would, in their simple story of simple fact, leave behind them that on which all generations would ponder, yet which they would never exhaust.

And indeed it is so. The more we contemplate it, look at it with believing eyes, warmed by love, stirred by hope and trust, the more vivid does the portrait grow, the more living are the features. They are, we know them; "we have found Him whom our soul loveth, we have held Him and will not let Him go." Other portraits help, copies, facsimiles, drawn by more recent artists; but all these have their limitations, some have their exaggerations, none are exactly accurate; all have what life they possess from the great original, and only in so far as they reproduce its fire have they any inspiration in themselves.

II

This is some little shadow of Jesus as the Gospels show Him to us; more if we like, and, above all, more of the details, we can gather for ourselves. These are four guiding lines; we can easily cluster much else around them. For He is not difficult to discover; He needs no great effort of psychology or analysis; He is Himself just simple and true, just meek and humble of heart, and by truth and simplicity, by humility and meekness, He is best to be found; let us not forget His own prayer of thanksgiving wrung from Him at a moment when the learned turned away in scorn: "Heavenly Father, I give thee thanks that thou hast hidden these things from the wise and prudent, and hast revealed them to little ones." Nor again His other words of warning: "Unless you become as little children, you shall not enter into the kingdom of God."

It is worth our while to weigh the meaning of these words. We complain of our want of fruit in prayer, of its dryness, its emptiness; often we only mean, but we do not know it, that we are looking for fruit, not of prayer, but of study; we are watching for that reflex knowledge that comes of thought and study, not for that deeper insight, that fuller understanding, that realization which is found in faith and love and hope, which is the real fruit of prayer, and which can no more be weighed and measured than life itself can be weighed in pounds or measured by yards. In other words, we judge by the standards of poor grown-up people, and not by the unerring standard of a child. A child needs but its mother's company to know her, to love her, and to trust her, yet its knowledge, and love, and trust are not less true, or less complete, or less admirable on that account.

And in precisely the same way there is a knowledge of our Lord which no books or pondering can give us; which can be gained only by living in His company; by living in His company as He glides through the pages of the Gospels; as he plies His daily trade at Nazareth, quiet, monotonous, till we become almost forgetful of His presence; or creeps away in silence up the mountainside, till that, too, becomes a habit with us; or walks by the riverside, unnoticed in the crowd, except by one who alone has eyes to see—how strange that those who fail to see Him claim this as proof of their superior knowledge!—or stands firm and frank before the people, now appealing, now commanding, now consoling, now rebuking, but always the same strong pillar on which all may lean; or sits at table, now with friends, now with enemies, familiarly treated, yet always reverenced, contemned by some, yet feared by others, held in awe, yet never losing that which is expressed in the phrase "only Jesus"; or sleeps in the boat, feeble, yet almighty; or compassionates by lowering Himself to the lowest, yet in such a way that because of it men would hail Him as their king; or denounces evil with a thunder that cows the most violent, yet all the while infants clamber on His knee—living with Him in the midst of all this, in busy streets or along lonely byways, in public Jerusalem or in the privacy of Bethany, we come to know Him as He is for ourselves, and we know that we know Him, whatever those who know Him not may say, and even though we have not, nor care to have, a single word with which to express it. "It is the Lord!" "I to my beloved and my beloved to me." "I know in whom I have believed." That is enough.

My Lord Jesus Christ, thou Wonder of the world, most beautiful among the sons of men, before whom thy very enemies bow down, acknowledging the marvel of thy countenance, the perfection of thy character, the invincible attraction of thy whole self, how strange a thing it is that there can be those who pass thee by unnoticed, how stranger still that even we can pass thee by! Yet is it even so. We believe, we are certain, we know; we build our life here, and our hope hereafter, on thee and thy claim; we own thee, not only to be perfect Man, but to be very God of very God; we see in thee alpha and omega, the beginning and the end, the climax of all for which this world was made, the source from which flows whatever of good this world contains; we can see all this, and know it to be true, and in our moments of emotion can think we would gladly give our lives to witness to its truth; and yet the next minute we can ignore thee; we can go counter to thee; we can go our way through life as if thou hadst never been.

More than this. We who have the light can reach behind the simple story of the Gospels; with thy Apostle St. Paul to guide us we can understand in part what thy resurrection signified; that "having once risen thou diest now no more, death can no more have dominion over thee"; that therefore thou art living now as thou wast living then, the same Jesus now as then, the same utter truth, the same fascination, the same understanding sympathy, the same beating heart: "Jesus Christ yesterday, today, and the same forever." We can realize all this, understand it sufficiently to know that it is true; we can accept the fact of thy being, and of thy nearness to us here and now; and yet we can think, and act, and build up our lives as if it were not or as if to us it meant nothing. We can, with eyes of faith, see thy face glowing in the darkness; with consciousness of hope we can feel thy hands stretched out to us to seize our own; with the instinct of love we can distinguish the very accent of thy voice, even as did thy fellow countrymen of Galilee, calling to us, whispering our very names, telling us of love that human words cannot express—all this is ours, and by its very clearness we know it to be true; it is no fancy, it is the offshoot of no mere sentiment; and yet withal we can turn away, our vision obscured by the fascination of a trifle; and we can act as if we preferred to walk with thee no more, as if we had never learnt to "taste and see how sweet is the Lord!"

Nay, there is something more. We can hear thee, in words that true hearing cannot misunderstand, giving thyself to us to be our slave, to be our food, our life, our abiding companion; yet we can still remain unmoved. One or two among men in the ages past we can see who have learnt thee, and, once they have learnt, have counted all else but refuse in comparison; who have loved thee, and, once they have begun to love, have known for certain that no other love could draw them away, with this no other love could compare; who have given themselves to thee, and, once they have made the surrender, have then proved what heroism, what a true man's strength can accomplish—the strength that conquers torture, that makes a toy of death; the strength that magically turns everything to gladness. We can all see this; we can admire and approve; we can say that here is a man at his best, because he has found the true goal of his being, has become infused with the very life of life, has attained to that likeness to Jesus which is man's ideal—all this we can see, and can say, and then can turn about upon our heel and go our way, as if for us these things had no meaning.

Truly, what a strange thing is man! Whether it be the man who believes, yet is not subdued, or the man who will not believe, as if to believe so grand and great a truth were in some way demeaning to himself. Demeaning to acknowledge Jesus Christ! Demeaning to own Him for my Brother, whose kinship makes me royal! To call Him my friend, whose great heart expands mine beyond the limits of the world! To take Him for my companion, whose comradeship gives life a new meaning! To accept Him for my leader, whose service is a hallmark of nobility! To set Him up for my ideal, than which neither God nor man could make anything more grand! Demeaning to be won by Jesus Christ! If man thinks so, or if in his meanness he acts so, can he be worth so great a gift? Can he be worth the offering of the life, the outpouring of the blood, of Jesus?

Yes; even to this Christ says, "Yes"; and it is a last disclosure of His character, the crowning feature of all, a revelation which breaks down the heart of St. Paul, and would break down the heart of every man who would let himself be penetrated by it. "Christ loved me, even me, and gave Himself for me, even for me."

III

When I was younger, a novice in religion, and knew myself less, and knew others less, and was full of high ambitions in the spiritual life, and sought in books and in study, in thought-out plans and schemes on paper for guides to the summit of perfection, I set virtues before me, and meditated on their beauty, and proposed to myself to acquire them, subdividing them, analyzing them, arranging their degrees as the steps of a ladder. This week, as the good spiritual writers bade me, I would acquire the virtue of patience; next week it should be a carefully guarded tongue; the week after should be given to charity; then should come the spirit of prayer; and in a month or two, perhaps, I might have an ecstasy and "see the Lord." But now, when I have grown older, and find myself still struggling for the first of these virtues, and that in a very elementary degree, and have been taught quite other lessons than I dreamt of, in part by the sorry disappointments in my own soul, in part by the progress seen in the souls of others, I am convinced that there is one road to perfection better than all else—in fact, that if we neglect this one no other will be of much avail. After all, it is possible to acquire perfection in virtues, and yet to be far from a saint; few men have made better use of the particular examination of conscience, for the acquiring of natural virtues, than a certain well-known atheist, and yet to the end he remained without a spark of religion in him. On the other hand, it is possible to be a great saint, and yet to be imperfect in many respects: ask the saints themselves and they will all tell you of their many failures and shortcomings. But one thing is not possible; it is not possible to grow in the knowledge, and love, and imitation of Jesus Christ, without at the same time growing in the perfection of every virtue and becoming more a saint every day.

This, then, if I were allowed to begin my spiritual life over again, is the line along which I would try to live it, and is the line along which I would try to lead the lives of any whom God gave into my care. Particular virtues are good things—of course they are; it is much to be always patient, to be diligent in the use of our time, to be considerate with those who try us, to keep our tongue in control; nevertheless, "Do not the heathens this?" And is it not possible to possess all these, and yet, on their very account, to remain as proud as Lucifer?

I would go further and say that the devil himself must possess many of these virtues; he can certainly bide his time, he can be very busy, he can speak honeyed words, he can accommodate himself to everybody's needs, he can be the most attractive of companions. But these things are not the main issue; they are often no more than the paint on the surface; and truth, sanctity, only begins when the core of the creature is affected. And this is done, almost alone, by love; when the creature loves, then it is changed, and till then scarcely at all. Thus it is that the knowledge and love of Jesus Christ goes deeper down than any Stoic striving after virtue; it is flesh and blood where the other is but bleached bones; it gives life and substance where the other is only dead perfection; the imitation of Jesus Christ includes every virtue, makes them unconsciously our own, produces them from itself, and does not merely put them on from without, even as the brown earth gives forth the beauty of spring flowers and does not know it.

Hence, in practice, were I to be asked for an application of all that I have been here pleading for, I would say:

1. Read spiritual books, yes, as much of them and as many as may be convenient; but do not measure growth in the spiritual life by the number of books you have read; do not even measure it by the amount of learning they give us. Remember the warning of St. Ignatius: "It is not abundance of knowledge that satisfies the soul, but to feel and to relish things with the inner man." Read to provide material for this inward perception and relish; but do not count it necessarily loss that there are books we have not read, or authors of whom we know nothing. And, above all, read the Scriptures, especially the Gospels, with an eye less upon ourselves, and more upon Him whom they describe; in that, more than in any other reading, shall we find that knowledge and true spirituality grow together.

2. Hold spiritual conferences, yes, but less about ourselves and our own despicable faults, or even our little virtues and ideals; more, far more, about Him and His superb perfection, forgetting ourselves in the glory of His sunshine. By so doing it is true we may lose the satisfaction of watching ourselves grow in holiness—that is dangerous satisfaction at the best—but instead we shall grow the more naturally and fully, and He will know it, and that is enough.

3. Make meditation, yes; pray, yes; give the thirsting soul as much of this as it can take. But do not spend all the time lamenting our own littleness and our own shortcomings, patching up our petty, threadbare resolutions and will-o'-the-wisp ideals which, experience has taught us, are only set up that they may topple down again each day. Instead fill the hours of prayer with His absorbing presence, with His invigorating company, the loving admiration of this beautiful of the sons of men, the joy of His friendship, the interpretation of His mind, sympathy with the gladness and sorrows of His heart. Fill our prayer with these things, creep through His wounds into His very

soul, thence look out through His eyes upon heaven and earth, and our little selves prone at His feet, and though by the process we may forget our own spiritual ambitions, we shall instead unconsciously become what He was.

4. Examine our consciences, yes; but do not turn it into an everlasting pecking at the soul, ceaseless beating of this poor creature, which time has long since shown us comes to little good. Instead, let the eyes of Jesus look at us, let us see ourselves through those eyes, the joy we are to Him for our encouragement, the sorrow for our trusting contrition, the smile on His face or the wistful look of disappointment at the sight of us; and it will be strange if the constant sight of Him does not produce its lasting effect. . . .

Editors' Note.—From A MORE EXCELLENT WAY (7th ed.; London: Burns Oates & Washbourne, 1952) *pp. 3-25.*

The Trinity

The Trinity: Mystery of Love
Gaston Salet, s.j.

PREFACE

Even as history speaks to us in many ways and yet there is, as we have seen, a special religious history, so too God speaks to us in many ways through nature to reveal Himself and yet there is also a special revelation of His interior life. There is nothing more important than the question: what is God? It is the greatest good fortune of the human race that the secret has not been kept and that Christ has been sent as teacher. It is He who has taught us, through His own being and through His own words; the doctrine of the Trinity is the beginning and the end of His revelation.

Fr. Salet begins his chapter with the following simple but powerful words:

"There is only one God.

"There are three divine Persons in God, truly distinct from each other, the Father, the Son, and the Holy Spirit.

"They are united by relations of origin: the Father begets the Son, the Holy Spirit proceeds from the Father and the Son.

"Each of these Persons is truly God. All of them and each of them possesses one and the same divinity.

"This is the dogma of the Blessed Trinity which every Christian must believe."

It is through an analysis of this Trinitarian mystery that he illuminates all the consolations behind the solemn declaration of St. John that "God is Love."

Gaston Salet, s.j.

The Trinity: Mystery of Love

There is only one God.

There are three divine Persons in God, truly distinct from each other, the Father, the Son, and the Holy Spirit.

They are united by relations of origin: the Father begets the Son, the Holy Spirit proceeds from the Father and the Son.

Each of these Persons is truly God. All of them and each of them possesses one and the same divinity.

This is the dogma of the Blessed Trinity which every Christian must believe. . . .

AT THE HEART OF CHRISTIANITY

This is not a question of only one important dogma among many others, but of the central dogma of religion. Sometimes people ask: "Why did God reveal the Trinity to us?" This is a naive question. If God wanted to take the trouble of speaking to us, what would He talk to us about if not about Himself? "My child," Péguy says so intimately, "Jesus did not come down to earth to tell us fairy tales."

Since heaven is the vision of God as He really is, and since our present existence is the apprenticeship for heaven, faith should give us some light on the inner life of God. "My whole life and being," said St. Bernard, "should be centered on the heights of the Trinity."

Further, the mystery of God in Himself is truly at the heart of those other mysteries which we might be tempted to call more "useful" or more "interesting" because they have reference to ourselves. The mysteries of our salvation, the Incarnation and the redemption, have their full explanation in the love which inflames the divine Persons. "For God so loved the world that He gave His only-begotten Son" (Jn 3:16). "When the fulness of time was come, God sent His Son in order to make us His adopted sons. And because we are sons, God has sent into our hearts the Spirit of His Son that makes us cry out 'Our Father'" (Gal 4:4). The dogma of the Trinity is the keystone of this whole marvelous building. Leave the Trinity out of it and everything falls to pieces.

Finally, let us add that the mystery of the Blessed Trinity is necessary not only to the Christianity which is the life of the Church, but to the Christianity of our own personal lives, every part of which should fall under its enlightening influence. . . .

GOD IS LOVE

Scripture gives us another definition of God: "God is Love." And this is, without a doubt, the most profound and most inspiring definition of all for us. St. Augustine said: "You wish to think of God. Why do you allow your thoughts to wander here and there? God is not at all what you imagine, not at all what you think you understand. Do you wish to have some foretaste of what He is? God is Love." And certain philosophers who worry very little about the catechism echo Augustine: "God is incomprehensible. But perhaps the two ideas which express God most reasonably are unity and love." "The great Johannine phrase is truly the most profound that man can utter and the only one, in the last resort, that is worth clinging to: God is Love."

Following the great theologians of the Middle Ages, then, we can examine genuine love to find in it, not a demonstration, but a way of picturing the Blessed Trinity for ourselves. We can discover in this divine Trinity the perfect realization of the dream which is pursued by every heart which loves, as well as the living model which every true love should imitate.

PERFECT LOVE

What is perfect love? It is a complete mutual giving. This supposes, at one and the same time, the presence of distinct persons and the absence among them of all selfishness: "To be aware of another in one's self and one's self in the other, to be united and joined together yet still distinct, to have all in common yet merging nothing." Love is union but not absorption. To give one's self totally, it is necessary to be and to remain completely one's self; to give one's self totally, it is necessary to keep nothing back for one's self.

Love is a "we." It demands, then, the "I" and the "thou." It also demands the suppression of the "mine" and "thine," those chilling words, St. Augustine would call them.

This is the ideal that orientates, sometimes completely unconsciously, sincere love in all its manifestations. It does not demand two beings who remain juxtaposed, nor two beings merged into one, but two beings who are distinct and conscious of their distinction in order to be united to each other in their very act of giving.

For human love, however, this ideal is only an inaccessible limit. We are always shut up within ourselves by a selfishness which is never completely destroyed. We are always hemmed in by the very circumstances of our nature, which makes us individuals incapable of communicating all that we are, and who remain completely unintelligible to one another. "Oh, union of two hearts that seek only to be one! Oh, hearts sighing after unity, you cannot discover it within yourselves," said Bossuet. And a modern analyst expresses the "drama" of love this way: "To be more the other than one's self in desire, and never to succeed in being anything but one's self!"

PERFECT LOVE IN THE TRINITY

Distinction, but not remoteness; union, but without confusion; "I" and "thou," but without "mine" and "thine"—what is idle fancy on the human level is a reality in God. The miracle of the Blessed Trinity is precisely this, that it is the complete realization of this perfect love.

The dogma tells us: only one God, only one nature, three Persons.

Here, then, are three Persons who really exist, who are distinct from each other in an irreducible fashion, and not by a mere metaphor or a way of looking at or imagining the mystery. Truly the Father is not the Son, the Son is not the Father, the Holy Spirit is neither the Father nor the Son. In other words, there are three "I's" set, as it were, opposite one another.

But these are not selfish egoisms that confront one another, nor juxtaposed beings that are mutually exclusive, but bountiful beings who are constantly giving themselves.

They possess the same divine nature, that infinite richness which can communicate itself entirely, since it is infinitely spiritual, and which forbids any idea of division and sharing, of joint ownership and participation, because it is infinitely simple. That divine nature cannot be possessed except in exactly the same way and integrally by each of the Persons and by the three Persons at the same time.

Accordingly, we ought not to speak of harmony, but rather of subsistent communion. For each of the divine Persons possesses this

136

richness only in an unselfish way, only in order to love the others in a total giving of Himself. For example the Father, in His entirety, is Paternity, and is not Paternity completely turned towards the Son? Thus each Person exists only in His relation to the others. It is in existing for the others that each one is in Himself. Since He does not seek His own reality in Himself, it is in the others that He finds Himself. Each of the Persons is not a selfish withdrawal into Himself, but a complete pouring out of Himself towards the others.

This plurality of Persons loving each other, however, does not result in a plurality of gods. If God is subsistent Love, how could He help but be infinite unity? All love is unifying; it brings about "unanimity" among the most dissimilar things. What should we say then of infinite Love? Is it not unity itself?

THE FATHER, THE SON, THE SPIRIT

Meditation on perfect love helps us to understand this statement of faith, that there are several Persons in God. But why three Persons? And why are these three Persons the Father, the Son, the Holy Spirit?

Our Lord, who is God-made-Man, knows everything, since He is God; and He can express what He sees and translate it into human language, since He is Man. He has chosen the words in our vocabulary that are best suited to express the divine reality of the Trinity.

The word "father" is the word which best expresses absolute generosity. A father wishes to produce another self in order to love him and because he already does love him. He desires to use his power of transmitting life in order to give the best of what he has, in order to give being to a person similar to himself. Richness, generosity, initiative in love—such is paternal love.

But paternal love here on earth is only the dim reflection of another love. "No one is Father as God is." Man is not always a father, he becomes father. Even then he is not solely father. His heart is divided and his daily life scatters his affections. His paternity is not complete; it does not define him adequately. The Father in the Trinity is solely Father, Father in a unique and total way, Father from all eternity. He is Paternity itself. He gives the divine nature: literally, all that He has and all that He is.

The Son who receives everything from the Father is His perfect Image. He responds to love which is infinite in its total giving by love which is infinite in its total response. Moreover, is not this the love which is revealed to us in so many little ways throughout the Gospels by the whole attitude of Christ Jesus, the God-made-Man, towards His Father? This Jesus has His eyes continually upon the Father, never saying or doing anything of Himself, receiving everything from the Father and rejoicing to possess everything only in order to give it all back to Him, nourishing Himself with His will and burning with the desire to glorify Him. This Jesus, who is humility itself and devotedness and filial obedience in His relations to the Father, what is He then if not the Son? He reveals to us by everything He does and says, and reproduces on the human level, the very essence of the mystery of His divine Person—an outburst of infinite response which is equal only to the paternal giving.

Moreover, this mutual love of the Father and the Son, which has nothing of self-love in one or the other, is not a selfish love of the two Persons. This is so far from being true that the mutual love of the Father and the Son produces by its very exchange of love the Third Person, the Holy Spirit. "For the love which is the Holy Spirit," says St. Bonaventure, "does not proceed from the love which the Father has for Himself, nor from the love which the Son has for Himself, but from the love by which the one loves the other. This love is a bond between them. It is the love by which the one who loves tends toward the other."

That is the unique character of the divine love. It is impossible for human love to be perfect and completely reciprocal between two hearts, for neither of these two hearts can fathom the depths of this exchange of love itself. But in God the intimacy and the perfection of the mutual love between the Father and the Son is so great that this love expresses itself in a living Third Person who is the Spirit of the Father and the Spirit of the Son, the encounter of Their charity, the mutual exchange of Their love. In the words of a theologian of the Middle Ages: "The love of the Two is fused in Them by the flame of a third love."

If the Holy Spirit Himself does not give rise to any other Person, we ought not to think of a self-complacency that selfishly retires within itself. The Spirit is a complete turning back, an unselfish pouring out of Himself towards the Father and the Son. With Him, the movement of divine love closes in again upon itself.

THE LIVING GOD AND PHILOSOPHY

Philosophy was able to suspect nothing at all of this mystery prior to its revelation, but it was enabled to broaden its ideas on God once the mystery had been revealed. "The mystery of the Holy Trinity has the effect of deepening the notion of God and carrying it well beyond what the most acute intellect could conceive." The Trinity introduces the living God to the philosophers.

In this way the danger is avoided, a danger which is far from imaginary, of looking upon the infinite and infinitely happy Being as a transcendent, selfish Ego, the Being that is immense as though He existed in a desertlike solitude, the personal Being as though He were a great God set apart and indifferent to everything outside Himself. The danger is also avoided of conceiving the Being that is infinitely one and simple as a supreme abstraction, the first of all beings as though He were the eternal axiom, the great X in the formula of the universe. "Our faith rejects a divine unity that would be solitude. It rejects just as vehemently a negation of the solitude that would be a negation of the unity," St. Hilary of Poitiers tells us. Thus we are preserved from what one writer calls "the all too simple affirmations of a cold and luminous deism."

Another danger, much more serious, is also avoided: the temptation to pantheism. Many philosophers feel that it is necessary to conceive God as an infinite Goodness that cannot exist except in giving itself. But since they fail to see how a solitary God could love and have awareness of Himself alone, they are driven to the affirmation that God, in order to be God, must overflow into the world, that the world is necessary to God.

But the dogma of the Blessed Trinity reveals to us that God Himself is as it were a living world, a unity that is infinitely simple to be sure, but a unity which involves the mysterious society of the Persons, Their mutual exchange of life, Their perfect happiness together. As a result, we look upon the universe not as necessary in order that God be God, but as an invention of His entirely gratuitous love and generosity, which freely gives itself to the world.

DIVINE LOVE AND OUR LOVE

For ordinary Christians like ourselves who are not philosophers, the dogma of the Trinity brings certain necessary insights into our lives. Our essential attitude, the great obligation which sums up all of Christianity, is love. Since the Blessed Trinity is divine Love itself, the dogma of the Trinity is the revelation of this Love; it is, as it were, the central message of the Trinity. "How can I recommend love to you in a more urgent way than by calling God Love?", asks a Father of the Church.

The love of the divine Persons for each other is poured out towards us. They have given us Themselves, Their very beings, no more, no less than that. "God so loved the world that He gave to it His only-begotten Son" (Jn 3:16). When the Father gave us His Son, who is His own Image, He gave us Himself. And the Son, who has brought us to an understanding of the love of the Father by sacrificing Himself even unto death, sends us His own Spirit, this Holy Spirit, who is the Spirit of the Father and of the Son, who is Their Love and who is called by His own proper name, the Gift.

In the face of this love of the divine Persons, how can we fail to understand that our service of God, our religion, does not consist in the love of slaves, in services and rents paid to the last penny, in rituals and empty forms, but that it is, above all and essentially, a personal love? Nothing can interest God more than this human person made in His own image, nothing can influence Him more than this heart which He has created. "Are you looking for something to give to God?", asks St. Augustine. "Give Him yourself!"

LOVE FOR OTHERS

The Blessed Trinity shows us, in the first place, what our love for others should be, that love which seems at the same time both natural and naturally impossible, desirable, even necessary, and yet only wishful dreaming.

It is the dogma of the divine Persons, in fact, which makes us recognize the value of the human person and which helps us discover most profoundly what the person really is. A person is not just an individual who possesses consciousness of the richness of his nature, a proprietor whose one great law is that of dogged self-defense against every possible invasion.

Certain modern philosophers tell us much more correctly that "the true being is the 'we,' " that "the act by which I am myself is the act of love and of giving," and that "isolation of the person is always an indication that its end is at hand." Thus, a person is a being who possesses his own richness only in order to give it to others. He is a being, moreover, who is completely himself only when giving himself and when, not selfishly seeking himself, he finally discovers himself in another.

How many new worlds open up in these lofty ideas when we examine them in the light of the Trinity! "May they be one, O my Father, as you and I are one" (Jn 17:22). That is the program which our Lord outlines for us. Like the divine Persons, each one of whom remains fully Himself, without the Father, for example, becoming the Son, we also must be entirely and magnificently ourselves in order to develop ourselves according to all our potentialities. The only way of being useful to others is by bringing to them in a complete communication of ourselves what we alone can give them. Each one of us must be a determined "I," which, in a sense, is irreplaceable. And what is true on the personal level is true also on the social and international level. Just as I will be useful to others only by being myself, so a nation will be useful to all mankind only by bringing to men its own individual value developed to the maximum, just as a musical note is helpful in harmony only by being itself, because if the individual note should cease, the harmony would not become more unified, but rather worse.

True love rules out the will for power and the desire for absorption. It excludes just as strongly the "will for weakness" and the cowardly willingness to be absorbed. Beyond this, and always in conformity with the perfect example of the divine Persons, I should desire that others remain and become more and more themselves. They are not for me riches that must be exploited. "We should not love men as epicures love thrushes," Augustine said in expressive terms. "Is love for men, then, only the desire to assimilate them?"

Man will find his true advantage, which is progress in the spiritual order, only in the real union between persons, with the respect and mutual generosity that it supposes.

THE TRINITY, SOURCE OF OUR LOVE FOR OTHERS

Selfishness has always been the only enemy of man's love, and selfishness has always yielded only to the love of God. The Blessed Trinity is not only the unique model of our charity towards others, but its sole source as well. In order to love as God does, we must love through God and with the heart of God. The grace which we need is the Blessed Trinity itself within us, coming to enkindle our hearts with love.

The Fathers of the Church come back to this point again and again: "We are not unified," says St. Fulgentius, "we are not sanctified except through the holy and natural unity, equality, and love of the three Persons who are alone true God." And St. Bernard: "It is love that gives birth to love, substantial Love that gives rise to participated love. The Holy Spirit is given to us in order to unite us to the Father and Son, whose bond of union He is, and in order to put us in communion with all men, whose principle of unity He is."

THE DIVINE PERSONS AND CHRISTIAN LIFE

For many Christians the divine Persons are unknown, as they were unknown to those pseudo Christians of Ephesus of whom St. Paul demanded, "Have you received the Holy Spirit?", and who answered, "The Holy Spirit? We do not even know that there is a Holy Spirit" (Acts 19:2).

There is no misunderstanding sadder than this. If Christ has come to reveal to us that the true God is Father, Son, and Spirit, if this is the fundamental truth, the substance of our dogma, and the basis of that love of ours which is the essential note of Christianity, how can one pretend to be a Christian and look upon this mystery as an abstract theorem, a thesis with no importance at all, an optional corollary to the chapter on "God," one more extra burden to be borne in the Christian's life?

In reality, this Christian life is an intimate union with the divine Persons. Everything in the Christian life unfolds and develops between two points: the baptismal formula, "I baptize you in the name of the Father and of the Son and of the Holy Spirit," and the moving plea which the Church addresses to God for the faithful Christian in his last agony, "He has sinned, it is true, but at least he has not denied his faith in the Father, the Son, and the Holy Spirit!" Between those two solemn moments all our days should be sanctified by a consideration of the Trinity. "The Trinity is our dwelling place, our home, our father's house which we should never abandon." This is, as a matter of fact, the desire of the Church manifested throughout the whole liturgy. St. Justin had already noticed it about the year 150: "In all the offerings that we make, we praise the Creator of the universe through His Son Jesus Christ and through the Holy Spirit." And the liturgists of the twentieth century underline the same idea: "All Catholic prayer is marked with this stamp—it is baptized in the Blessed Trinity." The Church does not pray to the Supreme Being, nor to the Eternal Axiom; it has its petitions ascend in the Spirit, through the Son, to the Father.

And this movement of prayer is only a reflection of the essential movement of the Christian life. The Father has sent us His Son, God made Man, who by His merits has gained for us the gift of the Holy Spirit—that is the epic story of redemption. Our sanctification, which is the result of the redemption, consists in receiving the Holy Spirit, the Spirit of the Son, who makes us like to the Son and, through Him and in Him, raises us up to the Father.

The three Persons act in us, and the Christian life is nothing more than their divinizing action in our souls. Let us leave it to the theologians to ask themselves whether each one of the Persons has a distinct action and whether, for example, the Holy Spirit has a sanctifying role which is proper to Him alone and a type of presence in our souls that is His alone. That is a very minute question. In any case, let us be careful not to imagine the divine Persons and their action in a way that would logically lead us to admit three Gods!

But it is very true to say that the three distinct Persons are within us, that the three really act in us, and that we have special relations with each one of them. We are truly sons of the Father, brothers of the Son, inhabited by the Spirit and stamped with His imprint. And these relations involve slightly different shades of attitude with regard to each of the divine Persons. The Holy Spirit is the soul of our souls, the master within us, the counselor who suggests and teaches, the inspirer of our prayer which He formulates in us and with us, the secret artist who plays on the keyboard of our souls in order to draw divine music from them. The Son is the revealer of the Father for us, the one who has made the Father visible by having His own beauty, the beauty of the only-begotten Son, shine through in the human nature that He has taken upon Himself. We are linked to Him by the inspiring bond of brotherhood. He is the companion of all our human wanderings. Since He is God-made-man, He is the head of that immense Body which is formed of all humanity. The invisible Father is the source of all life and of every good, to whom all gratitude should ascend. By giving us His Son and His Spirit, He has given us the ultimate proof of His own love.

In the ordinary life of faith, the divine Persons remain hidden. Union with them demands continual effort on our part. The graces of mystical union unveil the mystery to a certain extent. For on the testimony of St. Theresa and the Venerable Marie of the Incarnation, the most exalted of all these mystical graces are illuminations which reveal to the soul the divine Persons dwelling and living within the soul itself. Heaven will be nothing more than this union, which is already real, but which will bring us perfect happiness once it becomes fully conscious.

Our daily lives can only be a preparation for and continual progress in this happiness, but already it is a joy possessed. "To believe that a Being called Love dwells in us at every moment of the day and night, that is what has made of my life an anticipated heaven." Now we cannot yet see; for the time being we can only love. Is not the love which unites us to the divine Persons and, in Them and through Them, to all men, a confident anticipation of heaven and the only way to live a happy life here on earth?

St. Augustine has said: "Whether God be close to us or far away from us, depends upon us. Love, and He is there." And Bossuet echoes the same thought magnificently: "United as we are to God, let us form the Blessed Trinity in our hearts by knowing God and by loving God. And since our knowledge, which at present is imperfect and obscure, will soon pass away, and since love is the only thing that will never pass away and be lost, let us love, love, love. Let us do ceaselessly now what we shall do eternally; let us do forever in time what we shall do forever in eternity."

Editors' Note.—*From* RICHESSES DU DOGME CHRÉTIEN (Le Puy: Editions Xavier Mappus, 1945) *pp. 139, 149, 154-67;* translated for this volume by J. Galdon, s.j., and J. Nelson, s.j.

The Church of Christ and the Mother of Christ

The Church and Its Unity
Yves M.-J. Congar, o.p.

The Oneness of the Church
Yves M.-J. Congar, o.p.

Theotokos: The Mother of God
Walter J. Burghardt, s.j.

PREFACE

In our day there seem to be two main patterns of disturbance and concern whenever the subjects of Christ and history arise. One group of thinkers would protest that religious reality cannot possibly be so locked in this remote Jew of Nazareth as to exclude all the history that has intervened since then. Another group would protest with just as much strength that all the religious history in-between Christ and ourselves today is only a flight from Christ and a distortion of Him, that we must therefore keep perpetually returning to primitive Christianity for the truth.

It seems to us that both of these concerns would be alleviated by a careful understanding of the Church as Christ, as the first wonderful elaboration, in historical and community form, of the reality of that single figure who, being thus elaborated, has not tolerated remoteness from us. If the community of the Church is Christ, then all intervening history is alive and creative with Him. If Christ now has this larger form, then the strain and obscurity of constant crusading returns to the beginnings of religious history are no longer necessary.

Fr. Congar offers an analysis of the structure and the Christic nature of the Catholic Church.

Fr. Burghardt adds a study of Mary as constant type of the Church—in her motherhood, in her virginity, in her freedom from sin, in her ultimate destiny.

Yves M.-J. Congar, O.P.

The Church and Its Unity

I

The Church is the reality of the new covenant, the congregation of those men who have been reconciled with God in Christ, who died and rose for us, and have been called to live with God as His sons, as citizens of the heavenly city and as heirs to the legacy bequeathed by God. The mystery of this covenant begins to be realized and revealed from the time of the Old Testament in God's choice of a people. All is linked to the promises which God made to Abraham and the covenant which He struck with Abraham and his posterity (Gn 12:2, 3, 7; 13:14-17; 15:1 ff.; 17:1-8). God promises to Abraham a heritage and an heir. The heir is a son born of Sara and then his descendants, who will form a people which will become, as God shows Abraham, as numerous as there are stars in heaven. The heritage is the land of Canaan, which God bestows upon Abraham and his people as if by a will (1 K 8:36; Dt 1:8). This land for Abraham and his posterity is, as it were, both a heritage received from God and the fruit of the covenant which is signified by circumcision.

On Mount Sinai the covenant is renewed between God and Moses.

Here Moses represents the posterity of Abraham, which has become the people of Israel (Ex 19:1-6). This time the covenant is set upon a clearly defined basis: the Law given by God to His people, through the observance of which Israel will truly be the people of God.[1] In effect, the terms of the covenant are these: a mutual promise of personal fidelity, which will be expressed in the works of the Prophets through the symbol of betrothal between Israel and Yahweh. Israel will be the people of God among all the peoples of the earth, i.e., it will observe with an uncompromising zeal and a scrupulous fidelity the commandments and the wishes of Yahweh. In return Yahweh, who is the God of all the earth, will be in a more special way the God of Israel, *His* people. He will protect Israel and be with it against its enemies, who will also be His enemies. Beyond this promise of fidelity, moreover, there opens a perspective rich in religious values. Through its fidelity to Yahweh, through the observance of His wishes, Israel becomes a religious and a sacred entity which is raised, so to speak, to the sphere of God's own life. The covenant establishes between the people and God a bond which is like mystical parentage: Yahweh dwells in Israel (Lv 26:12; Ez 37:27; Is 60); He is *its* God. Israel itself is the people *of God*, His kingdom, His portion, His heritage, His personal possession, His vineyard. As a people living under God's rule, the theocracy is for God "a kingdom of priests and a holy nation" (Ex 19:6).

The promises which God makes to Abraham, the covenant which God strikes with him and renews with Moses and then later with David (in the promise of a perpetual throne), concern a heritage which is "the land" and an heir who is Israel, i.e., the lineage of Abraham. The ancient covenant is made with a people which is a historical race of men. Under the covenant, the gifts which God bestows are material and earthly goods. But through the preaching of the Prophets, especially when Israel was through its own fault deprived of "the land" and led into exile on a foreign soil, this double idea of the people of God and its heritage was enlarged and spiritualized. The heir was no longer only the historical people, a purely racial collectivity, but a completely religious Israel, a people of the meek, of the devout, of the holy.[2] God's call went out beyond the frontiers of the race to include every man and every people who desired to be obedient to Yahweh in justice (e.g., Is 21 f.; 56; etc.). At the same time the idea of the benefits of the covenant, God's legacy, became clearer and more spiritualized: over and beyond "the land," the benefits which God proposed to His people were a state of affairs in

●

[1] The ten commandments and the law "written on the book of the covenant," with the whole sealed by "the blood of the covenant": Ex 20; 24:7-8; 24:27. Cf. Heb 9:20.
[2] L. Cerfaux, "L'Eglise et le règne de Dieu d'après saint Paul," *Ephemerides theologicae Lovanienses* 2 (1925) 183, note 19.

which God would reign in justice. One had to submit to the yoke of His rule; those who bore this yoke would reign with God and inherit His glory. The fulfilment of the promises, the entry into possession of the true benefits of the covenant, are here deferred to the time of a Messiah-King still to come. Under the Messiah-King, who will be filled with wisdom and piety and wholly inspired with the spirit of Yahweh (Is 11), Israel will be, among the nations, the instrument and at the same time the privileged beneficiary of the kingdom of God.

Beyond even this inauguration of God's rule over the earth which a zealous, just, and religious Israel is to inherit from God, there is sketched the proclamation of an eternal rule. (Here we recall the astonishing seventh chapter of Daniel, whose exceptional importance for the New Testament idea of the Messiah and the Church F. Kattenbusch has brought to light.[3]) What is here announced is God's eternal rule. But who will share in this rule? On the one hand, we find that it will be an individual person, who comes "on the clouds as a Son of Man" (v. 13) and to whom are given "domination, glory, and royal power" for eternity. And at the same time, and just as truly, it will be the "nation of the holy ones of the Most High," who also receive "the royal power, the domination, and the grandeur of the kingdoms that are under all the heavens" (v. 27). As early as this we meet, in an extraordinary way, one of the features which will later become dominant and even decisive in the Christian idea of the kingdom and the Church: the real identity of an individual and a collectivity. As early as this, the full inheritance resides in an individual and belongs to an individual, and yet the full inheritance is also fulfilled in a collectivity and belongs also to a people.

At this point we can also see that the Pauline idea of the Mystical Body as the idea of a certain relation of identity between an individual and a group has a Jewish background and that it is based on the awareness, very much alive in the Old Testament, of the solidarity of the members of Israel among themselves and with God. Israel is a people of one blood ("those of my blood," St. Paul will say). The religious experience and the vocation of each Israelite are linked with the destiny of the people, and this destiny is expressed, is summarized, and is, as it were, concretized in the great religious personalities, the fathers of Israel. Because of the Patriarchs, in their persons, God looks with kindness upon His people.[4]

Finally, the reality of the ancient covenant, even spiritualized, is presented as something to be surpassed. Jeremiah (31:31-34, cited in

●

[3] F. Kattenbusch, "Das Messiastum Jesu," *Zeitschrift für neutestamentliche Wissenschaft* 12 (1911) 275 ff.; "Der Quellort der Kirchenidee," in *Festgabe für Adolf Harnack* (Tübingen, 1921) pp. 143-72. Cf. also M. Lagrange, *Le messianisme* (1909) pp. 224 ff.
[4] Cf. J. Bonsirven, *Le judaïsme palestinien* 2 (1935) 241, and W. Robinson, "The Hebrew Conception of Corporate Personality," in *Werden und Wesen des Alten Testaments* (Berlin, 1936) pp. 49 f.

Heb 8:8-12), Ezekiel (37:26-28), and especially Zechariah (2:5; 3:6-10; 6:12; 9:9; etc.) announce the formation of a new covenant, a new order of things which corresponds to the coming of the Messianic era and which will be characterized both by the extension of the rule of Yahweh, through Israel, to the entire world, and by a new regime of wisdom, meekness, and peace, which will result from an outpouring of the Spirit of God on the Messiah-King and on His people.

II

The realization of this new order is proclaimed by our Lord at the beginning of His public ministry (Lk 4:21, with reference to Is 51:1 ff.), and again by Peter on the day after Pentecost (Acts 2:16, with reference to Jl 3:1-5). The Messianic age has arrived, in truth "the last age," the eschatological age. This does not mean that the final catastrophe is necessarily imminent, but rather that humanity has now entered into the *last order* of things, into an age after which there is no other and could be no other age: for this is the order of *eternal life*. But it is indeed possible for this order to be as yet imperfect and, in this sense, awaiting fulfilment. The new order is, however, already inaugurated and established.

In fact, in the new order of things the heritage promised to Abraham as "the land" undergoes a radical change. It is still a heritage received from God; but that to which we are called, the inheritance which the people of the new covenant receive, is nothing less than the patrimonial blessings of God Himself. What the covenant, the blood of the new covenant, opens to us is access to the heavenly heritage (Heb 9:15; Col 3:24), the incorruptible heritage (1 Pt 1:4), the heritage of the kingdom (Eph 5:5; Jas 2:5), of eternal life (Tit 3:7). It is the access to the Holy Sion, the city of the living God which is the heavenly Jerusalem (Heb 12:22 ff.). We enter, by the new covenant, into the city of the holy ones (Eph 2:18-19; Phil 3:20); we share God's life (1 Cor 1:9; 1 Jn 1:3); we have eternal life (1 Jn 5:11-13; etc.).

But this unbelievable change in our heritage can be conceived only through the unbelievable change of heirs, in whom are wonderfully realized the promises made to Abraham. If we share in the patrimonial blessings of God, as it were in a heritage, it is in Christ Jesus. He alone is truly heir of God, since He is both Son of the Father by nature and descendant of Abraham according to the flesh, that flesh which he took from Mary. He is, then, at one and the same time natural heir of all the wealth of the Father ("all things that are thine are mine": Jn 17:10) and heir, through descendance, of the promises made to Abraham. These promises are going to be realized in Him, for "all that there is of promises of God become 'yes' in Him" (2 Cor 1:20). Thus, in his explanation of how we are justified by faith, St.

Paul gives arguments to show that the promises were made to Abraham and to his lineage, that is to say, to one alone, to Christ (Gal 3:8-18, 29). Heir by nature to the wealth of the Father, Christ is also the true beneficiary of the early promises. But the heritage, which was intended without being clearly signified in these promises, is now revealed as that of the saints in glory, the patrimonial blessings of God. We share this heritage in Christ, as His coheirs.[5] In Him we are heirs both of the promises made to Israel—for we are the new Israel, the new people of God (Rom 9:6-13)—and of the legacy natural to the Son. Christ alone has natural title to this heavenly heritage, "for no one ascends to heaven except the one who comes down from heaven, the Son of Man" (Jn 3:13). But if we become His members, we ascend there with Him and we have in Him access to the bosom of the Father. In Him we can lead the life of sons that we have received, the life of children in the family of God.

All this is the object of the faith and hope to which we have been called. St. Paul, who knew Christ glorified from the road to Damascus, speaks by preference of the completed redemption, that is, the redemption which involves the total transformation of man, the glorification of his body and the complete victory over death and sin. He is therefore more concerned with the future of this heritage of eternal life.[6] St. John, on the other hand, speaks more readily of eternal life in the present: we have eternal life now (1 Jn 3:1-2; 5:12, 13). Yet St. John is well aware that it awaits its consummation (1 Jn 3:2); and St. Paul knows very well that we have already entered on this life, since we have our life from Christ.[7] The riches of the kingdom have been given to us in a way that is precarious, incomplete, and hidden, but still real. Thus he speaks of the foretaste of the Spirit, which does not mean only a promise, but both a promise and a real beginning already of that which we await in faith and hope.[8]

Thus there are at least two sides to the mystery of the Church as revealed in the New Testament. In the Synoptic Gospels this mystery is revealed in terms of the kingdom. In St. John the mystery is revealed in terms of life.[9] In St. Paul the mystery is presented as the new creation, the restoration of all things in Christ, and ultimately as His Mystical Body. But no matter which tradition we consider, we discover these two features: (1) the city of God is whole and entire in an individual, and yet it is also a people, a multitude; (2) the city of God is already present, and yet it is still to be fulfilled, still to

●

[5] The principal texts are Rom 8:14-17; Eph 3:6; Tit 3:7; 1 Pt 3:22; 1 Jn 3:1.
[6] Cf. Rom 5:5; 8:19, 23; 13:11; 1 Cor 6:9-10; Eph 1:14; 5:30; 2 Th 2:11-14; 1 Tim 6:12.
[7] Cf. Cerfaux, *op. cit.*, pp. 191 ff.
[8] Cf. 2 Cor 1:22; 5:5; Eph 1:13-14. Compare Rom 8:23 and Eph 5:30.
[9] Cf. J. B. Frey, "Le concept de 'vie' dans l'évangile de saint Jean," *Biblica* 1 (1920) 37-58 and 211-39. Cf. also E. Tobac, "Grâce," in *Dictionnaire apologétique de la foi catholique*.

come. Since we are in the order of the new covenant, we are in the order of the last and definitive realities. But these realities are present to us and given to us in a limited and precarious way: we await their full manifestation.

We find these characteristics again in the sacraments, which are the signs of the covenant brought about through Christ. For the sacraments look to a triple reality: to the reality of the passion of Christ, which is past but always active and efficacious and by which we and the whole world are reconciled to God; to the present reality of grace, through which eternal life is now given to us and by which the Mystical Body is established; finally, to the future reality of the glorious consummation, which the sacraments announce and of which it is the pledge.[10]

III

The Church is first of all the Body of Christ. It forms a single reality with Him, a single beneficiary of the wealth of God: "coheirs, members of the same body, sharers of the promise: all that in Christ Jesus" (Eph 3:6). We are with Christ a single body, the members of this body.[11] St. Paul will go so far as to write that we are one single person in Christ (Gal 3:28). It is this reality of Christ *in us*, of the Mystical Body, of the change which Christ effects *in us* that we must now consider.

How does this happen? St. Paul tells us very clearly. On the one hand, "the first man, Adam, became a living soul; the last Adam became a life-giving spirit" (1 Cor 15:45). On the other hand, "as the body is one and has many members, and all the members of this body, many as they are, form a single body, so also is it with Christ. For in one spirit we were all baptized into one body, whether Jews or Gentiles, whether slaves or free; and we were all given to drink of one spirit" (1 Cor 12:12-13). There is only one Body of Christ because there is only one spirit animating this Body, the spirit of Christ. Have we not already seen that in the Old Testament the Messianic times were characterized by an outpouring of the spirit of God, with which the Messiah Himself first of all will be filled? [12] The risen and glorified Christ can give His Spirit. For now that He has brought about *in Himself, for us,* peace with God, in the three-sided mystery of His passion-resurrection-ascension, He has ascended into heaven "to fulfil all things" (Eph 4:10). That which He has accomplished in Himself for our salvation, He will now accomplish in us for His glory. Having become *Kyrios* and life-giving spirit, He becomes immanent in His body through His spirit. Pentecost follows the ascension. The Church which

[10] Cf., for example, St. Thomas, *Sum. theol.* 3, q. 60, a. 3; q. 73, a. 4.
[11] Cf. Rom 12:3 ff.; Eph 4:13, 25 ff.; Col 3:15 ff.
[12] Cf. T. Schmidt, *Der Leib Christi* (Leipzig, 1919) pp. 24 ff. and 63 ff.

He founded in Himself at the time of His passion which He suffered for us, He now founds in us and in the world through the sending of His Spirit. In addition, all that Christ Jesus did for the constitution of His Church which is His Body, whether in each of us or in the total life of the group, is henceforth attributed just as truly to His Spirit: it is the Spirit, the "other Paraclete," that is the agent of Christ in *His* Church.[13] The book of the Acts of the Apostles could thus be called the Gospel of the Holy Spirit. Indeed, all that St. Paul attributes to Christ in the life of the Christian, he attributes equally, save for a few nuances, to the Holy Spirit.[14]

This immanence of the living Christ in the Church, His Body, is expressed by Paul in two well-known expressions which signify ultimately the same reality: Christ in us—we in Christ. The formula "in Christ Jesus," if we take into account related formulas, is found 164 times in St. Paul. This formula expresses the fact of being under the influence of Christ, of receiving from Him life and movement, and therefore of acting in some way on His account by performing acts which belong to Him and are in the sphere of the reality which He animates. That is to say, we act as members of His Body, His *sōma*. The corresponding formula, "Christ in us," means that Christ is in us as a life, an interior principle of our activity. This is the basic expression of all that Pauline mystique of the Christian life[15] which consists in imitating Christ, in having in oneself the sentiments of Christ, the mind of Christ (1 Cor 2:16), and, ultimately, in forming Christ in us (Gal 4:19). The two formulas express the same fundamental reality: what the Christian does as a Christian is an act of Christ, because the Christian is a member of Christ. The totality of Christians, animated by the same spirit and acting in the name and under the impulse of the same Lord, from a single whole, the Body of Christ. But what does "Body" mean here? It seems to say that as our body is animated by our soul, renders it visible and expresses it in many different activities, so the Church is animated by Christ, renders Him visible and expresses Him in many different activities. In a sense, it adds nothing to Christ, for the Church is the visible and tangible Christ, it is a Christophany, the visible body of His Spirit, His *pneuma*.[16] In a sense, it does add something to Christ, for it is His

●

[13] Cf. A. Lemonnyer, "L'Esprit-Saint Paraclet," *Revue des sciences philosophiques et théologiques* 16 (1927) 293-307.

[14] Cf. A. Deissmann, *Paulus* 2, 110; F. Prat, *Théologie de saint Paul* 2, 352 ff.; Lemonnyer, *Théologie du Nouveau Testament*, notes carefully the nuances which Deissmann has somewhat neglected.

[15] Cf. O. Schmitz, *Die Christusmystik des Paulus* (Gütersloh, 1924) (Protestant); A. Wikenhauser, *Die Christusmystik des heiligen Paulus* (Münster, 1928) (Catholic); F. Jürgensmeier, *Das mystische Leib Christi* (Paderborn) (Catholic); J. Duperray, *Le Christ dans la vie chrétienne d'après saint Paul* (Paris) (Catholic); etc.

[16] St. Paul and the Fathers up until the tenth or eleventh century speak simply of the "Body of Christ." The term "mystical" was introduced in

plenitude and should, in realizing itself, realize Christ, "until we have arrived at the mature measure of the fulness of Christ" (Eph 4:13).[17]

In this way the mystery of the Mystical Body puts us, as does that of the kingdom, in the presence of the following double and dialectical truth: All is already accomplished in Christ, and the Church is only the manifestation of that which is in Him, the visible reality which is animated by His Spirit. And yet we have still to realize Christ and still to build up His body. We could easily call this double truth a dialectic of that which is "given" and of that which is "effected." We come very close here to the mystery of the theandric reality of the Church, which we will find again, especially in discussing the sacraments.

If we now ask ourselves how we make up the Mystical Body or how we become incorporated into this Body, we will have to speak with St. Paul of faith and charity, and then of the whole moral life conceived as a "life in Christ." There are so many texts that we would have to quote almost the whole of St. Paul, and even then we would have to add large sections from the letters of St. Peter and the wonderful writings of St. John. We will select only two summary texts: "That thus Christ may establish through faith His dwelling in your hearts, rooted and grounded as you will be in charity" (Eph 3:17-18), and "In view of the building up of the Body of Christ, until we attain to the unity of faith. . . . That professing the truth we may grow in every respect in charity, in Him who is the Head, that is to say, in Christ. It is under His influence that the whole body achieves its growth for the building up of itself in charity" (Eph 4:12-16). We will indicate later how faith and charity, that is, faith animated by charity and bearing fruit in good works through it, effectively procures the reality of the Mystical Body by realizing the *Christ in us* and *we in Christ*.[18] It is faith, in fact, that opens our souls to the point of view of *another* and brings to life in us *His* way of seeing. It is charity which makes us espouse *His* inclinations, *His* tendencies, *His* motives for action. Supernatural faith is, as it were, the outlook of Christ grafted onto us, and charity is, as it were, His living heart put in place of ours. By faith and charity our lives are

●
_____

contradistinction to the Eucharistic Body and means "pneumatic" or spiritual. Thus the Church as the Body of Christ is distinguished from the corporal reality of "Christ according to the flesh."

[17] Cf. also Col 1:24: "I help to pay off the debt which the afflictions of Christ still leave to be paid for the sake of His Body, the Church" (Knox). Modern Catholic piety considers the Church as an extension of Christ's humanity, but in a Pauline perspective this would be a subordinate notion.

[18] There are many statements of the theologians which make living faith the very substance of the Mystical Body. "We are incorporated with Christ through faith and charity," says St. Thomas, *Sum. theol.* 3, q. 80, a. 2, c., ad 3m, and ad 4m; *In 4 Sent.*, dist. 9, q. 1, a. 2, sol. 4; *In Ioan.*, c. 7, lect. 7, nn. 2, 3, 4, 6. Cf. *In Gal.*, c. 6, lect. 4.

handed over to Christ, so that in effect we lead a life in the name of Christ. "It is no longer I who live, it is Christ who lives in me. The life which I presently live in the flesh is a life in the faith of the Son of God, who loved me and delivered Himself up for me" (Gal 2:20). In this perspective we can understand a text of St. Ignatius of Antioch which more than one critic has stumbled over: "Faith, which is the flesh of the Lord, and charity, which is His blood" (*To the Trallians* 8, 1). By faith we are really members of Christ, and by charity we are living members. We bring Christ to live in us and we live in Him. We live a life in His name and under His life-giving action.

Faith and charity take hold of, and give form to, all our other activities. It is these virtues that animate the whole life of the Christian and will bring it about that all his actions, his sentiments, his thoughts will be accomplished *in Christ*. When living faith is the soul of all his actions, the Christian will realize all things in Christ. If he has friends, they will be his friends in Christ; if he works, he will work in Christ; if he walks, if he eats, if he is happy, he will do all that in Christ. In effect, he will bring Christ into his whole life by living faith, love, prayer, and grace. He will be saddened in Christ, sick in Christ, good and devout in Christ, chaste, patient, and mortified in Christ. And as a result our whole life, all that is in us from the first Adam and is animated by a "physical" life, becomes the life of the Second Adam, reality in Christ or reality of Christ in us. All things are in this way recapitulated in Christ, until "when all things are made subject to Him, then the Son Himself will be made subject to Him who subjected all things to Him, that God may be all in all" (1 Cor 15:27).

Thus does the Body of the Second Adam come to its fulfilment: through the progressive communication of His Spirit to all human matter, to all human activity which expands in the world through the growth of the first Adam. Can we therefore speak of separating Christianity from the professional, social, and cultural activities of humanity? To be sure, there is often a concrete antinomy between the carnal man and the spiritual man; to be sure, our natural activities proceed from a "body of sin" (Rom 6:6). But St. Paul invites us also to "put to death, by the Spirit, the works of the flesh" (Rom 8:13), to "live by the Spirit" (Gal 5:25) and to "offer our bodies [to God] as an offering living, holy, agreeable to God" (Rom 12:1).

The idea of the Mystical Body invites us to be very realistic about this. It teaches us that Christ wishes His life to continue in humanity, according to the logic of a genuine theandrism. He wishes to continue in us that which he first did for us. He wishes to be a child in the Christian child, obedient in the child's obedience, lead the life of the family in the Christian marriage, to be in the joy of those who are happy, to continue His passion in those who suffer, to teach in the

Christian teacher, to work in the Christian worker—in brief, to animate in us every living fiber of humanity, in order that all be "recapitulated" in Him.

The first Christian generations were very much aware of all that we have just said. In a very beautiful study of the Church, F. Kattenbusch has shown that the Church was for them a descent of the heavenly world onto the earth, the heavenly world being essentially that of the Spirit and of holiness. At the same time it was a gift from on high, the coming to us of the heavenly Jerusalem proceeding from the court of God; the Church was also, for them, essentially the Agape, that is to say, a fraternal community of free and spontaneous mutual assistance. Thus it was, according to the dialectic of the "given" and the "effected," both a gift of God which has come from on high and a co-operative effort of men, an acquired reality and a work which is effected, a Mystical Body and a society.

IV

The Church is not only sacramental and apostolic; it is obviously a real society, for it has the structure and qualifications of a real society.

The Church is the new Israel and it is, as Israel, a people of God having its existence as a people, with its social life, its legislation, its hierarchy. The Christians were conscious of forming this new Israel which God assembled no longer in the framework of the twelve tribes considered racially, but from the four corners of the world, under the government of twelve *apostoloi*. The pagans even mocked the Christians, whom they called with disdain a *tertium genus*.[19] When one reads with simplicity the New Testament texts and the earliest writings of Christianity before the peace of Constantine, one is struck by the clear simplicity with which the Mystical Body of Christ and the Church-society are, without distinction, fused in a single reality. The Mystical Body is not a spiritual thing without relation to the world of realities and human activities: it is the visible Church itself and can no more be disassociated from it than France considered in its spiritual reality can be really disassociated from the institutions and realities of the spatial and visible France with its laws, its constitution, its government, and so forth. Fortunately we are today well rid of the habit of reading the early texts through the glasses of the liberals with their "religion in spirit" or even through the eyes of the Lutheran tradition which disassociates the visible Church from the invisible Church. The works of a K. Holl [20] or F. Kattenbusch[21] separate us from those of

●

[19] For indications of the Christians' awareness of being the New Israel, cf. Rom. 9:6; 1 Cor 10:18; Gal 6:16; compare Jas 1:1.
[20] "Der Kirchenbegriff des Paulus in seinem Verhältnis zu dem der Urgemeinde," *Gessamelte Aufsätze* 1, 44-67.
[21] "Der Quellort," *op. cit.*

Hatch or R. Sohm. In particular, Kattenbusch has shown, in the study that we have already cited, that if the Church was, for the first Christian generations, a coming down from heaven on to earth, if it was a reciprocal *Ineinandersein* [literally, being-in-one-another] of Christ and Christians, it was also, at the same time and inseparably, *a society of faith and of the Holy Spirit in men's hearts* and *a society with external activity and rites.*

Some verses of the Acts of the Apostles (2:42-47) give us unquestionable testimony on the life of the Church in its very first years and bring to our eyes four of the characteristic acts of the new people of God.

They were, we are first told, *steadfast in the teachings of the apostles* It was not certain enlightened individuals who formed the community, but something which rather resembled a "Church taught" informed by a "Church teaching." *They were,* we are further told, *steadfast in the community,* that is to say, apparently in a regime of common life which, in these first times, generally went to the point of common life of material goods and which appeared as the Christian regime carried to its own natural conclusion. In any case, there was an ordered society which was ruled and directed by the apostles and which soon makes room for a hierarchical institution, that of the deacons. *They were,* we are told, *steadfast in the breaking of the bread,* which, if it does not signify the Eucharist exclusively, at the very least involves it.[22] Finally, *they were steadfast in prayer,* that is, as verse 46 makes clear, *in the temple.* These common activities, over which the apostles presided, brought it about that "the multitude of believers had only one heart and one soul" (Acts 4:32).

Evidently, human, geographic, cultural, and historical realities quickly imposed upon this ecclesiastical life developments, modifications, and adaptations. When the Church leaves Jerusalem to penetrate the Greek world; when it reaches generations who have not known Christ or the apostles, or, in a short time, even the immediate disciples of the apostles; when it grows until it is coextensive with the *Imperium Romanum,* then one day goes beyond it; when it quits the catacombs for the Constantinian basilicas; when it thrusts itself upon kings, creates Christendom, and has almost the monopoly of culture, then it will assume, quite evidently, exterior forms which are rather different from those of the community which issued immediately from Pentecost, was directed by the apostles, and counted still in its bosom the mother and the brethren of the Lord.

And yet, we will always find again, giving to all Christians one heart and one soul, the same elements of the *communion of the Church:* (1) a witness to the redeeming Incarnation, put forth by a hierarchical body in which is continued the apostolic witness, and received by the faithful in that unanimity of thought and expression

●

[22] Cf. Acts 20:7.

which St. Paul demanded;[23] (2) a common life, a life of mutual assistance and edification, the reality in all its degrees of the *communio sanctorum:* social life and religious life are so closely connected that nothing is more frequent in the writings of St. Paul [24] and in the earliest writings[25] than the idea of *a Christian life led socially,* a life of members in a body, each contributing a share to the progress of the whole—which is Christ;[26] (3) the participation in the sacraments and above all, after baptism (which made one to be a member of the Church), in the Eucharist around which . . . the whole liturgy came to be organized.[27]

The Christian life is a life in Christ which is nourished, maintained, and expressed in a spiritual life which is social and within the framework of the Church. The union with Christ, the interior life of each soul, is born and grows *socially* in the Church. Also, in the Church, the spiritual realities of the life in Christ are at once expressed, take flesh, and are nourished within the social life of the Church. Communion in the redemptive mystery of Christ is found in baptism, in the Eucharist, in the sacraments. Faith is expressed and nourished in dogma. Devotion is nourished and expressed in the liturgy. Love, which is engendered in mutual assistance and service, finds profit and support by letting itself be governed by law. The three principal elements of the ecclesiastical communion are at the same time served and ruled by a hierarchy invested with the triple power of teaching, of priesthood, and of pastoral government. All of this brings about a single Church which is at the same time spiritually and visibly one. In the Church the personal union of the souls with God and life in Christ is socially realized. For the Church is a body in which, according to the expression of St. Irenaeus, "has been organized our communion with Christ" (*Against Heresies* 3, 24, 1).

V

Finally, to summarize what we have said, we would like to put ourselves in the presence of the concrete reality of the Church and of its unity as we can see it.

The Church shows first of all a group life, which adapts itself in a

●

[23] There are many texts; cf., for example, 1 Cor 1:10; 1 Tim 4; etc.
[24] For the idea of mutual assistance, cf. Rom 15:25 ff.; 16:2; Gal 5:13; 1 Th 3:12; 2 Th 1:3. Cf. also 1 Pt 2:13-14. For the idea of mutual edification, cf. Rom 12:9 ff.; 14:19; 15:2; 1 Cor 8:9 ff. and 20-22; 10:23 and 32-33; Col 3:3; etc.
[25] For example, Clement, *To the Corinthians* 37, 5, and 38, 1; Ignatius, *To the Magnesians* 13, 2; Polycarp, *To the Philippians* 10, 2.
[26] See 1 Cor 12:4-30; etc. The practice of public penance in Christian antiquity shows that personal sins were considered as damaging the spiritual good of the society. No distinction was made between the interior dispositions of a soul and the common good of the Church as a society.
[27] Cf. Cabrol, *Le livre de la prière antique.*

certain measure to the development of human society, but which has its own proper rhythm, its special existence, its laws, its customs, its rites, its organization, its works, its hierarchy. One who forms part of this group lives in the heart of a parish community in which all the acts of life have their place: birth followed by baptism, childhood with the catechetical instruction and first Communion, Sunday Mass, various services, solemnities of the liturgical year, sermons for special occasions, marriage, introduction of another generation to prayer and the sacraments, preparation for death, anointing of the sick and viaticum, funeral prayers and ceremonies, and the cross in the cemetery where, several times a year, especially on Palm Sunday and All Souls' Day, the living visit those who have departed.

In the parish a man presides over the common prayer, administers the sacraments, teaches doctrine, gives counsels, sees to the observance of Christian obligations and the "laws of the Church"; for one who professes to be one of the faithful is held to certain practices and to profess a rather considerable body of doctrine.

Over and beyond the parish, a priest of higher rank, invested with more extensive powers and whom the others obey, is the guardian and the expression of a larger unity, that of the diocese. But the religious communion does not stop there, not even at the totality of all the faithful of the same nation. All Catholics, throughout the world, whatever their race, their language, their culture, their state in life, profess that they are a single people which lives the same life and is animated by the same hopes. Another man is the guardian of that unity and at the same time its symbol: the one whom all call "the Holy Father." If such a multitude, with all its differences, truly lives in unity, it is because the Church has in itself its visible head, its criterion of unity. Obedience is paid to him as to the visible Vicar of Jesus Christ.

But all this organization, all these laws and customs, rites and sacraments, works and co-operative enterprises of all kinds, all this has only one purpose: to effect, beyond all human possibility, even beyond all human likelihood, a life of faith and love hidden in God with Christ. All this display of ceremony, all this pomp, is intended only to rouse in the world faith and love for Jesus Christ and for God. Those demands of the Church, that unyielding claim of its right to teach the little children, that uncompromising stand on doctrine and that extreme reserve in regard to novelties, all that has only one purpose: to unite souls to God by making them, through faith, through the sacraments of faith and charity, living members of the Mystical Body of Christ. For this Church, organized for action and effectively structured as a society, is internally a community living mystically with the Christ who has died, has risen, and is glorious. The juridical implications of the ecclesiastical communion easily allowed internal development. Yet it is not substantially different from the community of the Cenacle which, steadfast in the teachings of the apostles, in the community life, in the breaking of the bread and in prayer, had only one heart and one soul in Christ. Here as there, we have always the assembly of those whom God calls to become beneficiaries of His heritage, with the saints in glory. All its exterior life, all its social display, are only an expression and an instrument of an interior life which is the life of Christ. All the exterior and visible activity of the Church exists only to bring to realization that which is its interior substance: the life of humanity in Christ.

Editors' Note.—From ESQUISSES DU MYSTÈRE DE L'ÉGLISE (rev. ed.; Paris: Editions du Cerf, 1953) *pp. 11-57;* translated for this volume by J. Healey, s.j., and J. Nelson, s.j.

Yves M.-J. Congar, O.P.

The Oneness of the Church

. . . The Church, as an institution, is the human form of the divine
interior unity of the Church as the Mystical Body. If anything be well
attested, it is this; but if there is one thing that has been lost sight of
through the historic divisions of Christianity and the inroads of liberal
relativism, it is equally this. And yet, theologically speaking, it is
perfectly clear—the visible and empirical Church is the visibility and
realization under human form of the Mystical Body. Christ compared
the unity for which He prayed to that which exists between His
Father and Himself, the Word *Incarnate*: He in His visibility did the
work of the Father, and the Father worked through Him. So also must
the Church—spiritual in substance and at the same time visible. St.
Paul and the early Fathers, as well as those of the fourth and fifth
centuries, had no notion whatever of a Mystical Body which was not
corporeally visible or was not a definite and individual reality, identical
with and indissociable from the apostolic Church. To break the unity
of the institutional Church was, for them, to break the unity of the
Mystical Body, or rather—since the heavenly unity of the Body cannot
be broken—to be separated from it. For the unity of the one was the

very form, on the human plane, of the other. "Have we not one self-same God, one selfsame Christ, one selfsame Spirit of grace poured out in us, one selfsame calling in Christ? How can we rebel against our own body? How can we perpetrate this folly of forgetting that we are members one of another?" said Clement to the Corinthians about a falling from unity in the Church.[1] Search as we may, we shall find nothing else in the authentic Christian tradition.[2]

It follows inevitably that we must belong to the Church in order to belong to the Mystical Body and that the two coincide. We shall discuss later the question raised by this statement, but whoever admits the doctrine of the Apostle set forth above can scarcely be in doubt of its truth.

We have so far considered (1) the supernatural character of the Church and its unity, (2) the human mode in which this is realized and expressed. We must now establish the concrete relation between the two, the substance and the human mode of its existence. This in fact results, in the Church, in two realities which have each their expressions, their exigencies, and their laws, and are nevertheless one Church. We will therefore consider first the twofold plane and law of unity and then the unique organic reality of the one Church.

THE TWOFOLD PLANE AND TWOFOLD LAW OF UNITY[3]

The Church may be regarded under two aspects, as being already the family of God and the community of those sharing the divine life, and as she is in this world, humanly conditioned and militant.

1. On one hand there is a divine unity, something simple, in that it is the communication of a simple Principle, as the life of the soul is communicated immediately and simply to the body.

1. On the other hand is a social unity, something complex, constituted in multiplicity by a consensus and an organized collaboration for a common good—a unity of order similar to a national unity.

2. An organism.

2. An organization.

3. From this point of view the Church is composed only of those incorporated as members in a liv-

3. From this point of view, because it is a society, there are in the Church rulers and ruled, in-

●

[1] Clement, *To the Corinthians* 46, 6-7.

[2] St. Irenaeus accused the Gnostics of wanting to divide "the great and glorious Body of Christ" (*Against Heresies* 4, 33, 7). There are many references in St. Augustine.

[3] Many references in this connection are to be found in the great medieval theologians, whether as regards excommunication or as regards the pope; e.g., St. Thomas, *In 4 Sent.*, dist. 18; *De verit.*, q. 29, a. 4; *In 2 Cor.*, c. 13, lect. 3; *In Rom.*, c. 12, lect. 2; Albert the Great, *De incarnatione* (ed. Backes) in *Florilegium patristicum* 40 (1935) 24.

ing body, animated by a spiritual life in faith and love.

4. The only hierarchy is that of holiness and virtue in accordance with a greater or lesser degree of living faith and union with Christ. The actual value of each member is a personal and interior thing inherent in himself: he is worth what he *is*. Here we are in the personal and moral order of the relation of each to his destiny and to the mystery of God in Christ, which is the concrete form of that destiny.

While, in the interior and moral order, nothing is taken into account by Christ in His Body but the fact of spiritual union with Him in living faith by charity. . . .

Therefore in this order a pope may be much less near to Christ than a humble and ignorant

volving, though in a community of spiritual life, commands and obedience.

4. A strictly social hierarchy, graded not according to personal worth but to functions, powers, and actual competence. The worth of each member is independent of his personal quality; he is worth not what he is personally but what he represents in relation to the common good. We are in an objective and juridical order, of the relation of each to a common good which is a means for the sake of persons. It is not so much a question of value as of validity and competence.[4]

Here, what a legitimate superior does is legitimately done. This is the basis of the validity of sacramental acts by ministers in themselves unworthy. "Peter baptizes," says St. Augustine, "it is Christ who baptizes. . . . Judas baptizes, it is Christ who baptizes."[5]

In the institutional Church superiors and clergy take a higher place merely because of their

●

[4] All this is precisely accurate of the Church, but must be understood in the light of more full statements regarding the relation of the institutional Church to the Mystical Body. This meets certain difficulties, those, for example, of Lacey (*Unity and Schism*, p. 123). The error which consists in transferring to the order of social functions the exigencies and conditions of the moral order has often appeared in the history of the Church; e.g., Tertullian, the Waldensians, Huss, Wycliffe. It is a natural temptation to religious souls, resting on the fact that the common good of the institution is itself essentially moral and religious. Yes, but social too. And no one has ever denied that there is a rigorous obligation for the members of the hierarchy to be holy in proportion to their responsibilities; the episcopate is bound up with the idea of perfection, and our Lord confided to Peter the charge of His flock only after having demanded the assurance of his love.

[5] Cf. St. Augustine, *Commentary on John* 5, 18 (*PL* 35, 1423) and *ibid.* 6, 7 (*PL* 35, 1428); cf. *On Baptism against the Donatists* 3, 10; 4, 4; 5, 19; *Against Crescentius* 4, 20; etc. This point of doctrine was one of the good results of the Donatist crisis and, though raised again later, it was established in Catholic dogma.

woman. This is a classic example for the Middle Ages. In the dooms painted in our churches and in the work of such artists as Fra Angelico we find bishops, popes, and monks carried off to hell.

function, apart from their personal holiness or unworthiness. Respect and obedience is due to them, for though the Samaritan may be worth more, morally, than the priest, yet it is not he who has been ordained. "He offereth the bread of God: he shall be holy unto thee" (Lv 21:8).

What counts is the spirit.

What counts is the commission.[6]

5. Here it is a matter of the communication of the life of God and its privileges. Christ is the only Head: He gives Himself as He will, and any co-operation by the creature in this life which is Christ's is only instrumental, in the exact theological sense of the word, i.e., not as having any innate virtue or efficacy, but simply serving as a channel of power or efficacy to the principal cause, to whom alone the effect is assimilated.

5. Here, since it is a matter of a society organized for the common good, though Christ is still the Head,[7] the Church has of right the sovereign powers necessary to her life as an institution. In the social order strictly so called, and in the exercise of juridical powers, the Church acts directly and with authority, not instrumentally. As a visible society of Christians corporately moving towards God she has a visible head, a central organ and regulator of her social life, the Bishop of St. Peter's see at Rome.[8]

6. From this point of view the Church has neither extension nor division, but is a living organism, simply and wholly realized where

6. From this point of view the Church has quantitative extension in the world and distinct parts. As my right hand is here

●

[6] This difference and relative antinomy presents a great problem. In the preaching of the prophets and in our Lord's teaching in face of the Pharisees we undoubtedly find the concern that "authority" should not quench the "spirit." On this, see P. Clerissac, *Mystère de l'église* (Eng. tr., *The Mystery of the Church*). In precise theological language he deals with sanctifying grace and graces *gratis datae*. See also St. Thomas, *Sum. theol.* 2-2, q. 3, a. 1; *Comp. theol.* 1, 214; *In Rom.*, c. 1, lect. 3; and *In 4 Sent.*, dist. 13, q. 1, a. 1.

[7] The pope is not the *successor* of Christ; he is His *vicar*. This distinction is often misunderstood; e.g., by Bulgakov, *L'Orthodoxie*, pp. 53 and 81, where under correct phraseology the two ideas are confused; and G. Hebert, *Intercommunion*, whose difficulties would be cleared up by this distinction between vicar and successor on the one hand and order and jurisdiction on the other.

[8] For an elaboration of the points touched on in 5, see M. J. Congar, "Ordre et juridiction dans l'église," *Irénikon* 6 (1933) 22-31, 97-110, 243-52, and 401-8.

men are united with God. It is the Mystical Christ.

and my left there, so there is the Church in France, the Church in England, and so on. But my soul is in my right hand as in my left, present and simple in both, just as is the soul of the Church, made up of the divine realities described.

7. The Church is a body in the vital sense of the word—a visible reality animated by an interior principle of life. The Holy Spirit and the grace of Christ are this soul, and the Mystical Body is mysteriously one with a simple living oneness which resembles the substantial unity of a living body.

7. The Church is a body in the institutional and legal sense of the word, i.e., a multitude organized in one by corporate activities and diverse functions.

8. The Church exists and will exist eternally, for she lives with an eternal life, typified in St. John's Gospel: "If I will that he tarry till I come. . . ." [9]

8. The Church on earth is in time, for the formation and gathering together of the members of Christ. She is necessary for so long as Christ is not fully come in us, that is, for the time of our pilgrimage. She is active and militant. She will cease to be, as such, when the work of God in humanity is complete and the Lord returns. Then the Church will give place to the kingdom, as prophecy and faith to open vision; when Christ will "deliver up the kingdom to God and the Father, having brought to nought all principality and power" (1 Cor 15:24). In heaven the Holy City will have no need of light, for

●

[9] Jn 21:22. The Fathers understood this text of the theological and contemplative life, which endures. Peter here symbolizes the active life. (Cf. St. Augustine, *Commentary on John* 124 [*PL* 35].) Both lives are necessary to the Church on earth, whose proper and specific form of life is more precisely "apostolic" (or, as is sometimes said today, quite incorrectly, the "mixed" life) as St. Thomas explains. Cf. Ch. Journet, "L'Occupation dominante ou la forme de vie de l'église," *Etudes carmélitaines* 19 (1934) 1-17. In heaven the Church will be no longer "Petrine" but only "Johannine," that is, no longer militant, but solely contemplative.

God Himself is the temple of it
and the Lamb is the light
thereof.[10]

THE UNIQUE ORGANIC REALITY
OF THE ONE CHURCH

This twofold plane and law of unity does not mean that there are two
Churches. There is not, on the one hand, an invisible, disembodied,
purely "mystical" Body, and on the other a lifeless corpse consisting of
the external ecclesiastical organization. For that which is thus organized is precisely the human fellowship of the friends of God, and
the Mystical Body *is* the ecclesiastical *societas* itself. The two compose
one organic structure, as soul and body are composites of one human
personality. A still better analogy, for He is the very archetype of
the Church, is that of the unity of the divine nature and the human
nature in the one Person of Christ. To exclude His human nature is
Monophysitism; to exclude His divine nature is Nestorianism. The
Church is analogous to the Christology of Ephesus as well as that of
Chalcedon, to that of St. Cyril as well as that of St. Leo.[11]

To sum up, the unity of the One Holy Catholic and Apostolic
Church is that of a clearly defined entity, consisting of human beings
united by a supernatural life proceeding from God and from Christ,
in an organized form of social life by means of which this supernatural
life is initiated and fostered. On its earthly side the Church is, so to
say, a vast sacrament in which everything is a sign and a means of an
inward unity of grace.[12] But this earthly reality only exists for the

●

[10] Ap 21:22, 23. The juxtaposition of the Church *societas* and the "temple"
does not seem to be fortuitous. Both are necessary, for the same reasons,
and the parallelism could be carried even further.

[11] Cf. Leo XIII: "The connection and union of both elements is as
absolutely necessary to the true Church as the intimate union of the soul
and body is to human nature. The Church is not something dead; it is the
Body of Christ endowed with supernatural life. As Christ, the Head and
Exemplar, is not constituted solely by His visible human nature, which
Photinians and Nestorians assert, nor solely by His invisible divine nature,
as the Monophysites hold, but is one, from and in both natures, visible and
invisible; so the Mystical Body of Christ is the true Church only because
its visible parts draw life and power from the supernatural gifts and other
things whence spring their very nature and essence . . ." (Encyclical Letter
Satis cognitum, June 29, 1896; tr. Messenger, *Rome and Reunion*, p. 35).
It is more appropriate to speak of the visible unity of the Church (as does,
e.g., The Lambeth Appeal of 1920) than the unity of the visible Church
or the unity of the invisible Church.

[12] "The real unity of the Church is sacramental . . . the Church itself is
the *sacramentum unitatis*. It is a visible human society informed by divine
grace" (Lacey, *Unity and Schism*, p. 156). Cf. G. Hebert, *Intercommunion*,
p. 39: "That a real relation of man to God is thereby established, in a
social fellowship or Kingdom." The law of incarnation, underlying such
quotations, is one of the strongest links in thought between us and Anglo-

sake of its heavenly substance, just as this exists only in its human embodiment. There are not two Churches, and never did the early Christians think that there could be two Churches. The unique Church, the Body of Christ, is at once heavenly and human, law and love, institution and fellowship, substantially divine but incorporate in humanity, at once and integrally *societas fidei et Spiritus Sancti in cordibus*, and *societas externarum rerum et rituum*, a unity at once corporeal and spiritual.[13] It is equally true to say of her, *Ubi Christus, ibi ecclesia*, because she has existed ever since the Spirit was given; and, *Ubi Petrus, ibi ecclesia*, because the inward fellowship is realized by human means, an apostolic ministry which has in Peter its visible standard of unity.[14]

●

Catholics.—In further elucidation of what has been said above we could apply theological categories which have been elaborated for the sacraments, such as *sacramentum tantum* (the ecclesiastical institution alone), *sacramentum et res* (the value of the institution in procuring the spiritual reality which it signifies), *res tantum* (the simple inward reality of the Church, the Mystical Body).

[13] St. Ignatius Martyr, *To the Magnesians* 13, 2.

[14] Nothing shows more clearly the unity of these two aspects than the actual context of the famous statements. St. Ambrose, *Commentary on Psalm 40* (*PL* 14, 1082): "Where Peter is, there the Church is; where the Church is, there is no death but eternal life." St. Ignatius, *To the Smyrneans* 8: "Let that be a valid Eucharist which is celebrated in presence of a bishop or one appointed by him. Where the bishop is, there also let the people be, even as where Christ Jesus is, there is the universal Church."

Editors' Note.—From DIVIDED CHRISTENDOM: A CATHOLIC STUDY OF THE PROBLEM OF REUNION, translated by M. A. Bousfield (London: Centenary Press, 1939) *pp. 74-88.*

Walter J. Burghardt, s.j.

Theotokos: The Mother of God

One of the most significant sermons of antiquity was delivered fifteen centuries ago. The date: early September, 431. The place: the Church of St. Mary at Ephesus on the west coast of Asia Minor. The congregation: almost 200 bishops of the East. The occasion: the dying hours of the Council of Ephesus, at which a virgin of Nazareth was proclaimed Mother of God. The preacher: Cyril, Patriarch of Alexandria in Egypt.

Cyril opened his sermon with a startling eulogy: "Hail, from us, Mary, Mother of God, majestic treasure of the whole world . . . crown of virginity, sceptre of orthodoxy . . . dwelling of the Illimitable, mother and virgin. . . ." Cyril closed his sermon with a remarkable sentence: "May we . . . reverence the undivided Trinity, while we sing the praise of the ever-virgin Mary, that is to say, the holy Church, and of her spotless Son and Bridegroom." [1]

The two facets of this essay are suggested by two appositive

●

[1] Cyril of Alexandria, *Homiliae diversae* 4 (ed. E. Schwartz, *Acta conciliorum oecumenicorum* 1, 1, 2, 104; *PG* 77, 996).

phrases with which Cyril dignifies Mary: (*a*) "Mary, Mother of God," and (*b*) "Mary, that is to say, the holy Church." More specifically, I submit that the significance of the divine maternity in 431, when it was equivalently defined, lay in its relationship to the *physical* Christ; and that its significance in 1960 lies in its relationship to the *mystical* Christ. In other words, the significance of the divine maternity in fifth-century Ephesus lay primarily in this, that it furnished a fresh insight into the *person* of Christ, into Christology; its added significance in twentieth-century America lies in this, that it suggests a fresh insight into the *work* of Christ, into soteriology.

I

First, then, 431. The Council of Ephesus is significant for a fact, and the fact itself has significance. The *fact* is simple enough. The title, Mother of God (*theotokos*), was expressly presented to the Council, in a letter of Cyril, as orthodox doctrine, and Cyril's letter was solemnly approved in the assembly.[2] This impressive approbation did not fall like a thunderclap on the Christian world; it had been prepared by three and a half centuries of theological development. That development is itself fascinating.[3]

Strangely enough, what was first denied to our Lady after she left this earth was not the prerogative, Mother of God, but what her contemporaries never dreamed of denying, that she was Mother of Jesus. The early crisis was Docetic—the affirmation that our Saviour simply did not have a genuinely human body, or at any rate, as Tertullian sums it up, that "He was born *through* a virgin, not *of* a virgin—*in* a womb, not *of* a womb."[4] In a word, He was not fashioned of Mary's substance. But there was a complementary denial. Where the Gnostics introduced a distinction between Jesus born of Mary and the Christ who descended into Jesus at baptism, they denied implicitly that the Child of Mary was God.

The Christian reaction in the first three centuries is expressive. Not that our Lady is categorically denominated Mother of God; there is no indisputable evidence for the title before the fourth century. But Ignatius and Aristides in the East, Justin and Irenaeus and Tertullian in the West, have a two-edged answer for the Gnostic position. On the one hand, they use expressions that equivalently affirm Mary's divine motherhood. On the other, they trumpet the twin premises for

●

[2] In a recent attempt to determine the precise theological value of Ephesus' first session (June 22, 431), I. Ortiz de Urbina concludes that the divine maternity was expressly and directly defined; cf. "Il dogma di Efeso," in *Mélanges Martin Jugie* (Paris, 1953) pp. 233-40.
[3] Cf., for example, W. J. Burghardt, "Mary in Western Patristic Thought," in J. B. Carol (ed.), *Mariology* 1 (Milwaukee, 1955) 109-55, esp. 132-37.
[4] Tertullian, *De carne Christi* 20 (*CSEL* 70, 238).

their conclusion: (*a*) Jesus was genuinely born of Mary; and (*b*) Jesus born of Mary is God.

With the fourth century the title, Mother of God, becomes a commonplace. As the evidence stands, we find it first in 319, when Alexander, Bishop of Alexandria, announces to his colleagues the deposition of Arius.[5] But even then the word flows from his pen so naturally, so spontaneously—I might almost say, so nonchalantly—that it leaves an impression of everyday usage. And soon the Christian world echoes with it. Athanasius in Alexandria, Eusebius in Caesarea, Cyril in Jerusalem, Epiphanius in Salamis, Hilary in Gaul, Ambrose in Milan, and Jerome in Rome—none feels he must justify it, none feels there is something to explain. So welcome is the word that in 382 Gregory of Nazianzus can hurl anathema at Apollinaris: "If anyone does not admit that holy Mary is Mother of God, he is separated from the divinity." [6] And while the theologian wielded the word as a weapon, the layman whispered it in accents of love. For from the same fourth century comes a precious papyrus leaf, from which we can reconstruct the original Greek of our lovely prayer, "We fly to thy patronage, O holy Mother of God"; and the word that stands out clearly is *theotoke*, Mother of God.[7] More eloquent than this love-call of Christians is Julian the Apostate's cry of despair: "You [Christians] never stop calling Mary Mother of God." [8]

Little wonder that, from 428 on, a rising reluctance to call Mary "Mother of God" provoked such violent reactions. Little wonder that, when Nestorius of Constantinople gave his blessing to a bishop who preached, "If anyone says that holy Mary is Mother of God, let him be anathema," Cyril of Alexandria retorted, "If anyone does *not* confess that . . . the holy Virgin is Mother of God . . . let him be anathema." [9] Little wonder that, when the Council of Ephesus convened in 431, Cyril could write of that first session to his flock in Alexandria:

"Know, then, that on the [22nd of June] the holy Synod met at Ephesus in the great Church . . . of Mary, Mother of God. We spent the whole day there, and finally . . . we deposed . . . Nestorius and removed him from the episcopal office. Now there were about 200 (more or less) of us bishops gathered together. And the whole populace of [Ephesus] was waiting tensely, waiting from dawn to dusk

●

[5] Cf. Alexander of Alexandria, *Epist. ad Alexandrum Constant.* 12 (*PG* 18, 568).
[6] Gregory of Nazianzus, *Epist.* 101 (*PG* 37, 177).
[7] Cf. G. Vannucci, "La più antica preghiera alla Madre di Dio," *Marianum* 3 (1941) 97-101; O. Stegmüller, "*Sub tuum praesidium*: Bemerkungen zur ältesten Überlieferung," *Zeitschrift für katholische Theologie* 74 (1952) 76-82. M. Gordillo, like Vannucci, believes it more probable that the papyrus belongs to the third century; cf. *Mariologia orientalis* (Rome, 1954) p. 7 and note 56.
[8] Quoted by Cyril of Alexandria, *Contra Iulianum* 8 (*PG* 76, 901).
[9] Cyril of Alexandria, *Epist.* 17, 12 (*ACO* 1, 1, 1, 40; *PG* 77, 120).

for the decision of the holy Synod. When they heard that the unfortunate fellow had been deposed, with one voice all started to shout in praise of the holy Synod, with one voice all began to glorify God, because the enemy of the faith had fallen. When we left the church, they escorted us to our lodging with torches; for it was evening. Gladness was in the air; lamps dotted the city; even women went before us with censers and led the way." [10]

That is the *fact* of Ephesus, and on the surface it is simple enough. A bishop had questioned Mary's most precious prerogative, and his brother bishops had banned him from their fellowship. But that is not quite the *significance* of Ephesus. Nestorius' concept of Mary stemmed from his concept of Christ. Similarly, what Ephesus determined with respect to Mary's motherhood was rooted in what Ephesus believed with respect to Christ's sonship. That is why Nestorius, for all his reluctance, could say to Cyril in all honesty: "It is not on the ground of a [mere] name that I part from you; it is on the essence of God the Word and on the essence of the Man." [11] What was at stake was the Incarnation itself. In what sense did God become man? In what sense can we say with St. John, "the Word was made flesh"? How were God and human nature made one in the womb of a virgin?

The solution of Nestorius is shrouded in uncertainty. How he conceived that incredible union is not at all clear; somehow God dwelt in flesh as in a temple. What is clear is the set of conclusions he drew therefrom. "Does God have a mother? [He does not.]" "I say it is the flesh that was born of the Virgin Mary, not God the Word. . . ." "It is not right to say of God that He sucked milk. . . ." "I do not say that God is two or three months old." "A born God, a dead God, a buried God I cannot adore." [12]

The answer of Ephesus was unequivocal. The flesh which Mary fashioned of her flesh, that flesh the Son of God took to Himself, took as His own, at the moment of its fashioning. At that instant, and forevermore, this flesh was as much God's flesh as my flesh is mine. This union of God's Son with a human nature was a far different thing from the presence of God in every corner of His universe, far different from His presence in my soul through grace, far different from His presence in my body through Communion, far different even from the Nestorian idea of God dwelling in a temple. This flesh fashioned of

●

[10] Cyril of Alexandria, *Epist.* 24 (*ACO* 1, 1, 1, 117-18; *PG* 77, 137).

[11] Nestorius, *Liber Heraclidis* 2, 1; my translation is based on the French version by F. Nau *et al.*, *Le Livre d'Héraclide de Damas* (Paris, 1910) p. 171.

[12] *Nestorii sermo* (*ACO* 1, 5, 1, 30); *Liber Heraclidis* 2, 1 (tr. Nau, p. 176); *Nestorii tractatus* (*ACO* 1, 5, 1, 38); J. F. Bethune-Baker, *Nestorius and His Teaching* (Cambridge, 1908) p. 71. Cf. also Nilus a S. B., *De maternitate divina b. Mariae semper virginis Nestorii Constantinopolitani et Cyrilli Alexandrini sententia* (Rome, 1944) pp. 1-19.

Mary is the only flesh that is strictly God's own. When Mary murmured, "Be it done unto me according to thy word," at that moment there were not two individuals, two persons in her womb: one of them God, the other a man. There was one individual, one person: the God-Man. The Man was God, and God was the Man.

That is why Ephesus could believe, against Nestorius, that *God* was conceived in Mary's womb and lay for nine months beneath her heart; that *God* was laid in a feeding-trough and exiled to Egypt; that *God* worked with His hands, learned what hunger tastes like, and thirst; that *God* was tired enough to sleep out a storm in an open boat; that *God* was slapped and spat upon, mocked for a fool, whipped like a dog, and nailed to a tree.

The man was God, and God was the Man. That is why Ephesus had to believe that the thoughts of Christ which cover the pages of the Gospel, the words which fell for thirty years from the lips of Christ, are God's thoughts and God's words. Not that God somehow reached out and claimed them, called them His own; but that these thoughts were framed in the human mind of God, these words hung on the human lips of God. It was not a man linked to God like other men, who whipped traffickers from a temple, who loved Martha and her sister Mary, who wept over Jerusalem and over Lazarus. It was God enfleshed.

It is only if you hold fast to this concept of Christ that you can call Mary unconditionally Mother of God; Nestorius saw that. And conversely, it is only if you cling unequivocally to the title, Mother of God, that you can find the Son of God in a human womb; Nestorius saw that too.

That is why Ephesus canonized the letter to Nestorius in which Cyril declared: "We must not . . . sever into two sons the one Lord Jesus Christ. Such severance will be no help at all to the correct expression of the faith, even if one allege unity of persons. Scripture, you see, has not said that the Word united to Himself the person of a man, but that He has been made flesh. Now the Word's being made flesh is nothing else than that He partook of flesh and blood in like manner with us, and made our body His own, and proceeded Man of a woman, without having cast away His divinity. . . . This is what the expression of the exact faith everywhere preaches; this is the mind we shall find in the holy Fathers. In this sense they did not hesitate to call the holy Virgin God's Mother (*theotokos*)—not as though the nature of the Word or His divinity took beginning of being from the holy Virgin, but that of her was begotten the holy body animated with a rational soul; to this body the Word was united personally, and so He is said to have been born according to the flesh." [13]

Briefly, then, Mary is Mother of God. She is Mother, because the

●

[13] Cyril of Alexandria, *Epist.* 4, 6 (*ACO* 1, 1, 1, 28; *PG* 77, 48).

flesh God took, He took from her flesh; and because Mary gave to her Son everything any mother gives to her child in its fashioning. She was pregnant with Christ. And she is Mother of God, simply because the human being who came forth from her womb was and is God.

It is understandable, then, why Ephesus was so exercised over a single word, *theotokos*. True, in the minds of some reputable historians Ephesus is synonymous with imprudence, intrigue, ecclesiastical politics. But, to its credit, Ephesus recognized that the denial or even the abandonment of *theotokos* was equivalent to a disavowal of Nicaea. Not that the Council of Nicaea had called Mary "Mother of God"; but that, unless Mary is God's Mother, you cannot confess, with the Fathers of Nicaea, "I believe in . . . Jesus Christ, God's Son . . . who for us men and for our salvation came down, was made flesh, became man. . . ." [14]

Call Ephesus, if you will, a war of words; we need not blush. For us, a word is the incarnation of an idea. A century before, in the Arian crisis, the Christian world had been ruptured by a word. With that word, *homoousios*, "consubstantial," Athanasius summed up orthodox belief on the Eternal Word, the Son of God. In the Nestorian controversy the Christian East was sundered once more by a word. With that word, *theotokos*, "Mother of God," Cyril summed up orthodox belief on the Word Incarnate, the Son of God made flesh. That is why Cyril could thunder: "To confess our faith in orthodox fashion . . . it is enough to . . . confess that the holy Virgin is Mother of God." [15] And three centuries later St. John Damascene, whose glory it is to have summed up in himself the theology of the Greek Fathers, wrote so simply: "This name contains the whole mystery of the Incarnation." [16]

It is a striking thing that a Mariological term should have been selected as the ultimate test of Christological orthodoxy. Striking, but not surprising. Our Lady's role at Ephesus is the spontaneous outgrowth of her role at Nazareth, of her role throughout history. Her deep significance has always been her relationship to Christ. At Ephesus it was the *physical* Christ her divine maternity revealed. In this human mother the Christian mind caught a vision of her divine Son.

II

So much for 431. It is the contention of this essay that in 1960 the divine maternity has an added significance. In 431 the significance of

●

[14] Cf. Cyril of Alexandria, *Epist.* 1, 5-6 (*ACO* 1, 1, 1, 12-13; *PG* 77, 16). For the text of the Symbol of Nicaea, cf. I. Ortiz de Urbina, *El Símbolo Niceno* (Madrid, 1947) p. 21.
[15] Cyril of Alexandria, *Homiliae diversae* 15 (*PG* 77, 1093).
[16] John Damascene, *De fide orthodoxa* 3, 12 (*PG* 94, 1029).

Mary's motherhood lay in its relationship to the *physical* Christ; in 1960 its significance lies in its relationship to the *mystical* Christ. At Ephesus the divine maternity furnished a fresh insight into the *person* of Christ, into Christology, into the fact of the Incarnation; in 1960 it suggests a fresh insight into the *work* of Christ, into soteriology, into the task of the redemption.

You see, in theological circles today there is a remarkable Marian movement. What this movement yearns for is a deeper penetration into the mystery that is Mary, the mystery that makes Mary the unique creature she is. It is not content to see in the Mother of God simply the object of a special veneration, of a warmer flame of love. It wants to insert our Lady in her proper place in the divine dream for our redemption.

To achieve this, theologians are aware that it is not sufficient to range privilege alongside privilege, mystery beside mystery, and say: that is Mary. It is not enough to plumb the depths of Mary's Immaculate Conception, her perpetual virginity, her divine maternity, her utter sinlessness, her glorious Assumption; it is not enough to penetrate the meaning and the beauty of each of these if you are to say: I know our Lady. For beauty and truth lie not so much in the isolated fragments as in the harmony of the whole. What is needed is a basic idea which gives meaning to all the rest, some tremendous insight into the mind of God which, while it welds together the scattered prerogatives that spell Mary, will, above all, explain her role in the divine design we designate redemption.

Basically, I believe, this insight will have to be achieved in terms of the divine maternity; that prerogative is, in some genuine sense, fundamental. But the contemporary theologian is asking: Is there something still more fundamental? What is it that lies at the core of Mary's motherhood? Why, for example, did God fashion Mary precisely as bridal Mother of God—as God's Mother and His bride as well? God wills it, yes; but God's will is not whim. It may be that we shall end by bending low before mystery. The point, however, is this: theologians believe they have caught a glimpse of the divine idea that gives ultimate meaning to the divine maternity, that sets the Mother of God in the center of God's plan for man.

The solution to the problem was suggested towards the close of the fourth century by St. Ambrose, Bishop of Milan, when he wrote: "Mary is type of the Church." [17] To have a type—as we are using the word here—four elements are desirable. In the first place, you have concrete representation, even at times personification. An idea, a spiritual reality is represented by something concrete, is represented by some palpable form, is made present at times by a human figure. Somewhat as we represent, personify the abstract idea of justice by a blindfolded lady with scales and a sword, so the early Christians

[17] Ambrose, *Expositio evangelii secundum Lucam* 2, 7 (*CSEL* 32/4, 45).

represented, personified the inner life of the Church by the human figure of our Lady.

The second requisite: a real relationship that links the two, an objective foundation for this representation. The relationship that links Mary and the Church, the relationship that makes Mary a type of the Church, is not a creation of the human mind, as is the case with justice and the visionless lady in white. It is not a casual, accidental likeness which invites the meditative mind to oscillate between Mary and the Church. The resemblance between the Church and the human figure of Mary is the consequence of an inner tie that is real, a deep-seated relation that is objective. The resemblance between the two is not put there by the human mind; it *is* there. The relationship is not invented; it is discovered.

The third requisite is the most significant, if only because it concretizes the second. A type cannot rest satisfied with two terms, the type and the antitype, the figure and the thing it prefigures, the human person and the spiritual reality it personifies. It demands a third term, a design which envelops the other two, a master plan which finds its first realization and revelation in the person who is the type, and its second revelation and realization in the antitype. In the concrete, when we say that Mary is type of the Church, we do not isolate Mary and the Church, as though they were related in some sort of vacuum. Mary is type of the Church in virtue of a divine design, an eternal plan in the mind of God which finds its realization first in bodily form in the person of Mary, then in the spiritual reality that is the Church. The resemblance between Mary and the Church is rooted in the divine dream of redemption. The third term is God—God's plan for man.

The fourth element follows from the second and third: the prototype is a moral pattern for the image. A *moral* pattern. The prototype, Mary, is a living individual. The image, the Church, is a collectivity, is actualized in the individuals who make up the Mystical Body of Christ. If Mary, as type of the Church, personifies the inmost essence of the Church, if the Church that unfolds in space and time exists in germ in Mary, then Mary is the model for the conduct of the Christian, the pattern of Christian living. Briefly, if by divine design Mary realizes in her own person what the Church is destined by God to be, then by divine design Mary realizes in her own life what the Christian is destined by God to do.

That much premised, the present essay will put forward a fact and an explanation. The fact: Mary is, in God's redemptive design, a prototype of the Church. The explanation: what this means in the concrete, how the Mary-Church idea lends meaning to the Mother of God and to her role in redemption.

First, then, is Mary a prototype of the Church? Did God plan redemption in such a way that, before the Church came forth from the pierced side of God's Son on Calvary, this Church somehow found its first realization in God's Mother? The answer will issue not from speculation but from revelation. God's mind is manifest in God's word.

In the twelfth chapter of the Apocalypse St. John has his celebrated Vision of the Woman. "In heaven a great portent appeared: a woman that wore the sun for her mantle, the moon under her feet, and a crown of twelve stars about her head. She had a child in her womb, and was crying out as she travailed, in great pain of her delivery. Then a second portent appeared . . . : a great dragon . . . fronting the woman . . . ready to swallow up the child as soon as she bore it. She bore a son, the son who is to herd the nations with a crook of iron. . . . In his spite against the woman, the dragon went elsewhere to make war on the rest of her children, the men who keep God's commandments, and hold fast to the truth concerning Jesus."[18]

Many Scripture scholars insist that in the woman of Apocalypse 12 you have the Church of God personified.[19] This woman, who has a vast progeny, whose children are the human beings who believe in Christ and live that belief, must be the Church of God. But this woman, who personifies the Church, is apparently the Mother of Christ: her son, says John, "is to herd the nations like sheep with a crook of iron." The Church of Christ, then, is personified by a woman, and the woman is the Mother of Christ. Somehow, therefore, in God's eyes, the Church and Mary are one.

This basic idea, that Mary is a type of the Church, recurs in patristic literature, in the theology of the first seven centuries, with an impressive constancy.[20] In the first place, the Fathers frequently describe the Church in language borrowed from the person of Mary. The Church, like Mary, is a virgin. The Church, Origen insists, "is a chaste virgin, by reason of her rectitude in belief and in morality."[21] The Church, like Mary, is a virgin mother. "Mary," says Augustine, "gave birth in body to the Head of this body; the Church gives birth in spirit to the members of that Head. In both [Mary and the Church], virginity is no hindrance to fertility; in both, fertility does not displace virginity."[22] The Church's virginal motherhood, like Mary's, involves a sponsal relationship: the Church, like Mary, is bride of God. Christ our Lord, Jerome remarks, "is bridegroom of the virgin Church—the Church which has neither spot nor wrinkle."[23] And

●

[18] Apoc 12:1-17; Knox translation.
[19] For example, Bernard J. Le Frois, in his recent extended treatment of the problem, *The Woman Clothed with the Sun (Ap. 12): Individual or Collective?* (Rome, 1954), concludes: "St. John under the figure of the Woman depicts Mary as the perfect realization of the Church" (p. 262).
[20] The most comprehensive investigation of this theme in the Fathers is to be found in A. Müller, *Ecclesia-Maria: Die Einheit Marias und der Kirche* (2nd ed.; Fribourg, Switzerland, 1955).
[21] Origen, *In Ioan. frag.* 45 (GCS, Orig. 4, 520).
[22] Augustine, *De sancta virginitate* 2 (PL 40, 397).
[23] Jerome, *In Ieremiam* 1, 44 (CSEL 59, 36).

though the Church's childbearing is consummated externally in baptism, as Mary's was in Bethlehem, at the basis of both is an inner act of conception: Christ is conceived in the soul of the Christian, as He was conceived in the body of Mary, in that the soul, like Mary, hears the word of God and believes it. In both there is a pregnant fiat: "Be it done unto me according to thy word." "That," as Chrysostom has it, "that is how the Church is wed to God." [24]

But the Fathers go further. They are not content to dignify the Church with the prerogatives of Mary; such a manner of speaking might be sheer metaphor. The Fathers are more explicit than that; they tell us it is more than metaphor. Some insist that God deliberately made the Church like His Mother. As Augustine puts it: "The most beautiful among the sons of men [is] the Son of holy Mary, the Bridegroom of holy Church. Her [the Church] He made like to His Mother, for He made her our mother and keeps her His virgin." [25] "Our Head," he claims, "had to be born of a virgin . . . in the way of the flesh, as a sign that His members were to be born of a virgin Church in the way of the spirit." [26] Some Fathers are more explicit still; they declare expressly that our Lady is type of the Church. Listen to Ambrose: "It is well that [Mary] is betrothed and yet a virgin, for she is type of the Church, which though wed is spotless." [27] And Ephraem, the most distinguished representative of Syrian Christianity: "The Virgin Mary is a prototype of the Church, because she received the beginnings of the Gospel." [28] And with no hesitation, no equivocation, comes the uncompromising affirmation: Mary and the Church are one; somehow Mary is the Church. Ephraem, for example, emphasizes the fact that beneath the cross Christ "gave to John Mary, His Church." [29] Cyril of Alexandria we have heard at Ephesus: "May we reverence the undivided Trinity, while we sing the praise of the ever-virgin Mary, that is to say, the holy Church." [30]

What Scripture hints at darkly, what the Fathers declare implicitly and explicitly, the Latin Middle Ages develop almost without interruption. Mary is type of the Church; she is its figure; she signifies it. The mystery of the Church is contained in the mystery of Mary as in its prototype and perfect exemplar. It is at once still hidden there and already revealed in advance, because it finds there its first and ideal realization. Our Lady, therefore, announces the Church and precedes it. She is its anticipation, and the remarkable things God accomplished in her He does not cease to reproduce in the Church. From the one

●

[24] Chrysostom, *In Ioan. hom.* 29, 3 (*PG* 59, 170).
[25] Augustine, *Serm.* 195, 2 (*PL* 38, 1018).
[26] Augustine, *De sancta virginitate* 6 (*PL* 40, 399).
[27] Cf. footnote 17.
[28] Ephraem, *Sermo ad nocturnum dominicae resurrectionis* 2 (ed. Lamy 1, 533).
[29] Ephraem, *Explanatio evangelii concordantis* 12, 5 (*CSCO* 145, 117).
[30] Cf. footnote 1.

to the other there is a real continuity; we cannot separate them; Mary and the Church are inseparably linked, because the same Christ links them to Himself.[31]

The fact, therefore, seems beyond dispute. In Christian tradition Mary is type of the Church. So was she destined by God; so was she in actuality. The more difficult question remains: what does this mean in the concrete? How does the Mary-Church analogy lend meaning to the Mother of God and to her role in the drama of redemption?

The fundamental principle which dominates this whole discussion was formulated by St. Augustine: "He who made you without your co-operation does not justify you without your co-operation." [32] It is the principle of human co-operation in the divine task of redemption: God has determined to save man by means of man. As in Paradise, so on earth, as in man's original fall, so in his later restoration, God would respect the inmost nature of His human creation, man's perilous power to say no. That divine decision spangles the pages of the Old Testament. Salvation is presented as a covenant, a pact, a contract offered by God and accepted by man. Or it is a marriage, wide-eyed and free, nuptials of love between God and Israel, and, in the New Testament, between Christ and the Church. The basic datum of this symbolism, exploited in Christian tradition till the Renaissance, is significant. In this marriage God is everywhere and always the man, the bridegroom; humanity is everywhere and always the woman, the bride. In this inspired figure of salvation it is the male who symbolizes the initiative and the power of God; it is the female who symbolizes the active receptivity of humanity and the fruitfulness which union with God communicates to it.

God saves man by means of man. In line with that design, God *became* man, asked of humanity the free gift of its flesh and blood. In harmony with that plan, Christ leaves His Church, the prolongation of His Incarnation, in the hands of men. The book that bears His name—the word of God—comes line by line from the pen of men. The grace He has won with His own body is communicated through the hands and lips of men. Nor will He come to the human heart unless the human heart whispers, "Come."

Now this co-operation of man with God is exercised in two ways: by faith and by ministry. Faith is primarily an interior thing, a drama within the soul; ministry is an exterior thing, a communication, an administration of words and sacramental signs whereby faith is born and grows. Faith is the task of the whole Christian community; ministry is the privilege of a segment within that community. Faith is

---

[31] For this summary of medieval thought on Mary and the Church I am indebted to H. Barré, "Marie et l'église dans la pensée médiévale," *Vie spirituelle* 91 (1954) 124-41.
[32] Augustine, *Serm.* 169, 13 (*PL* 38, 923).

receiving, an active receptivity; ministry is giving, an exercise of power in the name of God.

Precisely here we reach a conclusion of supreme significance. Mary cannot be a type of the ministering Church, of the Church in its hierarchical function. The hierarchical aspect of the Church is rather a prolongation of Christ's own activity, Christ's own power. It is the divine in the Church. Our Lady is type of the human element in redemption; she represents the believing Church, the whole community of Christians, men and women, hierarchy and laity, in so far as it hears the word of God and welcomes it within.

This personification of the Church finds its crucial hour at the Annunciation. That first Angelus, so simply told by St. Luke, veils a tremendous truth. It was not simply that God wanted Mary's motherhood to be a voluntary thing, uncompelled, unconstrained. Gabriel's role is more profound than that. The Son of God was about to wed human nature to Himself. Therefore, as St. Thomas phrases it, "what God was asking through the Annunciation was the consent of the Virgin *in the name of all humanity.*" [33] Or, in the lovely sentence of Leo XIII: "The eternal Son of God, when He wanted to take to Himself man's nature, and so enter a mystical marriage with the whole human race, did not do so before obtaining the perfectly free consent of His Mother-to-be, *who played as it were the role of the human race itself.*" [34] And, while a world waited breathlessly, Mary answered, "Be it done unto me according to thy word." Mary said yes. That whispered yes may well have been, in God's eyes, Mary's finest hour. At that moment she became bride of God and His Mother too: bride of God by her fiat, Mother of God whom she welcomed in her womb. At that instant was realized in Mary the substance of the mystery of the Church to come: the union of God and man in the Mystical Body of Christ.

This welcome given God by Mary was not a sheerly passive thing; it was incredibly active on all levels. In the spiritual order her faith, like all genuine faith, was the quickening response of her mind to a manifestation of God. In the moral order her consent was the loving response of her will to an invitation of God. In the physical order her conception was the living response of her body to the activity of God: "the Holy Spirit shall come upon thee."

Briefly, our Lady, as Mother of God and His bride, has a representative function. The task of the believing Church is to continue through space and time the sponsal fiat of Mary, her whispered yes. This community of the redeemed has for vocation to co-operate in the work of redemption by loving faith, and so bring God to birth in the

●

[33] St. Thomas, *Summa theologiae* 3, q. 30, a. 1 c.
[34] Leo XIII, Encyclical, *Octobri mense*, Sept. 22, 1891; ASS 24 (1891-92) 195.

human frame. The Church, therefore, is a collective Mary, and Mary is the Church in germ.

This vision of Mary's motherhood as a representative thing becomes clearer still if we see it in its virginal aspect. In our synthesis it is no longer satisfying to see in our Lady's virginity before and after Bethlehem little more than a privilege highly appropriate, perhaps indispensable in a girl who is God's Mother. It will not do to ask with St. Ambrose: "Would the Lord Jesus choose for Himself a mother who could defile heaven's court with the seed of man?" [35] From the vantage ground of history the answer is no. But the question is perilous. It might well leave the impression that the marital relationship is something less than good. Or it might, in reaction, revive a seductive fourth-century error, to the effect that marriage and virginity are equal in honor, that (as Helvidius claimed) Mary is doubly admirable for having been, in turn, virgin and mother: virgin till the birth of Jesus, then mother of the "brothers and sisters of Jesus" spoken of in Scripture. In any event, though the rhetoric of Ambrose may stimulate piety, it does not satisfy theology. The divine design goes deeper than that. Even in her virginity Mary is type of the Church; she represents the community of believers; her virginal motherhood is a first, a concrete, a symbolic realization of God's plan for redeemed humanity.

Womanly virginity, you see, has two facets. Negatively, it denies that intimate relationship with man which we term marital; it denies the initiative of man with respect to woman and woman's fruitfulness. But virginity, in the Christian concept, is not sheer negation, the absence of something. The negative aspect of virginity stems from something positive. The denial to man of any initiative in her fruitfulness must, if it is to be Christian, stem from a woman's total dedication to God, a complete openness to the divine, receptivity to God and to God alone. The denial of a bridal relationship to man is rooted in the affirmation of a bridal relationship to God.

And so it was with Mary. Her virginity meant, on the one hand, that no human being, no man, took the initiative in the bridal relationship which issued in the Son of God made flesh: "the Holy Spirit shall come upon thee." It meant, on the other hand—in fact, the denial of human initiative stemmed from—the total consecration of Mary to her Bridegroom, utter co-operation with God, an unfailing fiat, complete and exclusive.

And in this Mary is type of the Church; she represents the community of believers; she realizes in her own person what God intended for redeemed humanity. On the one hand, this union of God with man which is the Church denies to man the initiative in the task which links man to God. Not that man is purely passive; he must co-operate, else oneness with God is impossible. But his co-operation is a re-

●

[35] Ambrose, *De institutione virginis* 6, 4 (*PL* 16, 331).

sponse—a response to grace, a response to God's invitation. "If we but turn to God," Augustine insists, "that itself is a gift of God." [36] And that is the other aspect, the positive side, of the Church's virginity. The Church is linked to Christ as bride to groom. Her role, like that of Mary, is total consecration to Christ, a complete openness to the divine, a sensitiveness to the action of God's Spirit, an incredible readiness to respond, "Be it done unto me according to thy word."

The paradox is this. It is not simply that, as Augustine said, Mary's "virginity is no hindrance to fertility." For the Church as for Mary, it is only by reason of her virginity that she can achieve fertility. It was only by Mary's total response to God's invitation alone that the Son of God became flesh; it is only by prolonging this response through space and time that the Church, impregnated with the Spirit, is fruitful for the formation of Christ in individual souls. The words of Gabriel are expressive: "The Holy Spirit shall come upon thee, and the power of the Most High shall overshadow thee; and *therefore* the Holy One to be born shall be called the Son of God."

This vision of Mary's virginal motherhood as a representative thing grows clearer still if we ponder her Immaculate Conception. Here, too, our Lady is type of the Church. The Church, remember, is the Body of Christ. But it is a body redeemed; the members of that body have been touched with redemption. In the concrete, a human being enters the Church at a specific moment in time, by a baptism which weds him to Christ as it incorporates him into the Body of Christ. At that instant he *is* a person redeemed—at the instant he enters the Church. His redemption, however, has twin facets. Positively, he has captured Christ's life; negatively, he no longer has original sin. The two cannot coexist in the human soul: Christ's life and original sin. But notice: As God planned it, the Church does not take the human being, incorporate him into the Body of Christ, into the Church, and *then* remove original sin. At the moment he enters the Church he *is* free of original sin. That is why we say: the Church is a community of the redeemed, not a community of those who are to be redeemed.

But if it is of the Church's essence to be a community of the redeemed, of those who are free from original sin, then the Church herself has no part in original sin. That is her God-given nature. Therefore, at the first moment of her existence, at the instant of her incarnation on Calvary, she was sinless. In the womb of humanity, in the midst of a world estranged from God by the sin of Adam, the Church was conceived without original sin.

Here, too, in God's staggering design, the Mother of God is type of the Church. For, if the Church is to be personified, the human figure who personifies it must, like the Church, be free of Adam's sin. And not simply freed after being burdened with it. If it is of the Church's essence to be without original sin, to have no part in it,

●
[36] Augustine, *De gratia et libero arbitrio* 5, 10 (PL 44, 888).

then the individual who is type of the Church must be without sin from the first moment of her existence; she must be immaculately conceived. That person, alone among the children fashioned of human seed, is God's Mother. Mary conceived without sin is Mary redeemed; and Mary conceived without sin, Mary redeemed, prefigures the whole community of the redeemed which is the Church, fashioned without sin from the lanced side of the Crucified.

This vision of God's Mother as type of the Church grows in clarity if we study her perfect sinlessness, her freedom from actual sin. The inner essence of the Church, as community of the redeemed, means the participation of men in the redemption effected by Christ. All men who have been touched with redemption in baptism and are linked to the Church in submissive faith belong to this community of the redeemed. But redemption is a gradual process, a lifelong thing; it is not complete in baptism. We belong to this community of the redeemed more or less perfectly, we are more or less perfect members of the Church, to the extent that redemption has taken hold of us, in proportion as grace or sin dominates in our soul.

Because the redemption o fhumanity—in fact, the redemption of the individual—is not yet complete, the Church is not without sinners. Pius XII put it well: "One must not imagine that the Body of the Church, just because it bears the name of Christ, is made up during the days of its earthly pilgrimage only of members conspicuous for their holiness. . . . It is the Saviour's infinite mercy that allows place in His Mystical Body here for those whom He did not exclude from the banquet of old." [37]

The Church is not without sinners, but it is without sin. "I believe in the holy Catholic Church." This is the Church which Paul saw Christ summoning into His own presence, "the Church in all its beauty, no stain, no wrinkle, no such disfigurement . . . holy . . . spotless." [38] A paradox, yes: a Church of the sinful, yet herself without sin.[39] But nonetheless true. Where the Church is, there sin is, because man, though redeemed from sin, is still free to sin. Sin, however, stands in contradiction to the Church's essence, and the Church's essence stands in contradiction to sin. But her essence, as community of the redeemed, will be fully realized only when redemption is complete, and sin is no more, and the Church looks upon her Head in glory—the day when, as Augustine said, "there will be but one Christ loving Himself."

●

[37] Pius XII, Encyclical, *Mystici corporis*, June 29, 1943; AAS 35 (1943) 203; official English translation, *The Encyclical* Mystici Corporis *of Pope Pius XII* (New York: America Press, 1943) p. 12.
[38] Eph 5:26-27; Knox translation.
[39] The problem is real and does not admit of any facile solution. For two engaging approaches, cf. C. Journet, *L'Eglise du Verbe incarné* 2 (Bruges, 1951) 1115-29; R. Hasseveldt, *The Church: A Divine Mystery*, translated by W. Storey (Chicago, 1954) pp. 243-51.

Here again God's Mother is type of the Church. In her soul redemption found its perfect realization; in her soul there was never sin, there was only God. In our Lady we see God's design for redeemed humanity; in her we discover in its ideal state the sinlessness which is of the Church's essence, yet is realized not at once, but from day to day, through sin upon sin, till humanity be gathered up in Christ.

This vision of God's Mother as personification of redeemed humanity finds a final clarity in her bodily Assumption. There is a popular misconception among Christians with respect to the human body. For some, the body is nothing but an instrument, a tool of the soul. For others, the body is a burden from which the soul cries for release. All this is an echo of the third-century theory of Origen that the soul has been imprisoned in matter because it sinned in an earlier existence. Such an attitude pays slender homage to God. It fails to recognize that the body is an essential part of man; that without the body man is a creature incomplete; that, whether in heaven or purgatory or hell, a separated soul, as Jean Mouroux phrased it, "still longs for its body with a purely natural impulse of love." [40]

In somewhat the same way the visible structure of the Church is an essential part of the Church. Not merely because it is an instrument through which God's life is communicated to men. It is that, of course; but it is more. The Church is visible of her very nature because everything which is to absorb redemption must somehow be absorbed into the Church. As the body played its part in the first sin, as the body fell with the soul from God, so does the body yearn for redemption. In the inspired language of Paul, we "groan in our hearts, waiting for that adoption which is the ransoming of our bodies from their slavery." [41]

This redemption of the body, like all redemption, is achieved through the Body of Christ, through the Church. What is redeemed is absorbed into the Church, helps constitute her essence. That is why the Church is not simply a spiritual thing; she is visible, tangible, sensible, material. And when the body of man is absorbed into the visible structure of the Church, it ceases to be what St. Paul termed "the body of death"; it comes spiritually alive, because it is quickened by the Spirit of God. And the more fully grace permeates the Church and each member, the more intimately does the body partake of redemption, and the less the "law in my members" wars against the "law of my mind." This, however, is but the beginning of redemption. Redemption will find its consummation, its perfection, in the glory of the life to come—not merely in the soul's vision of God, but in the transfiguration of the body, when the whole material world will

●

[40] Jean Mouroux, *The Meaning of Man,* translated by A. H. G. Downes (New York, 1948) p. 108.
[41] Rom 8:23; Knox translation.

share in the perfection of redemption, and there will be "a new heaven and a new earth."

If Mary is type of the Church, of redeemed humanity, then this redemption of the body must appear in its perfection in her. The redemption operated by the Church will be consummated only after the general resurrection, when the body will be transformed, and the whole man, soul and body, will confront his Creator in an eternity of knowledge and love. That perfection of humanity redeemed, that consummation of the Church, finds its first purely human realization in the Mother of God, in Mary assumed into heaven, soul and body.

This vision of God's Mother as type of the Church has much to recommend it. To begin with, it preserves a perfect balance between Mary's humanness and her uniqueness. On the one hand, it curbs the anguished accusation, Mariolatry. Our Lady is seen as fully human. She is not equated with divinity, because she is essentially representative of humanity. She is not on a par with God the Redeemer, because she personifies man the redeemed. In her we glimpse not so much God's design for a single human being, as His plan for all human beings. If there is glory here and divinization, it is all humanity that is glorified in her, all humanity that is divinized. Granted she is, in Augustine's word, "supereminent" member of the Church;[42] she remains, for all that, a member. And still she is not depreciated. If it is true that she symbolizes humanity redeemed, that she represents in her person what God intended for the whole Church, it is equally true that redeemed humanity, God's plan for His Church, is realized in its perfection in no individual save her.

Secondly, this vision of Mary as type of the Church clarifies and unifies her role in redemption. In this synthesis there is no Marian prerogative that is merely "fitting," no need to range privilege alongside privilege with a more or less tenuous tie. Mary is the unique creature she is, because redemption is the unique program it is. Redemption is a master plan, divinely conceived, divinely executed. It finds its first, its ideal, its perfect realization in a single human being: Mary redeemed. It finds its ultimate realization in a community of human beings: humanity redeemed. What the Mother of God is, that the Church is destined to be. And what the Church is, that is already discoverable in God's Mother. When Léon Bloy saw the lesson of the Immaculate Conception in this, that the redemption was successful at its very outset, because it produced a Mary, he spoke more truly than he knew. For Mary is not simply redeemed; she is redeemed humanity.

Thirdly, this vision of Mary makes for authentic devotion. In attachment to the immaculate Virgin-Mother of God in glory, we are not simply bent low before mystery—mystery that is meaningless as

●

[42] Augustine, *Serm. Denis* 25, 7 (ed. Morin, *Miscellanea Agostiniana* 1 [Rome, 1930] 163).

far as contemporary living is concerned. We are not lost in wonder at an Immaculate Conception which can never be ours; at a wedding of perpetual virginity and physical motherhood unique in history; at a glorious resurrection not preluded, like ours, by the corruption of the tomb. Our devotion to God's Mother is the fruit not so much of mystery as of insight. In the Mother of God we encounter in human form the plan of God for man. In this one woman we see what the community of believers is and is destined to be. In her virginal maternity we glimpse in its perfection the role in which God casts every human being. What He asks of you and me is active receptivity—that, when we hear the word of God, we welcome it within. For on this depends our holiness, our oneness with God—the openness, the freedom with which we can respond, "Be it done unto me according to thy word."

Editors' Note.—From THE MYSTERY OF THE WOMAN. Essays on the Mother of God sponsored by the Department of Theology, University of Notre Dame; edited by Edward D. O'Connor, c.s.c. (Notre Dame, Ind.: University of Notre Dame Press, 1956) *pp.* 5-33.

The Sacraments

The Sacraments: The Christian's Journey
through Life
A.-M. Roguet, o.p.

PREFACE

*Our study of the Idea of Catholicism as
the religious journey of the human race,
planned by God in its patterns from the
beginning of time, brought to its perfect
point in the New Testament, and ever
growing since then in the life of the
Church, must now show how each one of
us as individuals shares in this Christic
journey.*

*For it is under the fascinating image
of a Christic journey that Fr. Roguet pro-
jects his study of the seven sacraments:
baptism, confirmation, the Holy Eucharist, penance, extreme unction, holy
orders, and matrimony. According to this
image, "The sacraments are themselves
the Christian life, the sacraments are
themselves a movement, a transition, a
voyage and—why not say it—an adventure." We will not be afraid of the passage of time if we deepen it with the
understanding that in the sacraments we
are also passing through Christic time to
our Father in heaven.*

*There was first the Exodus of the
Old Testament, in which the liberated
Jews passed over the Red Sea to the
promised land. There was then the life,
the Exodus of Christ, His triumphant
journey through the life of man to the
resurrection. There is now the individual
repetition of that journey by ourselves,
carried by the successive touches of Christ
in the sacraments. Thus life in the Church
is a vital and moving adventure "toward
the light and rest of the heavenly Jerusalem."*

A.-M. *Roguet*, O.P.

The Sacraments:
The Christian's Journey through Life

Too often we think of the sacraments, if not as magic signs, at least as formalities that mark certain fixed points of our existence. At birth we were baptized. Between the ages of seven and twelve years, we receive confirmation and make our first Communion. Regularly each year, the duty comes round with Easter, of going to confession and Holy Communion. Generally, between twenty and thirty years of age, one marries. When very ill, or when the end is approaching, we receive extreme unction. The sacraments in this way appear as realities, as firm and fixed as the civil registration of a newborn child, getting school certificate or a degree, the call-up to military service, income-tax returns, retiring from office, or the old-age pension.

You will say, this concerns Catholics who frequent the sacraments rarely, at certain seasons and perhaps with little fervor. Well, let us take the case of a Catholic who is assiduous in going to confession and Holy Communion. Is it not true that for him there are halts, more or less regular, but very much like each other when he makes up his accounts, makes good his losses and refreshes his strength; rather like a motorist testing and recharging his batteries and filling up with oil and petrol? This comparison is not at all derogatory. There is indeed something of all this in the sacraments. On life's way there are salutary and nourishing halts that let us start out again with greater strength and spirit, with a purer and more distinct view of the end to be obtained.

Nevertheless, sacraments are not only halts, milestones, or even landmarks placed all along a human life, to give it a certain Christian coloring. The sacraments are in themselves the Christian life, the sacraments are in themselves a movement, a transition, a voyage and —why not say it—an adventure.

We shall see in detail how the sacraments, if we do not extinguish their power by a formal and routine use of them, possess this internal dynamism according to the different rhythm and purpose of each. Let us try to see why.

First of all it is because the sacraments are the acts and gestures of Christ. They are Christ's acts, as we have already said, because in each of them it is Christ who is working, it is the personal and living Christ that we touch. The Gospel for Low Sunday shows us the apostle St. Thomas unwilling to believe in the risen Christ except that he touch Him, that he put his fingers into the wounds of His hands, feet, and side. Jesus gives way to these demands, but He adds: "Because thou hast seen me, Thomas, thou hast believed. Blessed are they who have not seen and have believed." This last sentence concerns ourselves. We cannot see Christ, but we must believe in Him. It is in the sacraments that we believe in Him without seeing Him. But if we do not see Him in the sacraments, we touch Him. He is there at work, to purify us, to heal us, to strengthen us, to deify us. We touch His adorable and life-giving flesh. For to believe in Him does not mean to say that we admit His existence, like that of some historical person who has once existed. It means that we believe in Him as in a living Saviour who calls us, who carries us along.

The sacraments are also the gestures of Christ. That is to say, they are not only mysterious actions, only accessible to faith, but visible, external actions whose outline and direction we can follow. Just as of old Christ touched and cured the blind, the paralytics, the feverish, just as He blessed His disciples, breathed upon them, laid His hands upon them, broke bread for them, so in the sacraments we are absolved, healed, and fed, hands are laid upon us and we are blessed in Christ's name. By the sacraments we are put into contact with the living Christ just as truly, although in another manner, as if we had escorted Him on the paths of Galilee or in the streets of Jerusalem.

Now, not only is Christ a living person but He is someone who walks, approaches, passes by. St. Peter sums up His mission by saying: "He went about doing good" (Acts 10:38). St. John begins his narrative of the Last Supper and the passion thus: "Before the festival day of the Pasch, Jesus knowing that His hour was come, that he should *pass* out of this world to the Father." The life and mission of

Jesus was a passing by. Easter, the Pasch, means just the "passage" of Jesus from this world to His Father, from death to life, a passing in which He draws us after Him.

This idea of the Pasch conjures up another "passover" that the Catholic must realize in his own life as he follows on the sacramental journey. The mission of Jesus, His passing, His journey through life, reproduce in a way the first Pasch, that of the Jews which was the passing of God over the Egyptian people to strike them and so to deliver the Jews from servitude. After that it was the passing of the liberated Jews across the Red Sea, across the desert for forty years until, one day of Passover, they passed over the Jordan and entered the Promised Land. The history of this people on the march, this people of God voyaging and on pilgrimage, is not a history that has grown old and come to an end. It is the ever-current history of each successive deliverance that God offers to His people. The prophets were untiring in bringing up this ancient epic of the Exodus as an image and parable of all the story of salvation. The Evangelists, particularly St. John, used it as the image and framework of the salvation brought about by Jesus in His life and sacraments. Finally, the Apocalypse will take again the theme of the Exodus to find in it once more, through all persecutions, the victorious progress of the Church towards the light and rest of the heavenly Jerusalem.

This great movement, this immense pilgrimage will be in vain if, in drawing along the Christian people as a whole, it does not really draw each one of us. We have been caught up, we have embarked. A Catholic is not a fixed and immovable being in an advanced world. His Church is not a lifeless building. It is a ship accomplishing an immense voyage. It is a gathering that will not be complete until the end of the world. It is a pilgrimage towards boundless horizons. The sacraments that cause us to complete this pilgrimage, which make us passengers in this vessel, living stones in this building that is perpetually growing (Eph 2:21, 22; Peter 2:5)—the sacraments, then, are themselves movement and life.

* * *

BAPTISM

The first stage of the Christian's journey through life that we are going to survey is obviously baptism, and to be precise, I want to point out to you that baptism is not only a starting point; it is already a journeying, a voyage. But you may say, I have assisted at many baptisms, and I have seen nothing of any voyage. It would take plenty of imagination to compare those few drops of water to the ocean!

It is true that the actual ritual of baptism by ablution does fall short of the full symbolism. It is even a real drawback; it suggests to everyone that baptism is chiefly a sort of cleansing, to purify man from original sin. Now, though this aspect of purification is not altogether wanting in baptism, it is not the primary nor the most important aspect. It does not even appear at all in the Gospel. The oldest rite is that of baptism by immersion, always practised in the East and moreover not forbidden in the West. . . . This rite corresponds better with the significance of the word "baptism," which means bath, plunging. Even in this rite, the quantity of water used is no reminder of the immensity of the sea, nor the importance of a river such as the Jordan. The important thing in this comparison with the sea is not the quantity of water, it is its nature and its symbolic value, which is the same in the baptismal baths of old or the smaller baptisteries of modern churches. The question that we are trying to answer might be put quite simply thus: Why do we baptize with water?

No doubt the effects of baptism could be obtained by a simple prayer, by a simple declaration on the part of the Church. But . . . if the sacraments procure spiritual effects, they do so by human and visible signs, often making use of some physical matter. And this is right and proper. It befits man, who has a body as well as a soul; it befits the Church, which is a supernatural society but also a human and visible one; and it befits Christ, the head of this Church, who is God made flesh and who died for us in the flesh. Moreover, it was Christ who ordered His apostles to baptize all men, that is, to immerse them in water.

What, then, is the significance of water? It is shown in many biblical accounts which are solemnly read precisely on the night of the Pasch before the consecration of the water that is going to be used directly for baptism.

The first of these accounts is the world's creation. It begins thus: "In the beginning God created heaven and earth, and the earth was void and empty, and darkness was upon the face of the deep, and the spirit of God moved over the waters" (Gn 1:1-2). Water is thus pointed out to us as the primordial, original, one might say material element. It is from it that all life comes. And if this is so, it is because "the Spirit of God moved over the waters like the bird hovering over the nest which contains her young." [1] . . . Here we have side by side two essential factors of baptism—water, and the spirit that makes it fruitful. We find them in Jesus' conversation with Nicodemus, which bears exactly upon baptism: "Amen, amen, I say to thee, unless a man be born again of water and the Holy Ghost, he cannot enter into the kingdom of God" (Jn 3:5). Baptism is carried out in water because it is the sacrament of a new birth, and it is because of that new birth that it effects our entrance into the kingdom of God.

The other biblical accounts will state precisely the manner in which this birth is effected. The next is the Deluge. . . . Mankind has sinned; God is angry with His corrupt creation and decides to destroy it by burying it under the waters. Nevertheless, one just man, Noah,

●

[1] Commentary of P. de Vaux on this verse in the *Bible de Jérusalem*.

with his family, is to escape His anger. God makes him build an ark which floats upon the water and which is the instrument of their safety. Noah learns that the water is subsiding, that God's anger is pacified, by the return of the dove carrying in its beak an olive branch, the symbol of peace restored. Noah and his family leave the ark, to find the earth purified and renewed by the flood. They will cause a new mankind to grow upon it. God repeats the order given to the first members of the human race: "Increase and multiply and fill the earth" (Gn 9), and He establishes a covenant with them by the sign of the rainbow. Here again, water is material, life-giving, but it has been death-dealing in destroying a wicked world. At the same time it has created a new world, a new humanity from one just man preserved miraculously. We might notice that the Spirit is represented here, with the water, by the dove that we shall find again at the baptism of Jesus in the Jordan, where it manifests the presence of the Holy Spirit.

The third narrative is that of the Passover and the crossing of the Red Sea. There again, as in the Flood, water is both death-dealing and life-giving. It is the cause of death because Pharaoh and his horsemen were swallowed up by the sea, which closed over them. It is life-giving because the crowd of wretched slaves, as were the Hebrews, subjected to drudgery, servitude, and idolatry in the land of Egypt, pass dry-shod across the sea and find themselves on the other side, made into a new people, into God's people. And here, too, the Spirit of God is present, but this time in a new way, in the pillar of cloud that guided the Hebrews by day and was transformed into a pillar of light to lead them at night. The birth of the people of God will be completed by another passing across water, the crossing of the Jordan which is the frontier between the desert and the Promised Land. In this last journey, the people of God are no longer led by Moses but by Joshua, whose name in reality is exactly identical with that of Jesus.

We must now speak of Jesus, who is the true author and the great model of baptism. Jesus Himself is to be baptized in the Jordan. His baptism is the model of ours, not indeed because He needs to be purified, but His going down into the water will be a primordial act in His great victorious struggle against the devil, the effects of which we shall reap in our own baptism. At the time of Christ's baptism in the Jordan, the Father will solemnly acknowledge Him as His Beloved Son: our baptism will make us children of God. The Spirit will rest upon Him in the form of a dove: it is always "birth by water and the Holy Ghost." Finally, at Jesus's baptism, the Evangelists say mysteriously "the heavens were opened." Baptism does in fact open to us heaven, which had been closed by sin. This baptism of Jesus in the Jordan was only the forerunner and figure of our baptism. To institute our baptism, something else was needed. Jesus Himself speaks of this other baptism which was more tragic and more mysterious: "I have a baptism wherewith I am to be baptized, and how am I straitened until it be accomplished" (Lk 12:50).

In another Gospel He gives us to understand what this baptism is. He replies to James and John, who are asking for the first places in His kingdom: "You know not what you ask. Can you drink of the chalice that I drink of, or be baptized with the baptism wherewith I am baptized?" (Mk 10:38).

This evidently meant the passion, which was for Jesus a chalice of bitterness, a being swallowed up by the waters of death (a current image in biblical language for great suffering: cf. 2 K 22:17; Jb 22:11; Ps 17:17; 31:6; 68:2; 123:4; 143:7). Jesus went through death and gave the sign of Jonah, the prophet who was three days in the sea, as the sign of His resurrection on the third day after His burial.

St. Paul says to those who are baptized that they have been "baptized in His death. For we are buried together with Him by baptism unto death: that, as Christ is risen from the dead by the glory of the Father, so we also may walk in newness of life. For if we have been planted together in the likeness of His death, we shall also be in the likeness of His resurrection" (Rom 6:3-4). Baptism, then, is both death and life, death and resurrection, as the waters of the Flood and those of the Red Sea were at the same time destructive of the old man, of sin, of evil, and of death and creative of a new man, a new people of God, and a new mankind.

These comparisons between the death and resurrection of Christ, the passage through the Red Sea and our baptism ought not to seem artificial to us. St. Paul again declares that "our fathers—the Hebrews—were all under the cloud, and all passed through the sea. And all in Moses were baptized in the cloud and in the sea"; and that "these things were done in a figure to us" (1 Cor 10:1-2, 6). Further, crossing the Red Sea was the great miracle of the Pasch, the passover. Now, Jesus celebrated His death and resurrection within the framework of the Pasch; and it was on the night of the Pasch that Christians were baptized. They went down into the baptismal bath by three steps, as a symbol of the three days passed by Christ in the tomb and in the realm of death (that is what we mean by "descended into hell"). After going through the water, they came out on the other side. Their immersion in the water re-enacted the death and burial of Christ; their emerging from the water re-enacted His resurrection.

However simplified may be the manner of celebrating it today, baptism is always a passage through the sea. We enter as sinners, slaves, we come out free and pure. We enter as subjects of death and the devil, we come out as sons of God. This sea, as we have seen, is at the same time both deadly and regenerating. The baptismal fonts, that is to say, the waters of baptism, are at the same time a tomb and a maternal womb of inexhaustible fruitfulness. For baptism is meant not only to redeem and renew us sinners individually. Like the Red Sea, it gives birth to a new people, the people of God. Like the waters of the Flood, it begets, from the one just man Christ, the new Noah, a new human race. . . .

Here we feel obliged to examine a very common idea that tends to make our Christianity insipid. Far too many people see the passion of Christ as something mournful and passive. It might be just an accumulation of sufferings undergone by an innocent and inoffensive prophet, the victim of an odious conspiracy. Faith and the most authentic Christian tradition, on the contrary, show us Christ as a courageous champion, a hero in battle, His passion as a duel to the death with the devil, His cross as the instrument of His triumph, a trophy of victory. His very burial is not a repose: it begins the descent into hell, by which Christ pursues Satan to his lair to confound him utterly. Baptism makes us partakers of the passion and cross of Christ. This plunging, this burial in the water, signified by the very word baptism, gives us a share in the descent into hell, and so, not only the preparations for baptism, but the act itself, is a battle. . . .

The cross of Christ, His passion and His resurrection were a complete defeat for the devil, death, and sin. Can we say that it is the same for those who, by baptism, share in this death and resurrection? We are obliged to acknowledge the contrary. All baptized people must die. All baptized people can fall back into sin and come under the sway of the devil again. We experience this every day around us and, first of all, within ourselves.

Does this mean that all these effects of baptism are illusory? By no means. The grace of God, all through life, will help us in the strife, but it is very true that not only the moment of baptism but all the life of the baptized soul is a warfare. When the Hebrews had been delivered from the Egyptians by crossing the Red Sea, they had to fight innumerable tribes one after another while they were crossing the desert. They were sustained by God, who had made a covenant with them, who "went with their armies" (cf. Ex 15:3; Ps 43:3; 59:12). And it is the same for us, the baptized people; all through life we have to fight, supported by the grace of our baptism. This struggle is hard and prolonged. The Catholic sighs for the time when Christ will reappear to establish supreme justice and definitive order, and annihilate death decisively by the general resurrection. This looking ahead to Christ's return, which will mark the end of our journey and of our warfare, is included in baptism. When the person being baptized is clothed again in a new garment, a white garment, as a sign of victory, he is told to "carry it unstained before the judgment seat of Christ." When he is given a lighted candle, he is recommended to keep it to meet Christ at His return like the wise virgins who kept their lamps burning for the coming of the Bridegroom. . . .

Baptism is a warfare: it opens up an earthly life of struggle, but it gives us a pledge that at Christ's return we shall possess total victory and unclouded joy: at baptism, in hope but also with certainty, man is born to everlasting life, to eternal joy, to the endless rest that will follow a combat valiantly sustained.

If baptism is a warfare, it is a victorious struggle; if it means a snatching away from the devil, it also means attachment to Jesus Christ. It is on this attachment to Jesus Christ that we must now insist. It is not merely a question of moral attachment by the determination to obey His commandments and to walk in His footsteps. It means to identify oneself with Jesus Christ, to become another Jesus Christ. Let us begin by briefly going over the teaching of the New Testament on this point.

Man is God's creature; more than that, he is made "to His image and likeness" like a son. To be truly the Son of God, we need grace, which makes us sharers in His life, just as a man's son has his father's blood in his veins and possesses a life that his father has given him. Sin has broken this link between God and man. Jesus Christ, the only Son and equal to His Father, came upon earth to re-establish this link, to make us into other sons, adopted sons, and so to become "the firstborn amongst many brethren" (Rom 8:29). St. John says this in a striking way in the Prologue of his Gospel, which is read at the end of Mass: The Word, the true light, "came unto His own, and His own received him not. But as many as received Him, He gave them power to be made the sons of God" (Jn 1:11, 12). And the same St. John marvels at this doctrine in his Epistle: "Behold what manner of charity the Father hath bestowed upon us, that we should be called and should be the sons of God" (1 Jn 3:1).

Baptism, as we have said at some length, is a new birth, a birth which introduces us therefore into a new life: the life of Jesus Christ, the life of the Son of God, consequently a life of intimacy with the divine Family of the Blessed Trinity. . . .

CONFIRMATION

The second stage of the Catholic's journey, of Christian initiation, the sacrament that takes second place in all the classic lists of sacraments, is confirmation. I do not hesitate to say that it is the least known of all the sacraments. Of course, confirmation is conferred exclusively by the bishop, who comes to the parish for that express purpose. However, that does not make it any better known, as most Catholics do not know what a bishop is; they see in him some high religious functionary in strange and sumptuous attire, to whom many bows and compliments are made. That will not help us to understand the true meaning of confirmation.

We must not think that this ignorance is merely superficial and that, for instance, a better organized religious instruction could give the faithful a better knowledge of confirmation. We must admit that this sacrament is far from well known to theologians themselves and that studies concerning it are almost nonexistent. Why is this? The very reason for the obscurity that envelops confirmation will make us begin to understand in what it consists. It is, in fact, the complement of baptism.

This is how it was administered in ancient times. During the night of the Pasch, the bishop had just consecrated the baptismal water himself. He would baptize the first catechumens. Then he gave place to priests, who continued the baptism in his name. This was evident, since it was he, the bishop, who had consecrated the water that they were all using, and since he had begun the series of baptisms. The bishop retired into a chapel of the baptistery, the chapel of the cross, or *consignatorium*, because it was there that he was to give the signing, which is the old word for our confirmation. The neophytes, emerging undressed from the baptismal piscina, had holy chrism poured over their bodies by the priest. Then they were reclothed in the white garment. They were given a candle. Then they came before the bishop, who gave them another anointing with holy chrism. Their whole body had already been anointed anyway and was now covered up again; so the bishop gave this second anointing on the uncovered forehead. This he did in the form of the cross on the forehead; that was the signing. That done, the new Christians had only to enter into the basilica, where they rejoined the congregation so as to take part in the Mass for the first time and to complete their Christian initiation by receiving their first Holy Communion.

This short description shows us confirmation linked up with the group of sacraments received at the paschal festivity; it is seen simply as a complement, a finishing-up, of baptism. That is, besides, the true meaning of the word "confirmation"; often it is interpreted as meaning a giving of strength, an act that confirms or fortifies the one baptized. In fact, we should understand it, not as a confirming of the one baptized, but as a confirming of the baptism, that is to say, it is the sacramental rite that finishes the work begun by the rite of baptism. . . .

In what actually does the sacrament of confirmation consist, what does it give to us? The answer is well known, it is classical: confirmation gives us the Holy Spirit. It is the sacrament of the Holy Spirit. So we can say that confirmation is like each Catholic's own Pentecost. A passage in the Acts of the Apostles is very clear on this point—the deacon Philip went to a city of Samaria and "preached Christ unto them." His teaching and his miracles made numerous conversions. The apostles, who had stayed in Jerusalem, hearing this good news, "sent unto them Peter and John, who, when they were come, prayed for them that they might receive the Holy Ghost. For He was not as yet come upon any of them: but they were only baptized in the name of the Lord Jesus. Then they laid their hands upon them, and they received the Holy Ghost" (Acts 8:5-6, 14-17). In this text baptism and confirmation are clearly distinguished; they are even separated by an interval of time; baptism is given by Philip, a simple deacon, whilst confirmation seemed to demand the presence of two apostles (predecessors of our bishops); finally, the giving of the Holy Spirit seems to be an effect reserved to the sacrament of confirmation only.

In this case it would be easy to distinguish confirmation from baptism, and certain theologians have not hesitated so to do. Baptism would have but a negative effect: it would only serve to free the soul from original sin. The sanctifying of the soul, its deification by the Holy Spirit, would be the effect of confirmation. Unfortunately, this dividing of the work is impossible. Baptism, as we have said again and again, gives divine life and consequently gives the Holy Spirit. At Jesus's baptism, the model of ours, the Holy Spirit appeared visibly under the form of a dove. The Church has always held that children who die directly after baptism, without having received confirmation, go straight to heaven. That is, then, because baptism gives them all they need to live a divine life in its fulness. . . . How can confirmation be said to be the sacrament of the Holy Spirit, if the Holy Spirit has already been given in baptism?

The Gospel of the Sunday that precedes Pentecost gives us the first hint: Jesus said to His apostles, "When the Paraclete cometh . . . the Spirit of truth . . . He shall give testimony. . . . They will put you out of the synagogues: yea, the hour cometh that whosoever killeth you will think that he doth a service to God" (Jn 15:26-27; 16:1-2). He is the Spirit of God, the life of God. The Holy Spirit is given in baptism to fulfil this vital function for each of us personally. "Unless a man be born again of water and the Holy Ghost" (that is to say, if he is not baptized) "he cannot enter into the kingdom of heaven." But alongside of this interior and personal role, the Holy Spirit has a social external role, that of a witness of Christ. He allows those who receive Him to become in their turn witnesses to Christ, in the face of a world that hates Him. These witnesses are what we call martyrs (the word "martyr" means "a witness"). Confirmation gives us the Holy Spirit not only that we may live by Him—that is the effect of baptism— but that we may profess our Christianity before the world, even were it necessary to become martyrs for the faith. . . .

We can now understand the present-day ritual of confirmation. The bishop extends his hands over all those to be confirmed, while reciting a prayer that calls down upon them the seven gifts of the Holy Ghost. However, this preliminary imposition of hands is not indispensable to the sacrament. The sacramental gesture, properly so called, concerns another imposition of hands: the bishop places his right hand on the head of each one being confirmed. At the same time he traces upon the forehead the sign of the cross—that is the signing—and he traces the sign of the cross with his thumb dipped in chrism—that is the anointing. This sign traced upon the forehead is full of meaning. It is the sign of the cross, the sign of Christ's victory. It is traced upon the forehead because the Christian should not be ashamed of it, but should on the contrary bear it proudly with head erect. We might explain confirmation by this saying of Jesus in the Gospel of St. Mark: "If any man will follow me, let him deny himself, and take up his cross and follow me. . . . He that shall be ashamed of me, and of my words, in this adulterous and sinful generation, the Son of Man also will be ashamed of him, when He shall come in the glory of His Father, with the holy angels" (Mk 8:34-38).

We know now the effect of confirmation and in what it is distinct from baptism. Baptism already makes us complete Christians, quickened by the Holy Spirit, who is the soul of our souls. That is our birth. Just as birth takes place in the bosom of the family, so baptism is received in the parish, which is the family cell of the Church, and the normal minister of baptism is the parish priest. But besides this, the Christian should be Christ's witness before the world: it is this that makes him a "perfect Christian," a grown-up Christian. It does not suffice for him to have received the Holy Ghost for his own personal life in the midst of the Christian congregation. He must receive Him again to become a witness, a prophet before an unbelieving world. This new consecration is not only for the sake of a limited congregation. It makes him the representative, the witness, the prophet of the whole Church before all the world. Thus it is fitting that this sacrament should be conferred upon him by one who is the head of the Christian community, by the one who holds the responsibility of the apostolate and of the conquest of the unbelieving world, the bishop. . . .

THE HOLY EUCHARIST

The third sacrament, not only in the classical enumeration of the sacraments but in the Christian's journey through life, is the Holy Eucharist. At the paschal vigil, catechumens took part in Christ's death and resurrection, or, to repeat St. Paul's expression, "they put on Christ," who died and rose again, by receiving in succession baptism, confirmation, and the Holy Eucharist. By baptism they were incorporated into the Church and with Christ; by confirmation they undertook to bear public witness to Christ by boldly professing their faith; finally, by the Holy Eucharist they ate the flesh and drank the blood of Christ so as to be united with him as intimately and really as was possible. These three sacraments, conferred successively in the same night, formed what we might call Christian initiation, that is to say that having once received them, and only then, one became completely a Christian.

It is still the same today, and it is that which explains the importance we give to the first Holy Communion of our children and the solemnity with which we surround it.

But though it is true that baptism, confirmation and the Holy Eucharist form between the three of them one single initiation, it would be a grave error—but alas a widespread one—to hold that the Eucharist is on the same level as baptism completed by confirmation. On the contrary, there is a great difference between them. Baptism and confirmation are given once for all, are never renewed, and their effects last a lifetime, but it is not the same with the Eucharist. If first Holy Communion forms part of Catholic initiation, it is still only a "first" Communion, which should be followed by many others. . . .

In the daily life of a Catholic, then, the Holy Eucharist holds a double place. As first Holy Communion it is a first step, a kind of unique sacrament, a sacrament especially for children or adult converts who are just beginning their Catholic life. This first step once taken, the Holy Eucharist becomes a daily sacrament, which is not the privilege of any particular age in life, which should be repeated indefinitely and become "our daily bread," or, as has been said, our "marching rations." . . .

Firstly, let us speak of the special nature of the Eucharist. What helps us most to know the nature of a sacrament is the human action which provides its matter, we might almost say its primary matter. Thus, baptism is an inaugurating bath, a new birth. Confirmation is a dedication and a being publicly admitted into the ranks of witnesses to the faith. Penance is the trial of a sinner who pleads guilty. The anointing of the sick is a remedy. Matrimony is a contract of partnership. Holy orders is a conferring of powers.

As for the Holy Eucharist, we can say without any hesitation, it is a meal. . . . Not only was it instituted at the time of the Last Supper, but it is itself a repast. It consists in bread and wine consecrated on a table covered with tablecloths. The priest, before the words of consecration properly so called, repeats Christ's own invitation: "Take and eat. . . . Take and drink. . . ." Now could anyone, short of an absurdity, talk of a meal which would only take place once and for all? Our bodily organism is incessantly spending itself, using itself up, getting weaker even when doing nothing. We must, then, at fairly frequent intervals, restore it, give it strength and cheer by rich and solid nourishment, by refreshing and sustaining drink. . . .

. . . It is not the incorporated nature of the soul that it is meant to keep up, but its supernatural life, which consists in union with God by charity. . . . It is not easy to love God and to remain united to Him. All sorts of enemies and obstacles set themselves up in opposition to it: sensuality, the formidable attractions of material and worldly things, ambition, egoism, money, sadness, weariness of life. A soul that is not constantly sustained by supernatural nourishment, that incessantly comes to revive its charity, is a soul that faints on the arduous way of Christian perfection; it is a soul that weakens and dies.

All during this long search for God, this hard and dangerous pilgrimage towards God, the faithful soul, then, needs to renew its strength regularly by the true and supernatural meal of the Holy Eucharist.

It is not, however, a common meal composed of ordinary bread and wine. Our faith teaches us that the consecration has made of this bread and this wine the body and blood of Christ, that Christ in person is really present in the Eucharist. . . . Do we not wrong Christ's power by thinking He is incapable of sanctifying us at one stroke and that we need to renew more than once, in the course of our life, the sacrament in which He is really present? In order to answer this objection, . . . let us go more deeply into things.

Who is Christ? What is His mission? Why did He come? Christ is God made man. That is a great mystery and we are quite incapable of explaining it. We can, however, try to discover in it something of God's designs. If God has thus united Himself to mankind, it is because God is Love. This means that, in spite of His perfection, God is not a being who remains shut up in Himself. We believe that God is Trinity. This dogma means that our God is a living God. In spite of His total and eternal perfection, He is at the same time, if one may say so, a God in expansion, one who seeks to communicate Himself, to give Himself. He gives Himself to Himself in the mystery of the Trinity, in which we see in Him one sole God who nevertheless unfolds Himself, so to say, in the richness of His thought and of His love, to the extent of forming in one sole Being three Persons in a permanent state of mutual exchange and giving. One sole God who is not a solitary God, but a family God.

That did not satisfy Him. So as to be able to communicate Himself, to shed His rays still further, God willed to be a Creator. He communicated His Being to other beings. He did this not because He needed to, but because of His generosity; not from poverty but from His richness. He called into existence creatures infinitely inferior to Himself, of course, but who share His Being, His beauty, and His happiness.

Still He was not satisfied. . . .[2] Still less was He satisfied when this beautiful creation was separated from Him by sin. The same impulse that caused God to give Himself as perfectly as possible, also led him to unite Himself to mankind. "God so loved the world as to give His only-begotten Son" (Jn 3:16), and that is Christ: God communicating Himself, giving Himself to humanity in a most complete union. Again, Christ, however great His holiness, which is the very holiness of God, is by no means an inactive or static being. He is acting, He is self-giving, He wants to unite Himself to men. He preached, labored, and indeed sweated blood, to draw mankind up to Himself. He carried this love even to the folly of the cross.

Even yet that was not all. Christ did not wish that this salvation through the cross should be a thing done once and for all. He wanted to give Himself yet more, His love drove Him to the institution of the Holy Eucharist, so that the fruits of His crucifixion could be ours, even to the end of time, so that His love could spread and grow, like a flame that only lasts while it is spreading. "I am come to cast fire on the earth: and what will I, but that it be kindled?" (Lk 12:49).

If you want to destroy the Holy Eucharist, make it a sacrament received but once and not a constant renewal of the cross of Christ, a communication of His love always growing in intimacy and strength, reduce the Eucharist to one solitary reception of the sacrament.

True enough, baptism is given once for all. That is no reason, how-

●

[2] This, of course, is putting it briefly: we ought really to mention here the gift of God by grace to the human creature, a gift refused by sin and restored by the Saviour.

ever, why it should be the same with the Eucharist. The exact aim of
the Eucharist is to let us renew our baptism incessantly. That is why,
on the day of first Communion, we make our children renew their
baptismal vows. That is why "making one's Easter duties" is to renew
one's baptism year by year, by receiving our Saviour in Holy Communion. If the Christ that we receive in the Holy Eucharist is a living
and working Saviour, we must needs often receive the Holy Eucharist,
so that our souls, weighed down by egoism and wearied with all the
burdens of life, should be in their turn acting and fervent living
souls. . . .

The Holy Eucharist cannot be a sacrament to be received once in a
lifetime. It makes us renew the covenant with God, brought about at
baptism, on certain great occasions: solemn Holy Communion, marriage, viaticum at the hour of death. It makes us celebrate the Pasch
each year, and that is why the Church has laid down the grave obligation of the annual Communion at Easter. However, anyone who
means to be a live Christian, who really wants to be filled with the
Spirit of Jesus, with His exacting and conquering love, should communicate much more often.

That is not all. Some pious people may have frequent recourse to
the Holy Eucharist as to a sacrament of their individual progress, of
their personal intimacy with Jesus, in which they seek a more or less
dreamy satisfaction of a certain ideal. Those who use the Holy Eucharist in this way, however devout they may be, only partially understand it. Holy Commuion ought not only to unite us to God by Jesus
and in Him. It should unite us to the people of God, strengthen and
enliven our union with our brethren. That is why this sacrament is not
celebrated in private and in silence, but in the popular rejoicing of a
family banquet in the hymns of the Church's liturgy. The charter of
the New Covenant is the new law, which is, as Jesus said, "that you
love one another as I have loved you," and that we thus make all together our Pasch, our passover, into the Promised Land.

THE SACRAMENT OF PENANCE

Baptism, confirmation, and the Eucharist, with which we have been
concerned thus far, are all obviously sacraments of life and progress;
they bring us a step forward. By receiving them we advance and grow.
But the sacrament of penance . . . ?

I am not asking this question as a rhetorical trick to furnish myself
with a preamble. The difficulty is a real one. In fact, I even think that
it explains in large measure the unpopularity of the sacrament of
penance among a great number of modern Christians.

People want an optimistic Christianity, glowing with vitality; positive, at all events. The sacrament of penance seems to belong to the
realm of pessimistic or negative religion.

Again, we are witnessing a rediscovery of the significance of the community in Christianity, whereas the sacrament of penance would appear to be strictly an individual affair. Finally, this sacrament seems to have no effect beyond that of removing stains, paying debts, and rebuilding ruins. Surely all this is a matter of standing still, or going back over the past, rather than a move forward.

All these difficulties must be met. We shall try, first of all, to see confession as the sacrament which, together with the Eucharist, shows us most vividly the merciful love of our Lord. Then we shall discover, I hope, that it is a community sacrament, and lastly we shall study it as the sacrament of spiritual progress.

Before being used as the name of a Christian sacrament, the word *poenitentia* ("penance" or "penitence") designated an attitude of soul, a virtue even, by which we detest and are sorry for our sins because they offend God and separate us from Him. We should not be surprised that the same word is used to designate both an inward disposition of the soul and a sacrament.

The relation between these two meanings of the same word is one of analogy, not ambiguity; in fact, they are related as cause and effect. The essential element of the sacrament, its primary matter, as indispensable as water is for baptism or bread for the Eucharist, is precisely sorrow for sin. Without this interior attitude, there is no sacrament.

Thus it is absolutely false to say that a Catholic needs only to confess his sins and receive the formula of absolution pronounced by a priest to become white as snow. Unless there is sorrow for sin present to begin with, absolution is completely ineffective. On the other hand, as we shall see, sorrow for sin, provided that it attains a certain purity and a certain intensity, can itself cleanse the soul, even before absolution has been given. . . .

If God looks upon sinners with such kindness, it is not because of their sin. God is bound to hate sin, because it is nothing other than separation from God. If God loves the sinner, it is because, far from wanting him to sink into sin, He wants to draw him out of it. The mercy of God is not a mere attitude of compassion; it is efficacious and in a sense creative. It has the power to bring back the sinner, to rescue him from his sin, and to make him as it were a new being. "As I live," says the Lord in Ezechiel, "I desire not the death of the wicked, but that the wicked turn from his way and live" (Ez 33:22). And in Isaiah: "If your sins be as scarlet, they shall be made white as snow" (Is 1: 18). . . .

This forgiveness is not mere agreement by which God decides not to see our sins any longer. It is a transformation, a re-creation of man. To quote Ezechiel again: "I will pour upon you clean water and you shall be cleansed from all your filthiness. . . . And I will give you a new heart and put a new spirit within you: and I will take away the stony heart out of your flesh and will give you a heart of flesh" (Ez 36: 25-26).

This change or turning back which takes place within the soul is exactly what repentance means; it is a conversion, that is to say, a complete change. Just as God alone can create the world, so he alone can perform this unheard-of operation which consists in the re-creation of a man's heart. And this is something so lovely that God and the angels know of nothing which gives them greater joy.

Our Lord said as much Himself, and in shattering terms. Jesus could not fail to renew, in all their fulness of meaning, the affirmations made by the prophets concerning the goodness of God. This is precisely because "God so loved the world as to give his only-begotten Son. . . . For God sent not His Son into the world to judge the world, but that the world may be saved by Him" (Jn 3:16-17). "For the Son of Man is come to seek and to save that which was lost" (Lk 19-10). And when the Pharisees are scandalized because "This man receiveth sinners and eateth with them," Jesus answers them with the parable of the lost sheep. "When he hath found it [the Good Shepherd will] lay it upon his shoulders rejoicing, and coming home call together his friends and neighbors, saying to them: Rejoice with me, because I have found my sheep that was lost. I say to you that even so there shall be joy in heaven upon one sinner that doeth penance more than upon ninety-nine just who need not penance" (Lk 15:1-10).

This Gospel taken from St. Luke, who is par excellence the Evangelist of mercy, is read on the Sunday within the Octave of the Sacred Heart. And after all, what is the Sacred Heart if not the symbol of God's pity towards mankind? In Maeterlinck's *Pelléas and Mélisande* there is a very beautiful sentence which has always struck me as a horrible blasphemy. Old Arkel says: "If I were God, I should have pity on the human heart." God has done precisely that: shown pity for the hearts of men, become incarnate for their sake, so that a human heart can beat in the breast of the Son of God, and be pierced by love for us and pour forth water and blood: water and blood so abundant and so powerful that they are able to wash away the stains of the whole world.

The very foundation of the sacrament of penance is this astonishing truth: God is capable of transforming the human heart, of turning a sinful heart into an innocent one, by the repentance of which He makes it capable. By looking at the sacrament of penance in this light, we can obviously clear away all the objections raised by people who reduce "confession" to an automatic device by which our sins are periodically wiped out.

"The remission of sins" in which we proclaim our faith every time we say the Credo is effected in the first place by baptism, which washes us once and for all in the blood of Jesus. But God knows our weakness, and in His infinite patience He has instituted another sacrament which places His inexhaustible mercy within our reach, so that we can be sure of being heard when we pray as David did after his great sin: "Wash me yet more from my iniquity and draw me from sin. . . . To thee only have I sinned. Thou shalt wash me, and I shall be made whiter than snow. Create a clean heart in me . . . and renew a right spirit (a firm good will) within. . . . Restore unto me the joy of thy salvation . . . a contrite and humbled heart, O God, thou wilt not despise. . . ."

It appears that the sacrament of penance has undergone a complete change of form between those days and our own: from being a community affair, it has become a matter for the individual. In point of fact, this contrast is far more apparent than real. Firstly because, if the penance was public in the old days, the confession was certainly not. Secondly, careful study of the sacrament of penance as it exists today will easily reveal its public character.

The penitent is, in the ordinary course of affairs, required to make his confession in a church. The church is the proper place for the confessional. In fact, this piece of furniture, which seems to exist for the sole purpose of guarding the privacy of the confession, is there primarily as an indication that the sacrament of penance is administered in the Church in both senses of the word. The priest who receives the penitent must be wearing not merely the surplice, but the stole which is the badge of his priestly power; it is as the Church's representative that he hears the confession and, if he sees fit, gives absolution. Another point, of which many of the faithful are ignorant, affords further proof of the fact that in the sacrament of penance the priest acts as the delegate of the Church. Any priest cannot hear the confession of any Catholic he chooses and give him absolution, except of course where there is danger of death. A priest can only administer the sacrament of penance in a diocese where the head of the diocese—that is to say, the bishop—has given him faculties to do so. Our penitent begins his confession with the Confiteor, in the course of which he is not content to confess his sins to Almighty God but includes the Blessed Virgin Mary and various saints, among whom we should notice St. Peter and St. Paul, mentioned as founders of the Church; perhaps especially St. Peter, the first Pope, who is usually represented carrying keys, of which we shall speak later on.

Lastly—a very important detail of which nearly all Catholics are ignorant—the priest usually gives two absolutions. The first is as follows: "May our Lord Jesus Christ absolve you, and I, by His authority, absolve you (that is to say, I release you) from every bond of excommunication and interdict, according to the extent of my power and of your needs." Only after this comes the absolution of sin properly so called: "Likewise I absolve you from your sins, in the name of the Father, and of the Son, and of the Holy Ghost." Why the first absolution? Because a priest can only absolve a sinner on condition that the latter is not cut off from the Church by any disciplinary measure such as excommunication or interdict. That is to say, in order to reconcile a man with God in the secrecy of his conscience, we have to begin by reconciling him with the Church, if he is cut off from it.

This brings to light a truth which is too little appreciated: sin is not only separation from God, but also separation from our fellows. All sin is separation, disintegration. That is the reverse, so to speak, of the doctrine of the communion of saints. Just as by charity we form a single body of which Christ is the head, a single vine, which is Christ; just as—to quote Elizabeth Leseur—"A soul which raises itself, draws the world upwards," so in the same way but inversely, sin is a mutilation of the whole body; it severs the branches from the vine, shakes the building, which is the Church; and every soul that falls, drags down the world. By sin we not only offend God, we not only injure ourselves by cutting ourselves off from God, but also we do an injury to our fellow men.

This is why the power to forgive sins, the sacrament of penance, was instituted by our Lord (as we read in the Gospel for the feast of St. Peter) at the time as He instituted the Church and its hierarchy. He told Simon, who from this moment is known as St. Peter: "I say to thee that thou art Peter, and upon this rock I will build my Church. And the gates of hell shall not prevail against it. And I will give to thee the keys of the kingdom of heaven. And whatsoever thou shalt bind upon earth, it shall be bound also in heaven; and whatsoever thou shalt loose upon earth, it shall be loosed also in heaven" (Mt 16: 18-19). Now this is precisely what makes penance a sacrament. It is a visible gesture—performed on earth—which has an invisible and supernatural power—it takes effect in heaven—and it is a gesture which is performed within the community of the Church, a power which is given to the head of the Church. . . .

After giving absolution the priest says a very lovely prayer, which far too many Catholics know nothing about: "May the passion of our Lord Jesus Christ, the merits of the blessed Virgin Mary and of all the saints, all the good that you do and all the evil that you bear, procure for you the remission of your sins, an increase of grace, and the reward of eternal life. Amen." Thus, far from being an isolated rite, a mere legal formality after which life goes along as before, or a sterile going back over the past, the sacrament of penance sheds its light upon our whole future, uniting our whole life with the passion of Christ, which was not only a death but a redemption, and the gateway to the resurrection and to new life.

ANOINTING OF THE SICK

The last of the sacraments destined for the good of the individual, in this Christian journey whose stages we are following, is extreme unction. I suppose that sounds like a truism. Surely extreme unction, as its name implies, is by definition the last sacrament. When we hear it said of someone who is dying that he has received "the last sacraments," are we not meant to understand that among them extreme unction held pride of place, and that we must now give up all hope of his recovery?

As a matter of fact, this does not follow at all. This view of things is slightly distorted, and we shall show that extreme unction, in spite of its name, is not exclusively, or even principally, the sacrament of the dying. Afterwards we shall see what are the helps which the Church reserves for people on their deathbed. For the moment, let us content ourselves with seeing extreme unction as the sacrament of the sick. And this is the reason—let us make the point once and for all—why we ought to drop the term "extreme unction," which is unsuitable and relatively modern, in favor of the more accurate and more traditional "anointing of the sick."

Like all the sacraments, this one must have been instituted by Jesus Christ. Now, what was our Lord's attitude to sickness and the sick? We should note, first of all, that Christ was never ill; sickness is one of the results of original sin. Our Lord, who took upon Himself all our miseries except sin, could never be ill; which does not diminish the fact that, by His cruel agony and His passion willingly borne in obedience to His Father's will and for love of us, He has given the sick a perfect example of brave and patient suffering.

Our Lord was not only a stranger to sickness, He treated it as an enemy, and this attitude is perfectly in harmony with His love for the sick. These come in crowds to block His path and pester Him so that He cannot even eat (Mk 3:20; 4:31), because He cures them in large numbers. It is in this way that He inaugurates, and in a sense carries on, His great struggle against death and sin, a struggle which is to end in a devastating victory, through His own death and resurrection. Never does our Lord say that sickness is a blessed thing, nor does He ever say that, for this or that individual, sickness is a punishment for sin. He simply takes pity on the sick and cures them on one condition: they must want to be cured and have faith in His power. Sometimes He adds forgiveness of sins (Mt 11:2) and the invitation to sin no more henceforward (Jn 5:14); because if there is no clear connection between any given sickness and a given sin, there is certainly a connection between sin and sickness in general. Both are the work of the devil. We must bear this principle in mind, as it is of primary importance in determining the effect of our sacrament.

Among the powers and functions which our Lord bids His apostles exercise after He has left them, the healing of the sick holds a prominent place. We even read in St. Mark that already on their first mission the disciples "cast out many devils and anointed with oil many that were sick and healed them" (Mk 6:13). Even if they were not as yet administering the sacrament, we can see it foreshadowed in this gift which was granted to the first disciples.

The Apostle St. James in his epistle, which is a reminder of the principal duties of the Christian life and which does not seem to embody any innovations, furnishes us with a text which has been regarded as a sort of "promulgation" of this sacrament. "Is any man sick among you? Let him bring in the priests of the Church and let them pray over him, anointing him with oil in the name of the Lord. And the prayer of faith shall save the sick man. And the Lord shall raise him up; and if he be in sins, they shall be forgiven him" (Jas 5:14-15).

In this text we find all the essential elements of the Catholic teaching concerning the anointing of the sick. First, as regards the people who are to benefit by it: these are the sick, not the dying. "Is any man sick among you? Let him bring in the priests of the Church." If the sick man has to ask for the priests himself, it means that he has to approach the sacrament of his own accord; it is not a magical remedy which the priest comes and thrusts upon a man in his last extremity. The ministers of the sacrament are "the priests of the Church," which does not prevent its being administered by a single priest or bishop. The matter of the sacrament is anointing with oil, since oil was in former times the standard remedy in Mediterranean countries. Tradition adds the condition that this oil must be blessed by the bishop. And in fact every year, at Mass on Maundy Thursday, the bishop, assisted by a number of priests, deacons, and subdeacons, blesses the oil of the sick, before he consecrates the holy chrism and blesses the oil of catechumens, all of which will be used throughout the year in all the parishes of the diocese. This gives the sacrament that official and public character, as something derived from the Church and the community, which St. James's words imply: "Let him bring in the priests of the Church." St. James also notes the "form" of the sacrament: "Let the priests pray over him, anointing him with oil in the name of the Lord." In practice the anointing is accompanied by a prayer: "May the Lord grant thee, through holy unction and His most tender mercy, forgiveness for whatever sins thou hast committed by sight, hearing, smell, taste, speech, and touch, and by thy steps," referring in turn to each of the sense organs or limbs as they are being anointed. As well as this, in the rite as it stands today, the anointings which form the essential part of the sacrament are preceded and followed by a number of prayers. We should notice at once that these prayers all ask for one and the same thing: the cure of the sick man, his return to normal life and his occupations; not a word about the last agony, death, or the judgment. . . .

Finally, St. James points to the effects of the sacrament: "The prayer of faith shall save the sick man. And the Lord shall raise him up; and if he be in sins, they shall be forgiven him." The primary effect of the sacrament, then, is the physical cure of the sick. A secondary effect is the forgiveness of sins. . . .

Since disease is fundamentally bound up with sin, and since body and soul are intimately united, anointing also has an effect upon the soul and completes the spiritual effects of the sacrament of penance. Even if it does not bring a complete cure—and in the opinion of doctors and nurses, this happens more often than people think—it brings an interior peace and purity. It sanctifies the state of the sick man and enables him to derive more merit from his sickness. It follows that it ought to be given as early as possible, to everyone who is ill enough to be in probable, even though not imminent danger of death. To act otherwise and postpone the sacrament until the last minute is to deprive the sick of the solace and help which the mercy of Christ has prepared for them.

Nevertheless, if there is a sacrament to help the Christian at each important stage of his journey through life, there must surely be one provided for this last and most important stage, the perilous journey of death. This sacrament does exist, and it is holy viaticum, whose name suggests a voyage and means precisely "provision for the journey." It is not an eighth sacrament. It is simply the Eucharist, but playing here a very particular role. We have already remarked that it is possible to distinguish, on the one hand, what I may call the ordinary Eucharist, our daily bread, and on the other hand the first Communion which completes the Christian's initiation and which is related for this reason with baptism and confirmation. The Eucharist also plays a third role, when it is given as viaticum; and in this form it might rightly be given the name of extreme Communion.

This is a role which finds a place quite naturally among the functions of the sacrament of bread. It is the sacrament of the Passover, or passing, and death is the last passover, the passing from this mortal life into true life. This sacrament enables us to renew throughout our life the sacrament of incorporation into Christ, which is baptism; and it is death that at last unveils all the hidden splendors which baptism has implanted within us, of which eternal life is the most important. Finally, our Lord, in His great discourse on the Bread of Life, emphasized the very special way in which this sacrament is connected with the resurrection: "I am the Bread of Life. Your fathers did eat manna in the desert (after the first Passover) and are dead. This is the bread which cometh down from heaven: that if any man eat of it he may not die. . . . He that eateth my flesh and drinketh my blood hath everlasting life; and I will raise him up in the last day. . . . This is the bread that came down from heaven. Not as your fathers did eat manna and are dead. He that eateth this bread shall live forever" (Jn 6:48-50, 55, 59). The Church has understood these solemn words of our Lord quite literally and she has always considered viaticum to be a "very necessary remedy" for the dying. This necessity is emphasized by an exceptional piece of legislation. To make sure that a sick person shall be able to receive viaticum, that is to say, Communion at the last moment, he is not required to observe a fast of any kind; if he has already received Communion on the same day, he can and ought to receive a second Communion as viaticum; a priest who is not fasting and has already said Mass may and ought to celebrate Mass again if this is necessary to consecrate a host to be given in a last Communion. And, of course, viaticum is always offered to those who are condemned to death, although these are never anointed.

Finally, at the supreme moment of death, the Church provides not a sacrament, but an appropriate sacramental, incomparably lovely in its confident serenity and motherly tenderness. This is the "Commendation of the Soul," made up of a Litany of the Saints and some long and beautiful prayers, reminding God that the departing soul who is being commended to His mercy has been baptized and marked with the sign of the cross and the seal of the Blessed Trinity; whatever may have been his faults, he had the faith, he belongs to Christ, he is enfolded in the Church's mantle; and these are all strong reasons for believing that God will receive him kindly. . . .

HOLY ORDERS

We have now examined the five sacraments which are necessary for every Christian: baptism, confirmation, and the Holy Eucharist secure his full supernatural vitality; penance and the anointing of the sick make good the loss caused by sickness. These five sacraments, as we have pointed out several times, are administered within the Church and make the Christian a living member of the Church. Nevertheless, their principal purpose is the personal salvation of the recipient. The last two sacraments differ from the other five in that their principal purpose is the prosperity, permanence, and good organization of the Church. The graces which these sacraments bestow are personal, as all graces are, but they do not only serve to secure the salvation of the recipients. They fulfil the further purpose of enabling men better to carry out their duties to other people and to hold worthily their place in Christian society.

What is the significance of the word "orders" when applied to a sacrament? And why not call it the sacrament of priesthood, which would seem to be clearer? The word "orders" shows that the Church is not a homogeneous mass, or a mob of people thrown together pell-mell, but an orderly and organized people, with their various functions duly distributed in a fairly complex hierarchy, built up of a fairly large number of different degrees. Nothing shows this more clearly than an ordination ceremony, which is one of the most beautiful in our liturgy. . . .

Let us now try to get beyond this narrow framework provided by the ordination ceremony, and see in all its splendid fulness this religious phenomenon, or rather this Christian mystery, which we call the priesthood. If we are to avoid mutilating this mystery, and discern the full magnificence of God's design in this regard, we must not limit the priesthood to priests properly so called. It is important to see that the priesthood extends far beyond those who are called priests: upwards, to the plenary priesthood of the bishop; downwards, to the priesthood that is common to all the baptized. To grasp this doctrine exactly is a delicate business; to make it clear we shall need to begin from the one and only real priesthood, the one which envelops all the others, and in which all the others are only a participation: the unique priesthood of Jesus Christ.

Jesus Christ is a Priest, he is the only Priest. For Him the priesthood is not a secondary attribute. It is His very mission and as it were the definition of His Person.

What is a priest? He is an intermediary between God and men, having the double duty of taking up to God the appeals, prayers, thanksgiving, and praise of men, and of bringing down to men the benefits of God. It is this twofold movement of going up and coming down which constitutes worship, and it is exercised above all in that mysterious act which we call sacrifice. A sacrifice is, in fact, both the homage which men pay to God and at the same time an act by which God shows to men that He has heard their prayers and accepted their offerings, and that He bestows upon them His friendship.

To play this part of go-between, a priest must belong to both domains, the human and the divine. This is true par excellence of Jesus Christ, who is truly and completely Man and at the same time truly and completely God. Because He is truly Man, born of a woman, He is capable of being our representative, our interpreter. But an ordinary man, a sinner, could not possibly be received by God. Jesus, though still a man, is the Holy One of God. God cannot fail to hear Him kindly and find His sacrifice fully acceptable and sufficient for the redemption of mankind. All the sacrifices which went before that of Christ were only weak foreshadowings of His unique and perfect sacrifice: the sacrifice of the cross. All the sacrifices offered since then are only images, participations, applications, and as it were the coinage minted by this unique sacrifice. Just as all the priests before Jesus Christ were priests only to announce His coming, likewise all the priests who come after Him are priests only to show forth and pass on His unique priesthood.

But if Jesus Christ is the one and only Priest, what is the good of having other priests after Him? The answer is that the priestly activity is not the invisible communication of invisible benefits. This bridge between earth and heaven which we call the priesthood must rest upon earth in an earthly and visible way. Jesus Christ did not begin to exercise His priesthood until the moment when He appeared among us to manifest God in the flesh: "The Word (invisible by nature) was made flesh and dwelt amongst us." Now that Christ has ascended to heaven and is with His Father, His priesthood has still to be exercised in a visible manner by means of other men, and among men. Jesus, having ascended to heaven, remains invisible in our midst in the person of the Church, that is to say, of all the men who are gathered together in His name animated by His spirit and who form His Body here on earth. This Church is His spouse, the heir to all His privileges and all His power. Since Christ was a Priest . . . likewise His Church (which could be called, like the Virgin Mary, the mirror of Jesus) is priestly. . . .

But what is the meaning of this statement that the Church is priestly? The people of Israel, the chosen race, beloved by God, which prefigured our Church, was already a "kingdom of priests" (Ex 19:6; cf. 1

Pt 2:9). It was not a mob of slaves; it was not even a profane people. It was a holy people, that is to say, a people consecrated in the worship of God and a permanent witness in the pagan world to the holiness of God. With even more justification the new people of God, the new Israel, may be called a priestly people, a people consecrated to worship, dedicated to praise and thanksgiving. It is here that the liturgy comes into the picture—this great mystery which is too often reduced to a sort of decorative appendage of the life of the Church. The liturgy is in reality nothing less than the priesthood of Christ, the Head (Jesus) and His members (the Church, the assembly of the baptized).

In the face of this statement, which is essential for a true appreciation of our dignity as Christians, it may be objected that only priests can actively carry out the worship of God, since ordinary Catholics have to benefit from it only in a passive way. Another possible objection is that a priest is a mediator, and that the Christian people cannot be a mediator: it is not in the middle of the relationship which unites God and the world, but at one end of it. It is not the bridge, but one of the extremities of the bridge.

Let us try to answer these objections. The whole Church is priestly, and all the baptized share in the priesthood of Jesus Christ: that does not mean that this share is distributed uniformly to all on an equal footing. The Church is not a lifeless mass; it is a people, a body, an edifice; all of which implies a structure, an organization, an architecture, and, in consequence, a hierarchy and an inequality.

The fundamental priesthood belongs to all, because all are members of Jesus, the Priest. But only those who are called "priests" are capable of representing Jesus Christ *personally*, of performing His saving actions, in particular of celebrating the Eucharistic Sacrifice and absolving sins. Also these "priests," since they hold personally the place of our Lord, represent all the baptized, the members of Jesus Christ, and gather up all their prayers and thanksgiving to offer them up to God. According to the double aspect of the priesthood which we have indicated, the "priests" are more especially charged with the duty of bringing down the gifts of God to men; and the "baptized" exercise their priesthood more especially in sending up prayers and thanks to God. But the distinction is not as simple as that: the priests, like the faithful, have to address prayers and thanks to God; and the ordinary baptized faithful, like the priests, can confer upon others the gifts of God. For example, in the sacrament of matrimony, as we shall see shortly, the two persons who are being joined in marriage actually confer the sacrament upon one another by virtue of their baptism. . . .

In order to arrive at a better understanding of all this—which is difficult, admittedly, but most important—it may help to put oneself in the place of a priest, and imagine that one is one of the young men upon whom the bishop laid his hand on the last feast of SS. Peter and Paul, asking God to give them "the dignity of the priesthood" and to "renew in them the spirit of holiness" (Preface for the Ordination of Priests).

One might say to oneself: "So here I am a priest! I now have the power, when I consecrate bread and wine, when a sinner asks me to forgive his sins, of personally taking the place of Jesus Christ. What an honor for a poor man like me! But also what a responsibility! All the same, I am not too terrified by it; first, because I did not ask for it myself, but was called by God speaking through His Church. Also, the sacrament of holy orders which I have just received has not only given me forever the powers of Christ, by means of the character which makes me a sharer in Christ's priesthood. This sacrament, if I lend myself to its influence, awakens in me grace which will make me share more fully in the holiness of Christ. The character makes me a priest forever; the priestly grace will make me a good priest, perhaps even a holy priest. And if it should happen—which God forbid—that I become a bad priest, even if I were to lose the faith, then since the solidarity of the Church and the salvation of souls can never be dependent upon the good or evil disposition of an individual, the baptisms, consecrations, and absolutions which I should perform would still be valid, because when I administer the sacraments, it is Christ in me who baptizes, Christ who consecrates, Christ who absolves.

"To think that I am another Christ! And yet, in fulfilling this unheard-of function, I am not alone. Above me, there is the bishop, who is Christ's representative par excellence in his diocese, the particular Church of which he is the head. Only he, the bishop, possesses the priesthood in its fulness, to the extent of being able to pass it on to other people. It is he who chose me for his collaborator. If I can hear confessions, it is because he has given me power of jurisdiction over the sheep of his flock. And if he has appointed me to be a parish priest, it is because he has confided to me the care and anxiety involved in the duty of exercising his authority over a department of his diocese. I am a priest, it is true, but in dependence on the high priest, the bishop, who with a sovereignty which places him on an entirely different level from myself, is another Christ.

"As a priest, I am also linked to the rest of the faithful. If I were not one of them, I should not have been capable of being ordained a priest. The baptismal character is the necessary support and foundation for the priestly character. I am a leader of these baptized souls, because I represent Christ; but, because I represent Christ, I am also their delegate and even their servant. I must exercise my priesthood in their service and in touch with them. At Mass I alone am capable of consecrating the body and blood of Christ, but if I have this power, it is, in the last analysis, in their service. One cannot imagine a priest of Christ without a Christian people from whom he has been drawn; and if the priest, personally, is another Christ, the whole Christian people, taken collectively, is the Body of Christ."

It is in this way that the mystery of the priesthood extends beyond the limits of the sacrament of holy orders, the ceremonies of which we have described. The mystery of the priesthood is the mystery of Christ visibly present in the world, first of all by His bishops, who are the successors of the twelve apostles, by His priests who renew His sacrifice and dispense His word and His mercy, but also by all the baptized.

Taken all together, we are the living Church, the house of prayer which the Temple of Jerusalem foreshadowed, the ceaseless circulation of divine life which foreshadows and builds up the lightsome city of the heavenly Jerusalem; for there, in heaven, we shall have no other light and no other food than the Lamb, Jesus Christ, Priest and Victim, slain and risen from the dead to reconcile mankind with the Father.

MATRIMONY

Matrimony comes last in the study of the sacraments. After holy orders, which organizes the supernatural society so far as worship is concerned, there comes a sacrament also entirely directed towards the good of society and towards its first and fundamental good, to secure its survival; the first aim of matrimony is, in fact, to supply the supernatural society with new members, without whom it must soon cease to be. This statement is not as ingenuous as it might sound; in the Middle Ages there were many heretics who condemned matrimony because it protracted an earthly progeny that they judged to be the work of the devil.

If matrimony comes last on the list of sacraments, it is not only for the reason of logical sequence that I have just given. There is also a historical reason.

Matrimony was the last sacrament that theologians consented to call by that name. They had hardly all agreed upon it by the twelfth century. We might also remark that it is a sacrament quite on its own.

First of all, it is of faith that the sacraments were instituted by Jesus Christ, that is to say, they have Jesus Christ as their author. It is obvious, for instance, that the Eucharist was really founded by Him, and that He has given quite new value to the ancient rites of bathing with water or anointing with oil. But marriage is as old as the human race. It was instituted by the Creator when He formed the first woman after saying: "It is not good for man to be alone" (Gn 2:18), and when He blessed them, saying: "Increase and multiply and fill the earth." Since that remote time, marriage has not changed its nature. Jesus Christ, it seems, only maintained it when He took up and confirmed the original words: "Have ye not read that He who made man from the beginning, made them male and female? And He said: 'For this cause shall a man leave father and mother, and shall cleave to his wife, and they two shall be in one flesh. Therefore now they are not two, but one flesh. What, therefore, God hath joined together, let no man put asunder" (Mt 19:4-6, quoting Gn 1:27; 2:24).

Can we even assert that marriage is a divine institution, part of our worship, as would seem necessary to merit the name of sacrament? It seems it is merely a natural function, common to all religious people and even to those without religion. Why should marriage be a sacrament any more than birth, death, or the succession of day and night? What chiefly prevented theologians from recognizing marriage as a true sacrament for a long time was an inveterate distrust of everything connected with procreation. Did not Jesus say that "the flesh profiteth nothing" (Jn 6:64), and St. Paul that "flesh and blood cannot possess the kingdom of God"? (1 Cor 15:50). Add to this general distrust the more precise motive that original sin is transmitted by human generation. How can a thing that passes on sin be at the same time a sacrament, that is to say, a remedy for sin? At the most one might admit—since Jesus sanctioned marriage, notably by being present with His mother at the marriage feast of Cana—that marriage was a last resort, the relief of concupiscence, but one could not imagine it positively giving grace and holiness and participation in the very life of God in Jesus Christ, which is the effect of every sacrament.

Let us begin by eliminating the most obvious of these objections. Christianity is not spiritualism, a religion for disembodied souls. God is the Creator of the flesh as well as the spirit. All the sayings of Holy Scripture that seem to condemn the flesh, only condemn it when it is in opposition to the spirit. The very word "flesh"—if it is sometimes used to denote carnal desire, the tyranny of the flesh that draws us away from God—can also be used to describe our natural earthly condition, which is itself blessed by God, since it is His own work. Human generation, the fruit of marriage, was willed by God, who, on the evening of the sixth day, after creating man and woman and ordering them to multiply, said not only that it was "good," as He had said of all the previous creations, but that it was "very good" (Gn 1:31), that is to say, very beautiful, very holy, truly worthy of Himself.

It is true indeed that we contract original sin by our birth, because every new member of Adam's race incurs the curse of Adam by entering into his lineage, but that does not signify that the act that gives us life is in itself evil. Did not God himself say, after blessing man and woman, "increase and multiply"? If the flesh was not evil from the beginning, still less is it evil since the coming of Christ, who is none other than the Word made flesh. Jesus is born of the Spirit, but also of the flesh, in the Virgin Mary. It was His flesh that saved us from damnation by being nailed to the cross. It was His flesh that opened heaven to us by rising again and sitting at the right hand of the Father to prepare a place for us. For we shall also rise again in our turn, and we shall be happy forever in heaven not only in our souls, but also in our bodies.

It is precisely because Christ inaugurated new relations between God and humanity that His coming has, without His having expressly said so, not changed but raised up tremendously the nature of marriage by making it a sign of a great mystery.

We say that by the Incarnation Christ became united to human nature. This union is indissoluble. Through its means the Son of God and the human race are no longer two, but one in the same flesh forever. This sublime model of marriage has, however, been perfected still more. When Christ died upon the cross, the human race was redeemed; it became the Church. By that one act Christ created His spouse, was united to her, and sanctified her. The Fathers in their teaching loved to recall that the first Adam gave birth in his sleep to Eve, the spouse drawn from his side, called the mother of all the living. In the same way, when the new Adam, the new head of the human race, Christ, was in the sleep of death upon the cross, water and blood gushed from His side, symbolizing the principal sacraments—baptism and the Holy Eucharist—in which is realized the incorporation of redeemed humanity into Christ which we describe in one word: the Church. It is a unique marriage, an indissoluble and fruitful marriage, since the Church, the Bride of Christ, will bring into eternal life an innumerable generation of redeemed souls.

This great mystery was expressed by St. Paul in a passage of his letter to the Ephesians (5:22) that is read as the Epistle at every Nuptial Mass. "The husband is the head of the wife, as Christ is the head of the Church. He is the Saviour of His body. . . . Husbands, love your wives, as Christ also loved the Church and delivered Himself up for it, that He might sanctify it, cleansing it by the laver of water in the word of life (baptism), that He might present it to Himself a glorious Church—holy and without blemish. So also ought men to love their wives as their own bodies. He that loveth his wife loveth himself. For no man hateth his own flesh, but nourisheth and cherisheth it, as also Christ does the Church, because we are members of His body, of His flesh, and of His bones. 'For this cause shall a man leave his father and mother, and shall cleave to his wife, and they shall be two in one flesh' (Gn 2:24). This is a great sacrament, but I speak in Christ and in the Church."

And so, since the beginning of mankind, by the law of nature as by the law of God, in the Old as in the New Testament, marriage has always been the same institution, the unbreakable union of man and wife for the increase of the people of God. In Christianity, when the bride and bridegroom are baptized souls, members of Christ, this natural and divine union is clothed moreover with incomparable splendor; it is a sign of the close union, in love and sacrifice, of Christ and His Church, of all the souls that He has saved by His precious blood. It is just this lofty significance, this deep symbolism, which makes matrimony a sacrament—for the word "sacrament" means a "divine sign." When two Christians marry, by that very fact and at that very time their union makes real upon earth and causes to be reflected in heaven the image of Christ united to His Church, sanctifying it and causing it to bring forth many children in the faith. This is because these married people are baptized, that is to say, members of the Body of Christ. It may even happen that instead of taking place simultaneously, natural marriage and the sacrament of matrimony succeed one another. If two pagans are united solemnly and for life, their union is a true marriage that the Church acknowledges as indissoluble. If afterwards these two pagans are converted and baptized, by that very fact their marriage is raised to the dignity of a Christian sacrament, without any need of a special ceremony to make it so. From that we see that Christian marriage is not the religious blessing that the priest adds to the natural contract to make it supernatural. Among baptized people it is the contract itself, the will to give themselves to one another, that constitutes the sacrament. . . .

In what, then, does this conjugal grace consist? What are its effects? We shall discover them by reminding ourselves of the nature and end of matrimony. It is instituted to perpetuate the human race, or, more exactly, for the expansion of the people of God. Actually, contrary to what is everywhere asserted, the Church is not out for keeping up the birth rate at all costs. She does not consider that it is always better to have as many children as possible, no matter what the conditions. It is true, she severely condemns married people who limit the number of their children for selfish or interested motives or to assure a more comfortable life materially for fewer children. She also condemns those who, in order to limit the family, make use of means that allow them to take their pleasure while preventing its natural consequences. Nor even does the Church expect the married couple to have the maximum number of children regardless of the mother's health or the resources of the household to bring up the children in a worthy Christian way. Matrimony is not merely a function for the reproduction of the human species, it is the means by which we can multiply the children of God. To have the courage to have as many children as can reasonably be managed, to bring them up as Christians to bear the troubles of which they are the cause or the occasion, the courage too to refrain when reason and charity require it: that is a very important function of the grace of the sacrament of matrimony.

This grace has other more pleasing aspects. Marriage is meant to produce happiness: not for each partner to be happy independently, but for both to be happy together. Married life should be a harmony in which two parties expand and flourish with the help of one another. "They are no longer two, but one single flesh!" This is not a juxtaposition nor even an association, it is the creation of a new being, the married couple; the home, its success, its happiness, its expansion is again an effect of matrimonial grace. Love of God and one's neighbor, which is the first duty of every Christian, when it concerns married Christians is a love and friendship of a unique quality, conjugal love. It may have sprung from passion; under the influence of divine love it becomes gentle, peaceful, purified, deepened. On the contrary, it may have begun with simple esteem or benevolence: under the influence of the sacrament it takes on a tint of tenderness, confidence, delicate and firm attachment.

We must make no mistake about conjugal love. It is not mutual selfishness, each seeking only his or her own completion in the other. It is another example of the deep saying of the Gospel: he who seeks his life shall lose it; who loses his life shall find it. The bride and bridegroom must really give themselves to one another in a way that is unselfish. It is in this forgetfulness of self that both are crowned. Neither should conjugal love become an egoism by two people living as if all but themselves had ceased to exist! On the contrary, it is of the very nature of marriage that the union of two beings should lead to the creation of another being apart from themselves: the child in whom they see themselves mingled, as it were, in a single person. And this child should not be coddled by them, brought up for their own pleasure, regarded only as their consolation or their plaything. They should love and bring up the child for its own sake, for God, for society. The word hearth and home (*foyer*) should not denote something enclosed and exclusive: it suggests a source of warmth and light radiating afar.

All this sounds very beautiful. In everyday life, however, conjugal love involves many clashes of temperament, deceptions, sometimes suspicions, even infidelity or breaking away. More often, deep love sustained by supernatural charity brings into harmony all these pulling, jarring notes inherent in nature, transfigures these little vexations, is strengthened by them, so as to become more deliberate, more meritorious, and finally happier. Sometimes also there may be a complete tragedy, hopeless incompatibility, betrayal, desertion. Or again there may be separation by death, the trial of widowhood. Here again the grace of matrimony brings its healing balm and its strength. All the sacraments draw their efficacy from the cross of Jesus, and we have seen that matrimony especially reproduces the bloody espousals of the Crucified with His Church. It is then that the grace of matrimony, accompanied by the grace of baptism, the Holy Eucharist, and penance, becomes a suffering grace, a grace of renunciation, expiation, redemption, a grace bringing peace and serenity. But, like every grace as well as every cross, it is the seed and the price of glory.

Editors' Note.—From CHRIST ACTS THROUGH THE SACRAMENTS, translated by Carisbrooke Dominicans (Collegeville, Minn.: Liturgical Press, 1954) *pp. 35-136.*

The Eucharist

The Sacrifice of the Mass
M. C. D'Arcy, s.j.

The Holy Eucharist
P. Benoit, o.p.

PREFACE

There is nothing so characteristic of our contemporary life as its ceaseless movement and effort—the giant strides forward it is always making, the price in tension and anxiety it is paying for every gain. It is impossible not to respect the dignity of these characteristics of activity, history, evolution. Yet the price we are paying will be too great if we do not also find a place for rest, for receptivity, for passivity, for knowing that history, which is always on the march, has also, with Christ, arrived at its final moment and there is nothing else to do but celebrate.

The form of celebration in the Church is the marriage feast of the Eucharist. Fr. D'Arcy's chapter on the Mass as perpetual renewal of the passion and death of Christ reminds us that the Eucharist is more than the commemorating prayer to which it was reduced by the Protestant Reformers. With the actual presence of the now glorified and happy Victim Christ in the Eucharist, His promise to striving man has come true: "So also you now indeed have sorrow; but I will see you again and your heart will rejoice, and your joy no man shall take from you" (Jn 16:20-22).

The forms of Christ are now everywhere and various. Fr. Benoit illuminates for us His real presence in bread and wine, the things of man, and the mode in which this central sacrament creates His collective and communal presence in the Church.

In the midst of all our movement and concern for the future there is an exultant note in the use of the present tense by the Church as spouse of Christ when she uses the following text: "He who eats my flesh and drinks my blood has life everlasting" (Jn 6:55).

M. C. D'Arcy, s.j.

The Sacrifice of the Mass

I

To grasp the full meaning of the Mass and its likeness to and contrast
with the rite enacted by Christ at the Last Supper, the significance
of the resurrection must be borne in mind, and also the object which
led the Son of God to become man. Some repetition, therefore, is required. The object of the Son of God was, as has been stated, to restore
man to the supernatural life of union with the Trinity, and to gain
this end He made propitiation for sin, and by the same act won as
prize from His Father the glorious state of Victim and the union of
mankind with Himself through His flesh. It is noteworthy that the sublime prayer of petition and thanksgiving in which the Father is asked
that Christ's chosen ones may be in Him as He is in the Father, comes
just before or after the institution of the Eucharist. Now this end so
desired by our Lord and confidently promised by Him is, as has also
been stated, gained by the reward for His propitiatory sacrifice—
namely, the resurrection. Acceptance, as we have seen, is the extrinsic
complement of sacrifice, God making known often by some visible
sign that the sacrifice is acceptable in His sight; and to such an extent

does God's benevolence stretch that the victim, which has become His property and gracious in every sense of the word, is permitted to be the sign and means of the new alliance between the creature and the Creator, the creature acquiring grace and sacrosanct prerogatives by partaking, after the sacrifice, of the victim as at a divine banquet. With regard to the sacrifice of Calvary, then, the resurrection to life of the dead body of Christ is the sign of the Father's acceptance; the Victim slain is endowed with a special title of holiness, and it is proposed to man that he should partake of that body which has redeemed him, and so pass into that special kinship with the Father, Son, and Holy Ghost, already indirectly signified at baptism.

We can consider, then, for convenience' sake, the effect of this acceptance, in respect to Christ and in respect to redeemed mankind. Christ, the Son of God, had a human nature which, despite the hypostatic union with the Word, was in everything save sin like to ours. The presence of divinity did not make itself felt normally in any external visible manifestation, although, as we can gather from the Transfiguration, it was connatural to that human nature to be irradiated with the divine beauty and to be immortal and glorious. That human nature had a task to perform, and the suitableness of the condition it wore is seen in the *Ecce Homo* of the passion. Only after the sacrifice did that body "put on incorruption" (1 Cor 15:53), when the latent divinity raised it from the tomb and shone through its texture. By an appropriation warranted by the words of Christ Himself and St. Peter at Pentecost and St. Paul in his epistles, this resurrection is attributed to the Father, to whom the sacrifice was offered, in whose power lay the acceptance or refusal. "Therefore God hath exalted Him and given Him a name which is above every name" (Phil 2:9). Correctly, therefore, the glory which belongs to the risen Christ is said to be the reward of the Father. That glory brings with it immortality and impassibility—that is, Christ can suffer no more, He can give but not lose, He can make others like to Himself, but no longer can He endure the result of sin and obloquy. Nevertheless, the past is not wiped out; the memory of the self-sacrifice and love strong as death is not effaced; the glory that is His has a particular connection with the act which entitled Him to it; in fact, that glory is just that title, that "new name" which makes of His shame an honor, and of His sacrifice a means of interceding forever for the brethren on whose behalf He died. And this new name is that of glorious Victim. By it He is the Lord of a new race bound to Him forever by the testament of blood, to be united still more closely by eating of that body and blood of the redemption. Connatural is it to Christ to possess a glorified human nature, but only by the redemptive sacrifice could He win from the Father the new prerogative in which He could eternally rejoice— the prerogative of Victim, of Saviour. And this prerogative it is which is His forever, given over to Him as the first fruits of the redemption, the spoil of the cross, which makes that cross the symbol of triumph and the emblem of Christ. For this reason He is depicted by St. John in the Apocalypse as the Lamb slain but living; for this reason, too, does the risen Lord bear on His body the everlasting marks in His hands and feet and side, and make it known that at the Last Day the Son of Man will appear with His cross to judge the living and the dead. Glorified Victim! It is these two words that sum up the redemption and explain the Sacrifice of the Mass and the revivifying power of the flesh of Christ when communicated to the faithful.

For us, the resurrection means life with Christ. What has been said of Him is true in a subordinate sense of us. There are, however, two big differences—the first, that our risen life is, so to speak, the complement of His, what St. Paul meant by the increase, and dependent entirely on Him as the branches on the vine. The second is that we are not decorated in the court of heaven with that glory (which is our promise sown in us by grace and the Eucharist) until we have on our part merited it by the trial of faith, that faith which is the substance of things hoped for. The real agony and death Christ bore, which we symbolically and in His person underwent, whereas the reward can be said to be really ours rather than His, inasmuch as He was stainless and the natural Son of God. But we could hardly be said to share in His glory, or belong to Him, were we not to understudy Him in some way in His redemption. We could hardly be admitted to His Mystical Body if we bore no trace ourselves of victimhood, "filling up those things that are wanting in the sufferings of Christ" (Col 1:24), carrying the cross in some fashion to Calvary. Hence it is that each Christian soul as it advances in the spiritual life puts off the "old man" more and more, and dies to itself in a mystical death, that Christ triumphant may live in it. And similarly the Church and the faithful enjoy the feast of the Lamb, the foretaste of the heavenly feast, by participating, after sacrifice, of the glorious Victim. In that sacrifice the Church appropriates to itself the Victim of Calvary and makes its own that divine offering to God, surrendering itself to God, making the all-holy words of self-oblation uttered by the High Priest at the Last Supper resound through the ages in one ever-swelling chord of praise and honor and sacrifice, until the Mystical Body of Christian folk has reached its completeness, and Christ is all in all at the end of time.

To return now to the explanation of the Last Supper as the inauguration of the Mass, and the questions involved in the rite followed by our Lord. It has been shown that at the Last Supper our Lord made, as High Priest, that oblation of himself as Victim which was a necessary part of the sacrifice completed by the immolation on Calvary. While making that oblation He made a symbolic representation of the future real immolation by the separate consecration of the bread and wine into His body and His blood to be shed for the remission of sins; and His apostles were ordained to perform the same rite in memory of Him. In obedience to His command, the Church has from

222

the beginning of her history reproduced this rite in the Mass. But now between this rite of the Last Supper and that of the Mass there are certain differences, despite the identity: the first being that the Last Supper offering looked to a Victim-to-be, whereas the Mass looks backward to a past Victim, or, as that is really incorrect, to a past act of immolation on Calvary. The second is, that instead of Christ Himself being the visible High Priest, the Church, through its priesthood in His name and with His words, even to the keeping of the first person, makes the oblation in the words of consecration. The interconnection, then, of the sacrifice of Calvary which began at the Last Supper, and that of the Mass instituted at the same time, may be shortly summarized as follows. There is identity of Victim and difference in the offerer. Moreover, the Mass is a sacrifice and yet no new sacrifice to be added to that of Christ, for it borrows its reality and efficacy from Calvary and has no meaning apart from it.[1]

Now the question may well be asked: How can a sacrifice be so intimately associated with a former one as to be essentially and perfectly a sacrifice and yet not new? Is there not, then, some subterfuge here, a subterfuge invented purposely so as to preserve the Mass, and yet at the same time keep the supereminent and sufficing one great sacrifice of Calvary? Moreover, the Epistle to the Hebrews is at pains to make clear that Christ died but once: "He entered once into the Holy of Holies, having obtained eternal redemption" (Heb 9:12). To say, then, that the Mass is a sacrifice is to forswear a central dogma of the Christian faith and to make Christ die again.

This is the sharp point of the Reformers' objection against the Catholic doctrine, and, as we shall see later, it led to new activity among Catholic theologians to parry the thrust. Not that for one

●

[1] The manner after which Christ is the offerer in the Mass will, I hope, by now be apparent. The whole of this book may be said to be an explanation of the relation of Christ's priesthood to our priesthood. Nevertheless, for the sake of convenience and clarity a short summary may be added here. According to the theory defended in the text every Mass is, in one sense, a new sacrifice, but this quality of "new" does not come from a new real immolation, but from a "new" offering of a perennial victim. This "new" offering is made by the Church. I say "new," but here further qualifications are necessary. The Church does not make a "new" offering in the sense that it can make an offering independent of that of Christ. Not only is the Victim the same, but the Church is Christ continuing in His Mystical Body. All the virtue of that Body comes from Christ, its Head. Christ, therefore, can be said to be the principal offerer in the Mass, in that the members are offering by virtue of the Head; and the priesthood of the Church is, so to speak, enveloped by, or a participation of, the priesthood of Christ. The priest, then, offers by virtue of Christ; he consecrates, as St. Paschasius says, in *sacerdotio ipso Christi*. "The part which Christ's offering has is that of the principal and universal cause in its own order; our part is that of a subordinate and particular cause. And so Christ offers through our offering without Himself making any new offering in His own person. From the Church comes all that is new; from Christ, all the virtue and power" (*Mysterium fidei*, p. 296). It will be clear, then, in what sense the Mass is said not to be a "new" sacrifice in the text.

moment was there a doubt about the sacrificial nature of the Mass. That truth was imbedded as deep in the Christian faith as the truth enunciated by St. Paul in the Epistle to the Hebrews, and the Reformers were rightly impugned for perverting an issue, for changing a problem of reconciliation between two certain facts into a denial of one fact by reason of the other.[2]

How, then, make this reconciliation? Let us begin with the question of sacrifice. That the Mass is a sacrificial act is clear, for all the requisites are present—priest, victim, and oblation in a visible rite. But now straightway the question arises: How is a victim present? There is no act of immolation, no new bloodletting. As the Council of Trent asserts, the Mass is an unbloody sacrifice. The answer is shown to us in the Last Supper. There our Lord, by means of the bread and wine, represented the immolation to come. Behind the appearances were His true body and blood, so that the passion was represented symbolically by the separate consecration and the Victim really offered. Similarly, in the separate consecrations at Mass there is a symbolical immolation which serves as a visible liturgical action necessary for a true sacrifice. But that action is only symbolical or mystical; no new *real* victimizing of the flesh and blood of Christ takes place, bloody or unbloody. And the reason is simple: if the body and blood of Christ are there present on the altar, they are there in a glorious state, *and in a Victim state*. The Victim being present, the rite representing a victim, the Victim being offered, all the requisites for a sacrifice are there.

Recollect what was said about the new title which our Lord acquired in His resurrection. His body rose glorious and beautiful, but that was not all. It was fitting that the human nature of Christ should be transfigured and become a fit vesture for the divinity abiding in it. This glory was in a sense its natural due, and withheld only because it was to be an instrument of the redemption. But that its glory should be the crown of the past, that the record of the sacrifice which saved man should be an everlasting testimony and testament imprinted in that risen body—this was the gift of the Father to the Son of Man, and through Him to His brethren. Christ our Lord is not only glorified,

●

[2] One may maintain rightly, I think, against all those who attack the Mass on the ground that it denies the oneness of Christ's redemptive sacrifice, that the objection shows a radical misconception of Christianity, while the answer helps to make the essential nature of that religion clearer. Suppose a man argued that contrary powers could not issue from the same source, and that, therefore, the soul of a man could not be one because reason, say, and feeling fought against each other—the answer would be simply that the critic was confusing material and spiritual unities. It is the very nature of the human soul to possess such powers. Similarly with Christianity—the answer would be that the unity which exists in the Church between the Head and the members is precisely such as to allow one sacrifice to be distributed as it were among the members, and the critic who has not realized this, be he Rationalist or Protestant, has still to learn what is the nature of Christ's redemption.

but He is the glorified Victim, and this new status acquired by Him is His prerogative forever, and the sealing of the New Covenant made between God and the human race. Therefore, when the Church celebrates in joy and thanksgiving the memory of Calvary, it is more than a memory, because the same Victim by the words of consecration is upon the altar; and the rite is more than a memory, because it continues Calvary through time. There is no need for a new real act of immolation, for a new victimizing, because the Victim of Calvary is there in His triumph, and that there should be sacrifice, Christ should offer up that same Victim which their High Priest offered at the Last Supper in the visible mode ordained by Him.

Visible rite, victim, and oblation, the first two now are clear. It remains to say some words on the oblation. Whereas Christ offered Himself at the Last Supper, now the Church, through the ministry of her priests, offers the same Victim. This privilege of the Church implies some mysterious identity between her and our Lord, and the identity is expressed in her title of the Mystical Body of Christ. The same truth we have so often had occasion to bring forward before is again the clue, a truth so pregnant with meaning that to pass it over as a luxury of our faith or to misconceive it as non-Catholics unfortunately do, is to miss the core of Christ's thought and intention in redeeming us and instituting the Christian religion.

In dying on the cross our Lord was the representative of man making atonement for sin against God. As He bore our sins, so His reward is ours; as we went with Him on the way of the cross to a mystical death of pain and a real death to sin, so we rose with Him really redeemed and mystically incorporated into His life. In the Epistle to the Ephesians St. Paul tells them that he is praying that they may come to know "the hope of God's calling and the riches of the glory of His inheritance in the saints, and what is the exceeding greatness of His power towards us who believe, according to the operation of the might of His power, which He wrought in Christ, raising Him up from the dead and setting Him on His right hand in the heavenly places, above all principality and power, and virtue and dominion, and every name that is named, not only in this world, but also in that which is to come. And He hath subjected all things under His feet and hath made Him head over all the Church, which is His body and the fulness of Him who is filled all in all" (Eph 1:18-23).

This Mystical Body, the Church, is, then, by its very name so one with Christ that it can offer the same Victim without multiplying the sacrifice. He is the Head and we are the members, and this Mystical Body grows until Christ reaches that plenitude at the end of the ages. St. Paul says that once he knew Christ according to the flesh, but knew Him so no longer, for the old things had passed away. The Jesus whom the apostles had known and touched before the resurrection did not stay amongst them during the forty days succeeding it, and at His appearances He was somehow different, so that it needed the eyes of faith to see Him. It behoved Him to go away, for otherwise the Holy Spirit would not come, the Holy Spirit that was to wed the risen Victim with those whose life was to be in Him, with the Church, His spouse. After Pentecost the risen Christ lives still amongst us, but invisibly in that visible body which is His, the Church, and in that source of life and union, the Eucharist, where He is disguised under the appearances of bread and wine. The Church, therefore, may be called the extension of Christ, the continuation of Christ, the Victim and Saviour, through time, visible as He was, holy as He is, and one in a sacred seamless union which must not be torn. And the Eucharist is the life of that body, the mode of incorporation or the marriage feast, where Christ and His spouse are made one flesh and one spirit.

It is in keeping, therefore, with God's plan that the Eucharist should have been instituted under the appearance of bread and wine. The risen Jesus was to be disguised, to be represented and made visible by those to whom He gave life. They had been the object of His love, they now were to play the part of Christ, to realize in themselves His love, to come to see for themselves the union that was theirs with Him and with one another. And this requires faith and hope and charity, the response and the acceptance of the inheritance. Jesus Christ is, as it were, passive, having done His part, having paid the price of sin and made the way to union easy through His flesh and blood. He is therefore passive—passive as a Victim which His people can actively offer. He stands at the door of the soul, but does not enter if the bride has fallen asleep or will not open for Him; His grace is there anticipating, collaborating, perfecting, but it requires collaboration. The saving of souls, the well-being of the Church, His spouse, are made dependent on the charity of the members—in fine, though redeemed, we are left with our free will to accept that redemption or not. Our Lord is a risen Victim, and therefore we are risen with Him, and our life is lived in the promise of full realization in heaven, but it is by faith. Our Lord is a Victim, but the servant is not greater than his Master, and consequently we have to go to the Mass and ourselves offer the Victim, joining our own body and soul with Him as a gift to God, and receiving in return the supernatural union with the Son of God. Through the emptying of ourselves, the pouring out of our gift, we pass to the plenitude of Christ.

That is one reason why the body and blood are hidden under the appearance of bread and wine. But if it be asked why bread and wine instead of any other forms, then the reply might be that bread and wine were offered in sacrifice by Melchisedech, according to whose order of priesthood was Christ. But as it was the offering of Christ which determined that of Melchisedech, the reality being the exemplar of the prophetic type, a simpler and better answer lies in the aptitude of bread and wine to signify the purpose of our Lord's choice. Bread and wine are the forms of food and drink which in all ages and in nearly every land have been the readiest and most common diet of mankind. So true is this that overhasty anthropologists have traced the divinities of various lands to the aboriginal tendency to create gods out of these necessaries of life, as a Ceres from corn and a Dionysus from the grape. Our Lord, then, who intended that His own body and blood should be the food and sustenance of our supernatural life, naturally chose what in a lower order were the equivalents. And this equivalence and analogy give us further insight into the purposes of Christ. The Victim is to be our food, the body that was to be the means of our redemption was to be the means, too, of our incorporation with the risen life, the reward of the redemption. And so in the Sacrifice of the Mass there comes a new note, a note of joy and exultation and thanksgiving, for the sacrifice is now pre-eminently eucharistic. "Amen, amen, I say to you that you shall lament and weep, but the world shall rejoice; and you shall be made sorrowful, but your sorrow shall be turned into joy. A woman when she is in labor hath sorrow, because her hour is come; but when she hath brought forth the child, she remembereth no more the anguish, for joy that a man is born into the world. So alas you now indeed have sorrow; but I will see you again and your heart shall rejoice, and your joy no man shall take from you" (Jn 16:20-22). The sacrifice begun at the Last Supper and continued through the passion to its bloody end on the cross was the travail of Christ that He might bring forth a new creature. And that these new creatures might enjoy the fruits of that passion and see Him again and be in Him and He in them, He instituted a rite under the symbols of food in which that body and blood of His, a Victim yet glorious and a principle of new life, might be the means of a joyous sacrifice offered by those incorporated with Him, and be the very means of incorporation into the superabounding divine life of peace and union with Himself.

This intricate and divinely contrived plan of God, whereof the Incarnation, death of Christ and resurrection, and Eucharist of the Church are the mysterious parts, is described in a way which recalls all that has been so far set forth by an unknown writer, once thought to be St. Augustine, in a sermon on the Nativity. "For today He cometh forth from the holy thalamus—that is, from the secret and uncontaminated hiding-place of the Blessed Virgin's womb. He cometh forth thence, the Son of a Virgin, the Spouse of a Virgin; the Son that is of Mary, the Spouse of the Church. For it was to the universal Church that the Apostle spoke when he said, 'I have mated you to one man to show yourself a chaste virgin to Christ.' It is to these nuptials of Christ that the peoples of all races are invited; it is they who have filled the Church, they who have received from the Lord's table no mean feast, no ignoble drink; but they have tasted in anticipation the flesh and blood of the slain Christ Himself. He, the innocent Lamb, was slain for His own marriage feast. He was slain for the nuptial feast, and whomsoever He hath invited He has fed on His own flesh. By dying He hath prepared the feast. In rising [from the dead] He hath celebrated the nuptials. By dying He endured the sufferings of His own free will. By rising he taketh the hand of the bride made ready. In the womb of a Virgin He took on human flesh as a pledge; on the cross He shed His blood, a dowry beyond price! In His resurrection and ascension He hath sealed the troth of an everlasting marriage." [3]

II

It is now time to gather up the various threads in the mystery of the redemption and point out one or two conclusions. The sacrifice of Calvary is an act begun at the Last Supper and ending with the death of Christ on Calvary, an offering of Himself-to-be-slain in a rite, and the long-sustained suffering which was closed by the slaying of the Victim after three hours upon the cross. That sacrifice is accepted by the Father, and in token of it the Victim is raised from the dead, clothed with honor, and made to sit at the right hand of God, the Lord of glory and of a new race, a Figure in perpetual intercession for those bought with a great price. The key to this sacrifice is the identity of Priest and Victim, the offerer with the offered, because owing to that identity the oblation once made persists and constitutes one moral action of a number of acts extending over many hours. Furthermore, that identity explains how it is that the Mass derives all its efficacy from the one sacrifice of the redemption and yet can continue through subordinate oblations as long as time shall last. There is one Victim forever, but because of the union signified at the resurrection and sealed by the coming of the Holy Ghost at Pentecost, Christians can offer in the present without making a new sacrifice.

The key, on the other hand, to the Sacrifice of the Mass is the new status of Christ risen from the dead—namely, that of glorious Victim. These two words are the alpha and omega of the New Testament, the two panels of the diptych of the redemption. Christ as High Priest offered Himself once as Victim; we can, so to speak, take the same Victim in our hands and offer up a gift of infinite value to God; we are admitted to the privilege of making a supreme act of worship. Again, as that Victim was the propitiation for sin, we, too, can offer up the same Victim of infinite value as a propitiatory offering in atonement and as satisfaction for our own sins and the sins of the world, and demand with an assurance warranted by the worth of an offering benefits for ourselves and others and greater love and union from the Father of the Victim. Lastly, our offering can and should be one of exultation and thanksgiving, a memorial of the love strong as death of God for us, and a bridal song of joy at the celebration of the marriage feast of the Son with His spouse the Church and our own selves. The Mass is, indeed, pre-eminently eucharistic, what Léon Bloy described as "an agony of holocaust accompanied by nuptial songs." St. Augustine I think it was who points out that whereas the

●

[3] Among the works of St. Augustine, *Serm.* 372, 2 (*PL* 39, 1662).

first consecration was in the evening, the night on which He was betrayed, the Mass is a sacrifice of the dawn and has in it the joy and ecstasy at the rising of the sun, that Daystar that knows no setting. "Maturatae resurrectionis laetabunda solemnia." And as we know from tradition that the early Church looked upon the Mass and spoke of it in terms of thanksgiving and praise, it is not farfetched to read into the words of St. Paul, in the very epistle in which the singleness of the sacrifice of the redemption is so thoroughly emphasized, a reference to the Mass: "By Him, therefore, let us offer up the sacrifice of praise always to God—that is, the fruit of lips confessing to His Name." [4]

And again, is there not a more than fortuitous consonance between the expression used, say, by Pliny in describing the morning meetings and prayers of the Christians, and the *sacrificium laudis* of the Mass, "qui tibi offerunt hoc sacrificium laudis tibique reddunt vota sua"? If we keep in mind that to the early Christians the Mass was preeminently a sacrifice of praise and thanksgiving prepared not with a knife or any real physical immolation, but by the all-holy words of consecration, we may be enabled to read the secret of many mysterious expressions to be found in the early literature of the Christian Church.

And now the reason why the Mass in distinction from the Last Supper is a joyous sacrifice is contained in the first epithet given to Christ the Victim. He is a perennial Victim, therefore a sacrifice; He is a glorious Victim, therefore a joyous sacrifice. The Church is the bride bought with a great price and introduced into the divine household. She has left the valley of the shadow of sin to dwell in faith in the paradise which the Bridegroom on the cross of pain saw awaiting Dismas, the good thief, and Himself, as the reward for this sacrifice. Dead to sin, she has risen with Christ and is incorporated in Him. Consequently, the Mass is the memorial of a sacrifice which has conquered death. It is the representation of the redemptive act, and a taste or foretaste by faith of its result. It is the act of the Mystical Body, of which Christ is the Head, and at the same time the very process of incorporation. The Head at the Last Supper consecrated His body to be slain on the morrow. The members consecrate daily the same body that was slain. The difference between past and future is the difference between sorrow and joy, between the travail to be

●

[4] The words "fruit of lips confessing" are at first sight disconcerting, but they refer probably to the Septuagint reading in Hos 14:3, ἀνταποδώσομεν καρπὸν χειλέων ἡμῶν: "We will make offering of the fruit of our lips." The "good news" of the Mass seems also indicated in Rom 15:15-16: "That I should be the minister of Jesus Christ among the Gentiles, sanctifying the gospel of God, that the oblation of the Gentiles may be made acceptable and sanctified in the Holy Ghost." The Greek word for "sanctifying" the good news is ἱερουργοῦντα, and that for oblation and sanctifying, προσφορά and ἡγιασμένη. In Père de la Taille's commentary on the passage (pp. 197-99), the words of St. Paul are shown to be closely connected with the sacrifice of our Lord as Victim. The words themselves are stronger in the Greek than in the translation: ἀναφέρωμεν θυσίαν αἰνέσεως.

undergone and the joy that a new child is born into the world. The Victim the Church offers is a glorious Victim, and the Church which offers is the *plebs sancta,* the people who have seen a great light and have been illumined by that light. To them it is given to celebrate in their turn the sacrifice which was for their salvation, in order that they may appropriate what is theirs by their own act, that they may play the part which really belongs to them, of being as gods, of participating in the divine drama of the redemption, and so putting on divinity. They can worship, satisfy, and demand as neither Abel nor Abraham nor Melchisedech were ever able to worship or demand, and the wonder and glory of the sacrifice is that they can in this way appropriate the sacrifice and make it separately and individually a means to merit and approach God, and yet rely on its divine properties as being the sacrifice of the Son of God. More than that, they can give thanks to God the Father that they are one with the Son, one because the sacrifice is theirs through their solidarity with Christ, and one really and by no figure of speech in the fruits indissolubly connected with that sacrifice, by the participation and transformation into the glorified body of their Redeemer.

In the first chapter, the redemption was portrayed as a plan of Almighty God to gain a certain end. That end was said to consist in the elevation of the finite creature man into the divine life of the Holy Trinity. The project seemed to involve insuperable difficulties, for how could a creature be finite and infinite at the same time—that is, keep his independent finite personality and still participate in the divine nature, especially, too, as that creature was alienated from God by sin and a debtor to His justice? The solution was worthy of God, and after the event we can have a never-ending delight in studying it and finding ever fresh manifestations of divine craftsmanship.

If we look at creation, there are clear indications, as St. Thomas Aquinas observed, of a hierarchy not only in kinds of being, but in primeval and elemental qualities and relations. There is, for instance, a gradual ascension in the purity and beauty of love and the kinds of union possible between one creature and another. That is to say that the most perfect love and union which will be found in the Godhead will have its analogy in the hierarchy of creation. Now we have an ineffable union in the Godhead, so close that it is a mystery, though a luminous mystery. On the other hand, starting from creation, we have a union between rational creatures by means of marriage, which adumbrates and symbolizes the mystery of the Trinity, though at such a remove that we might expect other forms of union to exist higher than that of marriage, bridging the gulf between human and divine love. This expectation is realized in the revelation of the Word made flesh and the redemption. A unity is achieved of which marriage is a symbol, where we find two in one flesh, one body, and one spirit, a derivative in turn of a union of two natures, one human and one divine, in a single Person; which in its own turn soars up to the consummate union of three Persons in one nature. The Word, the Second Person, is made flesh, and the whole world is affected by this condescension and suffers a change "into something rich and strange." The Incarnation, then, gives an indelible significance to all creation, but particularly will this be visible where the Word has fixed His abode, in the life He institutes, the life He chose to lead in a human nature, and in the life of that body which has been sanctified by the Holy Spirit and united with Himself for all time. If we look for Christ now, we shall not find Him far from the haunts of men, but still incarnate, one flesh and one Spirit with that visible body the Church, the bride. There, as in the old Arabian epilogue, the Lover has said to the beloved: "It is no longer I but you," and bidden searchers after Him look for Him where alone He makes Himself visible, in the Church, in the Mystical Body.

The Incarnation, therefore, revealed as possible, because real, a union between the finite and the infinite. Nevertheless this union was not the goal at which God was aiming. The Word made flesh was one person with two natures, and human personality, once given to human beings, was not to be withdrawn. Hence the Incarnation is the beginning of redemption, but not the end; the clue, but not the solution itself. In His human nature Christ suffered and atoned for sins, and the instrument of the atonement became by the Father's acceptance the instrument of communion with the Trinity. Being glorified, it generated new life; it could give of itself without diminution, for the higher the form of life the more is it communicative of itself; just as a human mind of a master communicates itself to a pupil without loss, whereas a natural human body has no such powers. The glorified body of Christ being next to God Himself in excellence, owing to the hypostatic union, communicates its life to those who participate of it, raising them to a level which can, with restrictions, be said to be as high as its own. And so it comes about that those initiated into the mystery of the risen Victim become His new body, His Mystical Body, as it is called, to mark the difference between what has no personality of its own but God's, and what is united corporally but with a finite personality left intact. The life of the Trinity is shared by the human nature of Christ, because that nature, though finite, belongs personally to the Son, and the life of the Trinity, too, is shared by all those who are one flesh and one spirit with Christ, for they are one with the body of Christ. They are, therefore, derivatively united with the Godhead, being heirs and coheirs with Christ.

Such is the plan of the redemption, and it is all, so to speak, codified and translated into the Mass. In that sacrificial action mankind stands before God, confessing its sins, but already forearmed against the wrath of God by the knowledge of what is to come. It is confident in the acceptable character of the Victim to be offered, the Son of Man, and the Word made flesh. The one sacrifice is enacted, the offering is made of the body and blood of Christ under the species of bread and wine, separated to symbolize ritually the immolation of Calvary; and we can picture the Last Supper with the High Priest giving thanks and blessing and breaking the bread, and watch the features of that High Priest change. The words remain, the first person singular of the Head and Author of redemption, but the face is the face of every Christian priest and every Christian offerer, the voice as of many waters, the new Mystical Body of Christ offering in His name, one with Him in that union indescribable, which allows of separate individuality and yet corporate identity, of private gain without addition to the merit and suffering of Calvary, of manifold, ever-growing membership with singleness of life. The Head and members meet together in that one oblation which brought redemption and union, and consummate that union in the divine feast which closes the Mass. The bride celebrates in her turn the victory through death which brought her a willing captive to Christ. She glorifies God and appropriates the fruits of the sacrifice and enters fully upon her divine life with the Godhead by becoming one flesh with the body of her Lord.

Many are the consequences of this ordinance of God and the privileges of Christ's Church. Some, indeed, are so illustrative of the argument just proposed that a word about them is required in the succeeding chapters, but there is one point which is in place here and now. The Reformers of the sixteenth century, in their zeal to purify the Church of the abuses and errors that had crept in, went back to the primitive conditions for their ideal, and among the superstitious and debased additions to the pure doctrines of Christ they counted the Mass. Hence, Protestantism has never been able to erect an altar to God or offer a real sacrifice. Its priesthood has confined itself, or should have confined itself, to a commemorative service, to the administration of the "Sacrament" and the ministry of the Word; so that, in the Reformation, Christianity lost its unity and the Reformers the Mass. The Reformers urged that the Mass as a sacrifice implied that the one sacrifice of Calvary was not complete, that it derogated from the dignity of the one redemptive act, whereas if the place and significance of the Mass have been rightly described, where they found disparity there the secret of Christian unity lay, the unity of membership with the Head. No wonder, then, that outside the Catholic Church there is no unity in Christendom, for human conceiving will never arrive at a substitute for the supernatural unity planned and supported by God. And that there should be a unity is so clearly demanded and promised by Christ, significantly enough, too, at the Last Supper, that its absence is a clear mark of the absence of Christ Himself. He intended but one division, and that a symbolic one—the separate consecration, to wit, of His sacred body and blood—a division signifying sacrifice and leading on to the reward of sacrifice, identification with Himself. His people are united as "living stones built up, a spiritual house, a holy priesthood," as the Mystical Body of Christ, so that it is as impious to cause dismemberment and schism in this Mystical Body and separate it from its High Priest, the glorious Victim, as it is to separate the human nature of Christ from His Godhead, claiming for it a personality of its own. The Church of Christ is inseparable from its Founder; it is visible as containing the mystery of the Incarnation, it is ever identical and yet ever increasing; it is holy because it is sanctified by the Holy Spirit, the bond of love between God and His elect; it is sacerdotal by right of adoption into the priesthood of Christ by its association with the blood of the Redeemer and its wedlock with the glorified perennial Victim. None of these prerogatives can be ignored, and justly the Church is jealous of its rights and will not sacrifice one or jot or tittle of them or make any bargain for the sake of bringing into the fold the warring sections of Christendom. There is no superfluous dogma which can be surrendered for the sake of peace. The supernatural life of union with Christ is as genuinely and fundamentally dependent on the supreme sacerdotal character and ecclesiastical lordship of the pope, the vicar of Christ, as on the divinity and body of Christ. The voice of God made man is heard in the Sacrifice of the Mass at the words of consecration, and the guarantee of that identity between the offerer and the High Priest is the sacerdotal dignity founded in the Mystical Body and dispensed by the successors of the apostles and by the chosen vicegerent of Christ, the successor of St. Peter. And the same infallible voice of God travels down the ages, the voice distinctly heard in the living traditions of the Church and today in the clear authority of the high priest, to whose care have been committed the keys of the kingdom of heaven.

III

The Sacrifice of the Mass is the offering of the Victim by the Church. Jesus Christ offered Himself at the Last Supper. He suffered once on the cross, and now He, the Victim of the passion, is offered by His Church. It is time, then, to consider what this privilege means to the Church.

The Mass is the centerpiece of the Church's devotion and the principle and assurance of its life, and in no way can the loving forethought of Christ be so well understood as in the realization of the significance of the Mass. Christ died at a certain place and at a certain time, and it might be supposed that even the work of a God made man would be restricted by the conditions of time and place. But it is not so. What concerns every Christian was to be made present in such a way that no one would have to look back upon a far-off event growing more and more dim as the years receded from it. The redemption had as its fruit salvation, but the fruit if severed from the tree, be it preserved ever so well, has not the freshness of an ever-present vine, and the means of salvation are a poor substitute for the Saviour Himself whom St. John saw and handled. Therefore, by an exercise of divine power instigated by love, Christ so provided that those who believed in Him should be able really and truly to offer Him up, to come to the foot of the cross and make Him their propitiatory Victim to the Father. He gave His life a ransom for many, but while this ransom was paid once and for all, nevertheless each and every purchased soul could offer in his own person, by offering the same infinite Victim for his own profit. The propitiation was made for no nameless multitude, for Christ calls His flock by name, and the redemption is as much whole and entire for each single soul as it is for the world at large. The Mass, therefore, is truly the center of the Christian life, because it is the continuation of the sacrifice of Calvary through time, the adaptation of the redemption to the needs of men born after the coming of Christ. All may drink of the chalice of His blood, because its fulness is never diminished, and its presence is ensured to mankind. In other words, all love is reciprocal. Our Lord loved His own to the extreme of love and showed it by the shedding of His blood. This is all that a lover could do; and for that act to be profitable, there was need of a response, an acceptance, an act on the part of the beloved. Therefore He continues as the passive Victim, and the Church is now active and does her part by reciprocating freely the love of Christ and so making it complete and efficacious for herself. This response is the Mass, which is the active offering by the Church of the Victim of Calvary and the appropriation of the infinite merits of the redemption by the priest and the faithful.

From this truth can be deduced the part of the Church, the priest, and the congregation in the Mass, and the fruits each can derive. But before this can be completely understood, the oblation of the Mass must be made clear as being that of the Mystical Body, otherwise a link in the argument would be missing. The Church has the power to offer the divine sacrifice, because it is one with Christ. The Christian is a suppliant at the shrine of God's mercy, but he approaches with confidence, not only because his offering is most acceptable, but because *personam Christi gerit;* he comes in the person of Christ and is, in fact, so intimately related to Christ that his supernatural life is not other than that of the High Priest. He is a living member of an organism whose Head is the risen Lord. This new status of mortal man is the fruit of the redemption given to him through the exaltation of Christ from the grave. The resurrection spelt a new status for our Lord, and that new status is conferred upon all who participate in the life-giving glorified body of the Victim by Communion and its antecedent and preparatory sacrament, baptism.

The Mass, therefore, may be said to be the holy place to which all the most sublime truths of the Christian faith converge and whence they issue. The sacrificial and a propitiatory aspect of the redemption is perpetuated by the presence of the Victim of Calvary. By offering up this Victim the world concurs with the wish of Christ to save it, and adds the assent which was necessary as a condition to make the living act of reparation by Christ efficacious. It follows, therefore, that the fruits of the redemption are laid at the disposal of the faithful in the Mass. Secondly, the primary effect of the redemption—namely, elevation into a supernatural order of union with Christ and so with the Blessed Trinity—is condition and consummation of the Mass. For only those who are so united with Christ as to be one with Him can offer a sacrifice which will be identical with that of Calvary. Were it not in some sort Christ who continued to offer, the Mass would be a new sacrifice and supplement that of Calvary, if such a thing were possible. In fact, it is impossible, for a new sacrifice, being human, would be incommensurate with that of the Son of God. Consequently, the Mass is subordinated to that of Calvary and yet can be said to be identical with it, inasmuch as the participation of the members in the infinite act of the Head is a subordinate act, whose value is derived from the virtue of that Head. The point is that the offerers of the Mass are participants of the grace of Jesus Christ and, in a limited though an exact sense, divine themselves. And the manner in which they are sharers of the divine nature is by their incorporation with Christ by becoming "one flesh and one spirit" with Him in the Communion, which ends the sacrificial action of the Mass, as the resurrection was the complement of the passion.

From these truths, which may be shortly summarized as the Church the offerer, and the offerer the Mystical Body, certain consequences can be drawn. The Church, under Christ, is the offerer in every Mass. The sacrifice is made by the Church by the means of priests, as the Council of Trent expressly declares. And the reason is that the Church is the Mystical Body of Christ, one and inseparable into parts or fractions. Apart from that Body no one can act representatively or by divine agency. The separated member is dead so far as the divine virtue infused into the Body is in question, whereas the member, when properly functioning, does so by the power of the whole Body. Hence, in every Sacrifice of the Mass, no matter whether the priest be without a congregation or accompanied by the multitudes that fill St. Peter's, it is the Church as one Body which offers through his ministry. In a true sense, then, the Church is composed of "a holy priesthood to offer up spiritual sacrifices acceptable to God, by Jesus Christ" (1 Pt 2:5). All who are baptized have what the theologians call an inchoative priesthood, for they participate in the life and power of Christ, who was the Victim and Priest, and are united with Him in the redemptive character. He "has made us to our God a kingdom and priests" (Ap 5:10).

This sublime dignity which belongs to the faithful is not always realized as it should be, for the laity are prone to forget that the Masses which are being celebrated throughout the world are being offered by them as members of the Mystical Body, and the fruit of these Masses is increased or diminished by the degree of holiness they possess. The Reformation is again to blame for the comparative ignorance of the laity of their sublime privilege, because the Reformers wished to destroy the distinction between priest and layman, apportioning to the latter what is not his—to wit, the full sacramental and sacerdotal character—and as a result the Church had to insist on the impassable abyss between the two states.

Nevertheless, it is sad that Catholics are not more aware of their intimate participation in the Mass. The prevalence of the phrase "hear Mass" is an indication how little they appreciate their privilege, for it suggests a service in which they have as little part as an audience listening to an oratorio, and the result is that a congregation is dissociated from its very life, while the Mass becomes for the slack a Sunday obligation, and for the pious an opportunity of practising their private and favorite devotions. This is not as it should be. And, again, how few Catholics encourage that supernatural sense that they are co-operators in the daily mystery of the altar as it is celebrated in every land and at every hour. Virtue goes out from them, for they are one with that company of the saints which continues the redemption to the end of time. Their lives are supernaturally a perpetual intercession; their strength is that of the Mystical Body, in which abides the spirit of the Redeemer, the glorious Victim. Hence the voice of the Church in the liturgy of the Mass is answered by the unceasing affirmative, Amen, inaudibly spoken in the depths of a soul living in sanctifying grace, and each Christian is invisibly present at the sacrifice of the Victim on earth as he will, in glory, be present at the adoration of the Lamb in heaven.

An appreciation of this truth makes a great difference to the outlook of the Christian. He can feel himself supported through the day invisibly by those who are one with him, by being one with the Victim, and himself can co-operate with his fellow Christians in the missionary endeavors in heathen countries, in the ministry of the sick, the oppressed, and afflicted, in the supplications to God to avert calamity and bring graces to strangers and friends. His life, too, is elevated to a higher order; it is being disposed of by the Holy Spirit in the ever-continuing redemptive work of Christ, and by union with Christ, the perpetual Victim, all that he does has a eucharistic value, a part in the voice of praise which goes up from the earth to the Father. The sentence of the New Testament, that we should take up our cross daily and follow Christ, is capable of indefinite application when taken in the context of the perpetual sacrifice of Christ. His Mystical Body not only offers, but is offered with Him, and this explains why the Church has always taught the value of vicarious suffering and nurtured special victim saints whose alliance with Christ upon the cross and in the Mass has averted the deserved chastisement from a sinning people. In this sense the agony of Christ, as Pascal rhetorically declared, is, in fact, continued to the end of the world.

That the Mass is the corporate action of the Church is indicated in various passages of the liturgy. The priest speaks in the Canon of the Mass of the gifts which "he offers to God for the holy Catholic Church, for the pope and bishop of the diocese, and for all true believers who keep the Catholic and apostolic faith." Again, just before the Consecration he asks God to receive the offering which "we thy servants and thy whole household make unto thee," and after the Consecration, the *plebs sancta* it is which is mentioned as offering. "We thy servants, as also thy holy people, do offer unto thy most excellent majesty of thine own gifts bestowed upon us. . . ."

It is to this *plebs sancta* incorporated in Christ, and bound thereby in the bonds of charity and peace, as the liturgy so admirably teaches after the Pater Noster, that every Catholic belongs, and the greater his holiness, the greater is the holiness of the holy people and the greater the power of the impetration of the Mass. It has been well said that the presence of our Lady on earth after the ascension must have made the offering of the sacrifice by the early Church ever so much more fruitful and helped to the rapid spread of the Christian faith; and in a less degree, the presence of hidden saints, and the sanctification of many souls in the Church of today, draw down upon the world with greater abundance the graces won by the Victim of infinite worth.

But besides being the corporate offering of the Church, the Mass is more particularly that of the congregation, the stipend offerer, and the priest. The priest holds a twofold function: he is the minister of Christ and also the minister of the Church. As Christ's minister he has the instrumental power derived from Christ of consecrating and doing what our Lord did. As the minister of the Church he is its procurator and stands in its place and in its name offering the infinite Victim. He is the *organum ecclesiae electum*, made sacred for the office and with the sole power of performing the symbolical immolation in which the Church's offering is fully expressed and realized. It is clear, then, that this participation in the sacrifice is the most intimate given to any human creature, and that the Mass can be said, in a sense, to belong to him, as, to use Père de la Taille's image, sight belongs perfectly to the eye, though it is the whole man who sees. For this reason the Church assigns to the officiating priest a grace which is his own and inalienable, and a power of applying the Mass to some particular intention of his own choosing or supplied to him by those whose stipends he accepts. For the same reason the Church demands uncommon holiness, as witness the words from the ordination service. In various places in the Mass he asks God to bestow on him the grace to be less unworthy, and naturally so, since the application of the infinite merits of the redemption depends in part on the holiness of the Church and of himself.[5]

●

[5] As all Catholics know, the merits of the redemption are infinite and the propitiatory value of the Victim is not affected by the good or bad estate of

Nearest to the priest in their share in the sacrifice come those for whose intention, as the expression goes, the Mass is offered. These are the stipend offerers, though that expression hides the full significance of their participation. The Sacrifice of the Mass is, it must be remembered, after the manner of Melchisedech, and therefore a sacrifice by means of the symbols of bread and wine. They are necessary materials which the priest consecrates by the form of words, changing them into the body and blood of Christ. The faithful, therefore, provide something. In a remote sense they can be said even to provide an offering; for though the real offering is Christ Himself, nevertheless, by the mode of offering instituted by Himself, that offering cannot be made unless there are present certain materials specified by Christ which are to be transubstantiated. The providers, therefore, of the bread and wine, or their equivalents, can be said to have prepared the sacrifice, made it possible, and to share by their gifts more intimately in the sacrifice.

Add to this another law, that these gifts or their equivalents save the priest the expense of providing for the sacrifice and enable him to live by the altar, as the minister of the congregation and the Church, and we can see how the custom of giving stipends came to be established. The priest dedicated to the service of the altar is free to discharge his duties, while the faithful provide for his wants by sustaining him with their gifts. These gifts are considered as the means whereby he can celebrate the Mass, and so these offerers share in the Mass by the right of their offerings, while the priest offers his Mass for their intentions. In this way it may be seen how the simplified method nowadays of allocating a definite sum of money in lieu of gifts represents the agelong practice of participating in the sacrifice by providing the material.

In the early days of Christianity it was considered a very high privilege to be allowed to join in this special way in the oblation of the Mass. One of the felt penalties of excommunication was the loss of this privilege, and public sinners also were deprived for a time of the right. Significantly St. Ambrose wrote to the Emperor Theodosius after the Thessalonian massacre: "Then will you offer when the power of offering the sacrifice shall have been granted to you. Then, when your Victim shall have become acceptable to God!" It is only natural, indeed, that this special offering should be esteemed highly. The return of the priest for the materials provided or the stipend is to offer the Mass for the intentions of the giver. By this act the fruit of the Mass is first and foremost, if not totally, applied to the benefit of the stipend giver; and since the Mass is the corporate act of the Church, the prayer and holy estate of all its members are directed to the advantage of one individual. His name appears in the liturgy at the

the priest, congregation, and Church. Nor, again, is the Eucharist as a sacrament affected. The degree of holiness in the offerer affects the application of those merits.

Memento, and his petition, instead of being that of a private and single almsman, becomes that of the holy and universal body of the faithful united to the sacrosanct and all-pleasing Victim, Jesus Christ.

Within, then, the Church—that is, the Body which offers the Victim —the priest holds by right the first position, and after him come the stipend offerers. Closely associated again with the priest in the Mass are those actually present at the sacrifice. They are better off than those who cannot attend, for not only does explicit and official union surpass the absent and collective assent, but they take an active part in the rite itself; just as, one may say, the server enables the priest to proceed by the responses. The Mass becomes, as it were, the special privilege of the group or family present; they are like the holy women who were near the cross and were the first to experience its power in their meeting with our Lord in the risen-Victim life. The server at Mass speaks for those present; they, through him, carry on the dialogue with the priest at the foot of the altar, telling him to be of good courage, and with him they implore the blessing of the Kyrie. In High Mass at the Offertory, the deacon recites with the celebrant the *offerimus tibi calicem*. A little later the priest turns round and begs his brethren to pray that the sacrifice may be acceptable; and at the beginning of the more solemn part of the sacrifice the faithful once more assure the priest of their collaboration and bid him, without fear, carry out his sacred function. Their Amen ratifies and almost commands. Comforted by their presence, the priest breaks out with the great preface of praise which preludes the coming of the Lord. Fittingly, at the end of this part of the Mass, priest and faithful again break the silence, kept so strictly save for the exclamation *Nobis quoque peccatoribus*. An Amen precedes the Pater Noster, and from then onward the congregation is at one with the priest, in the unity and kiss of peace and in Communion.

Such, then, are the varying degrees in which the Church and its members participate in the Sacrifice of the Mass. Christ, our Head, the High Priest and Victim, speaks to the Father the words of intercession and offers Himself through the Mystical Body, which is Himself, by the ministry of the priests and His holy people. All take part in the offering, and to make the sacrifice propitious in full measure for themselves they should, on their part, set themselves on the altar as victims united with the one Victim. All participate, but the closer one is to the mystery, the more does one ally oneself with Christ and share the fruits of the Mass, first by right of order and dignity the priest, then the stipend offerers, next the congregation, and last the body of the faithful who, when in grace, are never far from Calvary and the risen Victim.

Editors' Note.—From THE MASS AND THE REDEMPTION (London: Burns Oates & Washbourne, 1926) *pp. 58-90, 110-25.*

P. Benoit, O.P.

The Holy Eucharist

OUR LORD instituted the Holy Eucharist because He wished to remain with men until the end of the world, not only through the presence of His Spirit, but also of His body, and precisely of that body which was crucified and raised for them, that body from which their new life flows, as water from a spring. To reveal the theological riches of this mystery we intend to show that it brings about a *presence*: a presence *in time* first of all, namely, that time between the past of the cross and the future of our heavenly glory; a presence in space also, namely, a presence which *affects our bodily senses*; but more than that, a *physical and real* presence whereby we receive the Lord's body itself. And since this risen body is the nucleus of the new world, this mystery brings about a *collective* presence where we meet in Christ the whole of His body which is the Church. After considering these different aspects, we shall show in conclusion how this sacrament contains the *sacrifice* of Christ, His sacrifice which is also ours, and how this sacrifice is prolonged upon our altars by a *permanent* presence.

PRESENT HERE AND NOW

At first sight this might seem surprising: does not the rite suggest rather a remembrance of the past? "Do this in memory of me": we commemorate the death of our Lord, an event which took place two thousand years ago; how can we speak of His being present except in our memories of Him? It is true that our Lord also spoke of the new wine which He would drink with His disciples in the kingdom of the Father; but this leads us towards a future which only exists in expectation, that future when we shall be reunited with Him after the Parousia. Between our Lord's departure and His return there is only His absence.

As a matter of fact this is the impression given by the way the Supper is celebrated in certain Protestant circles. They recall that Christ died for us and rejoice at the prospect of rejoining Him some day; but in the meantime He is not there. The tension existing between the past and the future has even suggested a duality of sources to certain critics. According to them there were in the primitive Church two different ways of celebrating the Lord's Supper; in Jerusalem it was a joyful meal, taken with the risen Christ, and a meal during which they prepared themselves for His imminent return. But among the communities founded by St. Paul, such as that at Corinth, it was a funeral meal by which they commemorated the death of the Lord, and in which, according to a rite borrowed from the Hellenistic mysteries, they believed they were sharing in His sacrificed body. In the first case, then, the Lord's Supper was a simple fraternal banquet with no sacramental value, which was oriented towards the future, and in which they ate with the Lord; in the other, it was a mystic rite of Greek origin, which was oriented towards the past and in which they ate the Lord. These two concepts were later joined and the result was already to be seen in the Gospel accounts of the institution, where the perspective of the joyful eschatological future (Mk 14:25 par.) is found alongside the memorial of the past in the bread-body and the wine-blood (Mk 14:22-24 par.).

This ingenious hypothesis will not bear scrutiny, neither from the exegetical nor from the theological point of view. The exegesis of the texts runs contrary to such a dichotomy. The two aspects thus opposed are in fact already combined in each of the two sources. To the words "proclaim the death of the Lord" Paul immediately adds "until He come": in other words, he does not think of the past without reference to the future; on the other hand, the "breaking of bread" in the earliest Jerusalem community cannot be reduced simply to a feast of joyful expectation, for it is closely associated in the Acts with the apostolic kerygma in which the cross and resurrection form the central point; thus the future is not separated from the past.

In addition to these exegetical facts there is the theological truth of primary importance, that far from being in opposition, the past and the future of Christ, and in Him of Christian salvation, meet in a present which inherits the combined riches of them both. The past of Christ is not terminated like that of a creature who only belongs to this world's time; it continues in a present here and now, which stems from the new time inaugurated by the resurrection. Not only is God's action of granting pardon to mankind because of the cross as eternal as God Himself, and transcending all the centuries of human time; but also the action of Christ, though confined from one point of view within the progress of human history, surpasses it from another, because it brings the old era of this history to an end and inaugurates a new one. Through the resurrection, the life and death of our Lord overflows into a new world whose eternal present shares in a certain way the eternity of God. "Christ once risen from the dead dies no more; death no more wields power over Him. His death was death to sin, once for all; but His life is life to God" (Rom 6:9-10). Risen from the dead, Christ lives by a new life in which His past remains present. The Epistle to the Hebrews shows him entering the heavenly sanctuary through the veil of His flesh "in order that He might now appear before the face of God on our behalf" (Heb 9:24); for in virtue of His unchangeable priesthood and His sacrifice offered once for all, He is "always living to intercede on behalf of sinners" (Heb 7:25).

Christ's present is enriched by the past; it is also enriched by the future. The new era which He inaugurated is the eschatological era, the era of the final times which will change no more, and in which mankind, reconciled with God, will enjoy forever His love and company, in an eternal present. This era was begun by Christ and for Christ; Christ, "the first fruits of those that are asleep" (1 Cor 15:20), the risen Christ, has already taken His place in this new and final state, to which all who share in His salvation are called, in order that they may join Him there.

In actual fact, this eschatological present in which the past and the future meet is not yet fully realized, except in the case of Christ (and His mother, by virtue of the Assumption). The rest of men, even the faithful, are still hemmed in by the changing circumstances of the old order. Nevertheless the faithful, by their union with Christ, already in a certain sense have a share in the new order and the new era which He has established. One part of them is already dead to sin and risen with Christ, whilst the other is still subject to sin and condemned to death (cf. Rom 8:10-13; Eph 2:5-6); this is a violent, paradoxical, "amphibious" state, which is illustrated by the "You are dead . . . put to death then . . ." of Col 3:3, 5. Now this contact with Christ, which already places them partly in the eschatological era, is established by faith and by the sacraments of faith, of which the Eucharist is the center.

The Christ with whom we come into contact and whom we actually receive in the Eucharistic banquet is without doubt the Christ who died for us two thousand years ago, and He is the Christ who will raise us up and glorify us some day in the future, a day known to God alone; but He is the Christ who now lives with the Father, in possession of all the riches of His salvation and promises of glory. By the sacramental contact we enter in a mysterious fashion this present of salvation already realized, and we really share in it. We share in that sacrifice which Christ, after having offered it "once for all," offers at the present moment and always. We share in the Messianic feast already really begun, for the kingdom of God where it is celebrated is itself already begun: it is the Church, grouped round the risen Master. Jesus had already said: "The kingdom of God is among you" (Lk 17:21). This is particularly true after His resurrection, and we may surmise that Luke is thinking of this kingdom which is the Church when he tells us our Lord said: "I shall eat of this Pasch no more . . . I shall drink no more of the fruit of the vine until the kingdom of God be come" (Lk 22:16, 18), and then insists on the meals which the risen Master took with His disciples (Lk 24:30, 41-43; Acts 1:4). As in the case of the first disciples, it is Christ, dead and risen again, and alive at this very moment, whom we meet at the Eucharistic supper.

PRESENT TO THE BODILY SENSES

This is another trait which we must underline, for its necessity does not appear at first sight. Could not our Lord have remained near us simply by the spiritual presence of faith? Could not His word, received into our minds, have assured us of His permanent presence? That, at least, is how it is viewed by those who, in practice, misunderstand the sacramental order and allow of a contact with Christ and His salvation through faith alone. But this would not have been human. Man is a being endowed with bodily senses; his soul lives in a body. To establish real contact it is necessary to reach the body as well as the soul. Words are themselves in some measure dependent for their effect upon the senses, for ideas are only presented to the mind by way of sounds which play upon the ear. And even this is not sufficient to satisfy our needs; hence words are accompanied by expressive gestures or by symbols. God knows the ways of those He has created, and in His condescension He accommodates Himself to them. He revealed Himself by means of actions as much as words. A striking illustration of this is found in what we call the "types" of the Old Testament. He did not simply tell Israel that He was their saviour: He saved them by rescuing them from Egypt "with outstretched arm"; and He did not simply rescue them from Egypt: He made this act of salvation perceptible to the senses by the blood of the paschal lamb smeared on the doors, by the tables of the Law written by His hand, by the bronze serpent set up in the desert.

Our Lord, the supreme expression of God's nearness as far as it can

be perceived, did not act differently. In His speech He used images
and parables. He touched the bodies of those He healed, even using
such commonplace methods as saliva mixed with earth. It was by
taking hold of the whip or by prostrating upon the ground that He
taught His disciples the respect due to the divine majesty. When,
therefore, He takes bread and wine in order to attach to them the permanent presence of His sacrifice, He does so to make this presence
perceptible, tangible, striking. The words which explain the significance of His death will remain in the minds of His disciples, and of
their disciples after them; but to sustain these words in a tangible way
there will be this bread and this wine which are seen with the eyes,
grasped by the hands, tasted on the palate; they will provide man
with a more complete possession of the gift that has been made to
him. Yet this is not all. There is more, much more, in this bread and
wine.

PHYSICALLY PRESENT

The bread and wine here are not merely symbols. They are symbols,
but they are something more. They are really, although in a mysterious
manner, the body and blood of Jesus Christ. To establish this, it is not
enough to stress the form of Christ's words: "This *is* my body" or "this
is my blood," for philology would not adequately support such an
argument. In the first place we must remember that our Lord said
these words in Aramaic, and in this language the copula is not expressed; Joachim Jeremias[1] proposes for the original words: *den bisri*
(this my flesh) and *den idhmi* (this my blood). Secondly, the copula
which is understood need not necessarily signify a real identity. In
such phrases as "the one who sows the good seed is the Son of Man,"
"the field is the world," "the good grain are the members of the kingdom" (Mt 13:37-38), the verb is clearly not intended to mean more
than "signifies," "represents." It would therefore be possible to understand here, as some actually do, "This represents my body; this represents my blood." But there are other reasons which demand something
more in this particular case.

First of all, the value of bread and wine as a symbolic expression
is not sufficient to explain their use here. In a parable, spoken or acted,
an abstract idea, or something real but absent, is made clear by a
concrete image or something real that is to hand: the sowing of seed,
the field, the treasure, the leaven, the lamp, really help the mind,
through their well-known role in daily life, to grasp those more mysterious realities which are the kingdom of God and the teaching of
our Lord. But here, things are quite different. Our Lord speaks of His
body which He is going to give for His brethren, of His blood which

●

[1] *The Eucharistic Words of Jesus* (Oxford, 1955) pp. 140 f.

He is about to shed; there is nothing more concrete and more immediate; in what way would the bread on the table and the wine in
the cup help to convey this? It is possible to point out after the event
. . . that the red wine flowing from the crushed grape may evoke the
blood flowing from the body; or again, that the bread broken into
pieces can represent the body, broken and torn. The writers of the
Church went further along these lines and found, for example, in the
bread made from many ears of wheat and ground into flour, a beautiful symbol of the Christians whom Christ unites with Himself through
His passion into the one host He offers to the Father. These more or
less subtle allegories can be applied to the bread and wine used in
the Eucharist, but they do not give it its deep significance. Jesus did
not use these things as illustrations which made clear His coming
sacrifice; far from helping of themselves to explain the death of the
body and the shedding of the blood, it is precisely the bread and wine
which need explaining by means of the former.

The Eucharistic bread and wine, therefore, do not immediately
strike the mind as symbols; their immediate appeal is to the body as
food. It is as food that they first claim our interest. It is not an idea or
instruction that they are to convey to those who partake of them, but
a very concrete reality, the body and the blood of the Lord. This is
precisely the concrete and realist plane on which Christian salvation
is found, and it is important to insist on this, for this aspect is not
always appreciated as much as it ought. The salvation of Christ is
concerned with the body as much as the soul. This is an elementary
truth which we think we know perfectly well; but it has not in
practice the significance it ought to have, due to the Greek mode of
thought we have to some extent inherited. In Greek thought, influenced by Plato, the body is for the soul nothing but a prison, something bad in itself; the soul's salvation depends on getting rid of it.
The Greek idea of immortality only concerns the soul, freed at last of
its miserable burden. Many Christians unconsciously think somewhat
along these lines, not indeed that they deny the dogma of the resurrection of the body, but the latter seems very distant to them, and in the
meantime they are none too clear on what place to give to this troublesome companion, the body, in their striving after holiness. Often they
regard it as incurably bad; they reconcile themselves to the inevitable
and let it sin; or else they wish to master it and therefore have recourse
to an excessive asceticism. In both cases the body is not given its due
place, a wholesome and a holy place in the work of salvation; it
appears by the side of the soul like a poor relation; we dare not think
of it when it is a question of grace. We speak of "saving our souls,"
or of "saving souls," and seemingly forget that they dwell in bodies.
Does not the formula used these days in the distribution of Holy
Communion say *"custodiat animam tuam:* may the body of our Lord
guard thy *soul"*? It would be better to say, as in the Dominican rite:
custodiat te: guard *thee:* i.e., the whole man, soul and body. This

failure to understand the importance of the body is even to be detected in the way in which some Christians understand the resurrection of Christ: they see in this triumph of the flesh over death a personal compensation, a reward richly earned through torments generously borne; after such humiliations was it not fitting the body thus sacrificed should experience glory? These ideas are very narrow, and without being altogether false remain incomplete.

Biblical anthropology and the idea of salvation which it entails are quite different. In it the body is not pictured as an accidental companion, still less as something intrinsically bad. It is an essential element of man, created at the same time as the soul and as good as it. It is sin which came to disrupt this harmony, affecting the soul as much as the body; it separated the one from the other by an interior disorder to be made complete by the total separation which is death. But this is a violent state, for which the soul is to be held responsible, not the material nature of the body, and which will have to come to an end if man is to recover his pristine integrity. In biblical revelation, the only genuine "salvation" is that of the soul *with its body:* the one cannot be saved without the other. It is even going too far when, under pressure of language, we speak of them as two distinct parts. Actually man is his soul, and man is his body, in Semitic and biblical thought. They are two complementary and inseparable aspects of the one concrete being. This way of thinking, which is Semitic and not Greek, is essential if we are to understand the Incarnation and redemption, and also the sacramental dispensation. The Word did not take a human body simply to communicate with men at a level determined by the bodily senses. It was also, and indeed primarily, to take in hand the whole man, body and soul, and completely refashion him, body and soul. By yielding up His soul upon the cross, our Lord put to death the "flesh of sin" with which He was clothed (Rom 8:3; cf. 2 Cor 5:21; Col 1:22); by rising from the tomb He is the New Man whose soul and body are penetrated by the Spirit of the eschatological era (1 Cor 15:44-45). In Him who is the head of the new human race, the body is regenerated as much as the soul, and without it nothing would have been accomplished: "If Christ be not risen, your faith is vain; you are still in your sins" (1 Cor 15:17).

When, then, He communicates His life to the faithful, it is their bodies as much as their souls which He unites with Himself, in order to recreate them. It is His body as well as His soul which He puts in contact with theirs in order to make them share in His "passage" from death to life. The "grace" of Christ is His concrete life, that life which shines forth in His glorified body as well as in His glorified soul, and that life which He pours into the souls and bodies of those whom He unites to Himself. From this it is understandable why Christ, in order to establish such a contact and to exercise such an influence reaching man even in his body, uses these perceptible means, these physical means which we call sacraments. Salvation comes by faith and by the sacraments of faith; faith alone would have sufficed for disembodied souls, but the sacraments of faith are necessary if the body which supports the soul is to be reached at its own level. Notice that we are concerned here with something different; previously we spoke of ways of expressing things, of ways of enlightening the intelligence through the perception of the senses. Here it is precisely a question of transferring the new, recreated, pure life of the risen body of Christ to the contaminated flesh of the sinner. This demands a different contact from that of the Spirit; it demands a bodily contact, a physical contact which works in its own fashion. Such a contact by its very nature escapes the clear grasp of the intelligence; it is something experienced rather than capable of definition. But it is nonetheless real and indispensable. To bring it about, our Lord uses sacraments. Whether it be through the water of baptism or the oil of confirmation, whether it be through the tears of contrition and the gesture of absolution, in each of the sacraments His glorified and spiritual body comes into contact with our sinful body and heals it along with the soul which dwells in it. In the Eucharist, the central sacrament, it is not such or such an action of the body of Christ which has an effect upon us, but the body itself in its plenitude as the source of grace, which comes into us; it is not through a more or less superficial and ephemeral contact, but through the most intimate and lasting way there can be in this life: the assimilation of food. Our Lord does more than wash us with purifying water, or anoint us with strengthening oil; He nourishes us with His flesh. This demands that the bread and wine which we receive should be truly the flesh and blood of the Lord.

REALLY PRESENT

There is no doubt that the first Christians understood it in this way, and in particular the theologians Paul and John, whose teaching is part of divine revelation. After having quoted the account of the institution, Paul adds a realistic comment: "That is why whoever eats the bread or drinks the Lord's cup unworthily will have to answer for the body and blood of the Lord . . . for he who eats and drinks, eats and drinks his own condemnation, if he does not recognize the body therein" (1 Cor 11:27, 29). The fourth Gospel is even more categorical: "If you do not eat the flesh of the Son of Man and drink His blood, you will not have life in you. . . . For my flesh is truly food and my blood truly drink. He who eats my flesh and drinks my blood remains in me and I in him" (Jn 6:53-56). We must not pervert this realism into a gross materialism. The sacrament is nothing without faith, and the flesh of Christ would be nothing without the Spirit that dwells in it. Jesus Himself adds: "It is the Spirit that vivifies, the flesh counts for nothing" (Jn 6:63). It is the "spiritual" or "pneumatic" body of the risen Christ which is the channel of life; it is He whom we must put on (1 Cor 15:49). But whilst it differs in some way from the "earthly" or "psychic" body received from Adam, which Christ made to perish upon the cross, this spiritual body of the glorified Christ is nonetheless the same body, transformed from corruption to incorruption, from weakness to strength, from ignominy to glory (1 Cor 15:42-44). It is a spiritualized body, but still real, which could be touched (Lk 24:39-40; John 20:27), and it is in this state that it is found in the bread in order to be given to us.

"How can this thing be?" we would ask with Nicodemus. How can bread and wine become the body and blood of the Lord? It is a mystery of faith; we believe it because we believe in the Word of the Lord. He tells us that this is His body, that this is His blood, and we have just seen that His intention and the nature of His salvation cannot be satisfied by a merely symbolic representation. If He wishes this bread to give us really His body, He has the power to bring this about. His Word is powerful and creative. His words at the Last Supper are not an announcement but a decision. He does not merely state that the bread is His body; He decrees that this must come to pass, and that it has come to pass. His speech does not come after the event, it brings the event to pass, by giving to the bread and wine a new value. We have pointed out that the president of the Jewish Pasch commented upon the significance of the bitter herbs and the lamb, and thus gave these foods a real value they had not had before, so that when the guest ate them, he really shared in the deliverance of long ago and enjoyed the benefits which flowed from it. The efficacy of our Lord's words yields nothing to the realism of this biblical rite; it far surpasses it, for the object of the commemoration is of a completely new order. The elements which the new rite uses are no longer simply accidental details connected with a divine intervention and called to mind in order to help revive it; they are the essentials of a new and definitive intervention, the very substance of the sacrifice which redeemed the world, and their presence must be renewed in a real way, in order to reach the guests, body as well as soul.

Is it possible to scrutinize this mystery further and try to explain it to the rational mind? It was inevitable that this attempt should be made, and the effort is legitimate. With the help of philosophy it has been said that the "substance" of the bread and wine was changed into the substance of the body and the blood, whilst the appearance or "accidents" remained the same. This formulation is valid and the Church has sanctioned it by speaking of "transubstantiation." Nevertheless we must not forget the fact that even these philosophical notions are not free from mystery in this context. What they mean in the end is that the bread and wine, consecrated by the words of Christ, in a certain sense remain as they were in the old order of things; but on the other hand they become something more, as a result of their being elevated to the new order. What they are now so transcends what they were before that this loses its significance. In their new situation within the eschatological era, to which the whole of the sacramental dispensation belongs, they become the very body of Christ that died and was raised to life. The traditional dogmatic formula is expressed in terms of a philosophy of natures, and it has its value; nevertheless it is lawful to rethink and deepen it in terms of biblical thought, which is more clearly understood today. Biblical thought is concerned rather with existence and its transition from the old era of sin and death to the era of salvation and life. This transition which our Lord made first in His own person, from the cross to the morning of Easter, He brings to pass in the bread and wine, in order that through these He may bring it to pass in those who share them with faith.

A COLLECTIVE PRESENCE

When we receive Christ we do not receive Him alone. In accordance with the design of God He carries in Himself the whole of humanity of which He is the new head. By clothing Himself in our "body of flesh" He assumed all the descendants of the first Adam, led astray by sin, in order to punish them in His person upon the cross and thus reconcile them with the Father (Col 1:22); when He rose again on the morning of Easter as the Second Adam, created anew by God, the whole of the new humanity came out with Him from the tomb, as a regenerated stock, just and holy (Rom 5:12-19; 1 Cor 15:45-49; Eph 4:22-4). In Him was reunited all that sin had divided; sinners were reconciled not only with God, but also with each other. Thus St. Paul says, apropos of what he regarded as the two great divisions of mankind, namely, Jews and Gentiles: "Christ is our peace, He who of the two (Jewish and pagan worlds) has made one single people, destroying the barrier which separated them, in His flesh suppressing hate, this law of precepts with its ordinances, in order to make in Himself the two into one single new man, to make peace and to reconcile them both with God, in one single body, through the cross; in His person He has slain hate" (Eph 2:14-16). To understand this we must remember the very concrete realism of the Incarnation: the humanity of Christ, soul and body, is like a melting pot in which God has recast His work; it is like the clay from which He had remolded His "new creature." In it all men who are saved find themselves, body and soul, closely united in the same new life.

But however perfect and final it may be, this work of redemption could not be accomplished in our Lord except as in its principle, in its germ. Precisely because it is concrete, it still needs to be applied to all individual men, to successive generations through time and space. The risen Christ must touch every man who comes into this world, as formerly He touched the sick and the sinners of Palestine; His most holy soul and His divinity must touch the bodies and souls of those He saves through the intermediary of His glorified body. We saw that He does this through faith and the sacraments of faith. By physical contact He unites the faithful to Himself, even their bodies, and "incorporates" them into Himself. He makes of them the "members" of His body. This famous expression of St. Paul (1 Cor 6:15; 12:27; Eph 5:30) is not simply a metaphor borrowed from the classical comparison of the "social body"; on the contrary, it must be taken in a most realistic sense, and its real source lies in the doctrine we have been recalling. Christians are the members of Christ because their union with Him joins their bodies to His body in the same risen life, still hidden as far as they are concerned, but already completely real (Col 3:1-4).

Consequently the body of Christ, His personal body, crucified and raised up again, bears within itself the bodies of the brethren whom He forms to His image (Rom 8:29). The implications of this for the Eucharist are clear. Since this sacrament gives us the body of Christ, it unites us by that very fact to all our brethren whom it bears within itself. Already St. Paul taught this: "The bread which we break, is it not participation in the body of Christ? Since there is but one bread, we, all of us, form one single body, for we all share in this one bread" (1 Cor 10:16-17). It is this Eucharistic body of the Lord which was first called the "mystical body," and it is because it consummates the union of Christians with Christ and with one another that the expression was afterwards applied to the Church. In this Eucharistic body we meet our brethren, united by the love of Christ, and that is why the Eucharist is the sacrament of charity, its source and its nourishment. In this physical, penetrating, intimate contact which it brings about, we assimilate both the strength and knowledge to love Christ wholly, Him and His Father, and also the strength and knowledge to love the rest of mankind as He loves them, with His own heart. Through this sacrament the bonds of union are forged between all those who are united with Him. And since this union rests upon the physical basis of our bodies, it covers those mysterious exchanges where the suffering and death of one can satisfy in place of his brother.

THE SACRIFICE OF THE CHURCH

AND AN ABIDING PRESENCE

These two final characteristics follow from all that we have just said. We realize that the Eucharist contains the sacrifice of Christ, since it contains the body and blood of Christ in the very act of His immolation. That it contains Christ's sacrifice here and now we have concluded from the eschatological time into which Christ has entered. We are thus justified in saying that the Mass is a sacrifice which renews the sacrifice of the cross upon our altars: Christ is there, "always living to intercede on (our) behalf" (Heb 7:25). Can we go further and say that the Mass adds something to the cross? Protestants reproach Catholics for doing this, but their reproach is not justified; it is, however, important to see why.

In one sense it is certain that the Mass adds nothing to the cross. It is the same sacrifice which was already perfect in its historical realization. In contrast to the priests of the Old Covenant, who had to renew continually their insufficient sacrifices, Christ suffered "once for all, at the end of time . . . to abolish sin by His sacrifice" (Heb 9:26). The Church, therefore, does not renew her liturgical sacrifice in the manner of the Jews. And yet she renews it, by the very order of her Master; there must be a reason for this. From this angle, which must be accurately understood, it becomes lawful to say that the Mass adds something to the cross, and it does this in two ways.

First of all, it adds to it a concrete application, in time and space, the necessity of which we have already explained. The sacrifice of Christ merited to an infinite degree the benefits of pardon and life, needed for the salvation of mankind from the beginning to the end of the world; yet it is necessary for these benefits to be communicated to each and everyone, in the time and place of his own particular life. The Mass distributes these treasures, it releases this life-giving stream, for the small community grouped around the altar. Nothing is added to what flows from the spring, but a canal is made which enables the life-giving waters to reach to the very end of human time and space. Nothing is added to the action and words of Christ, except the action and words of one of His ministers, which only avail because Christ makes use of them; through them it is still He who acts.

Something else is added, which we must not be afraid to recognize, for it is admirable and detracts in no way from the absolute sovereignty of the one Priest. This is the offering of the Church. It is the active contribution to the sacrifice by the priest who offers it, and the faithful who communicate or assist at it. Their prayers and their own sacrifices, sinners as they are, add nothing to the efficacy of the cross; this much is clear. And yet they join to Christ's work a human participation which He desires. If He offered His love and acts of expiation in place of theirs, which sin made valueless, it was not to suppress them but to give them value. Now that He has accomplished His work, He does not wish to apply its benefits to them without their co-operation. That is why He gives to His Church not only His body and blood, but with them the whole of His sacrifice: in order that she may dispose of it and by its renewal associate with it all the sacrifices of her children. These sacrifices will add nothing, of course, to the one sacrifice of our Lord; on the contrary, they will receive from it everything of value they can have; but thus enriched, they will help in the sacramental application by allowing this saving contact which cannot be established without the active response of the redeemed to their Redeemer. This is the significance of the offering made at Mass; when she presents to God the elements for the sacrifice, the Church offers to God, through the hands of the priest, the faithful who have provided them; by accepting these humble gifts and making of them His body and blood, Christ incorporates into His sacrifice the sacrifices which these gifts symbolize. And He makes them share in this total sacrifice, with which He deigns to associate His Church, when He gives back to them the gifts they offered, but now transformed in His hands. The divine condescension which characterizes the whole plan of redemption, and which associates man in the working out of his own salvation, is seen here in a particularly striking way. Why must a misguided anxiety concerning the respect due to the divine autonomy and transcendence lead some to misunderstand the riches of this theological truth?

The gift of His body and blood which Christ has made to His followers brings with it a final consequence: their abiding presence among us. Certainly they are given us in the act of their being sacrificed; and that is why Protestants only admit their presence (more or less symbolically) in the bread and wine at the very moment of the action by which they are given. The sacramental realism of the Catholic faith does not allow such a way of thinking. Christ does not take bread and wine as ephemeral modes of expression; He gives them a new being, which derives from the eschatological era and has its permanence. Doubtless it is to commemorate His sacrificial act, but this act has become in Him a reality which ceases no more: His body and blood have become an offering constantly offered, constantly accepted, and constantly radiating life. The share in the old order of things which it still has prevents the sacrament from taking on fully this character of eschatological perpetuity. If the frail support of the bread and wine disappears, either by communion or by corruption, the presence of the body and blood by that very fact ceases. But as long as this support continues, the presence is maintained. Christ has donated this presence to the Church with a liberality such as is found in all His gifts. Not only can the Church renew the Supper as often as she wishes, but she can also make use of it as she desires. Thus it is that, whilst scrupulously respecting the essential words and actions which are its central point, she has been able in the course of centuries to order the words and actions which surround this central point as she pleases, and adapt it to the changing circumstances of time and place, of country, language, and customs. Thus, in the Mass as we have it now, she has introduced a certain interval of prayer and preparation between the words of consecration and the Communion. It is thus, finally, that even after the Communion she ventures to preserve the consecrated species. Her primary reason for this is to be able to feed her children apart from the time of Mass, if there be need; but it is also that she may offer to this presence, as she has done for centuries, a cult which prolongs that of the Mass. This custom of reservation is as ancient as it is universal in the Church. It is fully justified by our faith in a permanent presence. It satisfies our Lord's desire to remain always among us and gives to innumerable Christians a source of spiritual strength which is ever to hand. But we must not allow an unenlightened piety to dissociate the host reserved for adoration from the sacrifice it represents. The host in the tabernacle, in the monstrance, or carried in triumphal procession, is at all times the host of the Mass which is the host of the Supper, and this in turn is the host of the cross. Above all, it is a food, this bread and wine in which Christ placed at His last meal the power of His sacrifice, and it is this food we must eat if we would have life.

Editors' Note.—From SCRIPTURE 9, no. 5 (January, 1957) *1-14.*

Papacy and Episcopacy

The Church and Peter
Karl Adam

The Role of the Hierarchy in the Church
Yves de Montcheuil, s.j.

PREFACE

"Thou art Peter and upon this rock I shall build my Church."

The two chapters that follow, by Karl Adam and Yves de Montcheuil, summarize for us the theology of the structure of the Church in the papacy and the hierarchy of bishops.

At this stage of our discussion it will be far less difficult to understand and accept the extraordinary specificity and freedom with which God has introduced his order into the religious unfolding of man. From the very beginning we have been looking at the differences between the perfectly logical or rational forms of thought and the "scandalous" ways in which God, in the face of endless other alternatives, makes absolutely free elections of persons and places.

Therefore it makes sense, but divine sense and not mathematical sense, that Christ should have chosen Peter as His Vicar out of many men; that He should have chosen twelve apostles out of all possible numbers for His first episcopacy; that He should have guided the steps of His Church toward Rome; that, in a word, He should have said so often: "this and not that." For God is free.

But freedom, too, has its reasons. They are reasons of love and the exchange of common faith. For when Christ asked Peter: "Who do you say that I am?", Peter answered: "Thou art the Christ, the Son of the Living God."

Karl Adam

The Church and Peter

Our Lord's gospel of the kingdom pressed on to the foundation of a visible Church. The more definitely He opposed the ruling religious authority, and the clearer it became that He was dethroning the Law and setting His own word in its place, that the new kingdom was bound up with His Person and with faith in Him, that it was His kingdom (cf. Lk 22:29,30; 23:42; Mt 13:41), and that it was the New Covenant in His blood, so much the more inevitable was the gradual detachment of His disciples from their previous religious fellowship. "No man putteth a piece of new cloth unto an old garment." And naturally the fellowship which held His disciples together was bound to become all the more intimate and conscious. How often had He not told them: "By this shall all men know that you are my disciples, if you have love one to another." They shall call one another brethren, they shall be His family (cf. Mt 10:25), His marriage guests, who cannot be sorrowful so long as the Bridegroom is with them (Mt 9:15), who drink together out of the same cup of the New Covenant. And one day they are to be His elect, and at His table and in His kingdom to eat of the glad Messianic feast (Lk 22:29 f.; Mt 13:41).

256

The Messianic consciousness of Jesus necessarily led to the formation of a community. In His Person the judgment was already begun, the contrast of faith and unbelief, the separation of spirits. He told them quite plainly: "Do not think that I came to send peace upon earth; I came not to send peace, but the sword" (Mt 10:34; cf. Lk 12:51). In Him the City of God invaded the earthly city, and at once there began the process of discrimination, the formation of the new out of the old.

The first step was taken when Jesus began gradually to gather "disciples" about Him, and the Twelve are mentioned in twenty-nine passages of the Gospels. In St. Paul "the Twelve" are already a recognized body. However much it may be disputed whether the Twelve were named apostles by our Lord Himself, or whether this name became current first in Hellenistic surroundings, yet the fact that Jesus Himself selected the Twelve is indisputable. They were to be twelve in number, no more and no less. By being twelve they were—so He plainly intended—to signify the new twelvefold Israel and to be the germ of that holy people which He, as the Son of Man, foretold by the prophet Daniel, was come to establish.[1] As the new Israel they were the kernel of the new kingdom, its spiritual support, the authorized bearers of its message, the "salt of the earth," the "light of the world." They knew themselves as those who would one day judge the twelve tribes of Israel (Mt 19:28; Lk 22:30). So deeply were the Twelve permeated with the fundamental importance of their corporate union that after the ascension of Jesus they considered it their first business to fill the gap which the suicide of Judas had left in the apostolic college by electing Matthias (Acts 1:15 ff.). Therefore the Twelve were the original form and foundation of the new kingdom. That new kingdom entered history as an apostolic Church, built, as the Epistle to the Ephesians says (2:20), "upon the foundation of the apostles." The character of apostolicity, this real historical connexion with the Twelve, is essential to it and cannot be taken from it.

But already, at the election of Matthias, one of the Twelve is distinguished from the others by his self-assurance. This is Simon Bar Jona, surnamed Peter. He proposed the election and conducted it. On the day of Pentecost it was Peter again who by his stirring words brought the first Christian community into being (Acts 2:41). Both in the Temple (3:12) and before the Sanhedrin (4:8; 5:29) this same Peter was the spokesman of the Twelve. His miracles surpassed even those of our Lord. "The singular greatness of the marvels reported of him . . . shows that Christian tradition raised him above the rest of the Twelve." [2] It was he who by his reception of the Gentile Cornelius anticipated the decision of that question which was so vital

●

[1] Cf. F. Kattenbusch, "Die Vorzugsstellung des Petrus und der Charakter der Urgemeinde," in *Festgabe für Karl Müller* (1922) p. 341.
[2] *Ibid.*, p. 335.

for the young Church, that is, whether the Gentiles might be admitted directly into the Christian community. And he secured the general recognition of his policy in spite of all opposition (Acts 11:18). When the question was raised later whether Gentile Christians were under the law of circumcision, again his word was decisive (15:7). And when the controversy threatened to break out anew in Antioch, it was expected that his presence in person would produce peace. But the prestige of St. Peter was supreme not only in the original community, but also in those Hellenistic missionary churches where St. Paul exercised his apostolate to the uncircumcised (cf. Gal 2:7). St. Paul tells us that St. Peter was accounted one of the "pillars" of the Church, with James and John (Gal 2:9). He is one of the "authorities" (2:6). According to St. Paul, St. Peter is entrusted with the gospel to the circumcised, as he himself is the apostle of the uncircumcised, which means that St. Paul regarded him as the true founder and head of the Jewish Christian community (Gal 2:7). And so, on his first visit to Jerusalem, he sought out St. Peter especially. His visit, after his three years' sojourn in Arabia, was for the express purpose of "getting to know Peter personally" ($\iota\sigma\tau\sigma\rho\tilde{\eta}\sigma\alpha\iota$). And he abode fifteen days with him (Gal 1:18). Manifestly he considered it necessary to arrange matters with St. Peter and to be in agreement with him. And even when he can say that he did not agree with Peter, but had to "withstand him to his face" because he had wrongly withdrawn himself from social intercourse with Gentile Christians, and thereby practically belied his own principles (Gal 2:11-12), even then we discern his conviction that St. Peter's example is of especial authority even for Antioch, so that a public settlement with him is necessary.

And so St. Paul's attitude towards the apostles in general and towards St. Peter in particular confirms that picture of the Church which we derived from the original community in Jerusalem. It is clear that the governance of the Church appertained to the apostles, and that St. Peter was the most influential and esteemed of the apostles. The Twelve governed the Church under the leadership of St. Peter. Jerusalem, as the seat of the apostolic college with St. Peter at its head, was the metropolis of the Christian churches. As Karl Holl has lately demonstrated against Sohm, Jerusalem had a special competence to decide questions that arose and a formal right to supervise the whole Christian mission and to accredit the missionaries.[3] St. Paul himself tells us with obvious satisfaction that the authorities in Jerusalem recognized his mission to the Gentiles and gave him "the right hand of fellowship" (Gal 2:9), without laying more upon him (2:6). So the Pauline communities also were subject to the supreme control of Jerusalem. St. Paul adds: "Only that we should be mindful of the poor, which same thing also I was careful to do" (Gal 2:10). Not a

●

[3] In *Sitzungsberichte der preussischen Akademie der Wissenschaften*, 1921, p. lxxx.

few modern investigators see in these regular alms sent to Jerusalem a species of tax—Heiler even speaks of Peter's pence—which the Christian communities of the Diaspora had to pay in acknowledgment of their intimate dependence on Jerusalem, just as the synagogues of the Jewish Diaspora were bound to contribute to the Temple.

So if we consider the fundamental character of the original Christian Church, we can understand how Heiler can call those early years the "formative period of Catholicism," [4] and in what respect he can say of the primitive community in Jerusalem that it displayed the "unmistakable germs and fundamental elements of the coming Catholicism." [5] The most outstanding of these is St. Peter's pre-eminence in the apostolic college.

How are we to explain this pre-eminence of St. Peter? According to Wellhausen and his followers, it is simply due to the fact that St. Peter was the first to see the risen Christ. His faith awakened the faith of the rest, and so St. Peter's Easter faith was the creative cause and the root of all that Christianity which grew out of this Easter faith. Quite recently Holl has endeavored to improve this theory by modifying it as follows: St. Peter is not precisely the creator and enkindler of the Christian faith, but its re-creator. The events of the passion intimidated the disciples and extinguished their faith; that faith was re-enkindled by St. Peter's faith, and in that way the new faith is causally derived from St. Peter. Neither of these theories is admissible, because neither of them rests upon any secure historical basis. It is true that St. Peter was regarded by the primitive Christians as an important witness to the resurrection of our Lord. And it is indubitable that his testimony was valued more highly than the testimony of the other apostles. When St. Paul, in his argument against those who denied the resurrection, enumerates the most weighty witnesses to it, he mentions St. Peter first, and the Twelve as a whole only after him (1 Cor 15:5). It is significant also that the angel at the tomb (Mk 16:7) bade the women tell "the disciples and Peter" that Jesus would go before them into Galilee. So St. Mark also singles out St. Peter and distinguishes his testimony expressly from that of the other disciples. But nowhere, as Kattenbusch truly insists, is there any record of St. Peter's being the first to whom the Lord appeared. Nor is there any evidence whatever to show that the first disciples and the first communities expressly based their faith in the risen Christ on the testimony of St. Peter, that his faith begat theirs, and that their faith stood or fell with his alone. On the contrary, the narratives of the resurrection, and especially St. Paul's, are concerned to name a whole series of witnesses, and among them five hundred brethren, "of whom many remain until this present" (1 Cor 15:6). Not St. Peter singly, but all the living disciples as a body, are the witness and guarantee

●

[4] *Der Katholizismus, seine Idee und seine Erscheinung* (1923) p. 61.
[5] *Ibid.*, p. 49.

of the resurrection. The experience of Pentecost rests upon the basis of their common testimony.

Nevertheless, St. Peter's testimony has a special value and is expressly invoked before and along with the testimony of the Twelve. The reason is, not that St. Peter was the authentic and special, or the first, witness of the resurrection, but rather that his word and his testimony in general were more highly treasured and that he enjoyed a higher prestige than the other disciples. In other words, St. Peter's pre-eminence as a witness is not to be explained by his being the first to believe in the resurrection, but contrariwise it is by his already recognized pre-eminence that we must explain the special value which his testimony enjoyed. The high esteem and special consideration given to his testimony—as evidenced by St. Mark and St. Paul, and by St. Luke also (12:42)—compel the historian to conjecture the existence of some fact, existing before the resurrection of our Lord, which gave St. Peter a special standing in the primitive community, and which caused that community to give his testimony, though not an exclusive, yet an exceptional value. Is there such a fact?

The Evangelist St. Matthew records an event which of itself is quite sufficient to explain St. Peter's pre-eminence in the primitive community and the high value set upon his testimony to the resurrection. The scene is the neighborhood of Caesarea Philippi, by the southern slopes of Mt. Hermon, in sight of the mighty range in which the Jordan has its source. Our Lord put this question to His disciples: "Who do you say that I am?" Simon Peter made answer: "Thou art the Christ, the Son of the Living God." Jesus answered him: "Blessed art thou, Simon Bar Jona, because flesh and blood hath not revealed it to thee, but my Father who is in heaven. And I say to thee that thou art Peter [the rock], and upon this rock I will build my Church. And the gates of hell shall not prevail against it. And I will give to thee the keys of the kingdom of heaven. And whatsoever thou shalt bind upon earth, it shall be bound also in heaven; and whatsoever thou shalt loose upon earth, it shall be loosed also in heaven" (Mt 16:15 ff.). If we examine the linguistic idiom of these verses, it immediately becomes evident that they are Aramaic in origin. The play on the word Kephas is perfect only in Aramaic, for in the Greek *petra* (rock) has to be changed into Petros. The expressions, Simon Bar Jona, gates of hell, keys of the kingdom of heaven, binding and loosing, and the antithesis of heaven and earth, are all Aramaic in character. Semitic scholars are therefore emphatic in their denial that the passage is a Western, i.e., Roman forgery. On purely linguistic grounds that is an impossibility, and the hypothesis is now quite obsolete. The passage is native only to the soil of Palestine and to primitive Jewish Christianity. Is it genuine? That is to say, is it obviously an original part of the Gospel of St. Matthew, or does it betray the character of a later interpolation? In itself the whole passage is plainly very closely strung together, and there is no sign of any artificial patchwork. St. Peter's confession, "Thou art the Christ," is balanced by our Lord's attestation, "Thou art the rock." Our Lord's searching inquiry, "Who do men say that the Son of Man is?", and the exhaustive enumeration of the false opinions of the people lead up with psychological skill to St. Peter's correct answer and our Lord's commendation. "Other men judge falsely and in earthly fashion about me. But thou hast discerned my mystery: Blessed art thou," etc. The Protestant theologian Bolliger remarks of the verses that they "fit together as aptly as the members of a body. They have the quite inimitable flavor of a great historical moment. Moreover, they are expressed in words such as come only to the great ones of this world, and even to these only in the greatest moments of their life. No interpolator can write in this fashion." [6]

And if we consider the passage more broadly, in the light of the special tendency of St. Matthew's Gospel, its authenticity becomes manifest. It is the plain purpose of his Gospel to set forth Jesus as the Messiah foretold by the Old Testament, and in particular as the divine Lawgiver and Teacher who reveals the deepest meaning of the Old Testament and brings it to fulfilment. His new and perfect doctrine corrects and amends the false doctrine of the scribes and Pharisees, who strain out the gnat and swallow the camel (Mt 23:24). Therefore, the special tendency of St. Matthew, though not anti-Jewish, is certainly anti-Pharisaic. The true Teacher of the kingdom of heaven is Jesus alone. And in so far as His chosen disciples have to propagate His teaching of a justice superior to the justice of the Pharisees, they become a new teaching body and supplant the blind scribes and Pharisees. And so we see that the wider purpose of St. Matthew's Gospel is the institution of a new religious authority, a new teaching body, and consequently the establishment of a new Church which should replace the synagogue. And that disciple who grasped the mystery of the kingdom of God beyond all the rest and confessed it at Caesarea Philippi is appointed to be the foundation stone of the new Church, to be its steward and instructor in the kingdom, and is given the power of binding and loosing, that is, of forbidding and permitting, not according to the manner of the Pharisees, but according to the mind of Jesus. Thus the anti-Pharisaic tendency of the Gospel of St. Matthew culminates precisely at this point, in the foundation of a new Church and in the new authority granted to St. Peter. Our Lord's promise to St. Peter is undiluted anti-Pharisaism. And for that reason the passage may not be expunged from the Gospel; it belongs to the Evangelist's original plan.

But is it not conceivable that St. Matthew himself—let us say, in the Jewish and anti-Pauline interest—invented the words about the rock and the keys in order to secure St. Peter's teaching authority as against St. Paul, or the teaching authority of Jerusalem as against the pretensions of the Hellenistic communities? The passage would

●

[6] *Markus, der Bearbeiter des Mt.-Evangeliums* (1902) p. 86.

then be a product of Jewish Christians in Jerusalem, who wished to play off St. Peter against St. Paul; at the best a "pious fraud" of the author of our Gospel. It would take me too far were I to repeat the exhaustive proof adduced by Protestant as well as Catholic theologians to show that there is no evidence in the history of the primitive Church of any antagonism between St. Peter and St. Paul, or between Jerusalem and the Hellenistic communities. And the further demonstration that the Gospel of St. Matthew is inspired by no antagonism towards St. Paul is likewise quite unnecessary. It is decisive for our purpose to register the admitted fact that the fundamental word of our Lord's promise, His denomination of Peter as the "rock," was already current in primitive Christianity long before St. Matthew wrote his Gospel— i.e., shortly before the destruction of Jerusalem in A.D. 70—and that it was admitted and recognized not only among Jewish Christians, but also among the Gentiles, and not least of all in the churches founded by St. Paul. Not St. Matthew only, but St. Mark also (3:16) and St. John (1:42) record that St. Peter was originally called Simon, and that our Lord Himself first gave him the name of Peter (Kephâ = Petros = Rock). Mark (3:16) tells us further that Jesus substituted also for the names of James and John the designation Boanerges. Now it is surely very significant—Holl has recently pointed this out—that the name Boanerges did not become current among the primitive Christians, whereas Simon's designation as Kephâ, or the Rock, did. Simon's surname became for all Christendom his proper name. St. Paul scarcely mentions him except as Kephas, the Greek form of the Aramaic Kephâ. In his Epistle to the Galatians (1:18; 2:7, 8) he introduces the Greek translation, Petros. And that form Petros prevailed in the Hellenistic communities to the exclusion of any other. His own proper name, Simon, fell completely out of use. The fact is all the more striking because neither the Greek Petros, nor the Aramaic Kephâ, had been employed as proper names before the time of Christ. Therefore the early Christian communities, several decades before St. Matthew wrote, and in any case already about the year A.D. 35, when St. Paul was converted, were interested in Simon's being called, not Simon, but Rock. "All the faithful were meant to know that he was the rock" (Kattenbusch). And why? For no other reason that can be discerned save that the whole Christian body recognized that surname (Kephâ = Petros = Rock) as the expression of St. Peter's special function and importance for the Church, and was aware that this special position rested upon the original intention and deliberate, unequivocal decision of our Lord Himself. In other words, the central substance of this passage of St. Matthew, Simon's designation as the foundation stone of the Church and the Church's establishment on him, belongs in the closest possible way to the texture of the common Christian tradition, and, indeed, to that tradition even in pre-Pauline times. And so it cannot have been the invention of narrowly Jewish and anti-Pauline circles towards the end of the first century. And thus we understand how not only the alleged "anti-Pauline" St. Matthew, writing for Jewish Christians, speaks of Simon the Rock, but also the Hellenistic Luke, writing for Gentile Christians and closely associated with St. Paul, records a saying of our Lord which reads like a precise explanation of St. Matthew's passage: "And the Lord said: Simon, Simon, behold Satan hath desired to have you, that he may sift you as wheat. But I have prayed for thee, that thy faith fail not; and thou being once converted, confirm thy brethren" (Lk 22:31). So Christ prayed specially for Simon in particular, that he should not fail in the faith and should "confirm" his brethren. The word "confirm" ($\sigma\tau\eta\rho\acute{\iota}\zeta\epsilon\iota\nu$ = support) reminds us of the rock of St. Matthew. It is the special function of Simon to be the support and prop of the young Christian faith. Therefore St. Luke also implies Simon's vocation to be the rock. Nor is the case different with St. John. In the supplement to the fourth Gospel, which derives from the circle of St. John's disciples, the risen Christ asks: "Simon, son of John, lovest thou me more than these?" (21:15). Evidently our Lord expected a more faithful love from Simon than from the rest of His disciples. And on the basis of this more faithful love He deputed him, and him alone, to take His position as shepherd of His flock: "Feed my lambs, feed my sheep." We may turn these passages as we like, but we cannot escape the impression that the whole body of the early Christians knew that Simon bore a special relation to the stability of the Church, and derived this unique position of his from an express declaration of our Lord's. Consequently, the words of our Lord reported by St. Matthew are not isolated and baseless, but they are in their substantial content rooted in and authenticated by the common tradition of primitive Christianity, a tradition which is earlier than St. Matthew's Gospel and earlier than St. Paul. It is therefore evident, and we need not labor the point, that we are not dealing here with a pre-eminence of St. Peter which was confined to his peculiar gifts, as for instance to a special capacity for the interpretation of Scripture or to special eloquence in the exposition of the faith. In fact, St. Peter counts not merely as one stone in the newly-founded Church, nor merely as the first stone, but as the rock, the foundation stone which supports the whole Church. He is therefore intimately connected with the whole being of the Church, not only with its teaching activity and its faith, but also with the fulness of that life which springs from this faith, with its discipline, its worship, and its ordinances. The whole Church rests on Peter, and not merely its scriptural knowledge and its doctrine. Our Lord expresses this fact with even greater emphasis by the biblical image which he employs in the same context, promising Peter the keys of the kingdom of heaven. Peter is to be the steward of the house—the same figure is used by our Lord elsewhere (Mt. 24:45; Lk 12:42)—he alone has charge of the keys, and he has to supervise every department of the Church. The metaphor of binding and loosing points in the same direction. According to the rabbinical mode of speech from which it is taken, this signifies a power to forbid and to permit, to judge and to regulate, which is authoritative and valid in heaven, i.e., before God. Therefore, these three images really describe that plenitude of power (*plenitudo potestatis*) of which the Vatican Council speaks, and which comprises full doctrinal and disciplinary authority, the complete governance of the Church in the most comprehensive sense. And, as we have seen, St. Peter's influence was not in fact confined to the doctrinal sphere alone.

But—and here we come to the last question—have we not to deal here with a purely personal relation of St. Peter to the Church? The passage of St. Matthew and the conviction of the early Church testify to the precedence of St. Peter. Can we claim their testimony for his successors also? Do they support the exclusive precedence of the bishop of Rome?

A negative answer to this question can be given only by those who consider the scriptural texts in isolation and do not view them in relation to the divine Person of Jesus and His intentions. But those who really believe in Jesus, in His divine Personality, and in the necessarily imperishable character of His ideas and His works, in Jesus the Master and Lord of the future, cannot regard any of His works as transitory, or any of His words as spoken only for yesterday and today. All His words are instinct with eternal might, they are words of life, of creative power, they are promises which do not die until they are fulfilled.

And this is true of Matthew 16:18-19. What Jesus said and did on that occasion for His generation and His disciples, He said and did for all times, until He shall come again. When Jesus spoke the words, *Tu es Petrus*, He spoke them out of His triumphant Messianic consciousness that His Person and His work were imperishable. True, He Himself is now at the threshold of death, the "gates of hell"; but before His divine gaze all the dark shadows of death melt away. Down the long vista of time He sees the radiant picture of His eternal Church. Peter's confession gives Him the occasion to designate Simon and none other as the rock of His Church and to found His imperishable Church upon this imperishable rock. This Church will never perish, since it will always be a Church founded on a rock. There will always be a living Peter, whose faith will confirm his brethren. It lies at the basis of His words that His Church will never be without that strong foundation which He gave it at Caesarea Philippi, because its continuance depends upon this foundation. And so the continuance of St. Peter's office is derived immediately from the triumphant quality of the Messianic consciousness of Jesus. Because Jesus is sure that His Church, the most special creation of His Messianic consciousness, will never be overcome by the gates of hell, therefore the original Petrine form, with which He connected this imperishableness expressly and emphatically, Peter's office as "rock," must last on until He comes. So every successive generation of the disciples will have, like the first generation, its living Peter, its rock, which will enable it to triumph over all the assaults of the gates of hell.

So much we know from faith in Jesus. And from history we know that St. Peter, according to the wise designs of God's providence, died a martyr in Rome, and that the bishops of Rome have always regarded themselves, so far as historical record reaches, as possessors of his episcopal see. Nowhere throughout Christendom has another see been established which has claimed in the same sense as Rome to be the see of Peter. Though the theological basis of the Roman primacy and the exact definition of its meaning have been subject to some development, yet two facts belong to the solid substance of the ancient Christian tradition: first, that there has never been a Peter-less, non-Roman Catholic Church, and that communion with Peter and with the Roman church has been regarded from the earliest times as a fundamental necessity of the Catholic conscience; secondly, that Rome has been conscious from the most ancient times, from the days of Clement and Ignatius, of its pre-eminence, and has exercised as "president in love" (Ignatius) and "principal Church" (Cyprian) an authoritative and decisive influence on the development of doctrine, morals, and worship. Whence we hold it as an historical certainty, a certainty which is ultimately founded on faith in the rational nature of our Lord's work and on the conviction that He guards His Church, that Peter lives on in the bishops of Rome. We know no other Peter in our community, and no man knows of any other. It is our belief that we have in the bishop of Rome the Peter upon whom Christ at Caesarea Philippi established His Church.

In the light of this faith our Lord's words to Peter, "Thou art Peter and upon this rock I will build my Church," become at once promise and fulfilment. Has not history taught us, and are we not seeing every day, that it was, and is, and will be this one rock which supports the Church of Christ, and with that Church a living faith in the Incarnation of the Son of God? There is a sacred and profound significance in the fact that Simon's appointment to be the rock of the Church was preceded by his confession: "Thou art the Christ, the Son of the Living God." For faith in Christ, the Church, and Peter: these three things belong together. Where there is no Peter, where men have broken faith with him, there the fellowship of the faith perishes and along with it belief in Jesus Christ. Where there is no rock, there is no Church, there is no Christ.

And where Peter is, there of a truth the gates of hell rage against the fellowship of the faith. There Marcion comes, and Arius, and the Renaissance and Rationalism, and the gospel of worldly culture. But still we abide in the Upper Room, gathered round our Lord and Master. Where Peter is, there is Christ.

For us Catholics, faith in the Son of God, loyalty to the Church, communion with Peter: these things stand in an intimate and necessary connexion. And therefore, since we desire not to abandon Christ, we do not abandon Peter. And therefore is it our quiet but confident hope, a hope set in our souls by our Lord at Caesarea Philippi, that it cannot be otherwise, that it must be so again, that all who seek Christ shall likewise again find Peter. Heiler writes in moving language of the longing for the "angelic pastor" (*pastor angelicus*), to him a beautiful dream.[7] But for us it is no mere beautiful dream, but a certain expectation. The divine life, the life full of grace and truth, has been revealed and given to us once and for all in Christ. Nor can there be any permanent and fruitful life of nations and of men which is not nourished on that original divine life. There can be no unity of the West, no communion of souls, which does not draw all its motives, yearnings, and hopes from this divine source. Christ is and remains the heart of humanity, its true and only native land, wherein it shall find rest for its soul. That is our faith, though Western civilization should collapse and the prophets of its downfall are already with us—or though it should be born again in Him who is our life. And the organ and instrument of this Christian life will be that Church which He built upon Peter. For to her alone was made the promise that the gates of hell should not prevail against her. She alone possesses the guarantee of permanence, to her alone belongs the future. Just as the Church by the compact unity and strength of her Christian faith gave the Middle Ages their inward unity and their strength of soul, and just as in her severe and inexorable struggle with primitive pagan instincts and with the forces of extravagant imperialism she defended the sublimity, purity, and freedom of the Christian faith and of Christian morality, so she alone is able in our modern day to introduce again amid the conflicting currents, the solvent forces, and growing exhaustion of the West a single lofty purpose, a constructive and effective religious power, a positive moral energy and a vitalizing enthusiasm. And she alone can reunite the severed threads which joined our Western civilization to that great and rich past whence it sprang. Whether we look forwards or backwards, we realize that without the Church of Peter there will be no inward dynamic unity, no further "history" for the West, but only a succession of experiences without goal or purpose, the convulsive movements of a body that has lost its soul. We need the Church that we may live.

I grant that there are many who do not see the matter so. Nor is that their fault alone. When dark clouds of prejudice and misunderstanding obscure the fair image of our Church, we Catholics often must admit our guilt: *mea culpa, mea maxima culpa*. It is due in no small measure to our imperfections and frailties and sins that those dark clouds arise and conceal the countenance of the Bride of Christ. When God allowed great sections of the Church, containing an abundance of most noble and valuable elements, to separate from us, He punished not them only, but also us Catholics ourselves. And this

●

[7] *Op. cit.*, pp. 334 ff.

punishment, this penal permission of God, should, like all His permissions, cause us to look into ourselves and impel us to repentance. It should be an imperative "Do penance." The Spirit of Jesus is incarnate in the Church; we should all impress that Spirit on ourselves, and especially the spirit of love and brotherliness,[8] of loyalty and truth. And then it cannot be but that God, though after long wanderings and difficult inward crises of the Western soul, will graciously grant that we may all unite again, that our inward union with Jesus may become an outward fellowship also, that we may be one flock under one shepherd. Then will be fulfilled the sacred prayer which Jesus offered to His Father on the eve of His death: "And not for them only do I pray, but for them also who through their word shall believe in me, that they all may be one, as thou, Father, in me, and I in thee, that they also may be one in us, that the world may believe that thou hast sent me" (Jn 17:20, 21).

●

[8] Such is St. Augustine's admonition: "So then, brethren, be at peace. If you would draw others thereto, be you the first to be at peace, be you the first to lay hold of it" (*Serm.* 357, 3).

Editors' Note.—From THE SPIRIT OF CATHOLICISM, translated by Justin McCann, O.S.B. (rev. ed.; Image Books; Garden City, N. Y.: Doubleday, 1954) *pp. 85-101.*

Yves de Montcheuil, s.j.

The Role of the Hierarchy
in the Church

Christ is the Head of the Church, which is His Body. But, since His ascension, He is invisible, inaccessible to our senses. He makes the Church live by His Spirit, but we do not perceive Him in the same way the apostles saw Him guiding their little band. The Spirit He sends His Church, who is her soul and life-giving center, is Himself also invisible. Nevertheless, the Church is not a society whose members are left alone to themselves under the sole direction of the invisible Christ. All do not have the same role in it, all are not on the same level; just as there is among them a hierarchy of holiness—which is known to God—there is also a visible hierarchy, social and external.

The Church has never been, even for a short time, as some have imagined, a society in which religious enthusiasm, interior inspiration, was the only law, so that the determination of authority with its train of laws and regulations would have appeared only when the original fire had subsided, the first impetus died down. There did exist in the primitive Church a series of exterior spiritual manifestations, some of which are of a character quite disconcerting to us. St. Paul, who calls them "charisms," bears witness to their abundance, an abundance at times intemperate, since he sees himself obliged to regulate their expression (First Epistle to the Corinthians). Note, moreover, that he places charity above all the charisms. The habitual presence of these charisms in the first Christian communities is explained by providential circumstances and at the same time they bear the mark of the environment in which they appear. The disappearance takes nothing essential away from the Church. They are of value as helps, or as manifestations of the intensity of spiritual life, that is to say, in short, as manifestations of the intensity of charity. But charity, on the other hand, has value of itself. It is not necessarily diminished by their disappearance, for it can express itself in other ways.

Before or after the disappearance of the charisms, there has always existed in the Church a visible hierarchy not bound up with these charisms. Christ Himself is at its source by means of the functions He confided to the apostolic college, with Peter at its head. What is essential to this hierarchy has, therefore, existed since the beginning, although its forms and expression have varied very much in adapting themselves to the conditions in which the life of the Church was lived, to the very exigencies of her growth and to the complexity caused by her development. It is an important task to demonstrate the divine foundation of the ecclesiastical hierarchy, and its continuity in its essential organisms from the time of the apostles, in line with the expression of the Creed: *et apostolicam ecclesiam.* It is not the task I will take on here, at least directly. Our purpose is not to write history—though this is very necessary for apologetics and very useful for a wider knowledge—but rather to try to penetrate our faith.

The first thing for a Christian to do in the presence of the fact that there is a hierarchy whose subject he is, is to understand its meaning, to grasp its religious role. It is thus that he will see what his conduct towards it must be. The hierarchy must not be accepted simply as a fact, and especially must it not be endured as a fate involving a painful obligation to submit which is not really ratified deep down inside. Doubtless, it will always be more or less painful for us to obey. But if we have seen how the leadership of the hierarchy is necessary for our religious life, then we will love the sacrifice demanded of us. It will remain painful for the carnal man, but it will be a joy for the spiritual man. How, then, are we to understand the Catholic hierarchy?

THE MEANING OF THE HIERARCHY

There is, then, authority in the Church. This, we might think, is quite natural and contains no mystery. Only utopians can believe that a group of any sort can live without authority, and the fatal disintegration of all societies of any complexity at all which try to exempt themselves from this law removes this illusion. A religious society, therefore, must have, it is clear, a religious authority to insure order and common direction in it; an authority like all others except that it is exercised on the religious instead of the civil plane. It seems to me that that is the principle a liberal Protestantism might place as the basis of authority in the Church, when it does recognize one. In fact, if the Church is the grouping together of Christians who assemble to strengthen one another mutually in the spiritual life, we can scarcely see how there could be any other principle.

We could simply add that alongside the function of governing, other equally indispensable religious functions would have to appear. As a matter of fact, if there is worship at all complex in a somewhat numerous group, then it is necessary that someone be charged with it and consecrate himself to it, since the majority of the faithful are taken up with their particular occupations. From this there arises some sort of priesthood of service in worship, no matter what name we may give to it. Moreover, not all the faithful have the time or the chance to give themselves over to religious studies advanced enough to permit them to inventory for themselves the contents of revelation (represented, for the Protestants, by the Bible alone), to know how to find therein the answer to new questions, or at least the answer to the old questions asked in a new way. Certain persons will, therefore, have to consecrate themselves to this work, and they will then make the others benefit by their knowledge—in this sense, they will teach them. It seems, therefore, that authority and the functions of worship and teaching are necessary consequences of the existence of a religious society. If God has willed this religious society, He has also willed its conditions. It can, then, be said that this authority and these other functions which have in this way been set up within the society have a divine value. That much can be said of civil society, the state, whose existence is willed by God as necessary for the truly human existence of man, indispensable to humanity, which must pursue on earth the progress willed for it by God.

But this is borne out in another sense; for if a religious society be willed by Christ, to prolong the action which He began during the course of His earthly life, it must be said as a consequence that authority and the other religous functions of this society are equally willed by Christ.

What objection can we have against these considerations? Simply that they are *inadequate*. They have value, on the basis of experience and common thought, against those who might envision a religious society wherein there would be no differentiation. But they do not permit us to penetrate the meaning of the Catholic hierarchy. They do not reveal to us its relationship to Christ. That is because in this matter as elsewhere, if one wishes really to understand a reality which is "ecclesiastical" in the full sense of that word, that is to say, a reality belonging to and characteristic of the Church, then one has to begin by having a precise, exact idea of the Church. We must not consider her merely as a society which, having a religious purpose, must meet on the religious plane the requirements common to every society. *We must see her relationship to Christ,* a relationship which constitutes her in her original and unique reality.

Christ, we have already said, did not found the Church just once upon a time, as a man founds a human society which owes him its existence in the past but thereafter lives and develops without him. Jesus Christ remains the Head of the Church. He remains the Chief who instructs her, sanctifies her, directs her. He dwells with her "until the consummation of the world." It is true, in one sense, to say that He does this by means of His Spirit. But He also does it by means of the hierarchy which He established. Nor are these two separate means coming alternately into play. They are two means bound together, inseparable, representing as it were the visible and invisible aspects of the action of Christ on His Church. That is why, as Fr. Congar says in his *Esquisses du mystère de l'église,* p. 35: "It is not only sensible inanimate means, thing-sacraments, that Christ uses to perfect His Mystical Body, but it is also, and by the same logic, sensible animate means, person-sacraments. The Church is not only sacramental, she is apostolic and hierarchic." That is very exact—provided of course that it be properly understood. When the members of the Catholic hierarchy act in the exercise of the power confided to them by Christ, or, if you will, when they act under certain conditions which are not arbitrary but fixed by the will of Christ Himself, it is *the action of Christ which reaches us through them.* It is His teaching action, His sanctifying action, His commands.

God has not promised the men designated for such functions that He would take away their human weaknesses. What is more, even when they act rightly, their actions are not for all that always the vehicles of Christ's action. They have their personal opinions, their preferences, just as every man may have, and these, even when they are legitimate, are not necessarily Christ's ideas. We do not deify men even when they are irreproachable and virtuous. But what we are saying is that under certain given conditions, their acts, their teaching, their orders are the vehicles of Christ's action, of His teaching, of His will. They are not merely men who command other men because a religious society, as every other society, needs a specialized authoritative function. They bring down to us Christ's own action; through them this action reaches us. And that is what constitutes the proper characteristic of their authority. It is this particular link with Christ which gives the Catholic hierarchy its meaning. Even the action of Christ which He exercises through His Spirit is bound up with the intervention of these men.

Thus we are always coming back to the bond between the visible and the invisible in the Church, that is to say, in the action which Christ is exercising today in the midst of our humanity. The first of these two elements has no value and no meaning by itself, but only by means of the invisible element which it contains, which it secures, of which it is the means of realization. That is true of this matter, though in a different way, as it is of the water used in baptism or of the sensible species in the Eucharist. (Baptismal water, however, does not bear the same relationship to grace as the Eucharistic species bear to the body of Christ, but in the one case as in the other it is a matter of "signs," of "sacraments.") By the same token, the invisible element is normally bound up with the visible.

It is in this sense that we can speak of "person-sacraments"—not that all the actions of these persons are so many means whereby Christ leads His Church, but that this leadership is bound up with certain actions of these persons, actions which imply awareness, will, liberty. There is the reason why the existence of the hierarchy is not looked upon by the true Christian as a burden, a heavy drag on his religious life, but on the contrary as a help and a grace; for by means of it he comes in contact with Christ and puts himself under His vivifying and liberating influence. The hierarchy is not an intermediary that might prove to be an obstacle between Christ and himself; it is the means by which he is bound to Christ. Assuredly, it is only faith which makes him behold Christ's action in the action of the hierarchy. Just as in a sacrament the visible element veils over the invisible grace while at the same time it is its sign, it can also be said that the existence of the visible hierarchy is like a veil which hides from us the action of Christ. But we cannot say that it takes us far away or separates us from Him. And if we are asked why this veil, we must simply answer: *Because we are in a period of faith*, of trial; we are in the earthly stage. We must recognize Christ when He veils Himself in order one day to merit seeing Him face to face and experiencing His action directly, in all clarity.

Let us note also that the one who refuses the hierarchy because he wants direct communication with God, with Christ, hoping to find it in interior experience, that man is in the path of illusion. Interior experience is always a bit confusing—how to discern with accuracy the voice of God, that of Christ, from our own voice, the voice of our caprices or that of our human dreams? Catholicism does not deny at all that there is interior inspiration; however, when it has been nourished, it has still to be controlled, disciplined, corrected if need be. We have to make a distinction between what really comes from God, what we can have confidence in, and what comes from ourselves. But it is precisely the hierarchy which, with its teachings, and as a last resort its decisions, permits us to make this distinction. It therefore permits us to make use of interior inspiration; far from suppressing it, it uncovers it.

There again, it is important to understand clearly how a Catholic views the hierarchy, if we wish to understand the nature of the sentiments which attach him to it. This attachment is not found in the need for human support; it does not proceed from the fear of personal initiative (we will discuss this more at length); it is not the doing of a childish or a slavish soul. It has its source in *the will to submit oneself to Christ*, to remain subject to His illuminating and sanctifying action, to know what He expects from us, what is His will for us. Submission to the hierarchy, the acceptance of its decisions, may be difficult, because it is one of the means whereby Christ enters into our life, and this always wounds our egoism, always mortifies in us what St. Paul calls the "carnal man." But it is a joy for the spiritual man, whom it continues to liberate, a joy for whatever in us belongs to God or wants to belong to God.

That is the explanation also for the respect which the Christian has for all members of the hierarchy. He knows very well, as we have said, that they are not in every phase of their activity the representatives of Christ, and he retains his freedom with regard to the opinions and the preferences which they might manifest even in religious matters as private persons. But he everywhere and always respects them because of this action of Christ of which they are the instruments. Even outside of the Sacrifice, we never treat a chalice as an ordinary object. It is an analogous sentiment which inspires the attitude of the faithful not only towards the decisions or the teachings of the hierarchy, but towards the persons who have, in some degree, the mission of formulating and transmitting them.

Respect is never expressed by anything resembling flattery. That is even out of place with regard to human authority; a fortiori is it out of place with regard to those whom we venerate because of Christ whom they represent. The depth of the respect we have for them loses nothing by maintaining a certain sobriety in its expression, and it is to corrupt it to fall into obsequiousness—this latter is not religious, whereas the respect the faithful have for the members of the hierarchy is something of a religious nature. Naturally, this respect does not depend upon what they are themselves, and it must not be influenced by the human sentiments we may experience towards them.

The Catholic hierarchy was instituted by Christ when He established the apostles, the "Twelve," with Peter at their head. These transmitted their powers to their successors, who are the bishops. One of these, the bishop of Rome, is the successor of Peter. Always and in all places, in the exercise of their authority the members of the hierarchy are the "ministers of Christ." Whatever be the manner in which they are designated (that has changed very much in the course of twenty centuries of history), they are not delegated by the religious community to exercise the functions necessary for its existence. They are the means, the channels, which Jesus Christ uses to act in His Church. In her, everything comes from God through Christ. It is not of themselves, in virtue of their own efforts, that the members of the Church sanctify themselves, participate in divine life, are introduced into the life of the Trinity. It is God, it is Christ, who by His grace (with their free co-operation) sanctifies, elevates, divinizes them. The hierarchy, being the means by which grace is communicated to us, cannot be established except by Christ.

The hierarchy exercises a triple function and consequently is endowed with a threefold power: the power of teaching, which we also call the magisterium; the power of orders, which is concerned with the offering of sacrifice and the administration of the sacraments; the power of jurisdiction, which bears upon the internal government of the Church. Let us say a word about these three powers.

THE FUNCTIONS OF THE HIERARCHY

The Power of Teaching

The role of the magisterium is *to preserve intact the deposit of faith,* to keep it from all corruption, to teach the faithful, to prevent them from going astray in their beliefs, to make them grow in the faith. We can understand the importance and necessity of this function when we also understand the primal place of faith in the Christian life; it is to insure its exercise that the magisterium is endowed by the assistance of the Holy Spirit with the privilege of infallibility. Doubtless, the Church taken as a whole is infallible, in the sense that the Church as a whole will never accept a doctrine contrary to faith. But that does not exclude the fact that we must distinguish in her the teaching Church and the Church taught. The teaching Church is precisely the hierarchy in so far as it has the function of teaching the faithful. This teaching refers only to questions bearing on the religious life, that is to say, on the truths of faith, or truths accessible to reason the upholding of which is important for the preservation of the truths of faith (for example, the existence of God, the immortality of the soul). It is evidently necessary to include among the truths of faith those which refer to conduct.

The bishops reunited in general council ("ecumenical" council) are infallible, and their teachings do not need to be ratified by the assembly of the faithful in order to be infallible. The pope speaking *ex cathedra,* that is to say, as the teacher of the universal Church with the formal intention of teaching a point of doctrine as forming part of the faith, is infallible, and his teaching too, under these conditions, does not need to be submitted for the assent of the bishops in order to be binding.

Alongside these methods of proceeding, which are relatively rare, and which pertain to what is called the extraordinary exercise of the magisterium, there is its ordinary exercise, the one which is carried out by means of the teaching which the hierarchy on all levels gives in the ordinary course of the life of the Church. A teaching which comes from the whole hierarchy, that is, from the whole Church, through the ordinary magisterium, cannot be false, for that would indicate that those who are charged with stimulating the faith of the believers had themselves fallen into error. But the existence of a power of teaching founded by Christ has for its very purpose the avoidance of just such straying away. But we must nevertheless realize that many doctrinal decisions, either because they emanate from just a few members of the hierarchy, or if they come from the pope, because he does not intend to impose them on the universal Church, do not possess the note of infallibility. Often even, though their content is doctrinal, they are of a disciplinary nature; for example, it might be forbidden to teach, to propagate such and such a doctrine. Without wishing to commit itself as to the core of such doctrines, the hierarchy thinks that in certain determinate circumstances, given the state of the question and the condition of minds, they are dangerous to faith. Such decisions are obviously not irrevocable, which does not of course mean that we are not to pay any attention to them. In all this, we must neither try to exempt ourselves from the authority of the hierarchy nor give to its decisions a bearing which itself it does not give them. It is a common pitfall among zealous but little-informed laymen (as also among those on the outside), this exaggeration of the properly doctrinal scope of that type of decision. Trained theologians are generally more reserved. Let us always remember that the function of the magisterium is to bring down to us the teaching of Christ, the thought of Christ. It is in this way that we must see it in order to accept its decisions.

The Power of Orders

The second function of the hierarchy is one of sanctification and is insured by the power of orders. This power is essentially concerned with the administration of the sacraments. Of course, it is not only the members of the hierarchy, bishops or priests, who can administer the sacraments. All men can validly confer baptism and do so licitly in case of necessity; and it is the spouses who are reciprocally the ministers of the sacrament of matrimony. But to get right down to essentials, let us say that it is to the hierarchy, in so far as it is endowed with the power of orders, that our Lord has given power over His body in the Eucharist. This is so true that we can say that the power of orders is the power to consecrate the body of Christ and to prepare the faithful for the reception of the Eucharist, which is the center of the whole Christian sacramental mystery. The power of orders, we can also say, is the power of making Christ sacramentally present and active in the Church. Those who have received it in its plenitude, the bishops, can transmit it either in its fulness, by consecrating other bishops, or in part, by conferring holy orders. Among these latter, the priesthood and the deaconate are certainly also of divine institution. (We do not wish here to take sides in the question of ascertaining whether or not the episcopacy constitutes, properly speaking, a superior order with relation to the priesthood.)

When they act in accordance with the power of orders in administering the sacraments, the members of the hierarchy are the instruments of Christ, free, personal instruments, to the extent that the exercise of this power requires a free act on their part. A sacrament is valid only if its minister consciously wants to administer it. Nevertheless, he is still only an instrument. It is Christ who sanctifies by means of his ministry; through him the faithful are put in contact with Christ.

The power of orders was communicated to the apostles by Christ with the fulness of the priesthood. All of them received it directly from Christ, and not through the intermediary of Peter. They transmitted it to their successors, the bishops, and these can in turn transmit it also. They can do so licitly with the consent of the pope; they can do so validly even against his will. It is thus that the schismatical churches can perpetuate in themselves the episcopate and the priesthood. There is no superiority of the pope over the bishops from the point of view of the power of orders taken in itself. A simple priest cannot ordain another priest, since he has not received the fulness of the priesthood. He cannot licitly make use of his power of orders without the consent of his bishop, but he can do so validly. He can always, no matter what his situation may be, celebrate Mass validly. The power of orders has, therefore, as its end to insure our sanctification by Christ.

The Power of Jurisdiction
The third function of the hierarchy is the government of the Church. That is assured by what is called the power of jurisdiction. This deals with the social relations of Christians as Christians. Its purpose is the proper organization of the visible Church, the proper conduct of the Church as the people of God living in earthly conditions. It is exercised either by means of general laws (which make up canon law, the code of the Church) or by means of particular decisions. It pertains to the hierarchy, by virtue of its power of jurisdiction, to adapt the laws of the Church to times and places, to take all the means necessary for discipline and good order. All the same, this power is not unlimited; it is exercised only within the limits set up by Christ. The hierarchy cannot modify what is of divine institution in the make-up of the Church. In effect, it has received from Christ a power of jurisdiction in order to govern His Church during the time that His visible absence will continue, that is, as long as the world lasts.

The power of jurisdiction was given by Christ to the apostles, but dependent upon Peter. The bishops possess it, therefore, only dependent on the pope, which implies that a particular bishop has no legitimate jurisdiction unless it be confided to him by the pope, who can take it away from him, and that the pope always has the right to intervene directly in a diocese. Nevertheless, he cannot govern the Church without bishops, and they are not his delegates. It is not for reasons of mere practical convenience that there are bishops—their existence in the Church is of divine right. But the pope is superior to the bishops from the point of view of jurisdiction. It is in virtue of his pre-eminent place in this regard that he is called the Vicar of Jesus Christ. He is not His successor, as though he took His place, but only

His Vicar, the visible representative who governs in His name and by His actual, not past, authority. If there is at the head of the Church a bishop, the bishop of Rome, who has competence and authority not over just a portion of the Church, but over the whole Church, and is the only one to have it, the reason must not be sought primarily in the advantages of one-man rule; rather it is in this way, in accordance with the will of Christ, that the oneness of the Church and her invisible Head is visibly brought out.

It is well to insist on the difference of the relationship which the power of jurisdiction and the power of orders each have to Christ. Through the power of orders, the hierarchy is an instrument of sanctification in the hands of Christ in the administration of the sacraments; it places the acts through which the grace of Christ will flow. The power of jurisdiction also comes from Christ. The hierarchy receives it within certain limits, since, as we have said, it cannot modify the divine constitution of the Church which assures her her place. But within these limits it has full power to decide, and what it decides becomes for the faithful the will of Jesus Christ Himself. There is no doubt that God gives His graces to those who are thus charged with commanding in His name, no doubt that He watches over the Church to the extent that she cannot disappear. The assistance of the Holy Spirit is promised her, and the preparing of the kingdom of God will never cease being done through her. Our pastors will never render impossible the work they have the mission of promoting.

Nevertheless, Christ has not guaranteed that those whom He has set up in the Church will always make decisions which are objectively the wisest and best-suited; we need not create such an illusion in order to believe. Still, it is with reason that we admire canon law as being a marvelous work of wisdom. However, it is never claimed that all the desirable reforms have always been made as soon as it was opportune, and especially in the case of particular decisions it is never claimed that they have always been or will always be the best possible.

But what we have to maintain is that when the hierarchy gives us a command on its own ground, which is that of the religious and moral life (later on we shall see how the temporal order can be affected indirectly), as long as the fulfilling of the order it gives does not constitute a sin, it expresses the will of Christ for us. It is this will of Christ that we are fulfilling by obeying it. Without a doubt there is a profound mystery in seeing Christ's all-holy will thus hiding itself, so to speak, behind the imperfections and unavoidable insufficiencies of His representatives. But we are not obliged any the less to look for it where He has been pleased to put it, to listen to it wherever He is pleased to express it, and not where we would like to find it. We know that Christ watches over His Church and will never allow her to stop doing His work. We know that only in her is the coming of the kingdom being prepared. We know that nothing is to be preferred to unity, the bonds of which are loosened by all unruliness. By our obedience we are contributing to the preparation of the kingdom of God; by disobeying we only hinder it. It is in the power of jurisdiction, because the exercise thereof involves the intervention of a larger share of what is human, that Jesus Christ hides Himself more thoroughly behind the hierarchy He has instituted. But He is nonetheless present in it and acting through it. You see here to what extent the Church is a human-divine mystery. The divine makes use of the human, but it neither absorbs nor suppresses it.

This threefold function of the hierarchy has as its end the sanctification of souls. By their power of magisterium, of orders, and of jurisdiction, the apostles and their successors bring about the perfection of the Mystical Body. Entrance into the kingdom, the coming of the kingdom, is bound up with their ministry. It is not a question simply of governing an earthly society, no matter how august. In this also the visible and the invisible are united. That is why, too, the hierarchy knows it has received its powers for the service and the good of those whom it rules. One of the titles that the pope gives himself is that of *servus servorum Dei*. That is not an honorific title. The members of the hierarchy consider themselves as bearers of the action of Christ. They do not act by virtue of power which they have of themselves or which they merit by their personal qualities; it is Christ who wishes to make use of them to reach all the faithful.

Lastly, let us add that the exercise of these different powers is bound up with the state in which the Church finds herself on earth. There is no doubt that those who have received the sacrament of holy orders will always remain bishops or priests, since orders impress a character. But at the end, in the state of perfection, the power of teaching will no longer have any object, since vision will have succeeded faith. The power of orders will be superfluous, since we will be united directly, fully, and without any veils to the Source of holiness. The power of jurisdiction will no longer be needed—there will no longer be any need for anyone to take the place of Christ, who will no longer be invisible, and it will be charity in light which, possessed by all, will insure the unity, the cohesion of the Church. No longer will there be any need for a law, for an external command, since the living law, charity, will have become internal to each one, and no one will ever be in danger of taking anything at all away from it in himself. Every veil will be lifted, all vicariousness abolished, all "pedagogies" bypassed, and there will be only "Christ, all in all."

Editors' Note.—From ASPECTS OF THE CHURCH, translated by Albert J. LaMothe, Jr. (Chicago: Fides, 1955) *pp. 93-111.*

The Vision of the Way

The Vision of the Way
Gerald Vann, O.P.

PREFACE

Our present chapter, "The Vision of the Way," brings us to the end of our speculative journey through the Idea of Catholicism. The editors would like to point out what seems to them the critically important thing about this chapter. It is that it enables the first part of this book to end where it began, lodged deeply in the place of human personality in religion and in the role that Catholicism plays for the creation and fostering of human personality.

We began our total study with a section that insisted on the personal nature of religion as a relation between the soul and God. Every doctrinal study inbetween this and all that Fr. Vann will say has only deepened, strengthened, enlarged, and refined this relation. The personal factor in the basic religious equation has not been disturbed; rather, thought and doctrine have fortified it. It is only the superficial reader who will declare that real thought is an obstacle to, and not a friend of, real experience. We are all of one piece. Sensibility should not go off in one direction and doctrine in another.

So now again the soul confronts God. But now more surely and in a great enabling context: in Christ, in the company of the human community, in a sure march of history, with the strength of vigorous sacraments, in the light of wide-ranging truth. Now the soul can say even more firmly: "I to my beloved, my beloved unto me."

Gerald Vann, o.p.

The Vision of the Way

The way back to God is the way of worship. If all that we are and become and do in our many-leveled life could be made one in worship, we should be saints. Some people think that Christian morality is no more than a series of Don'ts; others a little less ill-informed think it is no more than a series of Do's. These things are included, for being and doing are interdependent; but it is being that comes first in importance; and Christian morality tells us first of all not what we should do, still less what we should not do, but what we should be.

That is why you cannot possibly separate, as some people would have us do, the Church's moral teaching from its beliefs about God's revelation of Himself to the world. You cannot possibly separate them, because the moral teaching is entirely determined by the doctrine; and if you try to isolate it, you destroy it. You could isolate this or that element in it; you could cling to the ideals of justice, kindness, generosity, fortitude; but these virtues would then cease to be the Christian virtues, because they would be divorced from worship.

You find a marked similarity on the surface between the *Ethics* of Aristotle and that part of the *Summa* of St. Thomas which deals with morality; but the similarity is far less striking than the difference. Aristotle will tell you how to act wisely and well in accordance with reason, and what he says is often so true and so salutary that St. Thomas is at pains to repeat it; but all that is secondary, all that is relatively unimportant; you can obey all these precepts and acquire all these good habits and still find at the end that the "good life" has been led by the false self and not by the true. These things are secondary; what is of first importance is the reality whose presence kindles and whose absence kills them: the rebirth of the self in God, the recognition that God and not the ego is the center of the self.

You remember the Pharisee and the publican in the Temple. The Pharisee was living the "good life"; but notice what he says: "I give thanks . . . I fast . . . I give tithes," and the good deeds turn to ashes because it is always "I"; it is the self which competently acts, the self which is served; there is no suggestion of need of the Other, the hunger of the heart is forgotten because pride has repressed it. The publican probably fails miserably to live the "good life," but he has the core of Christian as opposed to pagan morality, he has the one thing necessary, the pearl of great price, because he has learnt that he must say with his whole being not "I" but "Lord."

Christian morality is worship. There are prohibitions: they are the minimum, though many of us find that even this minimum is more than we can achieve. Thou shalt not kill, thou shalt not steal, thou shalt not commit adultery, thou shalt not covet: it is not always easy to keep these and all the lesser prohibitions of anger and injustice and intemperateness which they include. But notice how Christianity changes them. Thou shalt love: this is the essence of Christian morality; and to love is to dethrone the false self and be able to say, "It is thou." You are forbidden, then, to kill and steal and covet; but you are forbidden *because* these are sins against love, because they hurt those with whom you should be living in love. The proud man may refrain from these things because it is to his own interest; the Christian must refrain from these things primarily because if he does not he cannot love, he cannot live life in its wholeness, he cannot worship.

But a second thing follows. If it is love that leads you to refrain from injustice, it will lead you to more than that. As love grows deeper and wider in you and you come nearer to the fulness of life, you will find that this minimum becomes hopelessly insufficient; you will find the negative carried further and further over to the affirmation of its opposite. The saint's love prompts him not to kill in the service of the false self, but to sacrifice his own life if need be in the service of God and men; not to steal for himself, but to share all that he has with others; not to destroy a family life by wrecking its unity, but to give himself, even perhaps by forgoing his own family life, to restoring the family life of the world. Whatever he does is done thus as worship of the One and of the many in the One. How terrible when we find ourselves thinking of the moral law as a denial of freedom and happiness. These things are not wrong because they are forbidden: they are forbidden because they are wrong; and they are wrong because they are alien to the nature of man in general—because freedom and a full and dignified human life are impossible until they are outlawed; but principally because they make it impossible to escape from isolation, they make it impossible for us to love.

The lover does not find that love takes his freedom from him; on the contrary, he is tied and unhappy only if he is impeded from serving what he loves. If we obey the commandments because we fear that otherwise we shall be punished, we are not yet emancipated from the "bondage of the law" of which St. Paul speaks, we are not yet free. If we keep the commandments because we recognize that they are the necessary pattern of our own perfection, we are free but not yet happy, for we are still alone. But if, while accepting the commandments, as men, because they are the pattern of perfection, we yet obey them primarily because we are living in love, then we are fully free and fully happy, we are both man and child.

Christian morality tells us what we must be. We must be whole. If we are whole, or trying to be whole, we shall act in a certain way, the way of love and worship. If we love and worship, we shall refrain from acting in ways that hurt love and destroy worship. That is the Christian order. Our Lord did not say, "I am come that you may have a code of ethics," though He told us much about the way we should act; He said, "I am come that you may have life, and have it more abundantly."

The moral way is the way of rebirth. The new life is given chiefly through the sacraments; to receive it adequately and respond to it, we must be men of prayer and virtue; the power is from God, but God waits upon our will.

We must be men of prayer. Some people think that prayer just means asking for things, and if they fail to receive exactly what they asked for, they think the whole thing a fraud. Prayer does mean asking, though it means far more than that; but it must be not the proud self but the lover who asks. The lover may ask for gifts; but he will not want to ask against the will of the other, and he will not want to ask for gifts that would hurt love; he cannot, because his deepest wants are not his own. There is nothing very mysterious, still less is there anything superstitious, about the kind of prayer that is asking, if you accept the idea that there is spiritual energy and power as well as physical, and that the first can and does influence the second. Spiritual power unaided—the power of a personality—can produce physical changes in men and cause them to act uncharacteristically in this way or in that; and similarly the power of spirit in the universe may be taken to be capable of influencing physical events. One thing is immovable, being perfect, the will of God; but we do not suppose that prayer can alter God's providence, we believe that God's providence includes the power of prayer among the many converging influences which, under His will, produce events. What is superstitious is to suppose that prayer can, in fact, compel God's will, to suppose that prayer is magic, to suppose that if I pray for a coat, a coat will infallibly appear in my wardrobe. We pray within the design of God's providence, not against it.

But even if you take the superstition out of it, you are still far from real prayer unless you pray as a lover. "Give me this gift, but only if you want to." "Let this chalice pass from me, but not my will but thine be done." Love has such power that it can extort; but to extort is the last thing it wants to do. (That is why it is so terrible when the lover sinks back into the false selfhood which grasps and utilizes; for then he extorts, and perhaps only long after realizes he has hurt or destroyed love.) To pray is to ask as lover of God; it is also to ask as lover of the world. We are a family. Not only, "Give me this gift if you think it will be good for me," but also, "Give me this gift if you think it will be good for the family." We pray not for ourselves merely but for the world; and even when we pray for ourselves, we have to remember the good of the world.

But prayer is much more than asking. If we kept it to that, we might forget the Giver in our concern for His gifts. If we follow the example of the Church in the Mass, we shall begin with confession and penitence, the prayer of the publican; we shall go on to adoration and praise and the still, wordless prayer of wonder;[1] and only then shall we ask, when our attention is fixed on the true Center of the self; and even so, though we pray for our own private needs and desires, we shall remember the "Collects"—the united prayers for the united needs of the world. And indeed, just as we see things at their most real when we see them and love them in God, so our prayer is most powerful and most of value when it is gathered up into the cosmic prayer of Christ and His Church. As we take the whole world to the Mass to be offered and blessed and restored, so we take our prayer to be offered and empowered. The first thing that prayer can do for us is to make us humble: to make us realize that the source of power— the power to pray, the power to live the life of virtue—is not primarily in ourselves, but in God. When prayer has thus taught us the Christian approach to morality, we shall begin to turn the whole moral life into prayer.

The Christian life, then, is always the life of the child. Yes, indeed; but it is also and equally the life of the man. There is the twofold progress: to live more and more in the life and the power of God, to grow more and more in strength and maturity of mind and will and personality. The more deeply and fully you become the Other, the more deeply and fully you become yourself. And as the ultimate purpose and motive of all activity is the giving of glory to God's love, which is also and at the same time my own perfection and happiness,

●

[1] The wordless tapestry of sound woven, in the music of the Mass, on the final syllable of the word of praise, Alleluia; still more, the startling stillness that descends on a church at the elevation of the Host.

so the means to the end is worshiping obedience to God's power and will within me, which is also and at the same time my own labor and effort. We believe that through baptism we are given the power to live the life of virtue; but that I should act here and now virtuously depends on my own long and laborious efforts to translate the power into practice, to acquire the habit of so acting. We have to train ourselves to freedom, to think for ourselves and judge for ourselves and act for ourselves, for only free acts can be the material out of which the good life is fashioned; and the training consists in constantly acting as we ought so as to form the habit of acting as we ought, for acts are in the realm of doing but habits are in the realm of being, and it is only when we *are* good that we have the good life. So we become good in so far as we become free *men;* but the freedom we acquire is the freedom to obey love, the freedom to live the life of the *child.*

We believe that the moral life is the search for wholeness. Some have taught that the end in view is to become the perfectly rational man, and that the way is to suppress the passions and emotions lest they sweep like a gale through the trim temple of reason and disturb the worshipers. It is Talleyrand's *surtout point de zèle,* and the correctness of eighteenth-century religion and the eighteenth-century God. We have seen already what happens when you repress half the personality. But what a religion! You would be saying to God, "Oh yes, I worship you; but only with that portion of your handiwork which I find it possible to consider respectable." You might attempt to praise God thus: but you would stifle yourself with the starchy formalities of your illuminated address. You could praise Him with logic and science, never with timbrel and harp, never with poetry and ecstasy and ardor, never with love. Christian morality is worship: not the worship of the divine mind by the human reason, but the worship by the whole man of the whole God. You worship with the whole man in so far as instincts, passions, emotions, mind, will are integrated and fulfilled in the unity of the personality by being "harnessed to the service of the Light." And again, how is this process brought about? By childlike obedience to the power and sharing in the life of God; by laboriously acquiring the maturity and mastery of manhood.

Virtue is defined as the enduring possession of the power to act with facility and readiness in a certain way. You can speak instead, if you will, of a "good habit"; but it is not a question of a mechanical habit in the sense of a mannerism which is often unconscious and unconsciously acquired. The musician acquires by long hard practice the enduring ability to play well; if you have acquired the habit of temperateness or generosity you will normally and spontaneously be gentle and generous. But it is more than a technique. The musician must have the technical skill; but technical skill alone does not make the musician. To bring the technique to life, you must have music in the soul. Vision without skill is dumb; but skill without vision is dead. So with the moral virtues: there is the acquired skill, but underneath the skill, the vision. You must know the presence of God in the soul.

First, then, maturity of mind, mastery, autonomy: not the proud, assumed autonomy of the false self which tries to master God, but the real autonomy of the man who has learnt to master himself. You must acquire knowledge, you must be critical and learn to judge, you must be able to make up your own mind, you must try to be wise: because the judgment, "This is the right action and not that," must rest, in the last resort, with that power in the mind to make practical moral decisions which we call conscience. Then you find the four great modes of right action, prudence, justice, fortitude, temperateness, as elements in every virtuous action; but these things are the possession of the mature personality; they mean the exercise of reason, courage, and control. And each particular virtue in its turn means a similar mastery of the particular material involved. The man of virtue is master and maker; for he has mastered the material of life and acquired the art of living.

But behind the skill, the vision. The temperate man is usually absolved from the labor of reasoning out how to act temperately here and now; he knows by a kind of instinct; and he knows because he not only *has* tenderness and the humility of the flesh, but *is* humble and tender. So you find in him a childlike freshness and spontaneity that are denied to the purely rational man.

Then again, all virtue is grounded in humility and is a mode of worship; and again you have the dependence and smallness of the child.

There is a third thing. The moral life as a whole is rooted in the life shared directly with God, the life of faith, hope, and love. And by faith we are led, not against reason but beyond reason, to the knowledge of God in Himself and therefore of ourselves. By hope we are kept young of heart; for it teaches us to trust in God, to work with all our energy but to leave the future to Him: it gives us poverty of spirit and so saves us from solicitude. And by love we are not told about God, we are brought to Him; we are brought down into the depths of the soul to become one with Him there, to learn through sorrow and repentance to be reborn and say, "It is thyself"; and then it drives us out again to rediscover the world and to make all men and things our brothers, to show us the unity of the family of creation: and so we have still more emphatically the affirmation that God is the center and that, if we live, we live in Him.

And then, finally, there is the direct influence and impulsion of the Spirit upon the soul; for though the power of God that is given us is expressed through the virtues, the vitality of the virtues themselves is limited by the fact that they are the possession of finite human mind and will. We try to hold the infinite in human hands. We see as in a glass, darkly; however fervent the faithful Christian, there is an imperfection in faith itself because in itself it is obscure; there is an imperfection in the moral life because the apprehension of the good is limited in itself by the narrow compass of the human mind. But as the wind that bloweth where it listeth, so is everyone that is born of the Spirit: it is the breath of the Spirit that gives us the freedom of the sons of God because it raises human action above the confines of the purely human. All the powers of the personality will be given this enlightening and energizing impulsion if we can learn to accept and respond to it: the mind's darkness illumined by a direct experience of God, an intuitive perception of divine truth, a sense of the Christian life both in theory and in action; the moral life deepened and strengthened by an immediately God-given sense of worship and reverence, and by a childlike confidence that is proof against all dangers, together with an "insatiable desire" to overcome them all in His service.

Here, when this direct loving obedience to the Spirit is perfect (for here, too, God waits upon our will), we have the fulness of the moral life, the immensity of power and personality of the Christian saint. Think for a moment of a type of man with whom we are too familiar. At his most characteristic he is somewhat stout and red of face from heavy food; he is capable in office or shop or factory; when he leaves it he likes a good meal, though he is hardly discriminating; he reads the paper or glances at a magazine or two; he likes a tot of whisky, though he is inclined to bolt it a little thoughtlessly; he may while away the time uncritically at a cinema; if he talks about anything at all outside his own immediate work or pleasures, he will probably repeat in slightly garbled form the political views of his morning paper; he calls his friends "old boy" and his wife "old girl," and if he is what is known as a clean-living man he will probably develop an irritability or some other mild form of mental or physical disorder which he will ascribe to business anxieties; he will never get to know his son and daughter and would find it impossible if he tried, and when he is dying he will possibly shed a secret tear or two over his dog, whom he has never understood either. Could we say that this was a moral life? We could not, for the simple reason that it was not a life at all. Morality is a sort of life, not a sort of death.

If ever we feel forced to conclude that the great majority of a nation is like this, we shall have to conclude also that the nation is doomed. It is possible to be dead in every sense that matters and still go on catching the train to the office in the morning. When a whole nation does that, it is better perhaps that it should do the thing thoroughly. Thank God, there are still an enormous number who have not had life and wisdom smothered and killed by what is called education. The other day in a village inn an old man spoke to me of the farmlands in the village and the quality of the soil and the way the fields were being ruthlessly torn and plundered and left in ruin by the men who wanted the iron ore and had no concern for the land; he spoke with knowledge and sense and wisdom; he did not know about the land merely, he knew the land, he had the feel of the land in his soul, he was alive. Thank God, there are still many like him. But he was old.

"I have said, Ye are gods." And yet we have known men who were dead though the fact had not occurred to them; and we have seen squalor and stupidity and the pettiness that poisons and kills. Where are these gods? Look at the saints. We think of gods as having a greater intensity of life, a greater power and a greater freedom than we. And here in the saints we have the "insatiable desire" for meeting difficulties and braving dangers; we have the "hunger and thirst after justice"; we have the charity that reaches to the ends of the world; we have the fullest possible intensity of life because we have the infinity of the life and power of God. The man who is dead in spirit was once alive when he was a child and was one with the universe; and here we have the complete obedience to the Spirit, the power to see with the eyes of God and judge with the mind of God and desire with the will of God which mean that the life of the child is preserved and fulfilled in the heart of the saint. We think of the gods as having a greater intensity of life than we. And here we have the fulness of a life that is whole; a life in which instincts and emotions and desires and thought and will are all gathered up and given a more than human vitality by being made to share in the life and express and fulfil the purposes of the Infinite. We think of the gods as having a greater power than we; and here we have the faith that moves mountains, the strength that laughs at perils, the love that sweeps like a gale wind through the world because it is one with the Love that is a burning and a consuming fire. We think of the gods as having a greater freedom than we. And here we have the freedom that always does what it wants; the freedom that has gone beyond the freedom from the slavery of sin and the pseudo self, beyond the bondage of the law which seems like an external restraint because it is obeyed only from fear, beyond the clash of finite with infinite will, because we have here the man who has found that the heart is only fully free when it is living in love, and that then it is free because there are no longer two wills but only one. "I am come that you may have *life*, and have it more abundantly."

At the summit of the moral life you come to the point where lover and master, child and man, the man of vision and the man of power, meet and are one. And in so doing, you come also to the answer of the greatest paradox that confronts the moralist. "If I seek for virtue I seek for my own perfection; but if I seek for my own perfection I am selfish, and selfishness is the essence of vice." It is an argument that seems to hold against the ethic of Aristotle; it will not hold against the morality that is worship. When you speak of love, you cannot really distinguish giving from getting, for each is indistinguishably both. You cannot take the desire for joy out of love without destroying it; but the desire for joy is itself a desire to give, and the joy is desired only provided that it is a gift. *Nihil unquam in te nisi te exquisivi;* when you seek virtue you desire God, who is your joy; but the more deeply you are living in love, the more fully you will live in Him, and therefore, even though you more and more desire your own happiness with Him, you will more and more think of your happiness in terms of serving Him.

The end of the moral life is wholeness. But it is wholeness of life; and life is creative energy. All living is seeing and loving; but all living is also making. The vision of the artist impels him to express what he has seen; the love of the lover impels him to give. The man who is dead in spirit is not dead merely because only a minute fragment of his personality exists; he is dead because he leaves the world unenlarged. The morality which is worship is both vision and love; and you cannot see it fully unless you see it as it affects the world. The whole human being is more than an individual body-spirit, a closed system: he is an individual in an environment, and on every level he is related by a thousand bonds to that environment, which he must affect for good or for ill. To be just or temperate is to deal justly or temperately with persons and things. If you are unjust and cruel, you may ruin another human life; if you are gentle and generous, you may make it enduringly happy. We are individuals in an environment; we are individuals in an environment which is largely in the power of evil, and for which we are largely responsible. Morality, then, is worship; but that sort of worship which fulfils in the world the purposes of God. This is the insatiable desire of the saints: to help to restore the world to God. It is not enough to be all things; we have to help and to restore all things. It is not enough to "realize the idea of the Good" in our own lives; we have to realize the idea of the Good in our environment. For indeed, the Good we have to express in our lives is God; and God is self-diffusive Love.

The morality which is ultimately self-centered is of necessity individualist also—even the service of others can be a form of selfishness; but the morality which is God-centered, though it necessarily involves the perfection of the self, looks directly to the purposes of God. So when we think of the moral life from God's side, in terms of the giving of His power and life through the sacramental system, we cannot forget that this power is given not for ourselves alone. The Church's office is to bring the truth and the life of God to the world, to restore it; sometimes this power is given to individuals entirely for the sake of others; you read in the New Testament of the gifts of "tongues" and prophecy and the rest, which served and empowered the Church as a whole; you read especially of the gift of healing, the healing of body and soul alike, by prayer and the laying on of hands; and still today the Church's office and privilege is to bless and to heal—to bless the earth and the fruits of the earth, to bless the animals, to bless mankind, and to heal the sick in body and mind, to heal by prayer and blessing, to heal through the liturgy which has such power to restore and integrate the unconscious, to heal through the touch of the waters at Lourdes where faith makes whole. But that is not all. The life and power that are given to the individual for the individual are given to the man in his environment, are given to the man as taking part in the cosmic struggle, and so are given in their turn for the blessing and healing of all things.

Think first of baptism. It gives us the new life, which is to say precisely that it frees us from the bondage of the spirit of evil and makes it possible for us to live and work for the purposes of God. Its first concern is with the individual personality; but we necessarily affect our environment not only by what we do but by what we are; and as baptism creates in us the responsibility of being members of the Church, the responsibility of being lovers of one another, so it gives us the power to fulfil our responsibilities.

Faith is life, for it means living in God; but the life of God is something that has to be slowly and painfully realized in us—we have to do and experience in our own way what Christ did and experienced for us; and this personal progress is part of a much vaster cosmic process, the long travail whereby the world as a whole must learn eventually to "put on Christ" and to be made whole. As we are dependent on and determined by the past, so we, in our own lives, fashion the future. Just as we ourselves in the present are weakened (because the Church is weakened) by every individual betrayal and strengthened (because the Church is strengthened) by every individual fidelity, so if we succeed in realizing the life of God within us we build up the future, if we fail we destroy.

What Christ did for us, we in our own way must do. If you are a Christian, you must be a mediator. Living in union with Christ, you must labor to bring the life and power of Christ into the world to which you are bound by the solidarity of sin; the Church, like the individual, is not a closed system, but a power and an energy that come from God and go out to the world in order to bring the two together; by baptism you are made a sharer in the power and the energy and, therefore, in the work that has to be done.

The sacraments correspond to the deep enduring needs and also to the great landmarks of human life. Baptism is the sacrament of rebirth, the sacrament of the child. Confirmation is the sacrament of the youth approaching manhood, about to face the world as an independent person. He will have to face a world that is largely hostile to his true self; he may have to face an environment that will oppose all his deepest desires and dreams; and he will have to be strong if he is to resist submersion and retain his independence. This sacrament of strengthening is given us to bring about the victory of independence; it is given us to make us spiritually adult also. Catholics speak of the Church as a mother: her motherhood is the correlative of the humility of the child; but just as the growth of human life implies a growth of independence, of the power to make one's own life, so too we become spiritually adult in so far as we arrive at maturity of judgment and conscience and the ability to play our own part in the cosmic struggle on the side of the good—serving the Church and not merely relying on her. Hence the symbolism of this sacrament: oil denoting strength and the warrior spirit, the anointing on the forehead for courage, the tap on the cheek for endurance of hardship and suffering, the pentecostal fire which symbolizes growth as the water of baptism symbolizes birth. We are come to the fulness of social responsibility; we are to be masters and makers and not merely children; we are to bring holiness to others by being holy ourselves, to set others on fire by contact with the fire within us.

So the sacrament of confirmation is associated with the old traditional idea of the common priesthood of the laity: the official sharing in the priestly power and office of Christ. If you are looking for the essential meaning of the Church, do not stop short at the organization, the legal and juridical aspects, do not isolate the teaching authority, for this, too, is only a part: you will find the essential meaning of the Church and its claims when you see it as a torrent of life and power —the life and power that teach and sanctify and rule—descending from God to man.

The Church is essentially Christ living and acting in the world. But we must think of Christ as the "total Christ": Christ acting in and through the authority and power of the Church, and thence in and through the whole family of Christians. So that if His power is not opposed but on the contrary more and more fully recognized and received by the Christian—received precisely through loving obedience to the Church—then the Christian is fully a Christian at last because at last he is bearing the Christ within him out into the world which as yet knows not Christ; he is living the Christian life in something of its fulness because he is receiving from Christ in the Church the life and power that can restore the world, and turning with love to the task of restoring it. Notice how at the first Pentecost it is not to individuals merely but to the Christian family that the Spirit comes, and comes as fire: it is the bringing of a common power for this common task—the task of restoring all things in Christ.

But unhappily, we can never think of the cosmic struggle as though it were a clearly defined battle between the forces of good and the forces of evil. It is waged by the Church; but it is waged also within the Church. We betray what we love. We try to fight for the restoration of the world, for the coming of the kingdom; but the coming is postponed, and the power of the Church to heal and make holy is curtailed, by the persisting presence and power of evil within us. My personal sins reinforce the power of evil; but I am responsible for more than this. We are one in the love and life of God, but we are one also in the solidarity of sin. Whenever I sin I first of all weaken the Church; and through that weakening there are other sins, and I am in part responsible for them. But the mercy of God will repair this damage too. We see the sacrament of penance in its fulness and greatness if we see it thus against the background of the total struggle. It has as its first purpose to restore the individual to life in God; but it is medicinal also to the life of the Church as a whole. We retard the Church's work by our sins; we help it on by our use of this sacrament— building up our own health and power, we help to build up the corporate health and power of the community of Christians also.

Penance is the sacrament of healing, the healing of the individual for the strengthening of the Church. It is not a negative thing—the wiping out of something that is past; the past is never abolished. Its whole purpose is positive and creative. Just as personal sin repeats over again the primal sin, so penance repeats the work of baptism: freeing us from the power of evil, restoring us to the Church, strengthening us to overcome the weakness that sin leaves in us, so that we may work again in the Church for the victory of the Good. But the cross must precede the resurrection. Penance is given us not to lull us into a feeling that all is well, but to shake us from complacency into self-knowledge, into a realization of our responsibility for the continuing power of evil in the world, into a deeper realization of God's love for humanity and the shallowness and unreality of our love for Him. We can fight for the world only when the sense of sin has turned our half-hearted repentance into the sorrow of love, shown us to what extent we are traitors to God's purposes, and so caused us to begin with humility to put our trust not in ourselves but in Him. Unless the grain of wheat die, itself remaineth alone.

But after the death, the resurrection; after sorrow and repentance, the life and power of the living Bread. There follows the greatest of all the sacraments, which brings us not divine power merely, but the Source of divine power. It is the Eucharist above all which empowers us to fight for the Good, and to fight as a family. There are the two dangers: of independence in isolation, the man without the child; and of uniformity without maturity, the child without the man. The Eucharist is the supreme way to wholeness. The Mass is first of all a sacrifice, an affirmation that God and not the false self is the center; it is the sacrifice of the whole man gathered up into the sacrifice of the whole Church, which itself is gathered up into the sacrifice of Christ; and then again it is the sacrament which effects the oneness first of all of the individual with Christ and then of the family of Christians with one another—the Communion is preceded by the kiss of peace, as it was preceded in the primitive Church by the agape, the love feast. When the Mass is over and the *Ite missa est* is said, it is not simply a number of individuals who are sent out to serve and restore the world: it is a family.

True, a family is a unity, not a uniformity: there is diversity of gifts, even though the same Spirit; the first thing the Eucharist effects is the wholeness of the individual Christian. But it is the sacrificed Christ who is received; and it is part of the purpose of the receiving that through it the Body of Christ should be built up in love and unity, and that, through the unity of the Body, the restoring power of Christ should be made visible and active in the world.

What a tragedy when the immensity of this coming of the Infinite into the soul is made a purely individual thing and we forget the family! How can we fail to note the insistence of the liturgy on the fact that it is our *common* sacrifice that we are offering, and the *common* sacrament that we are receiving, a sacrament of unity symbolized in the kiss of peace; and how can we fail to realize that, when we come down from the altar after the Communion, it is in a wholly new and richer sense that we are "all one in that One!" But what a tragedy also if we forget the larger family of creation!

When a Christian is sick and bedridden it is the office of the priest to bring the sacramental Christ to the house; and the preparations that are made, the solemnity of the reception of the priest who bears the Host, enact once again the humility and wonder of the centurion, "Lord, I am not worthy that thou shouldst enter under my roof." But we do not always notice that, when we come down from the altar and return into our houses, the same thing is done; we in our turn are God-bearers; and if it must be with a new sense of reverence and a new sense of oneness that we salute one another, we cannot but remember also the thing that is done in and to the world. How terrible if we allow ourselves to sink back into the pettinesses that kill love and oneness, how terrible if we fail to find courage to meet and conquer the spirit of hatred and evil, since we bear within us the power of the presence of the Good Himself! How terrible if we are content to leave mankind in its loneliness, when we bear within us Him who came to take away the sin and, therefore, the loneliness of the world!

We are all meant to be mediators. But we need not think it necessarily our duty to be forever attempting to argue these things; we need never think it our duty to preach at others; nothing is more depressing and more illogical than aggressive Christianity; we preach as we ought if we are what we ought to be, and we preach best if we are what we most ought to be, a family living in love and in God. To the sacrament of marriage, with all that it has to tell us of the duties and power of love in the world, we turn later; but the root of the matter is already here. "See how these Christians love one another." If we who are Christians could make the world say the words again as it said them first, with awe and wonder, we should have fulfilled the first part of our work as Christians; and the second would follow automatically, for we could not to that extent love one another without loving the world.

But we shall not so love one another if, in fact, we adopt a selfish sectarian attitude to the world. When men see that the building of the Church is a labor of love, the labor of a family, and that it is the building not of a fortress but of a home whose doors are always open, an invitation to enjoy the light and warmth within; when they see that we are ready to live and die for one another because we know that our duty together as a family is to live and die for the world Christ came to restore, then they will begin to say seriously that Christianity is love in practice as well as in theory, and if they look for Christ they will not dismiss the possibility of finding Him, despite our sinfulness, in our midst.

The way back to God is the way of worship, the worship given by the whole human being, man and child, to God. But the whole human being precisely as such does not worship alone. When you are living in love you cannot live alone, you cannot think or will or act alone; when you live in Christ you think and will and act in Christ, and it is the "total Christ," it is Christ as gathering to Himself the totality of created things. In the prayers of thanksgiving after Mass is included the canticle, "Bless the Lord, *all* ye works of the Lord." We go back to God in company with those we love, helped and helping. To help all created things, that is the measure of our responsibility; to be helped by all, that is the measure of our hope. Do you think it childish and superstitious to look for help to the saints or the angels? We look to our friends for help; what is childish is to suppose that we cannot be helped except by things or persons we can see or touch. We live in the world of space and time, but we live in eternity too, in the eternal present; the world is a haunted house, but not all the spirits that inhabit it are mournful ghosts or spirits of evil; the mystery of iniquity is offset by the glory of the communion of saints. Do you think that the mother who dies is no longer in contact with her children, that lover is hopelessly separated from lover? And these great ones of God set no limit to their love of those who at any moment of our time-world are trying to play their part in the cosmic struggle. The modern West has reached a chilly cerebral stage in its evolution; think how it might be helped and perhaps saved from complete desiccation by the might of the seraphs, those spirits whom Christian tradition associates especially with fire, with the burning love which is the prayer of wonder.

We begin to live the moral life in the Christian sense when we begin to turn all that we do and are into worship; and if we do that, the false self will die within us, and we shall begin to be made whole; and we shall forget to be grasping, even about the things of the spirit, because we shall want to serve the world. But in fact we shall walk in all the power of God and His saints and angels, we shall walk in the company of all who love Him and of all the things He loves, and so we shall reach the breadth and height and depth of the infinite skies, and lose our fear of what can hurt us and our fear of what we can lose, and beneath all the pain of the world that is in us—for nothing now will suffer without our suffering too—there will be the unquenchable joy of the saints.

Then there will be only the final consummation to wait for, when, in the company of those who have loved and helped us and those we have loved and served, we shall enter into the ultimate fulness of integrity, we shall see Him as He is and all things in Him in their glory, and so we shall know at last the complete oneness for which we have been so long unsuccessfully striving because in the fulness of the vision of the Godhead we shall find at last that there is nothing that we cannot love.

Editors' Note.—From THE HEART OF MAN (New York–Toronto: Longmans, Green, 1945) *pp. 67-87.*

Part

Confessions and Creeds

PREFACE

Fundamentally, Catholicism is faith in Christ and faith in His revelation. It is a living faith that leads to salvation. At Bethany Christ told Martha: "I am the resurrection and the life; he who believes in me, even if he die, shall live; and whoever lives and believes in me shall never die" (Jn 11:23-26). The content of this faith is, therefore, a matter of prime concern to the Christian. The truths which had been taught to the apostles by Christ and the Holy Spirit were handed on by Peter and his companions to the faithful Christians whom they baptized. These truths were collected and preserved in the early Church in consecrated formulae, called symbols. Literally, the word "symbol" means a mark or sign, and a symbol of faith was the sign of recognition among Christians. It was a short formula which expressed in summary form the truths of the faith. In a more elaborate and longer form, the symbol was sometimes called a "profession of faith." But always it was the summary of the truths which Christians were to believe in order to attain salvation.

There are examples of these symbols and professions of faith in the Gospels and the Epistles of the New Testament. Some of them were undoubtedly recited by the catechumens at their baptism, or by the Christians themselves at the various liturgical functions of the early Church, or as forms of private prayer. The early Fathers of the Church formulated their own summaries of faith. At different times in the history of the Church, popes and councils elaborated professions of faith as tessera of orthodoxy.

The faith was and is always the same. It underwent no change in the course of history. But at different times, in the face

*of attacks from nonbelievers and in time
of crisis, different aspects of the faith
were emphasized and explicitated to
meet the changing needs of the times.
New facets of the truth were made clear
as the teaching Church reacted vitally
to the needs of the faithful. New expressions came into being, and new ways of
presenting the truth to the hearts and
minds of believing men. The Church,
too, was and is constantly growing in its
consciousness of the faith. This dynamic
vitality is the ultimate reason why the
profession of faith of the Council of Trent
is not a mere verbal repetition of the
preaching of St. Peter or St. Paul. For
by the very nature of Christ's revelation,
the depths of the faith can never be adequately exhausted or transmitted by any
one symbol or creed.*

*In the pages that follow, some few ex-
amples of confessions, symbols, and
creeds that have played important roles
in the developing history of the Catholic
Church have been selected, more or less
at random, to serve as representations of
the Church's vital and living tradition.*

Peter's Confession of Faith

From the Gospel according to St. Matthew 16:13-20.[1]
Now Jesus having come into the district of Caesarea Philippi, began to ask His disciples, saying, "Who do men say the Son of Man is?" But they said, "Some say John the Baptist; and others, Elias; and others, Jeremias, or one of the prophets."

He said to them, "But who do you say that I am?"

Simon Peter answered and said, "Thou art the Christ, the son of the living God."

Then Jesus answered and said, "Blessed art thou, Simon Bar-Jona, for flesh and blood has not revealed this to thee, but my Father who is in heaven. And I say to thee, thou art Peter, and upon this rock I will build my Church, and the gates of hell shall not prevail against it. And I will give thee the keys of the kingdom of heaven; and whatever thou shalt bind on earth shall be bound in heaven, and whatever thou shalt loose on earth shall be loosed in heaven."

Then He strictly charged His disciples to tell no one that He was Jesus the Christ.

●
[1] Confraternity of Christian Doctrine translation; 3rd ed.; 1953 printing.

Christ and Nicodemus

From the Gospel according to St. John 3:1-21.[2]

Now there was a certain man among the Pharisees, Nicodemus by name, a ruler of the Jews. This man came to Jesus at night, and said to Him, "Rabbi, we know that thou hast come a teacher from God, for no one can work these signs that thou workest unless God be with him."

Jesus answered and said to him, "Amen, amen I say to thee, unless a man be born again, he cannot see the kingdom of God."

Nicodemus said to Him, "How can a man be born when he is old? Can he enter a second time into his mother's womb and be born again?"

Jesus answered, "Amen, amen I say to thee, unless a man be born again of water and the Spirit, he cannot enter into the kingdom of God. That which is born of the flesh is flesh; and that which is born of the Spirit is spirit. Do not wonder that I said to thee, 'You must be born again.' The wind blows where it will, and thou hearest its

●

[2] Confraternity translation.

sound but dost not know where it comes from or where it goes. So is everyone who is born of the Spirit."

Nicodemus answered and said to Him, "How can these things be?"

Answering him, Jesus said, "Thou art a teacher in Israel and dost not know these things? Amen, amen I say to thee, we speak of what we know and we bear witness to what we have seen; and our witness you do not receive. If I have spoken of earthly things to you, and you do not believe, how will you believe if I speak to you of heavenly things? And no one has ascended into heaven except Him who has descended from heaven: the Son of Man who is in heaven.

"And as Moses lifted up the serpent in the desert, even so must the Son of Man be lifted up, that those who believe in Him may not perish, but may have life everlasting."

For God so loved the world that He gave His only-begotten Son that those who believe in Him may not perish, but may have life everlasting. For God did not send His Son into the world in order to judge the world, but that the world might be saved through Him. He who believes in Him is not judged; but he who does not believe in Him is already judged, because he does not believe in the name of the only-begotten Son of God. Now this is the judgment: The light has come into the world, yet men have loved the darkness rather than the light, for their works were evil. For everyone who does evil hates the light, and does not come to the light, that his deeds may not be exposed. But he who does the truth comes to the light, that his deeds may be made manifest, for they have been performed in God.

The Commission
of the Apostles

From the Gospel according to St. Matthew 28:16-20.[3]
But the eleven disciples went into Galilee, to the mountain where
Jesus had directed them to go. And when they saw Him they wor-
shipped Him, but some doubted.

And Jesus drew near and spoke to them saying, "All power in
heaven and on earth has been given to me. Go, therefore, and make
disciples of all nations, baptizing them in the name of the Father, and
of the Son, and of the Holy Spirit, teaching them to observe all that
I have commanded you; and behold, I am with you all days, even to
the consummation of the world."

●

[3] Confraternity translation.

Peter's Discourse at Caesarea

From the Acts of the Apostles 10:34-43.[4]

But Peter began and said, "Now I really understand that God is not a respecter of persons, but in every nation he who fears Him and does what is right is acceptable to Him. He sent His word to the children of Israel, preaching peace through Jesus Christ (who is Lord of all). You know what took place throughout Judea; for He began in Galilee after the baptism preached by John; how God anointed Jesus of Nazareth with the Holy Spirit and with power, and He went about doing good and healing all who were in the power of the devil; for God was with Him. And we are witnesses of all that He did in the country of the Jews and in Jerusalem; and yet they killed Him, hanging Him on a tree. But God raised Him on the third day and caused Him to be plainly seen, not by all the people but by witnesses designated beforehand by God, that is, by us who ate and drank with Him after He had risen from the dead. And He charged us to preach to the people and to testify that He it is who has been appointed by God to be judge of the living and the dead. To Him all the prophets bear witness, that through His name all who believe in Him may receive forgiveness of sins."

●

[4] Confraternity translation.

The Teaching of St. Paul

From the First Epistle of St. Paul to the Corinthians 15:1-11.[5]
Now I recall to your minds, brethren, the gospel that I preached to you, which also you received, wherein also you stand, through which also you are being saved, if you hold it fast, as I preached it to you— unless you have believed to no purpose. For I delivered to you first of all, what I also received, that Christ died for our sins according to the Scriptures, and that He was buried, and that He rose again the third day, according to the Scriptures, and that He appeared to Cephas and after that to the eleven. Then He was seen by more than five hundred brethren at one time, many of whom are with us still, but some have fallen asleep. After that He was seen by James, then by all the apostles. And last of all, as by one born out of due time, He was seen also by me. For I am the least of the apostles, and am not worthy to be called an apostle, because I persecuted the Church of God. But by the grace of God I am what I am, and His grace in me has not been fruitless—in fact, I have labored more than any of them, yet not I, but the grace of God with me. Whether then it is I or they, so we preach, and so you have believed.

●

[5] Confraternity translation.

The Hymn to Christ

From the Epistle of St. Paul to the Philippians 2:5-11.[6]
Have toward one another this attitude, which you also have in Christ
Jesus:

> Who, though of divine status,
> did not treat like a miser's booty
> His right to be like God,
>
> but emptied Himself of it,
> to take up the status of a slave
> and become like men;
>
> having assumed human form,
> He still further humbled Himself
> with an obedience that meant death,
>   even death upon a cross!

●

[6] Translation by Joseph A. Fitzmyer, S.J.

That is why God has so greatly exalted Him
and given Him the Name
which is above all others:

that everyone at Jesus' name
should bend his knee
in heaven, on the earth, and under the earth!

that every tongue should proclaim
unto the glory of God the Father
that Jesus Christ is LORD!

The Apostles' Creed

For many centuries there was no doubt that the apostles themselves had composed and authorized a summary of belief. The first serious questioning as to the authenticity of such a creed seems to have arisen at the Council of Florence (1438-45), and in the light of criticism of the ensuing centuries it seems rather unlikely that the apostles drafted an official summary of faith. The title "Apostles' Creed" is found for the first time in a letter sent by the Synod of Milan (390) to Pope St. Siricius (384-98). Though not written by the apostles, the Apostles' Creed is a faithful summary of the truths taught from the earliest days of the Church.[7]

I believe in God, the Father Almighty, creator of heaven and of earth. And in Jesus Christ, His only Son, our Lord, who was conceived by the Holy Spirit, born of the Virgin Mary, suffered under Pontius Pilate,

•

[7] Introduction and translation by John F. Clarkson, S.J., John H. Edwards, S.J., William J. Kelly, S.J., and John J. Welch, S.J., in *The Church Teaches* (St. Louis: Herder, 1955) p. 1.

was crucified, died and was buried; He descended into hell; the third day He arose again from the dead; He ascended into heaven, sits at the right hand of God the Father Almighty; from there He shall come to judge the living and the dead. I believe in the Holy Spirit, the holy Catholic Church, the communion of saints, the forgiveness of sins, the resurrection of the body, and life everlasting.

The Profession of Faith of Irenaeus

From Against Heresies *1, 10, 1.*[8]
*Irenaeus was a native of Asia Minor, a pupil of Polycarp of Smyrna
and through him a grand-pupil of St. John the Apostle. He was Bishop
of the Church at Lyons in the south of France in 177 A.D., wrote his
great work against the Gnostic heresies about 180 A.D., while Eleu-
therius (d. 185) was Bishop of Rome, and died about 202. He was
therefore a connecting link between the East and the West as well as
between post-apostolic and ante-Nicene Christianity, and altogether
the most important witness of the doctrinal status of the Catholic
Church at the close of the second century.*

The Church, though scattered through the world to the ends of the
earth, has received from the apostles and their disciples the faith in
one God the Father Almighty, who made the heaven and the earth
and the seas and all that in them is; and in one Christ Jesus, the Son

●
[8] Introduction and translation by Philip Schaff in *The Creeds of Christendom* 2 (New York: Harper, 1877) 13-15.

of God, who became flesh for our salvation; and in the Holy Ghost, who through the prophets preached the dispensations and the advent, and the birth from the Virgin, and the passion, and the resurrection from the dead, and the bodily assumption into heaven of the beloved Christ Jesus, our Lord, and His appearing from heaven in the glory of the Father, to comprehend all things under one head, and to raise up all flesh of all mankind, that, according to the good pleasure of the Father invisible, every knee of those that are in heaven and on earth and under the earth should bow before Christ Jesus, our Lord and God and Saviour and King, and that every tongue should confess to Him, and that He may execute righteous judgment over all; sending into eternal fire the spiritual powers of wickedness, and the angels who transgressed and apostatized, and the godless and unrighteous and lawless and blasphemous among men, and granting life and immortality and eternal glory to the righteous and holy, who have both kept the commandments and continued in His love, some from the beginning, some after their conversion.

The Church, having received this preaching and this faith, as before said, though scattered throughout the whole world, zealously preserves it as one household . . . and unanimously preaches and teaches the same, and hands it down as by one mouth; for although there are different dialects in the world, the power of the tradition is one and the same. And in no other manner have either the churches established in Germany believed and handed down, nor those in Spain, nor among the Celts, nor in the East, nor in Egypt, nor in Libya, nor those established in the middle of the world. But as the sun, God's creature, is one and the same in all the world, so, too, the preaching of the truth shines everywhere and enlightens all men who wish to come to the knowledge of the truth. And neither will he who is very mighty in language among those who preside over the churches say other than this (for the disciple is not above his Master), nor will he who is weak in word impair the tradition. For as the faith is one and the same, neither he who is very able to speak on it adds thereto, nor does he who is less mighty diminish therefrom.

The Niceno-Constantinopolitan Creed

There are various opinions as to the origin of the Niceno-Constantinopolitan creed. What is certain is that after the Councils of Ephesus (431) and Chalcedon (451), this creed made its way into the liturgy of the Eastern Church and soon became the baptismal creed. It was introduced into the Western liturgy towards the end of the eighth century.[9]

We believe in one God, the Father Almighty, Creator of heaven and earth, of all things both visible and invisible. And in one Lord Jesus Christ, the only-begotten Son of God, born of the Father before all time; light from light, true God from true God; begotten, not created, consubstantial with the Father; through Him all things were made. For the sake of us men and our salvation, He came down from heaven, was made flesh by the Holy Spirit from the Virgin Mary, and became man; and He was crucified for our sake under Pontius Pilate, suffered

●
[9] Introduction and translation by John F. Clarkson, S.J., *et al., op. cit.,* pp. 2-3.

and was buried. And on the third day He rose according to the Scriptures; He ascended into heaven, sits at the right hand of the Father, and is going to come again in glory to judge the living and the dead. His reign will have no end. We believe in the Holy Spirit, the Lord, the giver of life; He proceeds from the Father, is adored and honored together with the Father and the Son; He spoke through the prophets. We believe in one, holy, catholic, and apostolic Church. We profess one baptism for the forgiveness of sins. We expect the resurrection of the dead and the life of the world to come. Amen.

The Athanasian Creed

The Athanasian Creed—frequently called "Quicumque" from its initial Latin word—was not composed by St. Athanasius. Nevertheless, by reason of its clear presentation of the Trinity and Incarnation, it gradually gained such authority in the Western and Eastern Church that it was taken over into the liturgy and may be regarded as a genuine definition of Christian belief. Its authorship is still a matter of dispute among scholars; names proposed include Ambrose of Milan (382-83), Vincent of Lérins (d. ca. 450), Caesarius of Arles (d. 542).[10]

Whoever wishes to be saved must, above all, keep the Catholic faith; for unless a person keeps this faith whole and entire he will undoubtedly be lost forever.

This is what the Catholic faith teaches. We worship one God in the Trinity and the Trinity in unity; we distinguish among the Persons, but we do not divide the substance. For the Father is a distinct Per-

●

[10] Translation of Athanasian Creed *ibid.*, pp. 5-7.

son; the Son is a distinct Person; and the Holy Spirit is a distinct Person. Still, the Father and the Son and the Holy Spirit have one divinity, equal glory and coeternal majesty. What the Father is, the Son is and the Holy Spirit is. The Father is uncreated, the Son is uncreated, and the Holy Spirit is uncreated. The Father has immensity, the Son has immensity, and the Holy Spirit has immensity. The Father is eternal, the Son is eternal, and the Holy Spirit is eternal. Nevertheless, there are not three eternal beings, but one eternal Being. Thus there are not three uncreated beings, nor three beings having immensity, but one uncreated Being and one Being that has immensity.

Likewise, the Father is omnipotent, the Son is omnipotent, and the Holy Spirit is omnipotent. Yet there are not three omnipotent beings, but one omnipotent Being. Thus the Father is God, the Son is God, and the Holy Spirit is God. But there are not three gods, but one God. The Father is Lord, the Son is Lord, and the Holy Spirit is Lord. There are not three lords, but one Lord. For according to the Christian truth, we must profess that each one of the three Persons individually is God; and according to the Christian religion we are forbidden to say that there are three gods or three lords. The Father is not made by anyone, nor created by anyone, nor generated by anyone. The Son is not made or created, but He is generated by the Father alone. The Spirit is not made or created nor generated but proceeds from the Father and the Son.

There is one Father, not three fathers; one Son, not three sons; one Holy Spirit, not three holy spirits. In this Trinity there is nothing that precedes, nothing subsequent to anything else. There is nothing greater, nothing lesser than anything else. But the entire three Persons are coeternal and coequal with one another, so that, as we have said, we worship complete unity in the Trinity and the Trinity in unity. This, then, is what he who wishes to be saved must believe about the Trinity.

It is also necessary for eternal salvation that he believe steadfastly in the Incarnation of our Lord Jesus Christ. The true faith is: we believe and profess that our Lord Jesus Christ, the Son of God, is both God and Man. As God, He was begotten of the substance of the Father before time; as Man He was born in time of the substance of His mother. He is perfect God, and He is perfect Man, with a rational soul and human flesh. He is equal to the Father in divinity, but He is inferior to the Father in His humanity. Although He is God and Man, He is not two but one Christ. And He is one, not because His divinity was changed into flesh, but because His humanity was assumed to God. He is one, not at all because of a mingling of substances, but because He is one Person. As a rational soul and flesh are one man, so God and Man are one Christ. He died for our salvation, descended into hell, arose from the dead on the third day, ascended into heaven, sits at the right hand of God the Father Almighty, and from there He shall come to judge the living and the dead. At His coming all men are to arise with their own bodies; and they are to give an account of their lives. Those who have done good deeds will go into eternal life; those who have done evil will go into everlasting fire.

This is the Catholic faith. Everyone must believe it firmly and steadfastly; otherwise he cannot be saved.

The Profession of Faith
of the Fourth Lateran Council

More than four hundred bishops answered the summons of Innocent III (1198-1216) to the Fourth Lateran Council, the twelfth ecumenical council. In addition to the profession of faith and a definitive statement against the Albigenses and the Waldensians, the fathers of the Council defined the traditional Catholic faith in the Incarnation, the sacraments, and the resurrection of the body and life after death.[11]

We firmly believe and profess without qualification that there is only one true God, eternal, immense, unchangeable, incomprehensible, omnipotent, and indescribable, the Father, the Son, and the Holy Spirit: three Persons but one essence and a substance or nature that is wholly simple. The Father is from no one; the Son is from the Father only; and the Holy Spirit is from both the Father and the Son equally. God has no beginning; He always was and He always will be; the Father is the progenitor, the Son is the begotten. The Holy Spirit is the proceeding; They are all one substance, equally great, equally all powerful, equally eternal; They are the one and only principle of all

●

[11] Introduction and translation *ibid.*, pp. 132, 190, 347, 259.

things—Creator of all things visible and invisible, spiritual and corporeal, who, by His almighty power, from the very beginning of time has created both orders of creatures in the same way out of nothing, the spiritual or angelic world and the corporeal or visible universe. And afterwards He formed the creature man, who in a way belongs to both orders, as he is composed of spirit and body. For the devil and the other demons were created by God according to their nature, but they made themselves evil by their own doing. As for man, his sin was at the prompting of the devil. The Holy Trinity, indivisible according to its essence, and distinct according to its personal properties, first gave this teaching of salvation to the human race through Moses and the prophets and its other servants, according to a well ordered disposition of time.

And finally, the only-begotten Son of God, Jesus Christ, made incarnate by a common action of the Holy Trinity, and conceived by Mary ever Virgin with the cooperation of the Holy Spirit, became a true man composed of a rational soul and human flesh, one Person in two natures; and He pointed out the way of life more clearly. According to His divinity He is immortal and impassible, yet according to His humanity He became passible and mortal. He also suffered and died on the wood of the cross for the salvation of the human race; He descended into hell; He rose from the dead and ascended into heaven; but He descended with His soul and He rose in the flesh, and He ascended in both together. He will come at the end of the world; He will judge the living and the dead; and He will reward all, both the lost and the elect, according to their works. And all these will rise with their own bodies which they now have so that they may receive according to their works, whether good or bad; the wicked a perpetual punishment with the devil; the good, eternal glory with Christ.

Indeed, there is but one universal Church of the faithful outside which no one at all is saved and in which the Priest Himself, Jesus Christ, is the victim; His Body and Blood are truly contained in the sacrament of the altar under the species of bread and wine, transubstantiated by the divine power—the bread into His Body and the wine into His Blood—that, for the enacting of the mystery of unity, we may take from His substance as He Himself took from our substance. And no one can consecrate this sacrament except a priest who is rightly ordained according to the Church's powers that Jesus Christ gave to His apostles and their successors. But the sacrament of baptism (which is performed with water together with the invocation of God and the undivided Trinity; namely, the Father, the Son, and the Holy Spirit) is salutary both for infants and for adults, if it is administered correctly by anyone according to the form of the Church. And if, after receiving baptism, anyone shall fall into sin, he can always be restored by true contrition. Not only virgins and those who observe continence but also married people who please God by true faith and good works merit to come to eternal happiness.

The Creed of the Council of Trent

The Bull Injunctum nobis *was issued by Pope Pius IV (1559-65) on November 13, 1564. The profession of faith contained in this creed summarizes the doctrines which Catholics are to believe.*[12]

I, N., with firm faith believe and profess each and every article contained in the symbol of faith which the Holy Roman Church uses; namely: I believe in one God, the Father Almighty, maker of heaven and earth and of all things visible and invisible; and in one Lord Jesus Christ the only-begotten Son of God, born of the Father before all ages; God from God, light from light, true God from true God; begotten not made, of one substance with the Father; through whom all things were made; who for us men and for our salvation came down from heaven and was made incarnate by the Holy Spirit of the Virgin Mary and was made man. He was crucified also for us under Pontius Pilate, died and was buried; and he rose again the third day according to the Scriptures, and ascended into heaven; He sits at the right hand

●

[12] Introduction and translation *ibid.,* pp. 7-9.

of the Father, and He will come again in glory to judge the living and the dead, and of His kingdom there will be no end. And I believe in the Holy Spirit, the Lord, and giver of life, who proceeds from the Father and the Son; who equally with the Father and the Son is adored and glorified; who spoke through the prophets. And I believe that there is one, holy, catholic, and apostolic Church. I confess one baptism for the remission of sins; and I hope for the resurrection of the dead, and the life of the world to come. Amen.

I resolutely accept and embrace the apostolic and ecclesiastical traditions and other practices and regulations of that same Church. In like manner I accept Sacred Scripture according to the meaning which has been held by the Holy Mother Church and which she now holds. It is her prerogative to pass judgment on the true meaning and interpretation of Sacred Scripture. And I will never accept or interpret it in a manner different from the unanimous agreement of the Fathers.

I also truly acknowledge that there are truly and properly seven sacraments of the New Law, instituted by Jesus Christ, our Lord, and that they are necessary for the salvation of the human race, although it is not necessary for each individual to receive them all. I acknowledge that the seven sacraments are: baptism, confirmation, Eucharist, penance, extreme unction, holy orders, and matrimony; and that they confer grace; and that of the seven, baptism, confirmation, and holy orders cannot be repeated without commiting a sacrilege. I also accept and acknowledge the customary and approved rites of the Catholic Church in the solemn administration of these sacraments. I accept and embrace each and every article on original sin and justification declared and defined in the most holy Council of Trent.

I likewise profess that in the Mass a true, proper, and propitiatory sacrifice is offered to God on behalf of the living and the dead, and that the Body and the Blood, together with the soul and the divinity, of our Lord Jesus Christ is truly, really, and substantially present in the most holy sacrament of the Eucharist, and that there is a change of the whole substance of the bread into the Body, and of the whole substance of the wine into Blood; and this change the Catholic Church calls transubstantiation. I also profess that the whole and entire Christ and a true sacrament is received under each separate species.

I firmly hold that there is a purgatory and that the souls detained there are helped by the prayers of the faithful. I likewise hold that the saints reigning together with Christ should be honored and invoked, that they offer prayers to God on our behalf, and that their relics should be venerated. I firmly assert that the images of Christ, of the Mother of God ever Virgin, and of the other saints should be owned and kept, and that due honor and veneration should be given to them. I affirm that the power of indulgences was left in the keeping of the Church by Christ, and that the use of indulgences is very beneficial to Christians.

I acknowledge the holy, catholic, and apostolic Roman Church as the Mother and teacher of all Churches; and I promise and swear true obedience to the Roman Pontiff, vicar of Christ, and the successor of Blessed Peter, Prince of the Apostles.

I unhesitatingly accept and profess all the doctrines (especially those concerning the primacy of the Roman Pontiff and his infallible teaching authority[13]) handed down, defined, and explained by the sacred canons and ecumenical councils, and especially those of this most holy Council of Trent (and by the ecumenical Vatican Council). At the same time, I condemn, reject, and anathematize everything that is contrary to those propositions, and all heresies without exception that have been condemned, rejected and anathematized by the Church. I, N., promise, vow, and swear that, with God's help, I shall most constantly hold and profess this true Catholic faith, outside which no one can be saved and which I now freely profess and truly hold. With the help of God I shall profess it whole and unblemished to my dying breath; and, to the best of my ability, I shall see to it that my subjects or those entrusted to me by virtue of my office, hold it, teach it and preach it. So help me God and His holy Gospel.

●

[13] The words in parentheses in this paragraph are now inserted into the Tridentine Profession of Faith by order of Pope Pius IX in a decree of the Holy Office issued January 20, 1877; *Acta sanctae sedis* 10 (1877) 71 ff.

The Mass

The Christmas Mass at Midnight

PREFACE

The Mass, as we have seen in Part 1, is the renewal by the Church of the mystery of our redemption—the death, resurrection, and ascension of the Son of God. In it priest and people offer to God again the Victim of Calvary and in turn become one with their Victim by the reception of Holy Communion. It is God's "new and eternal covenant" with His Church, the new Israel; at the same time it is the Church's supreme act of worship and thanksgiving to God.

Like the paschal meal of the Last Supper, the essential Sacrifice-banquet of the Mass has been embellished with various rites and ritual. And yet, despite the constant development over the centuries and the significant differences even today among the various rites used by Catholics in East and West, the basic structure of the Mass has remained the same. Two fundamental divisions are always discernible: the Fore-Mass and the Sacrifice-Mass. The Fore-Mass comprises (1) an entrance rite made up of psalms, hymns, and a concluding prayer by the celebrant in the name of the people; (2) the service of the word: readings from Scripture and a short homily or sermon. The Sacrifice-Mass has three components: (1) the offering by the people of the gifts for the sacrifice; (2) the sacred narrative of institution, in which the gifts (bread and wine) are transformed into the body and blood of Christ—the heart of the Sacrifice, and therefore surrounded with hymns of praise, with prayers of petition and of offering; (3) the Communion service, preceded by the Our Father and other appropriate prayers of preparation, and followed by prayers of thanksgiving. The Mass concludes with a final blessing and dismissal.

The Mass reproduced in the following pages is the text of the first of the three Christmas Masses as celebrated in the Roman Rite today.

The Christmas Mass at Midnight[1]

THE PRAYERS AT THE FOOT OF THE ALTAR:

PRIEST: In the name of the Father, and of the Son, and of the Holy Ghost. Amen.
I will go up to the altar of God.
PEOPLE: To God, the giver of youth and happiness.
PRIEST:O God, sustain my cause; give me redress against a race that knows no piety; save me from a tremendous foe and cruel.
PEOPLE: Thou, O God, art all my strength, why hast thou cast me off? Why do I go mourning, with enemies pressing me hard?
PRIEST: The light of thy presence, the fulfilment of thy promise, let these be my escort, bringing me safe to thy holy mountain, to the tabernacle where thou dwellest.
PEOPLE: There I will go up to the altar of God, the giver of youth and happiness.

●

[1] From *The Missal in Latin and English* (ed. J. O'Connell and H. P. R. Einberg (Westminster, Md.: Newman, 1958) pp. 31-34, 677-717, 733-35.

PRIEST: Thou art my own God, with the harp I hymn thy praise. Soul, why art thou downcast, why art thou all lament?

PEOPLE: Wait for God's help; I will not cease to cry out in thankfulness: My champion and my God!

PRIEST: Glory be to the Father, and to the Son, and to the Holy Ghost.

PEOPLE: As it was in the beginning, is now, and ever shall be, world without end. Amen.

PRIEST: I will go up to the altar of God.

PEOPLE: To God, the giver of youth and happiness.

PRIEST: Our help is in the name of the Lord.

PEOPLE: Who made heaven and earth.

PRIEST: I confess to almighty God, to blessed Mary ever virgin, to blessed Michael the archangel, to blessed John the Baptist, to the holy apostles Peter and Paul, to all the saints, and to you, brethren, that I have sinned exceedingly in thought, word, and deed; through my fault, through my own fault, through my own most grievous fault. Therefore I beseech the blessed Mary ever virgin, blessed Michael the archangel, blessed John the Baptist, the holy apostles Peter and Paul, all the saints, and you, brethren, to pray to the Lord our God for me.

PEOPLE: May almighty God have mercy on you, pardon your sins, and bring you to everlasting life.

PRIEST: Amen.

PEOPLE: I confess to almighty God, to blessed Mary ever virgin, to blessed Michael the archangel, to blessed John the Baptist, to the holy apostles Peter and Paul, to all the saints, and to you, father, that I have sinned exceedingly in thought, word, and deed; through my fault, through my own fault, through my own most grievous fault. Therefore I beseech the blessed Mary ever virgin, blessed Michael the archangel, blessed John the Baptist, the holy apostles Peter and Paul, all the saints, and you, father, to pray to the Lord our God for me.

PRIEST: May almighty God have mercy upon you, pardon your sins, and bring you to everlasting life.

PEOPLE: Amen.

PRIEST: May the almighty and merciful Lord grant us pardon, absolution, and remission of our sins.

PEOPLE: Amen.

PRIEST: Thou wilt relent, O God, and bring us to life.

PEOPLE: And thy people will rejoice in thee.

PRIEST: Show us thy mercy, Lord.

PEOPLE: And grant us thy salvation.

PRIEST: Lord, heed my prayer.

PEOPLE: And let my cry be heard by thee.

PRIEST: The Lord be with you.

PEOPLE: And with you.

PRIEST: Let us pray. Take away from us our iniquities, we entreat thee,

Lord, so that, with souls made clean, we may be counted worthy to enter the Holy of Holies: through Christ our Lord. Amen.

We pray thee, Lord, by the merits of thy saints whose relics are here, and of all the saints, that thou wilt deign to pardon all my sins. Amen.

THE INTROIT:

Ps 2:7: Thou art my Son, the Lord's word came to me, I have begotten thee this day. What means this turmoil among the nations? Why do the peoples cherish vain dreams? Glory be to the Father, and to the Son, and to the Holy Ghost. As it was in the beginning, is now, and ever shall be, world without end. Amen. Thou art my Son, the Lord's word came to me, I have begotten thee this day.

THE KYRIE:

PRIEST: Lord, have mercy.
PEOPLE: Lord, have mercy.
PRIEST: Lord, have mercy.
PEOPLE: Christ, have mercy.
PRIEST: Christ, have mercy.
PEOPLE: Christ, have mercy.
PRIEST: Lord, have mercy.
PEOPLE: Lord, have mercy.
PRIEST: Lord, have mercy.

THE GLORIA:

Glory be to God on high, and on earth peace to men who are God's friends. We praise thee, we bless thee, we adore thee, we glorify thee, we give thee thanks for thy great glory: Lord God, heavenly King, God the almighty Father. Lord Jesus Christ, only-begotten Son; Lord God, Lamb of God, Son of the Father, who takest away the sins of the world, have mercy upon us; thou who takest away the sins of the world, receive our prayer; thou who sittest at the right hand of the Father, have mercy upon us. For thou alone art the Holy One, thou alone art Lord, thou alone art the Most High: Jesus Christ, with the Holy Spirit: in the glory of God the Father. Amen.
The Lord be with you.
PEOPLE: And with you.

THE COLLECT:

PRIEST: God, who hast made this most sacred night glow with the radiance of the true light, we pray thee grant that we may share to the full in heaven the joys of that Light whose mysteries we have

known on earth, and who is God living and reigning with thee in the unity of the Holy Spirit, world without end.
PEOPLE: Amen.

THE EPISTLE:

Titus 2:11-15: Beloved: The grace of God, our Saviour, has dawned on all men alike, schooling us to forgo irreverent thoughts and worldly appetites, and to live, in this present world, a life of order, of justice, and of holiness. We were to look forward, blessed in our hope, to the day when there will be a new dawn of glory, the glory of the great God, the glory of our Saviour, Jesus Christ; who gave Himself for us, to ransom us from all our guilt, a people set apart for Himself, ambitious of noble deeds. Be this thy message, this thy encouragement in Christ Jesus our Lord.
PEOPLE: Thanks be to God.

THE GRADUAL:

PRIEST: *Ps 109:3, 1:* When thou showest thy power, princely state shall be thine: amid the splendor of the holy places, thou art my Son, born before the day-star rises. To the Master I serve the Lord's promise was given, Sit here at my right hand while I make thy enemies a footstool under thy feet. Alleluia, alleluia. *Ps 2:7:* Thou art my Son, the Lord's word came to me, I have begotten thee this day. Alleluia.

PRAYER BEFORE THE GOSPEL:

Cleanse my heart and my lips, almighty God, who didst cleanse the lips of the prophet Isaiah with a live coal. In thy gracious mercy deign so to cleanse me that I may be able to proclaim fitly thy holy Gospel: through Christ our Lord. Amen.

Lord, grant a blessing. The Lord be in my heart and on my lips, so that I may fitly and worthily proclaim his Gospel. Amen.

THE GOSPEL:

PRIEST: The Lord be with you.
PEOPLE: And with you.
PRIEST: A passage from the holy Gospel according to Saint Luke.
PEOPLE: Glory to thee, Lord.
PRIEST: It happened that a decree went out at this time from the Emperor Augustus, enjoining that the whole world should be registered; this register was the one first made during the time when Cyrinus was governor of Syria. All must go and give in their names, each in his own city; and Joseph, being of David's clan and family, came up from the town of Nazareth, in Galilee, to David's city in Judaea, the

city called Bethlehem, to give in his name there. With him was his espoused wife Mary, who was then in her pregnancy; and it was while they were still there that the time came for her delivery. She brought forth a son, her first-born, whom she wrapped in His swaddling-clothes, and laid in a manger, because there was no room for them in the inn. In the same country there were shepherds awake in the fields, keeping night-watches over their flocks. And all at once an angel of the Lord came and stood by them, and the glory of the Lord shone about them, so that they were overcome with fear. But the angel said to them, Do not be afraid; behold, the news I bring you is good news of a great rejoicing for the whole people. This day in the city of David, a Saviour has been born for you, the Lord Christ Himself. This is the sign by which you are to know Him; you will find a child still in swaddling-clothes, lying in a manger. Then on a sudden, a multitude of the heavenly army appeared to them at the angel's side, giving praise to God, and saying, Glory to God in high heaven, and peace on earth to men that are God's friends.

PEOPLE: Praise to thee, Christ.

PRIEST: Through the Gospel words may our sins be wiped away.

THE CREED:

I believe in one God, the almighty Father, Maker of heaven and earth, Maker of all things visible and invisible. I believe in one Lord Jesus Christ, only-begotten Son of God, born of the Father before time began; God from God, light from light, true God from true God; begotten, not made, one in essence with the Father; and through whom all things were made. For us men, and for our salvation, He came down from heaven, took flesh of the Virgin Mary by the action of the Holy Spirit, and was made man. For our sake too, under Pontius Pilate, He was crucified, suffered death, and was buried. And the third day He rose from the dead, as the Scriptures had foretold. And He ascended to heaven, where He sits at the right hand of the Father. He will come again in glory to judge the living and the dead; and His reign will have no end. I believe too in the Holy Spirit, Lord and life-giver, who proceeds from the Father and the Son; who together with the Father and the Son is adored and glorified; who spoke through the prophets. And I believe in one holy, catholic, and apostolic Church. I acknowledge one baptism for the remission of sins. And I look forward to the resurrection of the dead, and the life of the world to come. Amen.

The Lord be with you.

PEOPLE: And with you.

THE OFFERTORY PRAYERS:

PRIEST: Let us pray.

Ps 95:11, 13: Rejoice, heaven, and let the earth be glad to greet the Lord's coming.

Holy Father, almighty, everlasting God, accept this unblemished sacrificial offering, which I, thy unworthy servant, make to thee, my living and true God, for my countless sins, offenses, and neglects, and on behalf of all who are present here; likewise for all believing Christians, living and dead. Accept it for their good and mine, so that it may save us and bring us to everlasting life. Amen.

O God, by whom the dignity of human nature was wondrously established and yet more wondrously restored, grant that through the sacramental use of this water and wine we may have fellowship in the Godhead of Him who deigned to share our manhood, Jesus Christ, thy Son, our Lord, who is God, living and reigning with thee in the unity of the Holy Spirit, for ever and ever. Amen.

We offer thee, Lord, the chalice of salvation, entreating thy mercy that our offering may ascend with a sweet fragrance in the presence of thy divine majesty for our salvation and for that of all the world. Amen. Humbled in spirit and contrite of heart, may we find favor with thee, Lord, and may our sacrifice be so offered in thy sight this day that it may please thee, Lord our God.

Come, thou Sanctifier, almighty, everlasting God, and bless these sacrificial gifts, prepared for the glory of thy holy name.

Ps 25:6-12: With the pure in heart I will wash my hands clean, and take my place among them at thy altar, Lord, listening there to the sound of thy praises, telling the story of all thy wonderful deeds. How well, Lord, I love thy house in its beauty, the place where thy own glory dwells! Lord, never count this soul for lost with the wicked, this life among the bloodthirsty: hands ever stained with guilt, palms ever itching for a bribe! Be it mine to guide my steps clear of wrong: deliver me in thy mercy. My feet are set on firm ground; where thy people gather, Lord, I will join in blessing thy name. Glory be to the Father, and to the Son, and to the Holy Ghost. As it was in the beginning, is now, and ever shall be, world without end. Amen.

Holy Trinity, accept the offering we here make to thee in memory of the passion, resurrection, and ascension of our Lord, Jesus Christ; in honor, too, of blessed Mary, ever virgin, of blessed John the Baptist, of the holy apostles Peter and Paul, of the martyrs whose relics are here and of all the saints. To them let it bring honor, to us salvation; and may they whom we are commemorating on earth graciously plead for us in heaven: through the same Christ our Lord. Amen.

Pray, brethren, that my sacrifice and yours may find acceptance with God the almighty Father.

PEOPLE: May the Lord accept the sacrifice at your hands, to the praise and glory of His name, for our welfare also, and that of all His holy Church.

PRIEST: Amen.

THE SECRET PRAYER:

Accept, Lord, this day's festal offering, and in thy gracious bounty grant that through this interchange of sacred gifts, we may grow to be like Him in whom our human nature is made one with thine: who is God, living and reigning with thee in the unity of the Holy Spirit, for ever and ever.

PEOPLE: Amen.

THE PREFACE TO THE CANON:

PRIEST: The Lord be with you.
PEOPLE: And with you.
PRIEST: Let us lift up our hearts.
PEOPLE: We lift them up to the Lord.
PRIEST: Let us give thanks to the Lord our God.
PEOPLE: That is just and fitting.
PRIEST: Just it is indeed and fitting, right and for our lasting good, that we should always and everywhere give thanks to thee, Lord, holy Father, almighty and eternal God; for through the mystery of the Word made flesh thy splendour has shone before our mind's eye with a new radiance, and through Him whom we recognize as God made visible we are carried away in love of things invisible. Therefore it is that with angels and archangels, thrones and dominations, and all the warriors of the heavenly array, we chant an endless hymn in praise of thee, singing:

Holy, Holy, Holy art thou, Lord God of hosts. Thy glory fills all heaven and earth. Hosanna in high heaven! Blessed be he who is coming in the name of the Lord. Hosanna in high heaven!

THE CANON OF THE MASS:

And so, through Jesus Christ, thy Son, our Lord, we humbly pray and beseech thee, most gracious Father, to accept and bless these offerings, these oblations, these holy, unblemished sacrificial gifts. We offer them to thee in the first place for thy holy catholic Church, praying that thou wilt be pleased to keep and guide her in peace and unity throughout the world; together with they servant our Pope N., and N. our Bishop, and all who believe and foster the true Catholic and apostolic faith.

Remember, Lord, thy servants N. and N., and all here present. Their faith and devotion are known to thee. On their behalf we offer, or they offer for themselves and for all who are theirs this sacrifice in praise of thee, for the redemption of their souls, for the hope of safety and salvation, paying homage to thee, their living, true, eternal God.

United in the same holy fellowship we celebrate that most sacred night on which the inviolate virginity of blessed Mary brought our Saviour into this world; we reverence also the memory, first, of the self-same glorious ever-virgin Mary, Mother of the same Jesus Christ, our God and Lord; and likewise that of thy blessed apostles and martyrs, Peter and Paul, Andrew, James, John, Thomas, James, Philip, Bartholomew, Matthew, Simon, and Thaddeus: of Linus, Cletus, Clement, Sixtus, Cornelius, Cyprian, Laurence, Chrysogonus, John and Paul, Cosmas and Damian; and of all thy saints. Grant for the sake of their merits and prayers that in all things we may be guarded and helped by thy protection: through the same Christ our Lord. Amen.

And so, Lord, we thy servants, and with us thy whole household, make this peace offering which we entreat thee to accept. Order our days in thy peace, and command that we be rescued from eternal damnation and numbered with the flock of thy elect: through Christ our Lord. Amen.

We pray thee, God, be pleased to make this offering wholly blessed, a thing consecrated and approved, making it reasonable and worthy of the human spirit and of thy acceptance, so that it may become for us the Body and Blood of thy dearly beloved Son, our Lord Jesus Christ.

He, on the day before He suffered death, took bread into His holy and worshipful hands, and lifting up His eyes to thee, God, His Father almighty in heaven, and giving thanks to thee, He blessed it, broke it, and gave it to His disciples, saying: Take, all of you, and eat of this,

For this is my Body.

In like manner, when He had supped, taking also this goodly cup into His holy and worshipful hands, and again giving thanks to thee, He blessed it, and gave it to His disciples, saying: Take, all of you, and drink of this,

For this is the chalice of my Blood,
of the new and everlasting covenant,
a mystery of faith.
It shall be shed for you and many others, so that sins may be for-
given.

Whenever you shall do these things, you shall do them in memory of me.

Calling therefore to mind the blessed passion of this same Christ, thy Son, our Lord, and also His resurrection from the grave, and glorious ascension into heaven, we thy servants, Lord, and with us all thy holy people, offer to thy sovereign majesty, out of the gifts thou hast bestowed upon us, a sacrifice that is pure, holy, and unblemished, the sacred Bread of everlasting life, and the Cup of eternal salvation.

Deign to regard them with a favorable and gracious countenance, and to accept them as it pleased thee to accept the offerings of thy servant Abel the Just, and the sacrifice of our father Abraham, and that which thy great priest Melchisedech sacrificed to thee, a holy offering, a victim without blemish.

Humbly we ask it of thee, God almighty: bid these things be carried by the hands of thy holy angel up to thy altar on high, into the presence of thy divine majesty. And may those of us who by taking part in the sacrifice of this altar shall have received the sacred Body and Blood of thy Son, be filled with every grace and heavenly blessing: through the same Christ our Lord. Amen.

Remember also, Lord, thy servants N. and N., who have gone before us with the sign of faith and sleep the sleep of peace. To them, Lord, and to all who rest in Christ, grant, we entreat thee, a place of cool repose, of light and peace: through the same Christ our Lord. Amen.

To us also, thy sinful servants, who put our trust in thy countless acts of mercy, deign to grant some share and fellowship with thy holy apostles and martyrs: with John, Stephen, Matthias, Barnabas, Ignatius, Alexander, Marcellinus, Peter, Felicity, Perpetua, Agatha, Lucy, Agnes, Cecily, Anastasia, and all thy saints. Into their company we pray thee to admit us, not weighing our deserts, but freely granting us forgiveness: through Christ our Lord.

It is ever through Him that all these good gifts created so by thee, Lord, are by thee sanctified, endowed with life, blessed, and bestowed upon us.

Through Him, and with Him, and in Him, thou, God, almighty Father, in the unity of the Holy Spirit, hast all honor and glory.

World without end.

PEOPLE: Amen.

THE LORD'S PRAYER

PRIEST: Let us pray. Urged by our Saviour's bidding, and schooled by His divine ordinance, we make bold to say:

Our Father, who art in heaven, hallowed be thy name. Thy kingdom come. Thy will be done, on earth as it is in heaven. Give us this day our daily bread. And forgive us our trespasses, as we forgive those who trespass against us. And lead us not into temptation:

PEOPLE: But deliver us from evil.

PRIEST: Amen.

Deliver us, we pray thee, Lord, from every evil, past, present, and to come, and at the intercession of the blessed and glorious ever-virgin Mary, Mother of God, of thy blessed apostles Peter and Paul, of

Andrew, and of all the saints, be pleased to grant peace in our time, so that with the help of thy compassion we may be ever free from sin and safe from all disquiet: through the same Jesus Christ, thy Son, our Lord, who is God, living and reigning with thee in the unity of the Holy Spirit, world without end.
PEOPLE: Amen.

THE PEACE OF THE LORD:

PRIEST: The peace of the Lord be always with you.
PEOPLE: And with you.
PRIEST: May this sacramental mingling of the Body and Blood of our Lord Jesus Christ be for us who receive it a source of eternal life. Amen.

THE AGNUS DEI:

Lamb of God, who takest away the sins of the world, have mercy on us. Lamb of God, who takest away the sins of the world, have mercy on us. Lamb of God, who takest away the sins of the world, give us peace.

THE COMMUNION OF THE PRIEST:

Lord Jesus Christ, who didst say to thy apostles: I leave peace with you; it is my own peace that I give you: look not upon my sins but upon thy Church's faith, and graciously give her peace and unity in accordance with thy will: thou who art God, living and reigning forever and ever. Amen.

Lord Jesus Christ, Son of the living God, who, by the Father's will and the co-operation of the Holy Spirit, didst by thy death bring life to the world, deliver me by this most holy Body and Blood of thine from all my sins and from every evil. Make me always cling to thy commandments, and never allow me to be parted from thee: who with the selfsame God the Father and the Holy Spirit art God, living and reigning forever and ever. Amen.

Let not the partaking of thy Body, Lord Jesus Christ, which I, unworthy as I am, make bold to receive, turn against me into judgment and damnation, but through thy loving kindness let it safeguard me body and soul and bring me healing: thou who art God, living and reigning with God the Father in the unity of the Holy Spirit, world without end. Amen.

I will take the Bread of Heaven, and will call upon the name of the Lord.

Lord, I am not worthy that thou shouldst enter beneath my roof, but say only the word, and my soul will be healed. (*Said thrice*)

The Body of our Lord Jesus Christ preserve my soul for everlasting life. Amen.

What return shall I make to the Lord for all that He has given me? I will take the chalice of salvation and invoke the name of the Lord. Praised be the Lord! When I invoke His name I shall be secure from my enemies.

The Blood of our Lord Jesus Christ preserve my soul for everlasting life. Amen.

THE ABLUTIONS:

That which our mouths have taken, Lord, may we possess in purity of heart; and may the gift of the moment become for us an everlasting remedy.

May thy Body, Lord, which I have taken, and thy Blood which I have drunk, cleave to every fiber of my being. Grant that no stain of sin may be left in me, now that I am renewed by this pure and holy sacrament: who livest and reignest world without end. Amen.

THE COMMUNION CHANT:

Ps 109:3: Amid the splendor of the holy places, thou art my Son, born before the daystar rises.

THE POSTCOMMUNION:

PRIEST: The Lord be with you.
PRIEST: Let us pray. Grant, Lord our God, that we who in this rite joyfully celebrate the birth of our Lord Jesus Christ may by worthy living become fit to obtain fellowship with him: who is God, living and reigning with thee in the unity of the Holy Spirit, world without end.
PEOPLE: Amen.

DISMISSAL AND BLESSING:

PRIEST: The Lord be with you.
PEOPLE: And with you.
PRIEST: Go, this is the dismissal.
PEOPLE: Thanks be to God.
PRIEST: May the tribute of my humble ministry be pleasing to thee, Holy Trinity. Grant that the sacrifice which I, unworthy as I am, have offered in the presence of thy majesty may be acceptable to thee. Through thy mercy may it bring forgiveness to me and to all for whom I have offered it: through Christ our Lord. Amen.

Almighty God bless you: the Father, the Son, and the Holy Ghost.
PEOPLE: Amen.

THE LAST GOSPEL:

PRIEST: The Lord be with you.
PEOPLE: And with you.
PRIEST: The beginning of the holy Gospel according to John.
PEOPLE: Glory to thee, Lord.
PRIEST: At the beginning of time the Word already was; and God had the Word abiding with Him, and the Word was God. He abode, at the beginning of time, with God. It was through Him that all things came into being, and without Him came nothing that has come to be. In Him there was life, and that life was the light of men. And the light shines in darkness, a darkness which was not able to master it. A man appeared, sent from God, whose name was John. He came for a witness, to bear witness to the light, so that through him all men might learn to believe. He was not the Light; he was sent to bear witness to the light. There is one who enlightens every soul born into the world; He was the true Light. He, through whom the world was made, was in the world, and the world treated Him as a stranger. He came to what was His own, and they who were His own gave Him no welcome. But all those who did welcome Him He empowered to become the children of God, all those who believe in His name; their birth came, not from human stock, not from nature's will or man's, but from God. And the Word was made flesh, and came to dwell among us; and we had sight of His glory, glory such as belongs to the Father's only-begotten Son, full of grace and truth.
PEOPLE: Thanks be to God.

The Sacraments

Baptism
Confirmation
Holy Eucharist
Penance
Holy Orders
Matrimony
Last Rites

PREFACE

The sacraments, in their own way, are revelations of God. For they are signs and tokens of God's dispensation and of His economy with reference to men. St. Thomas Aquinas says that the sacraments are signs of the past, of the present, and of the future. The past, inasmuch as they are signs of Christ's passion and resurrection. The present, in that they are efficacious signs of God's action and grace within the individual soul. The future, because they are signs of our own resurrection and glory to come.

But the sacraments are more than mere signs; they actually convey what they signify. In a very true sense the sacraments are the visible, outward manifestations of a whole attitude towards God and the world. They are the talismans of the Catholic's belief; for they mirror in concrete form the great mysteries of the faith: God and creation, the Incarnation and redemption, the Mystical Body, grace.

The Church surrounds each sacrament with ceremonies that are deeply moving and profoundly beautiful. The ordinary things of everyday life—water, bread and wine, oil, a gesture of the hand, a few simple words—are connected with symbolic rites that deepen the meaning of the sacramental signs themselves. The texts of the sacraments which are included here contain, on the level of symbolic action and word, the whole of the Catholic faith. Their careful study will deepen one's perception of the true life of the Christian soul as it moves through its mortal life towards its ultimate union with God.

Baptism

THE RITE FOR THE BAPTISM OF INFANTS[1]

At the threshold of the Church.

PRIEST (interrogates the child): N., what dost thou ask of the Church of God?

SPONSOR: Faith.

PRIEST: What does faith bestow on thee?

SPONSOR: Life everlasting.

PRIEST: If then thou wilt enter into life, keep the commandments: thou shalt love the Lord thy God with thy whole heart, and with thy whole soul, and with thy whole mind, and thy neighbor as thyself.

Then he gently blows three times on the face of the infant, and says:

[1] From *The Roman Ritual in Latin and English* 1: *The Sacraments and Processions,* translated and edited by Philip T. Weller (Milwaukee: Bruce, 1950) pp. 37-55.

PRIEST: Go out from him, thou unclean spirit, and make way for the Holy Spirit, the Consoler.

With his thumb he makes the sign of the cross upon the forehead and breast of the infant, saying:

PRIEST: Receive the sign of the cross upon thy brow and upon thy heart. Enter into the service of the heavenly commandments and be thou such in thy conduct that thou mayest deserve henceforth to be known as God's temple.

PRIEST: Let us pray. Graciously hear our entreaty, O Lord, we beseech thee, and with thine unfailing might guard thy chosen one, N., now signed with the seal of our Lord's holy cross. Help him to hold fast to this first acquaintance with thy majestic glory, that in keeping thy commandments he may deserve to attain the everlasting bliss destined for all who are born anew. Through Christ our Lord. Amen.

He now lays his hand upon the head of each child; then with outstretched hand he says:

PRIEST: Let us pray. Almighty, everlasting God, Father of our Lord, Jesus Christ! Deign to regard with favor thy servant, N., whom it has pleased thee to call to the beginnings of faith. Drive out from him all blindness of heart. Sunder all snares of Satan which hitherto bound him; open to him the gate of thy fatherly love, that dedicated with the seal of thy wisdom, he may remain unsullied from every evil desire. And inspired by the loveliness of thy precepts, may he serve thee with glad heart in thy church, advancing in perfection from day to day. Through the selfsame Christ our Lord. Amen.

The priest blesses salt, which once blessed may serve for future baptisms.

PRIEST: I purge thee of evil, thou creature of salt, in the name of God ✠, the Father almighty, and in the love of Jesus ✠ Christ, our Lord, and by the power of the Holy ✠ Spirit. I exorcise thee by the living ✠ God, by the true ✠ God, by the holy ✠ God, by the God who did provide thee in preservation of human needs, and did command that thou be consecrated by His servants for the people coming unto faith, that in the name of the Blessed Trinity thou mayest become an outward sign of salvation, repulsing the enemy. Wherefore, we beseech thee, O Lord, our God, to sanctify ✠ with thy sanctifying power, to bless ✠ with thy benediction this creature of salt, that it may be for all who receive it a sure remedy, ever enduring within them; in the name of the selfsame Jesus Christ, our Lord, who shall come to judge the living and the dead and the world by fire. Amen.

He puts a little of the blessed salt into the mouth of the child, saying:

PRIEST: N., receive the salt of wisdom; may it be unto thee a sign of reconciliation unto life everlasting. Amen.

PRIEST: Peace be with thee.

RESPONSE: And with thy spirit.

PRIEST: Let us pray. God of our fathers, O God, thou source of all truth, humbly we implore thee to look with mercy upon this thy servant, N., and no more let him hunger who now tastes this first nourishment of salt. But let him be enriched with heavenly food, so that he may ever be inflamed with zeal, joyous in hope, constant in serving thee. We bid thee, Lord, lead him to the bath where one is born anew, that in the company of thy faithful he may deserve to win the everlasting reward which thou hast promised. Through Christ our Lord. Amen.

PRIEST: I cast thee out, unclean spirit, in the name of the Father ✠, and of the Son ✠, and of the Holy ✠ Spirit. Depart and vanish from this servant of God, N. For it is He who commands thee, thou doomed and accursed one, He whose feet once trod the waves, who reached out His saving hand to Peter when he began to sink. Therefore, accursed fiend, admit thy doom, and pay honor to Jesus Christ, His Son, and to the Holy Spirit, and keep far from this servant of God, N. For Jesus Christ, our Lord and God, has graciously called him to His holy grace and blessing, indeed to the fountain of baptism.

> *Here he signs with his thumb the forehead of the child, saying:*

PRIEST: And this sign of the holy ✠ cross which we trace on his brow, do thou, accursed demon, never dare to violate. Through the selfsame Christ our Lord. Amen.

> *He lays his hand upon the child's head; then with outstretched hand he says:*

PRIEST: Let us pray. O Holy Lord, almighty Father, eternal God, Author of light and truth, I entreat for this thy servant, N., thine unfailing and righteous mercy. May it please thee to enlighten him with the light of thine understanding. Cleanse and sanctify him. Endow him with true knowledge, so that he may be made worthy of the grace of thy baptism, and thus remain steadfast in firm hope, right purpose, and holy doctrine. Through Christ our Lord. Amen.

> *The priest places the end of the stole, which hangs from his left shoulder, upon the child and leads him into the church, the while he says:*

PRIEST: N., enter into the temple of God, that thou mayest have part with Christ unto life everlasting. Amen.

> *After they have come into church, the priest leads the way to the font, praying aloud together with the sponsors:*

PRIEST AND SPONSORS: I believe in God the Father almighty, Creator of heaven and earth. And in Jesus Christ, His only Son, our Lord, who was conceived by the Holy Ghost, born of the Virgin Mary, suffered under Pontius Pilate, was crucified, died, and was buried. He descended into hell, the third day He arose again from the dead. He ascended into heaven and sitteth at the right hand of God the Father almighty; from thence He shall come to judge the living and the dead. I believe in the

Holy Ghost, the Holy Catholic Church, the communion of saints, the forgiveness of sins, the resurrection of the body, and life everlasting. Amen.

PRIEST AND SPONSORS: Our Father, who art in heaven, hallowed be thy name. Thy kingdom come. Thy will be done on earth as it is in heaven. Give us this day our daily bread. And forgive us our trespasses, as we forgive those who trespass against us. And lead us not into temptation, but deliver us from evil.

> *Then, before entering the baptistery, he turns to the candidate and says:*

PRIEST: I expel thee, every unclean spirit, in the name of God, the Father ✠ almighty, in the name of Jesus ✠ Christ, His Son, our Lord and Judge, and by the power of the Holy ✠ Spirit. Depart from this handwork of God, N., whom our Lord has deigned to call to His holy temple, that he may be made a temple of the living God, and the Holy Spirit may dwell within him. Through the selfsame Christ our Lord, who shall come to judge the living and the dead and the world by fire. Amen.

> *The priest touches the ears and nostrils of the child. He touches the right ear then the left, saying only once:*

PRIEST: Ephpheta, which means: Be thou opened!

> *Then he touches the nostrils, one after the other, adding:*

PRIEST: Unto the odor of sweetness. But thou, evil spirit, begone, for the judgment of God draws nigh!

> *Now he questions the candidate by name:*

PRIEST: N., dost thou renounce Satan?

SPONSOR: I do renounce him.

PRIEST: And all his works?

SPONSOR: I do renounce them.

PRIEST: And all his allurements?

SPONSOR: I do renounce them.

> *The priest dips his thumb in the oil of catechumens, and in the form of a cross anoints the child on the breast and between the shoulders on the back, saying only once for the two anointings:*

PRIEST: I anoint ✠ thee with the oil of salvation in Christ Jesus, our Lord, that thou mayest have life everlasting. Amen.

> *Thereupon he wipes his thumb and the places anointed with cotton or similar material.*
>
> *Remaining in the same place outside the baptistery gates, he exchanges the purple stole for a white one. Then he enters the baptistery, followed by the sponsor with the child. At the baptismal font he interrogates the candidate by name, with the sponsor giving the answer:*

PRIEST: N., dost thou believe in God, the Father almighty, Creator of heaven and earth?

SPONSOR: I do believe.

PRIEST: Dost thou believe in Jesus Christ, his sole-begotten Son, our Lord, who was born unto us and who suffered for us?

SPONSOR: I do believe.

PRIEST: Dost thou believe in the Holy Spirit, the holy Catholic Church, the communion of saints, the forgiveness of sins, the resurrection of the body, and life everlasting?

SPONSOR: I do believe.

He says to the candidate, calling him by name:

PRIEST: N., wilt thou be baptized?

SPONSOR: I will.

With the godfather or godmother (or both if two have been selected) holding the child, the priest takes baptismal water with the ladle, pours it thrice in the form of a cross upon the child's head, and simultaneously pronounces only once distinctly and attentively the following words:

PRIEST: N., I baptize thee in the name of the Father ✠ and of the Son ✠ and of the Holy ✠ Spirit.

Then the priest dips his right thumb into the holy chrism, and in the form of a cross anoints the child on the crown of the head, saying:

PRIEST: May God almighty, Father of our Lord, Jesus Christ, who has caused thee to be born anew by water and the Holy Spirit, and granted thee remission of all sins,

Here he anoints.

PRIEST: may He anoint thee ✠ with the chrism of salvation in the selfsame Christ Jesus, our Lord, unto life everlasting. Amen.

PRIEST: Peace be unto thee.

RESPONSE: And with thy spirit.

He wipes his thumb and the place anointed with cotton. Then he puts a white linen cloth (in place of the white garment) upon the child's head, saying:

PRIEST: Receive this white garment, and carry it unsullied unto the judgment seat of our Lord, Jesus Christ, that thou mayest have life everlasting. Amen.

Then he presents a lighted candle to the newly baptized or to the sponsor, saying:

PRIEST: Receive this burning light. Safeguard thy baptism by blameless life. Keep the commandments of God, that when our Lord shall come for the heavenly nuptials thou mayest meet Him together with all the saints in the court of heaven, and live forever and ever. Amen.

In conclusion he says:

PRIEST: N., go in peace, and the Lord be with thee. Amen.

Confirmation[1]

> *The candidates kneel, with hands joined, before the bishop,*
> *who, standing with hands joined, says:*

BISHOP: May the Holy Spirit come down upon you, and may the power of the Most High keep you from sin. Amen.

> *Then signing himself with large sign of the cross he says:*

VERSICLE: Our help is in the name of the Lord.

RESPONSE: Who made heaven and earth.

VERSICLE: O Lord, hear my prayer.

RESPONSE: And let my cry come unto thee.

VERSICLE: The Lord be with you.

RESPONSE: And with thy spirit.

> *Then with hands extended over the ones being confirmed,*
> *he says:*

BISHOP: Let us pray. Almighty, everlasting God, who has deigned to beget new life in these thy servants by water and the Holy Spirit, and

●

[1] From *The Roman Ritual in Latin and English* 1: *The Sacraments and Processions,* translated and edited by Philip T. Weller (Milwaukee: Bruce, 1950) pp. 219-23.

has granted them remission of all their sins, send forth from heaven upon them thy Holy Spirit, the Consoler, with His sevenfold gifts. Amen.

VERSICLE: The Spirit of wisdom and understanding.

RESPONSE: Amen.

VERSICLE: The Spirit of counsel and of fortitude.

RESPONSE: Amen.

VERSICLE: The Spirit of knowledge and of piety.

RESPONSE: Amen.

BISHOP: Fill them with the Spirit of fear of the Lord, and seal them with the sign of Christ's ✠ cross, plenteous in mercy unto life everlasting. Through the selfsame Jesus Christ, thy Son, our Lord, who liveth and reigneth with thee in the unity of the same Holy Spirit, God eternally.

RESPONSE: Amen.

> *Then the bishop confirms them. As he comes to each candidate who is kneeling and presented by the sponsor, he inquires for the name. And dipping the tip of his thumb in the holy chrism, he confirms the person as he says:*

BISHOP: N., I seal thee with the sign of the Cross ✠.

> *During these words he has his right hand resting on the head of the subject, while with his thumb he traces the sign of the cross on his brow, then continues:*

BISHOP: And I confirm thee with the chrism of salvation. In the name of the Father ✠, and of the Son ✠, and of the Holy ✠ Spirit.

RESPONSE: Amen.

> *And he lightly strikes the confirmed upon the cheek, saying:*

BISHOP: Peace be with thee.

> *After all have been confirmed, the bishop cleanses his fingers with bread and washes them over a bowl. During the washing of hands the assisting clergy sing or recite the following antiphon:*

ASSISTANTS: Strengthen, O God, what thou has wrought in us, from out thy holy temple which is in Jerusalem.

VERSICLE: Glory be to the Father, and to the Son, and to the Holy Spirit. As it was in the beginning, is now, and ever shall be, world without end.

RESPONSE: Amen.

> *The antiphon is repeated. And then the bishop, standing with hands joined and facing the altar, says:*

VERSICLE: Show us thy mercy, O Lord.

RESPONSE: And grant us thy salvation.

VERSICLE: O Lord, hear my prayer.

RESPONSE: And let my cry come unto thee.

VERSICLE The Lord be with you.

RESPONSE: And with thy spirit.

Keeping his hands joined, the while the newly confirmed are devoutly kneeling, the bishop continues:

BISHOP. Let us pray. O God, thou didst give the Holy Spirit to thine apostles, and didst will that He should be handed down through them and their successors upon the rest of the faithful. So now behold with favor our lowly ministration, and grant that the same Holy Spirit may come and abide in the hearts of them whose brow we have anointed with holy chrism and sealed with the sign of the holy cross. And by His indwelling, may He graciously cause them to become a perfect temple for His divine majesty. Thou who livest and reignest together with the Father and the selfsame Holy Spirit, God, forever and ever.

RESPONSE: Amen.

He then adds:

BISHOP: Behold, thus shall every man be blessed that lives in the fear of the Lord.

And turning toward the confirmed, he says as he makes the sign of the cross over them:

BISHOP: From Sion hence may the Lord send you His blessing ✠, so that all your days you may gaze upon the prosperity of Jerusalem, and may come to possess life everlasting.

RESPONSE: Amen.

The Holy Eucharist

The Mass is both the Eucharistic Sacrifice and a sacrament: it accomplishes what it signifies, the Sacrifice of Calvary. The reception of this sacrament is called Holy Communion. The priest who celebrates the Mass always receives Communion and it is customary that as many as possible of the faithful who join in offering the sacrifice also share in receiving the sacrament. But from the early days of the Church, because all Christians could not be physically present at Mass, it has been customary to "reserve" the Blessed Sacrament and to distribute Holy Communion also outside of Mass. The full text of this sacrament is therefore the text of the Mass. When Holy Communion is given outside of Mass the following rite is used.

The priest's assistant recites in the name of the people:

ASSISTANT: I confess to almighty God, to blessed Mary ever virgin, to blessed Michael the archangel, to blessed John the Baptist, to the holy apostles Peter and Paul, to all the saints, and to you, father, that I have sinned exceedingly in thought, word, and deed; through my fault, through my fault, through my most grievous fault. Therefore I beseech blessed Mary ever virgin, blessed Michael the archangel, blessed John the Baptist, the holy apostles Peter and Paul, all the saints, and you, father, to pray to the Lord our God for me.

The priest then turns to the people and says:

PRIEST: May almighty God have mercy on you, forgive you your sins, and lead you to eternal life.

ASSISTANT: Amen.

PRIEST: May the almighty and merciful Lord grant you pardon, absolution, and remission of your sins.

ASSISTANT: Amen.

Turning to the people with the Host in his hand the priest says:

PRIEST: Behold the Lamb of God, behold Him who takes away the sins of the world.

He then says three times:

PRIEST: Lord, I am not worthy that you should come under my roof; say only the word and my soul shall be healed.

Giving the Host to each of the communicants the priest says:

PRIEST: May the Body of our Lord Jesus Christ keep your soul for life unending.

The priest returns to the altar and says:

PRIEST: O sacred banquet, in which Christ becomes our food, the memory of His passion is renewed, the soul is filled with grace, and a pledge is given us of future glory.

PRIEST: You have given them bread from heaven.

ASSISTANT: Bread having in it all that can delight.

PRIEST: O Lord, hear my prayer.

ASSISTANT: And let my cry come unto you.

PRIEST: The Lord be with you.

ASSISTANT: And with your spirit.

PRIEST: Let us pray. O God, you have given us in this wonderful sacrament a memorial of your passion. We implore you, grant that we may so reverence the sacred mysteries of your Body and Blood that we may constantly feel within ourselves the effects of your redemption. Who lives and reigns for all eternity.

ASSISTANT: Amen.

The service is concluded with a blessing from the priest:

PRIEST: May the blessing of almighty God, Father, Son, and Holy Spirit, descend upon you and remain forever.

ASSISTANT: Amen.

The Sacrament of Penance

After the penitent has confessed his sins, the priest imposes a salutary penance and then pronounces the following words of absolution:

PRIEST: May almighty God have mercy on you, forgive you your sins, and lead you to eternal life.

May the almighty and merciful Lord grant you pardon, absolution, and remission of your sins.

May our Lord Jesus Christ absolve you, and I, by His authority, absolve you from every bond of excommunication, suspension, and interdict, in so far as lies within my power and you have need of it. Furthermore, I absolve you from your sins in the name of the Father, and of the Son, and of the Holy Spirit. Amen.

May the passion of our Lord Jesus Christ, the merits of the Blessed Virgin Mary and all the saints, the good you have done, and the ill you have endured profit for the remission of your sins, for an increase in grace, and for the reward that is eternal life. Amen.

The Ordination of a Priest[1]

PREPARATION

The first part of the rite of ordination is a preparatory ceremony in which the candidates are formally presented to the bishop. After the mandate authorizing the bishop to ordain has been read, the bishop first addresses the entire assembly and then the candidates directly, emphasizing the sublime dignity of the priesthood as well as its awful responsibility. When he has finished speaking, the Litany of the Saints is chanted, so that all present may pray to almighty God, imploring His grace for the young men who are about to be ordained.

The candidates are vested in amice, alb, maniple, and stole worn in the manner of a deacon. Over the left arm they carry a folded chasuble, the vestment of priesthood; and in the left hand (or attached to the cincture) the white linen bands for the binding of their hands. In the

[1] From Philip T. Weller, *The Ordination of a Priest* (Washington, D.C.: Saint Pius X Press, 1955) pp. 12-17, 25-36, 55-58.

*right hand they hold a lighted candle. As the ceremony be-
gins the bishop is seated on a faldstool placed on the altar
predella. The archdeacon calls the candidates, saying:*

ARCHDEACON: Let those come forward who are to be ordained to the
order of priesthood.

*As the notary now calls each candidate by name, the latter
answers:* Present. *Then all step toward the altar, arrange
themselves in a semi-circle before the bishop, and kneel
down. After this, one of the assistants reads the mandate.*

ASSISTANT: The most reverend father and ruler in Christ, His Ex-
cellency, N., by the grace of God and of the Apostolic See Bishop of
N., orders and enjoins under penalty of excommunication that no one
here present come forward to receive holy orders if he be irregular, or
excommunicated by canon law or by his superior, or interdicted, sus-
pended, illegitimate, infamous, or in any other way disqualified, or
from another diocese, unless he has the permission of his bishop. He
enjoins, moreover, that none of those ordained leave before the end of
Mass or before they have received the bishop's blessing.

*Now the archdeacon presents the candidates to the bishop,
saying:*

ARCHDEACON: Most Reverend Father, our holy Mother the Catholic
Church asks you to ordain these deacons here present to the office of
priesthood.

The bishop inquires:

BISHOP: Do you know if they are worthy?

ARCHDEACON: So far as human limitation allows, I am certain and I
vouch for the fact that they are deserving of the burden of this office.

The bishop says:

BISHOP: Thanks be to God.

*Next the bishop addresses the clergy and the people as
follows:*

BISHOP: My dear brethren, just as the captain of a ship and its passengers alike have reason to feel safe or else in danger on a journey, so
also ought all who have a common goal be of the same mind. Not
without reason, then, have the Fathers decreed that the people should
be consulted in the choice of those who are to be raised to the ministry
of the altar. For sometimes it happens that one or the other person
knows something about the life and character of the candidate that is
not generally known by the majority of men. And surely the people
will be more inclined to render obedience to a priest if they have been
allowed to have their say about his ordination.

So far as I can tell, the conduct of these deacons, who with God's
help are to be ordained to the priesthood, is commendable and pleasing to God. Hence, in my opinion, they are deserving of being promoted to a higher honor in the Church's ranks. Yet it is well to ask the

opinion of the people as a whole, for if only one or a few were to be allowed to voice their approval, there would be danger of a biased assent, influenced too much by friendship or by family ties.

Be perfectly free, then, to say what you know about the life and character of the candidates and what you think of their fitness. But let your approval of their elevation to the priesthood be based on their merits, rather than on your own affection and esteem for them. Consequently, if there is anyone present who has anything against them, let him for God's sake and in God's name come forward and speak. However, let that person keep in mind his own shortcomings.

After a brief pause the bishop continues, addressing himself now in exhortation to the candidates:

BISHOP: My dear sons, who are about to be consecrated to the office of priesthood, endeavor to receive it worthily, and once ordained, strive to discharge its obligations in a praiseworthy manner. A priest's duty is to offer sacrifice, to bless, to govern, to preach, to baptize. To advance to so high a position is a step that ought to be taken in great awe. Moreover, it must be our concern that those selected for it are recommended for it by the highest kind of wisdom, upright character, and a longstanding virtuous life.

When in olden times the Lord commanded Moses to choose as his helpers seventy men from all Israel, to whom He would impart the gifts of the Holy Spirit, He said to him:

"Choose the ones whom you know to be elders (leaders) of the people" (Nm 11:16). It is you yourselves who are prefigured in these seventy elders, if now, by the help of the sevenfold gifts of the Holy Spirit, you keep the ten commandments, and show yourselves both mature in wisdom and blameless in action.

By the same kind of sign and figure in the New Law, our Lord chose the seventy-two disciples, and sent them two by two before Him to preach the gospel. Thus He taught by word and deed that the ministers of His Church should be perfect both in faith and in works, well grounded in the twofold love of God and of neighbor. Strive, then, by God's grace to be that kind of priest, worthy of being chosen to assist Moses and the twelve apostles in the person of the Catholic bishops. For it is the latter, no less, who are prefigured in Moses and the apostles. And then, indeed, is Holy Church adorned and ruled by a remarkable variety of ministers, when from her ranks are consecrated, first the bishops, and under them the priests, deacons, and subdeacons, each in his own degree and dignity, yet all of them members making up the one body of Christ.

Therefore, my dear sons, chosen as you are by the judgment of our brethren to be consecrated as our helpers, let your conduct bespeak the integrity of a chaste and holy life. Realize fully how sublime are the acts you are to perform. Model yourselves on the holiness of the things you are to handle. Ordained to celebrate the mystery of the

Lord's death, see to it that by mortifying your bodies you rid yourselves of every inclination to vice and concupiscence. Let the doctrine
you expound be spiritual medicine for the people of God. Let your
good repute be the delight of the Church of Christ, so that by preaching and by example you help to build up the edifice which is the
family of God. May it never come about that we, for promoting you
to so great an office, or you, for taking it on yourselves, should deserve
to be condemned by the Lord. Rather, may we all be rewarded by
Him. This may He grant us by His grace.

RESPONSE: Amen.

> *If ordination to the priesthood was not preceded earlier
> in the ceremonies by the subdiaconate or the diaconate,
> then the Litany of the Saints is chanted at this time. During
> the Litany the candidates humbly lie prostrate on the floor
> of the sanctuary. The bishop kneels on the altar predella.*

RITE OF ORDINATION PROPER

The Laying on of Hands

*When the Litany is ended, the candidates rise and go in pairs to
kneel before the bishop. The bishop places both his hands on the head
of each candidate in turn, without saying anything. This very simple
yet impressive act, unaccompanied by prayer or chant, is called the
essential matter of the sacrament. It signifies that the power of priesthood is conferred by the bishop imposing hands on the candidate,
transmitting to the latter the power which the bishop himself has
received from Christ through the apostles and their successors.*

> *After the bishop has imposed hands on them, they return
> to their former place, and kneel. When all are in place, the
> bishop holds his right hand open and extended toward
> them. Next the priests who are present come forward and
> lay both their hands on the head of each candidate. Form-
> ing a semicircle beginning at the Gospel side, they stand
> behind the candidates, and hold their right hand extended
> toward them, the same as the bishop is doing. The bishop
> now says the following prayer:*

BISHOP: My brethren, let us beseech God the Father Almighty to multiply His heavenly gifts on these servants, whom He has chosen for
the office of priesthood. May they fulfil by His grace the office they
receive by His mercy. Through Christ our Lord.

RESPONSE: Amen.

Solemn Preface and Form of Sacrament

> *The bishop turns to the altar and says:*

BISHOP: Let us pray.

354

The assistants say:
ASSISTANTS: Let us kneel down.
And the bishop says:
BISHOP: Arise.
Next the bishop turns to the men being ordained, and says the following prayer and then chants the solemn Preface.
BISHOP: Hear us, we beseech thee, O Lord our God, and pour out on these thy servants the blessing of the Holy Spirit and the power of priestly grace. Accept them as we now offer them for consecration in the sight of thy benign presence, and assist them always with thy boundless favors. Through Jesus Christ, thy Son, our Lord, who lives and reigns with thee, in the unity of the Holy Spirit, God, forever and ever.
RESPONSE: Amen.
BISHOP: The Lord be with you.
RESPONSE: And with your spirit.
BISHOP: Lift up your hearts.
RESPONSE: We have lifted them up to the Lord.
BISHOP: Let us give thanks to the Lord our God.
RESPONSE: It is right and fitting that we do so.
BISHOP: It is truly right and fitting, worthy and salutary, that always and everywhere we give thanks to thee, O Holy Lord, almighty Father, everlasting God, the source of all honors and the dispenser of all dignities. Through thee all things make progress and become firmly established. In accord with thy perfect arrangement all rational creatures advance to a higher excellence. So also the various grades of priest and levites, instituted as sacred types, grew and developed. For after appointing chief priests to rule the people, thou didst choose men of lesser degree and second rank as their associates and helpers. So also in the wilderness thou didst promote Moses' spirit in the hearts of the seventy wise men, with whose help he was enabled to govern without difficulty the countless multitude. For a like purpose thou didst pour out on Eleazar and Ithmar, the sons of Aaron, the superabundant graces enjoyed by their father, in order to assure a sufficient number of priests for more frequent offering of the saving sacrifices and other sacred rites. With equal concern, Lord, thou didst give the apostles of thy Son other teachers of the faith, who would fill the whole world with the preaching of salvation. Hence, we beseech thee, Lord, give this same aid to us weak servants, who need it so much more, because we lack their strength.
The bishop at this point interrupts the chant and recites the following words, which constitute the form of the sacrament.
BISHOP: Almighty Father, we beg thee to bestow on these thy servants the dignity of the priesthood. Renew in their hearts the spirit of holiness. Help them to be steadfast in the office of second priestly rank

received from thee, and to inspire others to strive for perfection by their example. May they become zealous fellow workers in our ministry. May they shine in all the Christian virtues, so that they will be able to give a good account of the stewardship entrusted to them, and finally attain the reward of everlasting life. Through the same Jesus Christ, thy Son, our Lord, who lives and reigns with thee, in the unity of the Holy Spirit, God, forever and ever.

RESPONSE: Amen.

Investiture of the New Priests

> *Now the newly ordained go before the bishop. The bishop takes the stole, until now worn by the newly ordained on the left shoulder, draws it over the right shoulder, and arranges it in the form of a cross over the chest (in the manner worn by a priest). As he does so he says to each one:*

BISHOP: Take the yoke of the Lord, for His yoke is sweet and His burden light.

> *Next he invests each one with the chasuble, leaving it folded and pinned at the back but hanging down in front. As he does so he says:*

BISHOP: Receive the vesture of priesthood, which is a symbol of charity. God is well able to increase charity in you and make perfect your works.

> *To this the new priest replies:*

RESPONSE: Thanks be to God.

> *The bishop rises and says the following prayer, during which the people kneel:*

BISHOP: O God, author of all holiness, from thee alone we receive true consecration and perfect benediction. Pour out on these thy servants, whom we now raise to the dignity of the priesthood, the gift of thy blessing. By their noble and exemplary lives, let them prove that they are really elders of the people, and true to the norms laid down by Paul to Timothy and Titus. Let them meditate on thy law day and night, so that they will believe what they read, teach what they believe, and practice what they preach. May justice, steadfastness, mercy, fortitude, and all the other virtues be reflected in their every way of acting. May they induce others to the same by their example, and hearten them by their admonitions. May they keep pure and undefiled the gift of their high calling. For the benefit of the people may they always be ready to change bread and wine into the Body and Blood of thy Son by a holy consecration. May they through persevering charity mature "unto the perfect man, unto the measure of the age of the fulness of Christ," and rise on the day of the just and eternal judgment of God with a good conscience, true faith, and the full gifts of the Holy Spirit. Through the same Jesus Christ, thy Son our Lord, who lives and reigns with thee, in the unity of the same Holy Spirit, God, forever and ever.

RESPONSE: Amen.

CONCLUDING RITES SYMBOLIC OF PRIESTHOOD

The Anointing of Hands

> *The bishop kneels and intones the hymn:* Veni Creator, *which is then continued by the choir:*

BISHOP: Come, Holy Ghost, Creator blest,
And in our souls take up thy rest,
Come with thy grace and heavenly aid
To fill the hearts which thou hast made.

> *After the first strophe of the hymn, the bishop anoints the hands of the newly ordained with the Oil of Catechumens. First he anoints the inside of the hands, tracing a cross from the thumb of the right hand to the index finger of the left, and from the thumb of the left hand to the index finger of the right. Then he anoints the entire palms. He says as he performs the anointings:*

BISHOP: May it please thee, O Lord, to consecrate and hallow these hands by this anointing and our blessing.

RESPONSE: Amen.

> *And having made the sign of the cross over the hands of the ordained he continues:*

BISHOP: That whatsoever they bless may be blessed, and whatsoever they consecrate may be consecrated and hallowed, in the name of our Lord Jesus Christ.

> *The newly ordained says:*

RESPONSE: Amen.

> *The bishop folds the hands just consecrated, and one of the assistants binds them together with a white linen cloth. In the meantime the choir is singing the remaining strophes of the* Veni Creator:

CHOIR: O Comforter! to thee we cry,
Thou heavenly gift of God most high!
Thou font of life and fire of love,
And sweet anointing from above!

Thou in thy sevenfold gifts are known;
Thee, finger of God's own hand we own,
The promise of the Father, thou
Who dost the tongue with power endow.

Kindle our senses from above,
And make our hearts o'erflow with love;
With patience firm and virtue high
The weakness of our flesh supply.

Far from us drive the foe we dread,
And grant us thy true peace instead;
So shall we not, with thee for guide,
Turn from the path of life aside.

Oh, may thy grace on us bestow
The Father and the Son to know;
And thee, through endless times confessed,
Of both the eternal Spirit blest.

All glory while the ages run
Be to the Father and the Son,
Who rose from death; the same to thee,
O Holy Ghost, eternally. Amen.

Presentation of the Host and Chalice

> *The bishop now presents each of the newly ordained with a chalice containing wine and water and a paten upon it with a host. The newly ordained touches with the fore and middle fingers both the paten and the cup of the chalice. During this ceremony the bishop says:*

BISHOP: Receive the power to offer sacrifice to God and to celebrate Mass, both for the living and the dead, in the name of our Lord.

RESPONSE: Amen.

> *Thus the main rites of ordination come to an end, and the Mass is resumed. This Mass is celebrated by the bishop together with the newly ordained priests. After the Communion of the Mass occur the concluding rites of ordination.*

CONCLUDING RITES OF ORDINATION

Bestowal of Power to Forgive Sins

> *After the bishop has washed his hands, he stands at the Epistle corner and intones the following responsory, which is continued by the choir:*

BISHOP: I will no longer call you servants but my friends. For you know all that I have done in your midst. Alleluia. Receive the Holy Spirit, the Advocate, within you. It is He whom the Father will send you. Alleluia. You are my friends if you do the things that I command you. Receive the Holy Spirit, the Advocate, within you. Glory be to the Father, and to the Son, and to the Holy Spirit. It is He whom the Father will send you. Alleluia.

> *The bishop now turns to the newly ordained. The latter recite the Apostles' Creed, the profession of faith which they will henceforth explain to the people.*
>
> *Then the bishop sits down, and as the new priests come to kneel before him, he places both his hands on the head of each one saying:*

BISHOP: Receive the Holy Spirit. Whose sins you shall forgive, they are forgiven them; and whose sins you shall retain, they are retained.

> *Now that the newly ordained have been given full priestly powers, the bishop unfolds the chasuble, which so far they have worn folded on the shoulders; and as he lets the chasuble drop at the back, he says:*

BISHOP: May the Lord clothe you with the robe of innocence.

The Promise of Obedience

> *Again the newly ordained come before the bishop, kneel in front of him, and place their hands folded between the hands of the bishop, who puts the following question to each one:*

BISHOP: Do you promise me and my successors reverence and obedience?

RESPONSE: I promise.

> *Still holding the priest's hands within his own, the bishop kisses him on the right cheek, saying:*

BISHOP: May the peace of the Lord be ever with you.

RESPONSE: Amen.

Admonition and Blessing

> *When the newly ordained have returned to their former place, the bishop addresses them as follows:*

BISHOP: My dear sons, the office you are going to perform is surely a difficult one. For that reason let me admonish you, before you begin to celebrate Mass, learn carefully from other experienced priests the rites of the whole Mass—the consecration, the breaking of the Bread, and the Communion.

> *The bishop then solemnly bestows the blessing on them:*

BISHOP: May the blessing of almighty God, Father, Son, and Holy Spirit, come upon you, that you may be blessed in priestly orders, and offer for the sins and transgressions of the people atoning sacrifices to God Almighty, to whom be honor and glory forever and ever.

RESPONSE: Amen.

Matrimony[1]

The sacrament of matrimony is usually administered before a nuptial Mass celebrated for the newly married and including a special nuptial blessing for them. Sometimes circumstances require that the ceremony be had independent of the nuptial Mass. In all cases the ceremony is essentially the same.

The bridal couple approach the altar with customary solemnity. The priest ascends the altar, turns, and faces them. He may read the following instruction or he may give one of his own composition. The marriage rite follows immediately upon the instruction.

Instruction Before Marriage
PRIEST: My dear friends: You are about to enter into a union which is most sacred and most serious. It is most sacred, because established

●

[1] From *The Sacristy Manual,* compiled by Paul Griffith (rev. ed.; New York: Kenedy, 1947) pp. 60-66, 68-69.

by God Himself; most serious, because it will bind you together for life in a relationship so close and so intimate, that it will profoundly influence your whole future. That future, with its hopes and disappointments, its successes and its failures, its pleasures and its pains, its joys and its sorrows, is hidden from your eyes. You know that these elements are mingled in every life, and are to be expected in your own. And so, not knowing what is before you, you take each other for better or for worse, for richer or poorer, in sickness and in health, until death.

Truly, then, these words are most serious. It is a beautiful tribute to your undoubted faith in each other that, recognizing their full import, you are nevertheless so willing and ready to pronounce them. And because these words involve such solemn obligations, it is most fitting that you rest the security of your wedded life upon the great principle of self-sacrifice. And so you begin your married life by the voluntary and complete surrender of your individual lives in the interest of that deeper and wider life which you are to have in common. Henceforth you belong entirely to each other; you will be one in mind, one in heart, and one in affections. And whatever sacrifices you may hereafter be required to make to preserve this common life, always make them generously. Sacrifice is usually difficult and irksome. Only love can make it easy; and perfect love can make it a joy. We are willing to give in proportion as we love. And when love is perfect the sacrifice is complete. God so loved the world that He gave His only-begotten Son; and the Son so loved us that He gave Himself for our salvation. "Greater love than this no man hath, that a man lay down his life for his friends."

No greater blessing can come to your married life than pure conjugal love, loyal and true to the end. May, then, this love with which you join your hands and hearts today, never fail, but grow deeper and stronger as the years go on. And if true love and the unselfish spirit of perfect sacrifice guide your every action, you can expect the greatest measure of earthly happiness that may be allotted to man in this life. The rest is in the hands of God. Nor will God be wanting to your needs; He will pledge you the lifelong support of His graces in the holy sacrament which you are now going to receive.

The priest asks the bridegroom:

PRIEST: Wilt thou take N., here present, for thy lawful wife, according to the rite of our holy Mother the Church?

RESPONSE: I will.

Then the priest asks the bride:

PRIEST: Wilt thou take N., here present, for thy lawful husband, according to the rite of our holy Mother the Church?

RESPONSE: I will.

The priest bids them join their right hands. Then the man repeats after the priest:

RESPONSE: I, N.N., take thee, N.N., for my lawful wife, to have and to hold, from this day forward, for better, for worse, for richer, for poorer, in sickness and in health, until death do us part.

The woman repeats after the priest:

RESPONSE: I, N.N., take thee, N.N., for my lawful husband, to have and to hold, from this day forward, for better, for worse, for richer, for poorer, in sickness and in health, until death do us part.

The priest, as witness to their marriage, joins them together in the name of the Blessed Trinity:

PRIEST: I join you together in marriage in the name of the Father ✠, and of the Son, and of the Holy Ghost. Amen.

He then sprinkles them with holy water. Following this, he blesses the ring, saying:

PRIEST: Our help is in the name of the Lord.

RESPONSE: Who hath made heaven and earth.

VERSICLE: O Lord, hear my prayer.

RESPONSE: And let my cry come unto Thee.

VERSICLE: The Lord be with you.

RESPONSE: And with thy spirit.

PRIEST: Let us pray. Bless ✠, O Lord, this ring, which we bless ✠ in thy name, that she who is to wear it, keeping true faith unto her husband, may abide in thy peace and obedience to thy will, and ever live in mutual love. Through the same Christ our Lord.

RESPONSE: Amen.

The bridegroom puts the ring on the third finger of the left hand of the bride, saying:

BRIDEGROOM: With this ring I thee wed, and I plight unto thee my troth.

The priest continues:

PRIEST: In the name of the Father, and of the Son, and of the Holy Spirit. Amen.

VERSICLE: Strengthen, O God, what thou has wrought in us.

RESPONSE: From out thy holy temple which is in Jerusalem.

Lord, have mercy on us. Christ, have mercy on us. Lord, have mercy on us.

Our Father . . . *inaudibly until:*

VERSICLE: And lead us not into temptation.

RESPONSE: But deliver us from evil.

VERSICLE: Preserve thy servants.

RESPONSE: Who place their confidence in thee, my God.

VERSICLE: Send them, Lord, aid from on high.

RESPONSE: And from Sion watch over them.

VERSICLE: Be unto them, O Lord, a tower of strength.

RESPONSE: In the face of the enemy.

VERSICLE: O Lord, hear my prayer.

RESPONSE: And let my cry come unto thee.

VERSICLE: The Lord be with you.

RESPONSE: And with thy spirit.

PRIEST: Let us pray. Look down, we beseech thee, O Lord, upon these thy servants, and graciously protect thy institutions whereby thou hast provided for the propagation of mankind, that those who are joined together by thine authority may be preserved by thy help. Through Christ our Lord. Amen.

The nuptial Mass follows immediately. At its conclusion the following prayer may be said:

PRIEST: O God, who has ordained and sanctified the holy state of matrimony for replenishing the earth, for mutual consolation, and as a type of the union of Christ and His Church, give to these here present who have this day entered into this sacred relation, grace to both thankfully accept its blessings and faithfully to fulfil its duties. Accompany their union with thy constant assistance, to enable them to live together in peace and love, in the careful discharge of all their duties to thee and to each other.

Deliver them from all evil temper, from every heedless action which may in any way embitter or weaken the tie by which thou hast bound them together. Make them true and affectionate, studious to please, and ready to deny their own will and inclination in all things. Let not the trials and crosses of this life induce them to murmur, nor let their earthly prosperity cause them to forget thee, the Author and Giver of all blessings, but by patience and meekness, by prayer and thankfulness, may all blessings be sanctified unto them, and fit them for an eternal union with thee. Through the same Christ our Lord. Amen.

Last Anointing[1]

Arriving at the place where the sick person is confined, the priest as he enters the room says:

VERSICLE: Peace be unto this home.

RESPONSE: And unto all who dwell herein.

He then places the oil upon the table, and vested in surplice and purple stole presents the crucifix to be devoutly kissed by the sick person. Thereafter he sprinkles with holy water in the form of a cross the patient, the room, and the bystanders, saying the antiphon:

Sprinkle me with hyssop, O Lord, and I shall be clean; wash me, and I shall be whiter than snow.

If the patient wishes to go to confession, he hears his confession and absolves him. Then he addresses to him some

[1] From *The Roman Ritual in Latin and English* 1: *The Sacraments and Processions,* translated and edited by Philip T. Weller (Milwaukee: Bruce, 1950) pp. 337-45.

pious words of consolation, and if time permits briefly explains the power and efficacy of this sacrament. When necessary, he adds words of encouragement and directs the person's mind to hope of everlasting life.

Next he says:

VERSICLE: Our help is in the name of the Lord.

RESPONSE: Who made heaven and earth.

VERSICLE: The Lord be with you.

RESPONSE: And with thy spirit.

PRIEST: Let us pray. Along with our lowly coming, O Lord Jesus Christ, let there enter into this home unending happiness, divine blessing, untroubled joy, charity which is fruitful, continual health. Drive forth from this place the spirits of evil, let thine angel of peace come hither, and banish all harmful dissension from this house. O Lord, extol thy holy name in our esteem, and bless ✠ what we are about to do. Sanctify the coming of thine unworthy servant, for thou art holy, thou art kind, thou art abiding with the Father and the Holy Spirit through all eternity.

REPONSE: Amen.

PRIEST: Let us pray to our Lord, Jesus Christ, and beseech Him to bless ✠ with His abundant benediction this home and all who dwell herein. May He appoint over them a good angel as a guardian, and assist them to serve Him, to contemplate the grandeur of His law. May He turn away all powers that would harm them, free them from all anxiety and distress, and keep them in well-being within their home. Thou who livest and reignest with the Father and the Holy Spirit, God, for all eternity.

RESPONSE: Amen.

PRIEST: Let us pray. Hear us, O holy Lord, Father almighty, eternal God! And deign to send thy holy angel from heaven to guard, cherish, protect, abide with, and defend all who dwell in this home. Through Christ our Lord.

RESPONSE: Amen.

Before the priest begins to anoint the sick person, he invites all present to pray for him. And if circumstances of time and place are favorable, as well as the number and capability of the bystanders, they should recite the Seven Penitential Psalms and the Litany of the Saints or other prayers while the priest is administering the last anointing. First he extends his right hand above the head of the sick person, and says:

PRIEST: In the name of the Father ✠ and of the Son ✠ and of the Holy ✠ Spirit! May all power of the devil become extinct in thee through the laying on of my hand and through the invocation of the glorious and blessed Virgin Mary, Mother of God, of St. Joseph, her illustrious spouse, and of all the holy angels, archangels, patriarchs, prophets, apostles, martyrs, confessors, virgins, and all the other saints. Amen.

> *Next he dips his thumb in the holy oil, and anoints the sick person in the form of a cross on all members indicated below, pronouncing in each case the respective form as follows:*

Anointing the Eyes (on the Eyelids)
PRIEST: Through this holy anointing and through His tender mercy may the Lord forgive thee whatever sins thou hast committed by the sense of sight. Amen.

> *After every unction the priest wipes the part anointed with a fresh pellet of cotton or similar material.*

Anointing the Ears (on the Lobes)
PRIEST: Through this holy anointing ✠ and through His tender mercy may the Lord forgive thee whatever sins thou hast commited by the sense of hearing. Amen.

Anointing the Nose (on each Nostril)
PRIEST: Through this holy anointing ✠ and through His tender mercy may the Lord forgive thee whatever sins thou hast committed by the sense of smell. Amen.

Anointing the Mouth (on Closed Lips)
PRIEST: Through this holy anointing ✠ and through His tender mercy may the Lord forgive thee whatever sins thou hast committed by the sense of taste and the power of speech. Amen.

Anointing the Hands (on the Palms)
PRIEST: Through this holy anointing ✠ and through His tender mercy may the Lord forgive thee whatever sins thou hast committed by the sense of touch. Amen.

Anointing the Feet (Either on the Instep or Sole)
PRIEST: Through this holy anointing ✠ and through His tender mercy may the Lord forgive thee whatever sins thou hast committed by the power of walking. Amen.

> *The anointing of feet may be omitted for any good reason. When the priest has finished the anointings, he rubs his thumb with particles of bread, then washes his hands and wipes them with a towel.*
> *Afterward the priest says:*

PRIEST: Lord, have mercy on us. Christ, have mercy on us. Lord, have mercy on us.

> Our Father . . . *inaudibly until:*

VERSICLE: And lead us not into temptation.
RESPONSE: But deliver us from evil.

VERSICLE: Save thy servant.

RESPONSE: Who places his confidence in thee, my God.

VERSICLE: Send him, Lord, aid from on high.

RESPONSE: And from Sion protect him.

VERSICLE: Be unto him, O Lord, a tower of strength.

RESPONSE: In the face of the enemy.

VERSICLE: Let the enemy have no power over him.

RESPONSE: And the son of iniquity do nothing to harm him.

VERSICLE: O Lord, hear my prayer.

RESPONSE: And let my cry come unto thee.

VERSICLE: The Lord be with you.

RESPONSE: And with thy spirit.

PRIEST: O Lord God, who didst say through thine apostle, James: "Is any man sick among you? Let him call in the priests of the Church, and let them pray over him, anointing him with oil in the name of the Lord. And the prayer of faith shall save the sick man, and the Lord will raise him up; and if he be in sins they shall be forgiven him": Cure, we beseech thee, O our Redeemer, by the grace of the Holy Spirit, the ailments of this sick man, heal his wounds, and forgive his sins. Deliver him from all miseries of body and mind, and mercifully restore him to perfect health inwardly and outwardly, that having recovered by an act of thy kindness, he be able to take up anew his former duties. Thou who with the Father and the selfsame Holy Spirit livest and reignest, God, forevermore.

RESPONSE: Amen.

PRIEST: Let us pray. Look down with favor, O Lord, we beseech thee, upon thy servant, N., failing from bodily weakness, and revive the soul which thou hast created, that reformed by thy chastisement, he may acknowledge himself saved by thy healing. Through Christ our Lord.

RESPONSE: Amen.

PRIEST: Let us pray. O Holy Lord, Father almighty, eternal God! In pouring forth thy plenteous grace upon our ailing bodies, thou dost encompass thy creature with abounding love. Wherefore, graciously hearken as we call upon thy holy name, and do thou raise him up—freed from sickness and restored in health—by thy right hand, strengthen him by thy might, protect him by thy power, and give him back in all desired vigor to thy holy Church. Through Christ our Lord.

RESPONSE: Amen.

Prayers of the Church

Canticles of Sacred Scripture
Liturgical Prayers of East and West
Familiar Prayers and Devotions

PREFACE

"He went up the mountain by Himself to pray." Part of the mystery of the Incarnation is the fulness and perfection of the prayer of Jesus Christ. His mind and His will were ever in union with the mind and will of His Father. *"Watch and pray."* It is of the Christic nature of the people of God that they be a prayerful people. Without prayer they would not *"put on the Lord Jesus Christ."*

The Church never leaves off praying. Her highest prayer is the continuing sacrifice of praise in the Mass. Again, her voice is ever singing the psalms and hymns and prayers of the Office. Finally, Christians the world over continually turn their hearts and minds to God in the countless possible ways of speaking with Him.

The present section offers brief samples of Christian prayer-forms. Other sections —the creeds, the Mass, the sacraments, spiritual documents—illustrate in themselves the different types and spirit of Christian prayer. Here we isolate various prayer formulas to suggest the depth and breadth of the Church's prayer.

They are arranged in three categories, each explained in its place: Scripture, liturgy, private devotion. Admittedly this classification is somewhat artificial and can be misleading: both liturgical prayer and private prayer of the Church are thoroughly scriptural, often in the words themselves. Moreover, the use of such categories compels us to omit great areas of the prayer life of the Church: meditation, contemplation, mystic union with God.

Indeed, there is only one true prayer of the Church, and that is the prayer of Christ. All the words of the Church are but an echo of His voice; she speaks always through and in and with Christ.

Canticles of Sacred Scripture

Man speaks to God in song—that is a fact of religious history. Many of the most beautiful songs to God were composed under His inspiration: the psalms and canticles of the Old and New Testament. That most of these songs were anonymous and many attributed to such national leaders as David and Solomon tells much about them: they were the religious songs of a nation, of the People of God. Praise, thanks, pleas—all the prayer-needs of individual and nation found expression in these hymns. They were recognized as from God; they were incorporated into the canon of Scripture. The Old Covenant canticles found their fulfilment in their New Covenant use. They were the daily prayer of our Lord, our Lady, the apostles; they became the national prayer of the new People of God, the Church. They find frequent use in every Mass; together with the fresh canticles found in the New Testament they are the substance of the Office, the official prayer of the Mystical Body.

PSALM 50
Confession of a Penitent Sinner: His Promises and Petitions[1]

> Have mercy on me, God, for you are merciful;
> blot out my sin, for you are richly merciful.
> Completely cleanse me from my guilt,
> and purge me from my sin.
>
> Yes, I acknowledge my iniquity;
> my sin at all times stares me in the face.
> 'Twas you alone 'gainst whom I sinned;
> what in your sight is evil—that I did!
> You must be shown to have been in your sentence just,
> and in your judgment, right.
> Alas, I was in sin when I was born,
> in sin, too, when I was conceived.
> But now—sincerity of heart is your delight;
> deep-searching wisdom you impart to me.
>
> With hyssop sprinkle me: I shall be clean;
> wash me: and I shall whiter be than snow.
> O let me hear the good and joyful word;
> you crushed my frame: O let it now be thrilled!
> O turn your face away from my misdeeds,
> and blot out all my guilt.
>
> A heart all pure create in me, O God;
> a spirit new and firm breathe into me.
> No, do not from your presence banish me;
> your Holy Spirit do not take away from me.
> Restore to me the joy which your salvation brings;
> and by a generous spirit make me strong.
>
> I will instruct the wicked in your ways;
> and sinners will turn back to you.
> Free me from the penalty for bloodshed, God, my savior
> God;
> and let my tongue exult by reason of your clemency.
> Open my lips, O Lord;
> my tongue will hymn your praise.
> 'Tis not with sacrifice that you are pleased,

●

[1] This Psalm and the following are from *The Psalms*, tr. James A. Kleist, S.J., and Thomas J. Lynam, S.J. (Milwaukee: Bruce, 1954) pp. 73-75, 159-61, 29-30, 236. 211-12.

and if I offered holocausts, you would not care for them.
A contrite spirit is my sacrifice, O God;
a crushed and humbled heart, O God, you will not loathe.

Deal kindly, Lord, with Sion in your graciousness;
rebuild the ramparts of Jerusalem.
And then you will receive the lawful sacrifices, offerings
    and holocausts;
then bullocks will be on your altar laid.

PSALM 102

Praises of God's Mercy

O bless, my soul, the Lord;
and all that is within me bless His holy name!
O bless, my soul, the Lord;
do not forget His blessings, each and all.
'Tis He that pardons all your faults;
that heals all your infirmities;
that saves your life from death;
that crowns you with His mercy and His grace;
that fills your life with all good things.
Renewed by Him, your youth is eaglelike.

The Lord does what is right and just,
sees justice done to all oppressed.
To Moses He revealed his ways,
to Israel's children all His deeds.
The Lord is merciful and kind,
to anger slow, and rich in clemency.
He is not finding fault perpetually,
nor does He bear a grudge for aye.
He does not deal with us according to our sins,
nor punish us according to our faults.

As heaven towers above the earth,
so toward His worshipers His mercy wins the day;
as far as Orient is from Occident,
so far does He remove from us our sins;
as sire is merciful to son,
so does the Lord show mercy to His worshipers.
He knows the stuff of which we are made,
and He remembers we are dust.
Man's days are like to grass;
like flower in field—so does He bloom:
the breeze has hardly brushed it—it is no more;
its very place no longer knows it!

The Lord's eternal mercy shields His worshipers eternally;
His justice shields their children's endless line,
if they observe His covenant, remember His
decrees, and keep them faithfully.

The Lord has fixed His seat in heaven;
His kingship rules the universe.
O all His angels, bless the Lord;
you, mighty princes, carry out His orders
and obey His word!
O bless the Lord, all you, His hosts,
His ministers, who carry out His will.
All you, His creatures, bless the Lord
in every place of His domain!
O bless, my soul, the Lord!

PSALM 22
The Lord Is My Shepherd

The Lord is my shepherd, and nothing do I want:
He bids me to repose in verdant pastures;
to springs where I may rest He leads me on,
and there refreshes me.
He leads me onward over safe, straight paths
to manifest His holy name.
And should I cross a gloomy vale,
no evil shall I fear, because you are with me.
Your crook and staff—
they comfort me.

You spread for me a feast
for all my foes to see;
and you anoint my head with oil;
my cup is full up to the brim.
Kindness and grace will wait on me
through all the days of my life;
and I shall dwell in the house of the Lord
forever and evermore.

PSALM 150
A Solemn Concert of Praise for God

O praise the Lord within His holy shrine;
praise Him in His majestic firmament.
Give praise to Him for His grand works;
praise Him for His transcendent majesty.
Give praise to Him with blast of horn;

praise Him with harp and psaltery.
Praise Him with tambourine and dance;
praise Him with flute and stringed instrument.
Praise Him with sounding castanets;
with crashing cymbals give Him praise.
May every breathing thing give praise to the Lord.
Alleluia!

PSALM 129

Man's Sins; God's Mercy

Out of the depths I cry to you, O Lord;
Lord, hear my voice!
O be your ears attentive
to the voice of my entreating!

Should you keep record of transgressions, Lord,
then who, Lord, could endure?
But in your gift is pardon of sins,
so that you may be served with reverence.

My trust is in the Lord;
my soul trusts in His word.
My soul awaits the Lord
more eagerly than watchman waits for dawn.

More eagerly than watchman waits for dawn
may Israel await the Lord.
For in the gift of the Lord is mercy,
and in His gift is plentiful ransom;
and He will ransom Israel
from all its wickedness.

The best summary of the chief themes of the Old Testament and their opening-out into fulfilment in the New is to be found in the three Psalms or "Canticles" of the New Testament: the Benedictus, *sung by the father of St. John the Baptist in thanksgiving for the vocation of his child; the* Magnificat, *our Lady's song of praise for the Incarnation; and Simeon's song of thanksgiving for having seen Christ, the* Nunc Dimittis.[2]

●

[2] This introduction and the following three canticles are from *The Psalms: Fides Translation,* introduction and notes by Mary Perkins Ryan (Chicago: Fides, 1955) pp. xxxv-xxxvii.

SONG OF ZACHARY (BENEDICTUS)
From the Gospel according to St. Luke 1:68-79.

> Blessed be the Lord, the God of Israel,
>> for He has visited His people and redeemed them,
>
> And He has raised up for us a mighty Saviour
>> in the house of David, His servant,
>
> As He promised through the mouth of His holy ones,
>> His prophets in past ages,
>
> That He would deliver us from our enemies
>> and from the hand of all who hate us,
>
> To be merciful to our fathers,
>> remembering His holy covenant,
>
> And the oath He swore to Abraham our father,—
>> that He would grant us,
>
> Freed from the hand of our enemies,
>> fearlessly to serve Him,
>
> In holiness and justice before Him
>> all our days.
>
> And you, child, shall be called the Prophet of the Highest,
>> you shall go before the Lord, to prepare His ways,
>
> To give His people knowledge of salvation,
>> forgiveness of their sins;
>
> This the work of the depths of our God's mercy,
>> the mercy with which He will visit us, He the Dayspring
>>> from on high,
>
> To shine on those who sit in darkness and death's shadow,
>> to guide our feet into the way of peace.

SONG OF OUR LADY (MAGNIFICAT)
From the Gospel according to St. Luke 1:46-55.

> My soul proclaims the Lord's greatness,
>> and my spirit rejoices in God my Saviour:
>
> For He has looked upon the lowliness of His handmaid,
>> and behold, now all generations shall call me blessed!
>
> Great things has He done for me, He the Strong,
>> His name is holy:
>
> His mercy extends from generation to generation,
>> to those who fear Him:
>
> He has shown the power of His arm
>> and scattered the proud of heart:
>
> He has cast down the mighty from their thrones
>> and lifted up the lowly:
>
> He has filled with His bounty those who hunger,
>> and sent the rich away empty:
>
> He has raised up Israel His servant,

remembering His mercy—
As He promised to our fathers—
toward Abraham and his race forever.

SONG OF SIMEON (NUNC DIMITTIS)

From the Gospel according to St. Luke 2:29-32.

Now, Lord, you let your servant go
in peace, according to your word:
For my eyes have seen the salvation
that you have prepared in the sight of all peoples,—
The light of revelation for the nations,
and the glory of your people, Israel.

Liturgical Prayers of East and West

Liturgy is the public worship of the Mystical Body. We have already seen liturgical prayer in the texts of the Mass and sacraments. There follow samples of individual prayers selected from the liturgy. There are "collects" with their severe Roman structure, in which the priest at Mass collects the voices of the congregation and speaks them together as the voice of the Mystical Christ. There is the summation of the Advent liturgy in the "O Antiphons," which address Christ with deliberate joy by the types and figures of Him in the Old Covenant, then summon Him: "Come!" The Good Friday adoration of the cross, sorrowful but not despairing, reveals a faith in the meaning of the cross that overrides the grief. The Easter Exsultet sums up in a song the theology of Christian joy. The Te Deum is the Church's hymn of praise and gratitude. The few examples of the Eastern liturgies may give some idea of their sweep and majesty, tempered with a certain filial tenderness.

COLLECTS[3]

As a rule the Church directs her prayers to the Father, through the mediation of the Son, in union with the Holy Spirit. Hence the following prayers are concluded with some such formula as: "Through our Lord Jesus Christ, thy Son, who is God, living and reigning with thee, in the unity of the Holy Spirit, forever and ever. Amen."

God, who on this day through thy only-begotten Son hast vanquished death and unlocked for us the gate of everlasting life: help us to fulfil the longings thou hast thyself planted in our hearts. (*Prayer for Easter Sunday, the Resurrection of Our Lord*)

Grant, we beseech thee, almighty God, that we, who believe thy only-begotten Son our Redeemer to have ascended into heaven on this day, may ourselves dwell there in spirit. (*Prayer for the Feast of the Ascension of Our Lord*)

God, who on this day didst teach the faithful by sending the light of the Holy Spirit into their hearts, grant that, by the gift of that Spirit, right judgment may be ours, and that we may ever find joy in His comfort. (*Prayer for Pentecost Sunday*)

O God, by whose action the faithful are united in good will, incline thy people everywhere to love what thou commandest and to desire what thou dost promise, so that, among the changes of this world, our hearts may be set upon the one true home of joy. (*Prayer for the Fourth Sunday after Easter*)

God, who desirest that all men should be saved and that all should come to know the truth, we pray thee send forth laborers to thy harvest, and give them strength to proclaim thy word with all confidence, so that thy teaching may be received with honor throughout the world and all nations may acknowledge thee, the true and only God, and Him whom thou hast sent, Jesus Christ, thy Son, our Lord. (*Prayer from the special Mass for the Spreading of the Faith*)

O God, by whom error is righted, who mendest what is shattered and preservest what thou hast mended, we pray

[3] From *The Missal in Latin and English*, ed. J. O'Connell and H. P. R. Finberg (Westminster, Md.: Newman, 1958) pp. 415, 462-53, 487, 450, 162°, 168°-69°, 478.

thee in thy mercy to imbue Christian people with the grace of unity in thee, so that they may put aside all divisions, attach themselves to the true shepherd of thy Church, and be thereby enabled to render thee due service. (*Prayer from the special Mass for the Healing of Division among Christians*)

Almighty, ever-living God, who through thy only Son hast shown thyself to be the cultivator of thy Church, tending with loving care each fruitful branch of that true vine which is thy Christ, so that it shall bear more abundant fruit; allow no thorny sins to choke thy vineyard, the faithful whom thou broughtest out of Egypt through the waters of baptism, but let them be so strengthened by thy Spirit's hallowing grace that their vintage time may last for ever. (*A prayer from the pre-Mass liturgy of Pentecost Eve*)

O ANTIPHONS[4]

December 17: O Wisdom, you came forth from the mouth of the Most High, and reaching from beginning to end you ordered all things mightily and sweetly. Come, and teach us the way of prudence.

December 18: O Adonai, and Ruler of the house of Israel, you appeared to Moses in the fire of the burning bush and on Mount Sinai gave him your Law. Come, and with an outstretched arm redeem us.

December 19: O Root of Jesse, you stand for an ensign of mankind; before you kings shall keep silence and to you all nations shall have recourse. Come, save us, and do not delay.

December 20: O Key of David, and Scepter of the house of Israel: you open and no man closes; you close and no man opens. Come, and deliver him from the chains of prison who sits in darkness and in the shadow of death.

December 21: O Rising Dawn, Radiance of the Light eternal and the Sun of Justice: come, and enlighten those who sit in darkness and in the shadow of death.

[4] From *A Short Breviary*, ed. William G. Heidt, O.S.B. (Collegeville, Minn.: Liturgical Press, 1954) pp. 276, 543, 545.

December 22: O King of the Gentiles and the Desired of all, you are the Cornerstone that binds two into one. Come, and save man whom you fashioned out of clay.

December 23: O Emmanuel, our King and Lawgiver, the Expected of nations and their Saviour. Come and save us, O Lord our God.

ADORATION OF THE CROSS[5]

REPROACHES

During the rite of adoration the choir sings the "Reproaches": quoting Ps 135, in which God had enumerated the benefits He had heaped on His chosen race, Christ reproaches us, His people, for our ingratitude and sinful rebellion. In the third part, the joy of Easter, gained for us by the cross, already shines through.

I

O my people, what wrong have I done you? When have I ever grieved you? Answer me! I led you out of the land of Egypt: is this why you have prepared a cross for your Saviour?
REFRAIN: O holy God! (*twice:* first in Greek, then in Latin).
　　　　　O holy, mighty God! (*twice*).
　　　　　O holy, immortal God, have mercy on us! (*twice*).
Forty years I led you through the desert, fed you with manna, and then brought you into a fair and fertile land: is this why you have prepared a cross for your Saviour?
REFRAIN: O holy God! . . .
What more should I have done for you that I have not done? I planted you to be my very own and most choice vine, but you have borne me bitter fruit: for with vinegar you have quenched my thirst, and with a spear you have pierced your Saviour's side.
REFRAIN: O holy God! . . .

II

For your sake I scourged Egypt and its first-born and you have handed me over to be scourged.
REFRAIN: O my people, what wrong have I done you? When have I ever grieved you? Answer me! I led you out of the land of Egypt: is this why you have prepared a cross for your Saviour?
I led you out of Egypt and drowned Pharaoh in the Red Sea: and you have handed me over to the chief priests.
REFRAIN: O my people. . . .

●
[5] From *The Masses of Holy Week and the Easter Vigil*, ed. Godfrey L. Diekmann, O.S.B. (Collegeville, Minn.: Liturgical Press, 1957) pp. 117-18.

I opened up the sea as a path before you: and you have opened up my side with a spear.
REFRAIN: O my people. . . .
I went before you in a pillar of bright cloud: and you have led me to the judgment hall of Pilate.
REFRAIN: O my people. . . .
I nourished you with manna in the desert: and you have rained blows and stripes upon me.
REFRAIN: O my people. . . .
I gave you life-restoring water from the rock to drink: and you have quenched my thirst with gall and vinegar.
REFRAIN: O my people. . . .
For your sake I struck down the kings of Canaan: and you kept striking me on the head with a reed.
REFRAIN: O my people. . . .
I gave you a royal sceptre: and you have placed a crown of thorns on my head.
REFRAIN: O my people. . . .
I raised you up above all others by my mighty power: and you have hung me on the high gibbet of the cross.
REFRAIN: O my people. . . .

III

We adore thy cross, O Lord, and praise and glorify thy holy resurrection: for behold! by the wood of the cross joy came into the whole world. *Ps 66:2:* May God have pity on us and bless us; may He let his face shine upon us, and have pity on us.—We adore thy cross. . . .

THE EASTER SONG—THE EXSULTET[6]

Rejoice, you hosts of heaven, rejoice, all ministers of God!

Let trumpets sound the triumph of the mighty King, for He has wrought salvation.

Exult, O earth, made brilliant by such splendor, and illumined by the brightness of the eternal King, know that darkness has everywhere been overcome.

Be glad, O Church our Mother, adorned with the radiance of so great a Light, and let your temple ring with the loud song of this great multitude.

And you, beloved brethren, who are gathered near the brightness of this holy flame, invoke with me, I beg you, the mercy of almighty God:

That He who willed to number me, all unworthy, among His levites, may enlighten me with His bright light and thus enable me to sing due praises of this candle.

●

[6] *Ibid.*, pp. 133-36.

Through our Lord Jesus Christ His Son who is living and reigning with Him in the unity of the Holy Spirit, one God,

PRIEST: Forever and ever.

PEOPLE: Amen.

PRIEST: The Lord be with you.

PEOPLE: And with your spirit.

PRIEST: Lift up your hearts.

PEOPLE: We have lifted them to the Lord.

PRIEST: Let us give thanks to the Lord our God.

PEOPLE: It is meet and just.

PRIEST: Truly meet it is and just, with all our strength of mind and heart and with our voice as instrument, to praise the invisible Father almighty, and His only-begotten Son, our Lord Jesus Christ, who paid to the eternal Father in our stead the debt of Adam, and with His own blood shed for love of us erased the ledger of ancient guilt.

For this is that Easter feast in which the true Lamb is slain, whose blood hallows the doorposts of the faithful.

This is the night in which thou of old didst lead our forefathers, the children of Israel, out of the land of Egypt dry-shod through the Red Sea.

This is the night which scattered the darkness of sin by means of the pillar of fire.

This is the very night which delivers all who believe in Christ from worldly vice and from darkness of sin, which restores them to grace and makes them cosharers with saints.

This is the night in which Christ burst the bonds of death and came forth as Conqueror from the grave. For unless we had been redeemed, it would avail us nothing to be born.

O wondrous condescension of thy mercy toward us!

O incomprehensible goodness of love: to redeem a slave thou didst deliver up a Son!

O truly necessary sin of Adam, which the death of Christ has blotted out!

O happy fault, that merited a Redeemer so holy and so great!

O truly blessed night, which alone merited to know the time and hour when Christ rose from the dead!

This is the night of which it is written: "The night shall be light as the day," and: "Then shall my night be turned to day, in my rejoicing." For the holiness of this night drives out wickedness and washes away guilt; it restores innocence to the fallen and joy to the sorrowful. It banishes enmities, establishes peace, and brings low the pride of tyrants.

Wherefore, in this night of grace, receive, O holy Father, this evening sacrifice of burning light; holy Church, by the hands of her servants, offers it to thee in the solemn oblation of this candle wrought by the labor of bees. For now we have heard the praises of this column of wax which the sparkling fire lights to the honor of God. And though the fire was spread to kindle other flames, such sharing does not lessen the force of its light. For it is constantly fed by the melting wax which the mother bee wrought to form this precious candle.

O truly blessed night, when Egypt was despoiled and Israel enriched!

O night, when heaven is wedded to earth, and God to man.

We pray thee, therefore, Lord: may this candle consecrated to thine honor continue with undiminished light to dispel this night's darkness. Receive it as a fragrant and pleasing offering, and let its light mingle with the lamps of heaven.

May the Morning Star behold its flame—that Morning Star who knows no setting, who rose from hell and gently shines on man.

In this festival of Easter joys, we beseech thee, therefore, Lord, for ourselves thy servants, for all the clergy and thy most devoted people, for our Holy Father, Pope N., and for our Bishop, N.: grant peace to our days; guide, govern and protect us by thy constant care.

Look with favor, too, upon our rulers. Assist them with thy boundless love and gracious mercy; direct their hearts toward justice and peace, that after this life of earthly labors they may attain, together with all thy people, to the heavenly fatherland.

Through the same Jesus Christ, thy Son, our Lord, who is living and reigning with thee in the unity of the Holy Spirit, one God.

PRIEST: Forever and ever.

PEOPLE: Amen.

TE DEUM[7]

We praise you, O God; we acclaim you Lord and Master.
Everlasting Father, all the world bows down before you.
All the angels sing your praise, the hosts of heaven and all the angelic powers;
All the cherubim and seraphim call out to you in unending chorus:
Holy, Holy, Holy is the Lord God of angel hosts!
The heavens and the earth are filled, Lord, with your majesty and glory.
Your praises are sung by the renowned apostles;
By all the prophets who themselves deserve our praise;
By that mighty white-robed army who shed their blood for Christ,
And to the ends of the earth the holy Church proclaims her faith in you:
Father, whose majesty is boundless;
Your only Son, who is true God, and who is to be adored;

●

[7] From *A Short Breviary*, ed. William G. Heidt, O.S.B. (Collegeville, Minn.: Liturgical Press, 1954) pp. 8-10.

The Holy Ghost, sent to be our Advocate.

O Christ, the King of glory! You alone are the Father's eternal Son.

When you were to become man so as to save mankind, you did not shrink back from the chaste Virgin's womb.

When you triumphantly destroyed death's sting, you opened up to believers the kingdom of heaven.

You are now enthroned at God's right hand, in the Father's glory.

We believe that you will come for judgment.

We therefore implore you to grant your servants grace and aid, for you shed your precious blood for their redemption.

Admit them all to the ranks of your saints in everlasting glory.

Be the Saviour of your faithful people, Lord; grant them your blessing, for they belong to you.

Be their Shepherd, Lord, uphold and exalt them forever and ever.

Day by day we praise you, daily we acclaim you.

We will confess and glorify your holy name, now and for all eternity.

In your great mercy, Lord, throughout this day keep us free from sin by your protection.

Have mercy on us, we humbly pray; Lord, have mercy on us.

May your mercy, Lord, your loving kindness, always remain with us; for we have placed our confidence in you.

In you alone, Lord, I have hoped; may I not be disappointed.

THE TRISAGION HYMN[8]

Holy God, holy Strong One, holy Deathless One, have mercy on us (*thrice*).

Glory be to the Father and to the Son and to the Holy Ghost, now and forever, world without end. Amen.

Holy Deathless One, have mercy on us.

Holy God, holy Strong One, holy Deathless One, have mercy on us.

O God, who art holy and restest in the holy, who art hymned by the seraphim with the cry of the *trisagion*; who art glorified by the cherubim and adored by all the hosts of heaven; thou who didst bring all things from nothing into being; who didst make man to thine own

●

[8] From *Prayers from the Eastern Liturgies*, ed. Donald Attwater (London: Burns Oates & Washbourne, 1931) pp. 46-47.

image and likeness, and didst adorn him with all gifts of thy grace, who givest to him that askest wisdom and understanding, and dost not despise the sinner, but hast ordained repentance unto salvation; thou who hast granted unto us thy humble and unworthy servants to stand before the glory of thine holy altar, and to offer thee due worship and honor; do thou, O Lord, receive from the mouth of us sinners the hymn of the *trisagion* and look down upon us in goodness. Forgive us all our sins, voluntary and involuntary, sanctify our souls and bodies, and grant that we may serve thee in holiness all the days of our life, by the prayers of the holy Mother of God and of all the saints who have pleased thee from the beginning of the world. For thou art holy, O our God, and we give glory to thee, Father, Son, and Holy Ghost, now and for ever, world without end. Amen.   (ST. JOHN CHRYSOSTOM)

A HYMN FROM THE EVENING OFFICE
OF THE BYZANTINE RITE[9]

Φῶς ἱλαρόν

Hail, gladdening Light, of His pure glory pour'd
who is immortal Father, heavenly, blest,
holiest of holies, Jesus Christ, our Lord.
Now we are come to the sun's hour of rest,
the lights of evening round us shine,
we hymn the Father, Son, and Holy Ghost divine.
Worthiest art thou at all times to be sung
with undefiled tongue,
Son of God, giver of life, alone!
Therefore in all the world thy glories, Lord, they own.

O Lord, who dost bless them that bless thee, and dost sanctify them that trust in thee, save thy people and bless thine inheritance. Guard the company of thy Church, sanctify those who love the beauty of thy house. Give them honor by thy divine power, and forsake us not who hope in thee. Give peace to thy world, to thy churches, to the priests, to our sovereigns, to the army, and to all thy people. For every good gift and every perfect gift is from above, and cometh down from thee, the Father of light, and to thee we render glory and thanksgiving and worship, Father, Son, and Holy Ghost, now and for ever, world without end. Amen.   (ST. JOHN CHRYSOSTOM)

●

[9] *Ibid.*, pp. 51-52.

HYMN TO OUR LADY
FROM THE MARONITE LITURGY[10]

Hail, Mary, ever virgin, mother of the Almighty who fills both the heavens and the earth.

Hail, Mary, ever virgin, mother of the Ancient of Days whose name was before the sun was created.

Hail, Mary, ever virgin, mother of Him who made Adam from the mold of the earth.

Hail, Mary, ever virgin, mother of Him who formed Eve and gave her to Adam.

Blessed art thou, Mary, the mother of Him who gave righteousness and virtue to the sons of Levi.

Blessed art thou, Mary, for within thee dwelt the Only-begotten, the Light of the Father, the Child of the Godhead.

Blessed art thou, Mary, for thou hast fed Him who giveth to all creatures to eat.

Blessed art thou, Mary, who hast carried in thy lap and arms the Son of the Most High whom the powers of heaven acclaim.

All generations bless thy maidenhood, for He who is born of thee hath driven the curse of fear from the earth. We too bless thee, O holy Virgin, here kneeling before thee. Intercede with the Lord who was born of thee that He may bestow His graces on all people and ever have pity on us. Praise to thee, O Lord, born of a virgin, who became Man, uniting two natures and two wills in one Person. Glory be to thee, to thy Father, and to thine Holy Spirit, three Persons in one undivided God. Amen.

THE CHERUBICON PRAYER
FROM THE BYZANTINE RITE[11]

O King of glory, no one is worthy to come to you, to draw near to you, to perform a service for you when he is bound down by desires and pleasures of the flesh; for to serve you is something grand and awe-inspiring even for the heavenly powers themselves. And yet, because of your ineffable and boundless love for mankind, you became man without changing or diminishing your divinity, and you became our high priest; and acting as master of all creation you granted to us the sacred power of offering up this public sacrifice without any new shedding of blood. For you alone, O Lord our God, are master over

●

[10] *Ibid.,* pp. 17-18.
[11] From *Byzantine Liturgy* (New York: Russian Center, Fordham University).

all things in heaven and on earth—You who are borne upon the throne of the cherubim, you who are the Lord of the seraphim and King of Israel, you alone are holy and rest among the holy. Still I make my prayers to you, who alone are good and graciously ready to hear me. Turn your eyes upon me, your sinful and unprofitable servant, and cleanse my soul and heart from any thought of evil. By the power of the Holy Spirit, render me also worthy. And so it is to you that I come with my head bowed low and beseech you not to turn away your face from us, but to allow these gifts to be offered to you by me, your sinful and unworthy servant; for it is really you who offers and are offered, you who receives the offering and are given back to us, Christ our God—and to you we render glory, with your eternal Father, and with your most holy and gracious and life-giving Spirit, now and ever and for ages of ages. Amen.

(AUTHOR UNKNOWN)

Familiar Prayers and Devotions

The two-thousand-year experience of a praying people has left a legacy of prayer and prayer-forms that is a library in itself. Here all we can do is sample. The prayers here included are the ones that are part of every Catholic. Many of them go back in his life as far as his memory will bring him. So often they are the spontaneous vocabulary of his conversation with God in his private prayer. They have become part of Catholic tradition. They give familiar and frequent contact with Father, Son, and Holy Spirit; with Mary, the Mother of God and the Christian's mother; with the holy ones of God who are with Him now.

ACT OF FAITH

O my God, I firmly believe that you are one God in three Divine Persons, Father, Son, and Holy Spirit. I believe that your divine Son became Man and died for our sins, and that He will come to judge the living and the dead. I believe these and all the truths which the holy Catholic Church teaches, because you have revealed them, who can neither deceive nor be deceived.

ACT OF HOPE

O my God, relying on your almighty power and infinite mercy and promises, I hope to obtain the pardon of my sins, the help of your grace, and life everlasting through the merits of Jesus Christ, my Lord and Redeemer.

ACT OF LOVE

O my God, I love you above all things with my whole heart and soul, because you are all good and worthy of all love. I love my neighbor as myself for the love of you. I forgive all who have injured me and ask pardon of all whom I have injured.

ACT OF CONTRITION

O my God, I am heartily sorry for having offended you, and I detest all my sins, because I dread the loss of heaven and the pains of hell, but most of all, because I have offended you, my God, who are all good and deserving of all my love. I firmly resolve, by the help of your grace, to confess my sins, do penance, and amend my life. Amen.

DIVINE PRAISES

Blessed be God.
Blessed be His holy name.
Blessed be Jesus Christ, true God and true man.
Blessed be the name of Jesus.
Blessed be His most Sacred Heart.
Blessed be Jesus in the most holy Sacrament of the Altar.
Blessed be the great Mother of God, Mary, most holy.
Blessed be her holy and immaculate conception.
Blessed be her glorious assumption.
Blessed be the name of Mary, virgin and mother.
Blessed be Saint Joseph, her most chaste spouse.
Blessed be God in His angels and in His saints.

MORNING OFFERING

O Jesus, through the Immaculate Heart of Mary, I offer you all my prayers, works, joys, and sufferings of this day for all the intentions of your Sacred Heart in union with the holy Sacrifice of the Mass throughout the world, in reparation for my sins, for the intentions of all our associates, and, in particular, for the intentions of the Holy Father. . . .

THE HAIL MARY

Hail Mary, full of grace, the Lord is with thee; blessed art thou amongst women, and blessed is the fruit of thy womb, Jesus. Holy Mary, Mother of God, pray for us sinners now and at the hour of our death. Amen.

THE ANGELUS

The Angelus is said three times a day, at dawn, at noon, and at dusk, to recall the Incarnation of Christ, the great mystery by which God became man. The Angelus is a beautiful prayer in honor of Mary, for through her Christ came to us.

The angel of the Lord declared to Mary.
   And she conceived of the Holy Spirit.
Hail Mary.
Behold the handmaid of the Lord.
   Be it done to me according to your word.
Hail Mary.
And the Word was made flesh.
   And dwelt among us.
Hail Mary.

Let us pray. Pour forth, we beseech you, O Lord, your grace into our hearts; that we, to whom the Incarnation of your Son was made known through the message of an angel, may by His passion and cross be brought to the glory of His resurrection, through the same Christ our Lord. Amen.

QUEEN OF HEAVEN (REGINA COELI)

During paschal time the Regina Coeli is substituted for the Angelus, to recall Mary's joy for the triumph of her Son in His resurrection.
   O Queen of heaven, rejoice, alleluia;
   For He whom you did merit to bear, alleluia;
   Is risen as He said, alleluia.
   Pray for us to God, alleluia.
   Rejoice and be glad, O Virgin Mary, alleluia.
   Because our Lord is truly risen, alleluia.
Let us pray. O God, who by the resurrection of your Son, our Lord Jesus Christ, has been pleased to fill the world with joy, grant, we beseech you, that through the Virgin Mary, His Mother, we may receive the joy of eternal life, through the same Christ our Lord. Amen.

HAIL, HOLY QUEEN

Hail, holy Queen, Mother of Mercy, our life, our sweetness, and our hope. To you do we cry, poor banished children of Eve; to you do we send up our sighs, mourning and weeping in this valley of tears. Turn then, most gracious advocate, your eyes of mercy toward us, and after this our exile show us the blessed fruit of your womb, Jesus. O clement, O loving, O sweet Virgin Mary.

MEMORARE

Remember, O most gracious Virgin Mary, that never was it known that anyone who fled to your protection, implored your help, or sought your intercession, was left unaided. Inspired by this confidence I fly to you, O Virgin of virgins and Mother; to you I come, before you I stand, sinful and sorrowful; O Mother of the Word Incarnate, despise not my petitions, but in your mercy hear and answer me. Amen.

PRAYER FOR GENEROSITY

Dearest Lord, teach me to be generous. Teach me to serve you as you deserve; to give and not to count the cost; to fight and not to heed the wounds; to toil and not to seek for rest; to labor and not ask for reward, save that of knowing that I am doing your will. Amen.

(SAINT IGNATIUS LOYOLA)

PRAYER BEFORE A CRUCIFIX

Behold, O good and sweetest Jesus, I cast myself upon my knees in your sight and with the most fervent desire of my soul I pray and beseech you to impress upon my heart lively sentiments of faith, hope, and charity, true repentance for my sins and a most firm purpose of amendment; while with deep affection and grief of soul I consider within myself and mentally contemplate your five most precious wounds, having before my eyes that which David, the prophet, long ago spoke in your own person concerning you, my Jesus: They have pierced my hands and my feet; they have numbered all my bones.

SPIRIT OF JESUS

Dear Jesus, help me to spread thy fragrance everywhere. Flood my soul with thy spirit and life. Penetrate and possess my whole being so utterly that all my life may be only a radiance of thine. Shine through me and be so in me that every soul I come in contact with may feel thy presence in my soul. Let them look up and see no longer me but only Jesus. (CARDINAL NEWMAN)

SOUL OF CHRIST (ANIMA CHRISTI)

Soul of Christ, sanctify me.
Body of Christ, save me.
Blood of Christ, inebriate me.
Water from the side of Christ, wash me.
Passion of Christ, strengthen me.
O good Jesus, hear me.
Within your wounds hide me.
Permit me not to be separated from you.
From the wicked foe defend me.
At the hour of my death call me.
And bid me come to you.
That with your saints I may praise you
Forever and ever. Amen.

STATIONS OF THE CROSS

These fourteen incidents or episodes in the Good Friday journey of Christ are usually arranged in pictorial form around the walls of a church. They are visited in order, with a pause at each for prayer and meditation. The very early custom that pilgrims had of retracing the steps of Christ in the Holy City led Christians to reproduce this analogous devotion in their own churches.

FIRST STATION—Jesus is condemned to death.
SECOND STATION—Jesus carries His cross.
THIRD STATION—Jesus falls the first time beneath the cross.
FOURTH STATION—Jesus meets His afflicted mother.
FIFTH STATION—Simon of Cyrene helps Jesus to carry the cross.
SIXTH STATION—Veronica wipes the face of Jesus.
SEVENTH STATION—Jesus falls the second time.
EIGHTH STATION—The daughters of Jerusalem weep over Jesus.
NINTH STATION—Jesus falls the third time.
TENTH STATION—Jesus is stripped of His garments.
ELEVENTH STATION—Jesus is nailed to the cross.
TWELFTH STATION—Jesus dies on the cross.
THIRTEENTH STATION—Jesus is taken down from the cross.
FOURTEENTH STATION—Jesus is laid in the sepulcher.

THE MYSTERIES OF THE ROSARY

The practice of the Rosary dates back to the twelfth century. With the aid of beads to help the memory, one recites the Our Father, the Hail Mary ten times, and the Glory Be to the Father, all the while meditating on one of the fifteen mysteries listed below. Ordinarily only a third part of the Rosary (five decades) is said on any one occasion.

JOYFUL MYSTERIES

1. Annunciation
2. Visitation
3. Nativity
4. Presentation in the Temple
5. Jesus with the Doctors

SORROWFUL MYSTERIES

1. Agony in the Garden
2. Scourging at the Pillar
3. Crowning with Thorns
4. Carrying of the Cross
5. Crucifixion and Death

GLORIOUS MYSTERIES

1. Resurrection
2. Ascension
3. Descent of the Holy Spirit
4. Assumption
5. Coronation of the Blessed Virgin Mary

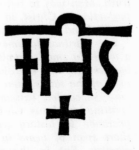

Spiritual Documents

Christ our Lord: The Beatitudes
St. Paul on Charity
The *Didache*: The Way of Life
St. Basil the Great on Religious Solitude
St. Augustine on Love of God
St. Benedict's Rule for Monks
St. Bernard on the Reward of Loving God
Thomas a Kempis on Imitating Christ
and Despising Vanities
St. Ignatius Loyola: First Principle and Foundation ·
St. Ignatius Loyola: Choice of a Way of Life
St. Theresa of Avila on Mental Prayer
St. John of the Cross: The Communion
of the Divine Persons
St. Francis de Sales on Christian Devotion
St. Theresa of Lisieux: The Story of a Soul

PREFACE

God's gradual revelation of Himself to the Jewish people culminated in the birth, the life, and the teaching of Jesus Christ, Son of God made man, perfect reflection of the Father. He is the book in which man can read the full revelation. God did not unveil Himself to satisfy man's speculative curiosity; man was to live this truth. Man was to reflect in himself the perfection of Christ, in this way glorifying God and achieving salvation.

The spiritual documents that follow—a woefully small sampling from an embarrassingly rich tradition—are from the pens of the saints, men and women who have succeeded extraordinarily well in "putting on Jesus Christ." Christ's appearance in history was limited to a short span of years in an insignificant country. But in the members of His Church, and especially in His saints, He has reached every land and every age. No one saint could show forth completely "the unfathomable riches of Christ." The brilliant and passionate ex-sinner Augustine does not look like Theresa of Lisieux pious from childhood, nor barefoot Francis of Assisi like the aristocrat Francis of Sales. There is Benedict's flight from the world and Ignatius' confrontation with it. Every temperament, passionate, unimaginative, or sentimental, every type of intelligence, speculative, intuitive, or practical, every era, whether of peace or crisis or war, every culture, be it primitive or sophisticated, Oriental or Occidental, has mirrored forth with unique brilliance some aspect of the limitless perfection of Christ. No less than the Bible and the tomes of the theologians, the lives and writings of these good people are a living book in which the faith is written for all to read.

Christ Our Lord: The Beatitudes

From the Sermon of Christ our Lord on the Mount, as recorded by the Evangelist St. Matthew 5:3-10.[1]

Blessed are the poor in spirit,
    for theirs is the kingdom of heaven.
Blessed are the meek,
    for they shall possess the earth.
Blessed are they who mourn,
    for they shall be comforted.
Blessed are they who hunger and thirst for justice,
    for they shall be satisfied.
Blessed are the merciful,
    for they shall obtain mercy.
Blessed are the clean of heart,
    for they shall see God.
Blessed are the peacemakers,
    for they shall be called children of God.
Blessed are they who suffer persecution for justice' sake,
    for theirs is the kingdom of heaven.

●

[1] Confraternity of Christian Doctrine translation; 3rd ed.; 1953 printing.

St. Paul on Charity

From St. Paul's First Letter to the Corinthians 13:1-13, written at Ephesus in Asia Minor, probably in the beginning of the year 57 A.D. "Charity" here means the supernatural virtue comprising love of God above all things and love of neighbor for God.[1]

If I should speak with the tongues of men and of angels, but do not have charity I have become as sounding brass or a tinkling cymbal. And if I have prophecy and know all mysteries and all knowledge, and if I have all faith so as to remove mountains, yet do not have charity, I am nothing. And if I distribute all my goods to feed the poor, and if I deliver my body to be burned, yet do not have charity, it profits me nothing.

Charity is patient, is kind; charity does not envy, is not pretentious, is not puffed up, is not ambitious, is not self-seeking, is not provoked; thinks no evil, does not rejoice over wickedness, but rejoices with the

●

[1] Confraternity translation.

truth; bears with all things, believes all things, hopes all things, endures all things.

Charity never fails, whereas prophecies will disappear, and tongues will cease, and knowledge will be destroyed. For we know in part and we prophesy in part; but when that which is perfect has come, that which is imperfect will be done away with. When I was a child, I spoke as a child, I felt as a child, I thought as a child. Now that I have become a man, I have put away the things of a child. We see now through a mirror in an obscure manner, but then face to face. Now I know in part, but then I shall know even as I have been known. So there abide faith, hope, and charity, these three; but the greatest of these is charity.

The Didache: The Way of Life

The Didache *is an early Christian manual on morals and Church practice, which may go back to the first century but is usually dated towards the middle of the second. The metaphor of Two Ways for two modes of living was familiar to Greeks and Jews.*[1]

ONE. Two Ways there are, one of Life and one of Death, and there is a great difference between the Two Ways.

2 Now, the Way of Life is this: *first, love the God who made you; secondly, your neighbor as yourself* (Mt 22: 37, 39): do not do to another *what you do not wish* to be done to yourself (Mt 7:12).

3 The lesson of these words is as follows: *bless those that curse you,* and *pray for your enemies*; besides, fast *for those that persecute you.* For *what thanks do you deserve when you love those that love you? Do not the heathen do as much?* For your part, *love those that hate you* (Mt 5:44, 46-47; Lk 6:27-28, 32-33); in fact, have no enemy.

●

[1] Translated by James A. Kleist, S.J., in *Ancient Christian Writers* 6 (Westminster, Md.: Newman, 1948) 15-18.

4 *Abstain from gratifying the carnal* [and bodily] *impulses* (1 Pt 2:11). When anyone gives you a blow *on the right cheek, turn to him the other as well,* and *be perfect* (Mt 5:39, 48); when *anyone forces you to go one mile with him, go two with him*; when anyone takes *your cloak* away, give *him your coat also* (Mt 5:40); when anyone robs you of *your property, demand no return* (Lk 6:30). You really cannot do it. 5 *Give to anyone that asks you, and demand no return* (Lk 6:30); the Father wants His own bounties to be shared with all. Happy the giver who complies with the commandment, for he goes unpunished. Trouble is in store for the receiver: if someone who is in need receives, he will go unpunished; but he who is not in need will have to stand trial as to why and for what purpose he received; and, if he is thrown into prison, he will be questioned about his conduct, and *will not be released from that place until he has paid the last penny* (Mt 5:25-26). 6 However, in this regard, there is also a word of Scripture: *Let your alms sweat in your hands until you find out to whom to give.*

TWO. A further commandment of the teaching: 2 *Do not murder*; *do not commit adultery*; do not practice pederasty; do not fornicate; *do not steal*; do not deal in magic; do not practice sorcery; do not kill a fetus by abortion, or commit infanticide. *Do not covet your neighbor's goods.* 3 *Do not perjure yourself*; *do not bear false witness* (Mt 5:33, 15:19; 19:18); do not calumniate; do not bear malice. 4 Do not be double-minded or double-tongued, for a double tongue is *a deadly snare* (Prv 21:6). 5 Your speech must not be false or meaningless, but made good by action. 6 Do not be covetous, or rapacious, or hypocritical, or malicious, or arrogant. Do not have designs upon your neighbor. 7 Hate no man; but correct some, pray for others, for still others sacrifice your life as a proof of your love.

THREE. My child, shun evil of any kind and everything resembling it. 2 Do not be prone to anger, for anger leads to murder. Do not be fanatical, not quarrelsome, not hot-tempered; for all these things beget murder. 3 My child, do not be lustful, for lust leads to fornication. Do not be foulmouthed or give free rein to your eyes; for all these things beget adultery. 4 My child, do not be an augur, because it leads to idolatry. Do not be an enchanter, not an astrologer, not an expiator, and do not wish to see <and hear> these things; for they all beget idolatry. 5 My child, do not be a liar, for lying leads to theft. Do not be a lover of money, or a vain pretender. All these things beget thievery. 6 My child, do not be a grumbler, because it leads to blasphemy; or self-willed, or evil-minded. All these things beget blasphemy.

7 On the contrary, be gentle, for *the gentle will inherit the land* (Mt 5:4). 8 Be long-suffering, and merciful, and guileless, and quiet, and good, and *with trembling treasure* forever *the instructions* (Is 66:2) you have received. 9 Do not carry your head high, or open your heart to presumption. Do not be on intimate terms with the mighty, but associate with holy and lowly folk. 10 Accept as blessings the casualties that befall you, assured that nothing happens without God.

FOUR. My child, day and night *remember him who preaches God's word to you* (Heb 13:7), and honor him as the Lord, for where His lordship is spoken of, there is the Lord. 2 Seek daily contact with the saints to be refreshed by their discourses. 3 Do not start a schism, but pacify contending parties. *Be just in your judgment* (Dt 1:16-17; Prv 31:9): make no distinction between man and man when correcting transgressions. 4 Do not waver in your decision.

5 Do not be one that opens his hands to receive, but shuts them when it comes to giving. 6 If you have means at your disposal, pay a ransom for your sins. 7 Do not hesitate to give, and do not give in a grumbling mood. You will find out who is the good Rewarder. 8 Do not turn away from the needy; rather, share everything with your brother, and do not say: "It is my private property." If you are sharers in what is imperishable, how much more so in the things that perish!

9 Do not withdraw your hand from your son or your daughter, but from their youth teach them the fear of God. 10 Do not, when embittered, give orders to your slave, male or female, for they hope in the same God; otherwise, they might lose the fear of God, who is the Master of both of you. He surely is not coming to call with an eye to rank and station in life; no, He comes to those whom the Spirit has prepared. 11 But you, slaves, be submissive to your masters as to God's image in reverence and fear.

12 Abhor all sham and whatever is not pleasing to the Lord. 13 Do not by any means neglect the *commandments of the Lord,* but *hold fast* to the traditions, *neither adding nor subtracting anything* (Dt 4:2; 13:1). 14 In church confess your sins, and do not come to your prayer with a guilty conscience.

Such is the Way of Life.

St. Basil the Great on Religious Solitude

The monastic Rule of St. Basil (ca. 330-379)—in two forms, the
Long Rules *and the* Short Rules—*is the basis of the usual Rule still
followed by religious in the Eastern Church. Basil frowns on extreme
austerities, commends community life under obedience. The following
passages from the* Long Rules *discuss the need of solitude and the
hazards of solitary life.*[1]

QUESTION. *Concerning the necessity of living in retirement.*

RESPONSE. A secluded and remote habitation also contributes to the
removal of distraction from the soul. Living among those who are un-
scrupulous and disdainful in their attitude toward an exact observance
of the commandments is dangerous, as is shown by the following
words of Solomon: "Be not a friend to an angry man and do not walk
with a furious man, lest perhaps thou learn his ways and take snares

●

[1] Translated by Sister M. Monica Wagner, C.S.C., *Saint Basil: Ascetical
Works* (= *Fathers of the Church* 9; New York: Fathers of the Church,
1950) pp. 246-52.

to thy soul" (Prv 22:24-25). The words of the Apostle, "Go out from among them and be ye separate, saith the Lord" (2 Cor 6:17), bear also upon this point. Consequently, that we may not receive incitements to sin through our eyes and ears and become imperceptibly habituated to it, and that the impress and form, so to speak, of what is seen and heard may not remain in the soul unto its ruin, and that we may be able to be constant in prayer, we should before all things else seek to dwell in a retired place. In so doing, we should be able to overcome our former habits whereby we lived as strangers to the precepts of Christ (and it is no mean struggle to gain the mastery over one's wonted manner of acting, for custom maintained throughout a long period takes on the force of nature), and we could wipe away the stains of sin by assiduous prayer and persevering meditation on the will of God. It is impossible to gain proficiency in this meditation and prayer, however, while a multitude of distractions is dragging the soul about and introducing into it anxieties about the affairs of this life. Could anyone, immersed in these cares, ever fulfil that command: "If any man will come after me, let him deny himself" (Lk 9:23)? For we must deny ourselves and take up the cross of Christ and thus follow Him. Now, self-denial involves the entire forgetfulness of the past and surrender of one's will—surrender which it is very difficult, not to say quite impossible, to achieve while living in the promiscuity customary in the world. And in addition, the social intercourse demanded by such a life is even an obstacle to taking up one's cross and following Christ. Readiness to die for Christ, the mortification of one's members on this earth, preparedness for every danger which might befall us on behalf of Christ's Name, detachment from this life—this it is to take up one's cross; and we regard the obstacles springing from the habits of life in society as major impediments thereto.

And in addition to all the other obstacles, which are many, the soul in looking at the crowd of other offenders does not, in the first place, have time to become aware of its own sins and to afflict itself by penance for its errors; on the contrary, by comparison with those who are worse, it takes on, besides, a certain deceptive appearance of righteousness. Secondly, through the disturbances and occupations which life in society naturally engenders, the soul, being drawn away from the more worthy remembrance of God, pays the penalty of finding neither joy nor gladness in God and of not relishing the delights of the Lord or tasting the sweetness of His words, so as to be able to say: "I remembered God and was delighted" (Ps 76:4), and "How sweet are thy words to my palate! more than honey to my mouth" (Ps 118: 103). Worse still, it becomes habituated to a disregard and a complete forgetfulness of His judgments, than which no more fatal misfortune could befall it.

QUESTION. *On the necessity of living in the company of those who are striving for the same objective—that of pleasing God—and the difficulty and hazards of living as a solitary.*

Since your words have convinced us that it is dangerous to live in company with those who hold the commandments of God in light regard, we consider it logical to inquire whether one who retires from society should live in solitude or with brethren who are of the same mind and who have set before themselves the same goal, that is, the devout life.

RESPONSE. I consider that life passed in company with a number of persons in the same habitation is more advantageous in many respects. My reasons are, first, that no one of us is self-sufficient as regards corporeal necessities, but we require one another's aid in supplying our needs. The foot, to cite an analogy, possesses one kind of power and lacks another, and without the co-operation of the other members of the body it finds itself incapable of carrying on its activity independently for any length of time, nor does it have wherewithal to supply what is lacking. Similarly, in the solitary life, what is at hand becomes useless to us and what is wanting cannot be provided, since God, the Creator, decreed that we should require the help of one another, as it is written, so that we might associate with one another. Again, apart from this consideration, the doctrine of the charity of Christ does not permit the individual to be concerned solely with his own private interests. "Charity," says the Apostle, "seeketh not her own" (1 Cor 13:5). But a life passed in solitude is concerned only with the private service of individual needs. This is openly opposed to the law of love which the Apostle fulfilled, who sought not what was profitable to himself but to many that they might be saved. Furthermore, a person living in solitary retirement will not readily discern his own defects, since he has no one to admonish and correct him with mildness and compassion. In fact, admonition even from an enemy often produces in a prudent man the desire for amendment. But the cure of sin is wrought with understanding by him who loves sincerely; for Holy Scripture says "for he that loveth correcteth betimes" (Prv 13:24). Such a one it is very difficult to find in a solitude, if in one's prior state of life one had not been associated with such a person. The solitary, consequently, experiences the truth of the saying, "Woe to him that is alone, for when he falleth he hath none to lift him up" (Qoh 4:10). Moreover, the majority of the commandments are easily observed by several persons living together, but not so in the case of one living alone; for, while he is obeying one commandment, the practice of another is being interfered with. For example, when he is visiting the sick, he cannot show hospitality to the stranger and, in the imparting and sharing of necessities (especially when the ministrations are prolonged), he is prevented from giving zealous attention to [other] tasks. As a result, the greatest commandment and the one especially conducive to salvation is not observed, since the hungry are not fed nor the naked clothed. Who, then, would choose this ineffectual and unprofitable life in preference to that which is both fruitful and in accordance with the Lord's command?

Besides, if all we who are united in the one hope of our calling are one body with Christ as our Head, we are also members, one of another. If we are not joined together by union in the Holy Spirit in the harmony of one body, but each of us should choose to live in solitude, we would not serve the common good in the ministry according to God's good pleasure, but would be satisfying our own passion for self-gratification. How could we, divided and separated, preserve the status and the mutual service of members or our subordinate relationship to our Head which is Christ? It is impossible, indeed, to rejoice with him who receives an honor or to sympathize with him who suffers when, by reason of their being separated from one another, each person cannot, in all likelihood, be kept informed about the affairs of his neighbor. In addition, since no one has the capacity to receive all spiritual gifts, but the grace of the Spirit is given proportionately to the faith of each, when one is living in association with others, the grace privately bestowed on each individual becomes the common possession of his fellows. "To one, indeed, is given the word of wisdom; and to another, the word of knowledge; to another, faith, to another, prophecy, to another, the grace of healing" (1 Cor 12:8-9), and so on. He who receives any of these gifts does not possess it for his own sake but rather for the sake of others, so that, in the life passed in community, the operation of the Holy Spirit in the individual is at the same time necessarily transmitted to all. He who lives alone, consequently, and has, perhaps, one gift renders it ineffectual by leaving it in disuse, since it lies buried within him. How much danger there is in this all of you know who have read the Gospel. On the other hand, in the case of several persons living together, each enjoys his own gift and enhances it by giving others a share, besides reaping benefit from the gifts of others as if they were his own.

Community life offers more blessings than can be fully and easily enumerated. It is more advantageous than the solitary life both for preserving the goods bestowed on us by God and for warding off the external attacks of the Enemy. If any should happen to grow heavy with that sleep which is unto death and which we have been instructed by David to avert with prayer: "Enlighten my eyes that I never sleep in death" (Ps 12:4), the awakening induced by those who are already on watch is the more assured. For the sinner, moreover, the withdrawal from his sin is far easier if he fears the shame of incurring censure from many acting together—to him, indeed, might be applied the words: "To him who is such a one, this rebuke is sufficient which is given by many" (2 Cor 2:6)—and for the righteous man, there is a great and full satisfaction in the esteem of the group and in their approval of his conduct. If in the mouth of two or three witnesses every word shall stand, he who performs a good action will be far more surely corroborated by the testimony of many. Besides these disadvantages, the solitary life is fraught with other perils. The first and greatest is that of self-satisfaction. Since the solitary has no one to appraise his conduct, he will think he has achieved the perfection of the precept. Secondly, because he never tests his state of soul by exercise, he will not recognize his own deficiences nor will he discover the advance he may have made in his manner of acting, since he will have removed all practical occasion for the observance of the commandments.

Wherein will he show his humility, if there is no one with whom he may compare and so confirm his own greater humility? Wherein will he give evidence of his compassion, if he has cut himself off from association with other persons? And how will he exercise himself in long-suffering, if no one contradicts his wishes? If anyone says that the teaching of the Holy Scripture is sufficient for the amendment of his ways, he resembles a man who learns carpentry without ever actually doing a carpenter's work or a man who is instructed in metal-working but will not reduce theory to practice. To such a one the Apostle would say: "Not the hearers of the law are just before God, but the doers of the law shall be justified" (Rom 2:13). Consider, further, that the Lord by reason of His excessive love for man was not content with merely teaching the word, but, so as to transmit to us clearly and exactly the example of humility in the perfection of charity, girded Himself and washed the feet of the disciples. Whom, therefore, will you wash? To whom will you minister? In comparison with whom will you be the lowest, if you live alone? How, moreover, in a solitude, will that good and pleasant thing be accomplished, the dwelling of brethren together in one habitation which the Holy Spirit likens to ointment emitting its fragrance from the head of the high priest? So it is an arena for the combat, a good path of progress, continual discipline, and a practicing of the Lord's commandments, when brethren dwell together in community. This kind of life has as its aim the glory of God according to the command of our Lord Jesus Christ, who said: "So let your light shine before men that they may see your good works and glorify your Father who is in heaven" (Mt. 5:16). It maintains also the practice characteristic of the saints, of whom it is recorded in the Acts: "And all they that believed were together and had all things common" (Acts 2:44), and again: "And the multitude of believers had but one heart and one soul; neither did anyone say that aught of the things which he possessed was his own, but all things were common unto them" (Acts 4:32).

St. Augustine on Love of God

From the tenth book of the Confessions, *the autobiography of Augustine's soul, written about the year 400. Augustine interrogates creation: "What is it I love when I love my God?" The last paragraph below is Augustine's cry of anguish as he recalls the God he has fled, his tortured quest for truth and love, the heart that was restless because it did not rest in God.*[1]

It is with no doubtful knowledge, Lord, but with utter certainty that I love you. You have stricken my heart with your word and I have loved you. And indeed heaven and earth and all that is in them tell wherever I look that I should love you, and they cease not to tell it to all men, so that there is no excuse for them. For *you will have mercy on whom you will have mercy, and you will show mercy to whom you will show mercy*: otherwise heaven and earth cry their praise of you to deaf ears.

●

[1] Translated by F. J. Sheed, *The Confessions of St. Augustine* (New York: Sheed & Ward, 1943) pp. 215-17, 236.

But what is it that I love when I love you? Not the beauty of any bodily thing, nor the order of seasons, not the brightness of light that rejoices the eye, nor the sweet melodies of all songs, nor the sweet fragrance of flowers and ointments and spices: not manna nor honey, not the limbs that carnal love embraces. None of these things do I love in loving my God. Yet in a sense I do love light and melody and fragrance and food and embrace when I love my God—the light and the voice and the fragrance and the food and the embrace in the soul, when that light shines upon my soul which no place can contain, that voice sounds which no time can take from me, I breathe that fragrance which no wind scatters, I eat the food which is not lessened by eating, and I lie in the embrace which satiety never comes to sunder. This is it that I love, when I love my God.

And what is this God? I asked the earth, and it answered: "I am not He"; and all things that are in the earth made the same confession. I asked the sea and the deeps and the creeping things, and they answered: "We are not your God; seek higher." I asked the winds that blow, and the whole air with all that is in it answered: "Anaximenes was wrong; I am not God." I asked the heavens, the sun, the moon, the stars, and they answered: "Neither are we God whom you seek." And I said to all the things that throng about the gateways of the senses: "Tell me of my God, since you are not He. Tell me something of Him." And they cried out in a great voice: "He made us." My question was my gazing upon them, and their answer was their beauty. And I turned to myself and said: "And you, who are you?" And I answered: "A man." Now clearly there is a body and a soul in me, one exterior, one interior. From which of these two should I have enquired of my God? I had already sought Him by my body, from earth to heaven, as far as my eye could send its beams on the quest. But the interior part is the better, seeing that all my body's messengers delivered to it, as ruler and judge, the answers that heaven and earth and all things in them made when they said: "We are not God," and, "He made us." The inner man knows these things through the ministry of the outer man: I the inner man knew them, I, I the soul, through the senses of the body. I asked the whole frame of the universe about my God and it answered me: "I am not He, but He made me."

Is not the face of the earth clearly seen by all whose senses function properly? Then why does it not give the same answer to all? Animals great and small see it, but cannot interrogate it. For reason does not preside in them to judge upon the evidence their senses bring. But man can interrogate it, and so should be able clearly to see *the invisible things of God understood by things which are made;* but they love these last too much and become subject to them, and subjects cannot judge. All these things refuse to answer those who ask, unless they ask with power to judge. If one man merely sees the world, while another not only sees but interrogates it, the world does not change its speech—that is, its outward appearance which speaks—in such a way as to appear differently to the two men; but presenting exactly the same face to each, it says nothing to the one, but gives answer to the other: or rather it gives its answer to all, but only those understand who compare its voice as it comes through their senses, with the truth that is within them. For truth says to me: "Your God is not heaven or earth or any corporeal thing." So their very nature tells us. For clearly there is less bulk in the part than in the whole. And I tell you, my soul, you are better, since you vivify the whole bulk of the body: you give the body life, which no body can give to a body. But your God is the Life of your life. . . .

Late have I loved thee, O Beauty so ancient and so new; late have I loved thee! For behold thou wert within me, and I outside; and I sought thee outside and in my unloveliness fell upon those lovely things that thou hast made. Thou wert with me and I was not with thee. I was kept from thee by those things, yet had they not been in thee, they would not have been at all. Thou didst call and cry to me and break open my deafness: and thou didst send forth thy beams and shine upon me and chase away my blindness: thou didst breathe fragrance upon me, and I drew in my breath and do now pant for thee: I tasted thee, and now hunger and thirst for thee: thou didst touch me, and I have burned for thy peace.

St. Benedict's Rule for Monks

The monastic Rule drawn up by St. Benedict (ca. 480-ca. 550), patri-arch of Western monasticism, to regulate the life of his monks, is de-rived in part from the earlier Rules of John Cassian, Basil the Great, and Caesarius of Arles. Perhaps its outstanding feature is the wise balance it invariably strikes between excessive rigor and unwarranted leniency. The following extract offers the Prologue to Benedict's Rule.[1]

Hearken, my son, to the precepts of the master and incline the ear of thy heart; freely accept and faithfully fulfil the instructions of a loving father, that by the labor of obedience thou mayest return to him from whom thou hast strayed by the sloth of disobedience. To thee are my words now addressed, whosoever thou mayest be, that renouncing thine own will to fight for the true King, Christ, dost take up the strong and glorious weapons of obedience.

●

[1] Translated by Justin McCann, *The Rule of St. Benedict* (London: Burns Oates, 1952) pp. 7, 9, 11, 13.

And first of all, whatever good work thou undertakest, ask him with most instant prayer to perfect it, so that He who has deigned to count us among His sons may never be provoked by our evil conduct. For we must always so serve Him with the gifts which He has given us, that he may never as an angry father disinherit His children, nor yet as a dread lord be driven by our sins to cast into everlasting punishment the wicked servants who would not follow Him to glory.

Up with us then at last, for the Scripture arouseth us, saying: *Now is the hour for us to rise from sleep* (Rom 13:11). Let us open our eyes to the divine light, and let us hear with attentive ears the warning that the divine voice crieth daily to us: *Today if ye will hear His voice, harden not your hearts* (Ps 94:8). And again: *He that hath ears to hear, let him hear what the Spirit saith to the churches* (Mt 11:15; Ap 2:7) And what doth He say? *Come, ye children, hearken unto me: I will teach you the fear of the Lord* (Ps 33:12). *Run while ye have the light of life, lest the darkness of death overtake you* (Jn 12:35).

And the Lord, seeking His workmen among the multitudes to whom He thus crieth, saith again: *What man is he that desireth life and would fain see good days?* (Ps 33:13). And if hearing Him thou answer, "I am he," God saith to thee: *If thou wilt have true and everlasting life, keep thy tongue from evil and thy lips that they speak no guile. Turn away from evil and do good: seek after peace and pursue it* (Ps 33:14-16). And when you have done these things, my eyes will be upon you and my ears open unto your prayers. And before you call upon me, I shall say to you, "Lo, here I am." What can be sweeter to us, dearest brethren, than this voice of our Lord inviting us? Behold, in His loving mercy the Lord showeth us the way of life.

Let us, therefore, gird our loins with faith and the performance of good works, and following the guidance of the Gospel walk in His paths, so that we may merit to see Him who has called us unto His kingdom. And, if we wish to dwell in the tabernacle of His kingdom, except we run thither with good deeds we shall not arrive. But let us ask the Lord with the prophet: *Lord, who shall dwell in thy tabernacle, or who shall rest upon thy holy hill?* (Ps 14:1). Then, brethren, let us hear the Lord answering and showing us the way to that tabernacle and saying: *He that walketh without blemish and doth that which is right; he that speaketh truth in his heart, who hath used no deceit in his tongue, nor done evil to his neighbor, nor believed ill of his neighbor* (Ps 14:2-3). He that taketh the evil spirit that tempteth him, and casteth him and his temptation from the sight of his heart, and bringeth him to naught; who graspeth his evil suggestions as they arise and dasheth them to pieces on the rock that is Christ. Such men as these, fearing the Lord, are not puffed up on account of their good works, but judging that they can do no good of themselves and that all cometh from God, they magnify the Lord's work in them, using the word of the prophet: *Not unto us, O Lord, not unto us, but unto thy name give the glory* (Ps 113:9). So the Apostle Paul imputed nothing of his preaching to himself, but said: *By the grace of God I am what I am* (1 Cor 15:10). And again he saith: *He that glorieth, let him glory in the Lord* (2 Cor 10:17).

Wherefore the Lord also saith in the Gospel: *He that heareth these my words and doth them, shall be likened to a wise man that built his house upon a rock. The floods came and the winds blew, and they beat upon that house, and it fell not, for it was founded upon a rock* (Mt 7:24-25). Having given us these instructions, the Lord daily expects us to make our life correspond with His holy admonitions. And the days of our life are lengthened and a respite allowed us for this very reason, that we may amend our evil ways. For the Apostle saith: *Knowest thou not that the patience of God inviteth thee to repentance?* (Rom 2:4). For the merciful Lord saith: *I will not the death of a sinner, but that he should be converted and live* (Ez 33:11).

So, brethren, we have asked the Lord about the dwellers in His tabernacle and have heard what is the duty of him who would dwell therein; it remains for us to fulfil this duty. Therefore our hearts and bodies must be made ready to fight under the holy obedience of His commands; and let us ask God that He be pleased, where our nature is powerless, to give us the help of His grace. And if we would escape the pains of hell and reach eternal life, then must we—while there is still time, while we are in this body and can fulfil all these things by the light of this life—hasten to do now what may profit us for eternity.

Therefore must we establish a school of the Lord's service; in founding which we hope to ordain nothing that is harsh or burdensome. But if, for good reason, for the amendment of evil habit or the preservation of charity, there be some strictness of discipline, do not be at once dismayed and run away from the way of salvation, of which the entrance must needs be narrow. But, as we progress in our monastic life and in faith, our hearts shall be enlarged, and we shall run with unspeakable sweetness of love in the way of God's commandments; so that, never abandoning His rule but persevering in His teaching in the monastery until death, we shall share by patience in the sufferings of Christ, that we may deserve to be partakers also of His kingdom. Amen.

St. Bernard on the Reward of Loving God

St. Bernard (1090-1153), first abbot of the Cistercian monastery of Clairvaux, exercised a powerful influence on secular and religious affairs in Europe by his holiness and forceful personality. The following passages, excerpted from his classic De diligendo Deo *(On Love for God), give some little insight into the man and his spiritual doctrine.[1]*

Something having now been said of the merit of God, not indeed worthily but in such terms as have been granted me, it remains that I should say something, as it is granted me, of the reward of loving God.

For it is not without reward that God is loved, although He ought to be loved without looking for reward. And this is because true love cannot be empty of effect, nor yet is it mercenary. We know that *it seeks not the things which are its own* (1 Cor 13:5). It is a disposition of the emotions, not a legal contract; it is neither acquired by mutual

●

[1] Translated by Watkin Williams, *St. Bernard: The Man and His Message* (New York: Spiritual Book Associates, n.d.) pp. 58-61.

agreement, nor does it acquire after such a fashion. It affects a man freely, and it makes him free. True love finds satisfaction in itself. It has its reward, which is the object of its love. For whatever you appear to love for the sake of something else, it is plain that what you really love is not the mere means of loving, but the final object of your love. Paul does not preach the gospel in order that he may eat, but he eats in order that he may preach the gospel (1 Cor 9:18), for the reason that he loves not food but the gospel. True love does not seek a reward, but it does deserve one. In fact, it is when a man has not yet learned to love that a reward is set before him; when he loves it is due to him; when he perseveres it is given to him. Finally, when persuading people in quite little matters, it is the reluctant and not the eager whom we entice by promises or rewards. For who would think that a man must be tempted by rewards in order that he may do what of his own accord he desires to do? For example, no one either pays a hungry man to eat or a thirsty man to drink, and certainly not a mother to suckle the little son of her womb (Is 44:15).

You may see men who inhabit royal homes and spacious palaces nevertheless to be daily joining house to house (Is 5:8), and building with restless anxiety—scattering and turning things upside down. What do we see, if not men exalted by honors—what do we see, if not such men striving their utmost with insatiable ambition to attain yet greater heights? And of all this there is simply no end, because in no single one of these objects is found anything of the highest or the best. And what wonder is it if that which is unable to find rest anywhere short of the highest or the best should not be satisfied by lower or by worser things? But this is folly and utter madness to be always longing after what never, I do not say, satisfies but even allays the appetite, while, whatever you may possess of such a kind, you nevertheless lust for what you do not possess and are forever restlessly sighing after what you lack. For thus it comes about that the wandering mind, running in empty effort hither and thither through the diverse and deceptive delights of the world, is wearied, not satisfied; while, whatever the famished creature gorges, it thinks to be very little in comparison with what remains to be devoured, and never less feverishly desires what is still wanting by reason of its joyful possession of what is already supplied. For who is there that gains the whole world? Although we may be by no means certain when we shall lose with grief even that little which each of us has gained by labor, which he possesses in fear, we are certain that at some time we shall lose it.

But the righteous does not do that. Hearing, forsooth, the blasphemy of the multitude as they loiter on their wandering way—for they are many who follow the broad path which leads to death—he chooses for himself the King's highway, declining neither to the right hand nor to the left; as the prophet testifies: *The way of the righteous is a direct way, his path is straight to walk* (Is 26:7). These are they who, by taking the saving direct way, are careful to avoid such troublesome and unprofitable wandering, choosing the short and summary word of exhortation, which is—not to grasp everything which they see, but rather to sell their possessions and give to the poor (Mt 21:21). Plainly *the poor are blessed, for theirs is the kingdom of heaven* (Mt 5:3). *All indeed run* (1 Cor 9:24), but there is a difference between the runners. Lastly: *The Lord knows the way of the righteous, and the way of the ungodly shall perish* (Ps 1:6). Therefore *to the righteous man his modest means are better than the great wealth of sinners* (Ps 36:16), seeing that, as the wise man tells us and the fool finds out, he who loves money shall not be satisfied by money; but *they who hunger and thirst after righteousness, they it is who shall be satisfied* (Mt 5:6). If righteousness is really the vital and natural food of the reasonable spirit, then certainly money does not relieve or lessen the hunger of the mind, any more than does wind the hunger of the body.

I have said above that the cause of loving God is God. I have spoken truly, because He is both the efficient and the final cause of so doing. He Himself provides the occasion; He Himself creates the affection; He Himself fulfils the desire. His works are done or, rather, His very existence is—to the end that He should be the object of love; His hope is that He will be so fruitfully loved as not to be loved in vain. His love for us both prepares and rewards our love for Him. And so He goes before us the more kindly, He rewards us the more justly, He awaits us the more graciously. He is rich unto all who call upon Him, but He has nothing better to give them than Himself. He gave Himself to merit for us; He keeps Himself to be our reward. He supplies Himself as the refreshment of the souls of the saints; He distributes Himself as the redemption of every captive. *Thou art good, O Lord, to the soul which seeks Thee* (Lam 3:25). What then art thou to the soul which finds thee? But here what is so wonderful is that no one is able to seek thee, save only he who has already found thee. It is thy will, therefore, to be found in order that thou mayest be sought, to be sought in order that thou mayest be found. Thou canst, indeed, be sought and found, but thou canst not be anticipated.

Thomas a Kempis on Imitating Christ and Despising Vanities

The Imitation of Christ, *probably the work of Thomas Hemerken (ca. 1380-1471) of Kempen near Cologne, is a famous manual of spirituality in which the Christian is instructed to seek perfection by following Christ as his model. The following extract is the first chapter of Book 1.*[1]

"He who follows me walks not in darkness," says the Lord (Jn 8:12). By these words of Christ we are advised to imitate His life and habits, if we wish to be truly enlightened and free from all blindness of heart. Let our chief effort, therefore, be to study the life of Jesus Christ.

The teaching of Christ is more excellent than all the advice of the saints, and he who has His spirit will find in it a hidden strength. Now, there are many who hear the Gospel often but care little for it because they have not the spirit of Christ. Yet whoever wishes to understand

●

[1] Translated by Aloysius Croft and Harry F. Bolton, *The Imitation of Christ* (Milwaukee: Bruce, 1940) pp. 1-2.

fully the words of Christ must try to pattern his whole life on that of Christ.

What good does it do to speak learnedly about the Trinity if, lacking humility, you displease the Trinity? Indeed, it is not learning that makes a man holy and just, but a virtuous life makes him pleasing to God. I would rather feel contrition than know how to define it. For what would it profit us to know the whole Bible by heart and the principles of all the philosophers if we live without grace and the love of God? Vanity of vanities and all is vanity, except to love God and serve Him alone.

This is the greatest wisdom—to seek the kingdom of heaven through contempt of the world. It is vanity, therefore, to seek and trust in riches that perish. It is vanity also to court honor and to be puffed up with pride. It is vanity to follow the lusts of the body and to desire things for which severe punishment later must come. It is vanity to wish for long life and to care little about a well-spent life. It is vanity to be concerned with the present only and not to make provision for things to come. It is vanity to love what passes quickly and not to look ahead where eternal joy abides.

Often recall the proverb: "The eye is not satisfied with seeing nor the ear filled with hearing" (Qoh 1:8). Try, moreover, to turn your heart from the love of things visible and bring yourself to things invisible. For they who follow their own evil passions stain their consciences and lose the grace of God.

St. Ignatius Loyola:
First Principle and Foundation

This basic principle in the spiritual life is taken from the Spiritual Exercises of St. Ignatius Loyola (1491-1556), a famous series of meditations and rules designed to lead souls to conquer their passions and give themselves to God.[1]

Man is created to praise, reverence, and serve God our Lord, and by this means to save his soul.

The other things on the face of the earth are created for man to help him in attaining the end for which he is created.

Hence, man is to make use of them in as far as they help him in the attainment of his end, and he must rid himself of them in as far as they prove a hindrance to him.

Therefore, we must make ourselves indifferent to all created things, as far as we are allowed free choice and are not under any prohibition.

[1] Translated by Louis J. Puhl, S.J., *The Spiritual Exercises of St. Ignatius* (Westminster, Md.: Newman, 1954) p. 12.

Consequently, as far as we are concerned, we should not prefer health to sickness, riches to poverty, honor to dishonor, a long life to a short life. The same holds for all other things.

Our one desire and choice should be what is more conducive to the end for which we are created.

St. Ignatius Loyola:
Choice of a Way of Life

From the Spiritual Exercises of St. Ignatius Loyola.[1]

INTRODUCTION

In every good choice, as far as depends on us, our intention must be simple. I must consider only the end for which I am created, that is, for the praise of God our Lord and for the salvation of my soul. Hence, whatever I choose must help me to this end for which I am created.

I must not subject and fit the end to the means, but the means to the end. Many first choose marriage, which is a means, and secondarily the service of our Lord in marriage, though the service of God is the end. So also others first choose to have benefices, and afterwards to serve God in them. Such persons do not go directly to God, but want God to come straight to their inordinate attachments. Consequently, they make of the end a means, and of the means an end. As a result, what they ought to seek first, they seek last.

●

[1] Translated by Louis J. Puhl, S.J., *op. cit.*, pp. 71, 75-77.

Therefore, my first aim should be to seek to serve God, which is the end, and only after that, if it is more profitable, to have a benefice or marry, for these are means to the end. Nothing must move me to use such means, or to deprive myself of them, save only the service and praise of God our Lord and the salvation of my soul.

FIRST WAY OF MAKING A GOOD AND CORRECT CHOICE OF A WAY OF LIFE

This contains six points.

FIRST POINT. This is to place before my mind the object with regard to which I wish to make a choice, for example, an office, or the reception or rejection of a benefice, or anything else that may be the object of a choice subject to change.

SECOND POINT. It is necessary to keep as my aim the end for which I am created, that is, the praise of God and the salvation of my soul. Besides this, I must be indifferent, without any inordinate attachment, so that I am not more inclined or disposed to accept the object in question than to relinquish it, nor to give it up than to accept it. I should be like a balance at equilibrium, without leaning to either side, that I might be ready to follow whatever I perceive is more for the glory and praise of God and the salvation of my soul.

THIRD POINT. I should beg God our Lord to deign to move my will, and to bring to my mind what I ought to do to promote His praise and glory with regard to the matter in question. Then I should use the understanding to weigh the matter with care and fidelity, and make my choice in conformity with His most holy will.

FOURTH POINT. This will be to weigh the matter by reckoning the number of advantages and benefits that would accrue to me if I had the proposed office or benefice solely for the praise of God our Lord and the salvation of my soul. On the other hand, I should weigh the disadvantages and dangers there might be in having it. I will do the same with the second alternative, that is, weigh the advantages and benefits as well as the disadvantages and danger of not having it.

FIFTH POINT. After I have gone over and pondered in this way every aspect of the matter in question, I will consider which alternative appears more reasonable. Then I must come to a decision in the matter under deliberation because of weightier motives presented to my reason, and not because of any sensual inclination.

SIXTH POINT. After such a choice or decision, the one who has made it must turn with great diligence to prayer in the presence of God our Lord, and offer Him his choice that the Divine Majesty may deign to accept and confirm it if it is for His greater service and praise.

SECOND WAY OF MAKING A CORRECT AND GOOD CHOICE OF A WAY OF LIFE

This contains four rules and a note.

FIRST RULE. The love that moves and causes one to choose must descend from above, that is, from the love of God, so that before one chooses he should perceive that the greater or less attachment for the object of his choice is solely because of his Creator and Lord.

SECOND RULE. I should represent to myself a man whom I have never seen or known, and whom I would like to see practice all perfection. Then I should consider what I would tell him to do and choose for the greater glory of God our Lord and the greater perfection of his soul. I will do the same, and keep the rule I propose to others.

THIRD RULE. This is to consider what procedure and norm of action I would wish to have followed in making the present choice if I were at the moment of death. I will guide myself by this and make my decision entirely in conformity with it.

FOURTH RULE. Let me picture and consider myself as standing in the presence of my Judge on the last day, and reflect what decision in the present matter I would then wish to have made. I will choose now the rule of life that I would then wish to have observed, that on the Day of Judgment I may be filled with happiness and joy.

Note

Guided by the rules given above for my eternal salvation and peace, I will make my decision, and will offer it to God our Lord as directed in the sixth point of the First Way of Making a Choice of a Way of Life.

St. Theresa of Avila on Mental Prayer

From the Way of Perfection *of St. Theresa of Avila (1515-1582), cofounder with St. John of the Cross of the Discalced Carmelites. She was gifted with mystical prayer, deep knowledge of spirituality, and practical administrative ability, all to a high degree.*[1]

1. Now, my daughters, mental prayer is not a question of praying simply with our mouths shut. If when I pray vocally, I am thoroughly aware that I am speaking to God and am more conscious of this thought than of the words I am saying, then I am uniting mental and vocal prayer. But if anyone says that you are speaking to God while you say the Our Father and think of the world, I have nothing further to say. Actually, if you are going to speak with so great a Lord with the consideration due Him, you must stop to reflect who it is you speak

●

[1] Translated by Alice Alexander, *The Way of Perfection by St. Theresa of Jesus* (Westminster, Md.: Newman, 1946) pp. 136-41. The extract we reproduce here is chapter 24 of the *Way.*

to and who you are, merely as a matter of propriety. Could you call the king "Highness," and know the ceremonial protocol to be observed in speaking to a great person, if you were not aware of his position and of your own as well? The honor shown him must accord with his rank and with custom. You must know the custom and not fail to observe it; otherwise you will be taken for a boor and gain no hearing. Furthermore, if you are not acquainted with ceremonial usages, you must find out how you should act and even, if necessary, write out what you should say.

2. This is what happened to me once. I was not in the habit of speaking with the nobility, but one day necessity required me to speak to a lady who should be addressed as "Your Ladyship." I had been carefully coached in using the title but, not being too intelligent and being unaccustomed to it, once I reached her presence I became confused. I decided to tell her what my trouble was and to laugh at it, begging her not to be offended if I called her "Your Grace." And that is what I did.

3. But what is all this, my Lord? What is it, my Sovereign? How canst thou endure it, thou Prince of all creation? Thou art the Eternal King, my God, whose kingdom is no borrowed one, but thine own! It will never end. Blessed be God! Almost always, when the Creed is said, I feel a special joy at the words: "of whose kingdom there shall be no end." I praise thee, O Lord, and bless thee. May all things praise thee forever! Thy kingdom shall last forever. Never, my Lord, let anyone think that he can praise thee only with his lips.

4. What does it mean, Christians, when you say you have no need of mental prayer? Do you understand what you are saying? I cannot believe you do understand and thus you would lead us astray too. You do not even, I am sure, know what mental prayer is, or how to practice vocal prayer, or what contemplation is. If you did understand, you would not condemn on one hand what you praised on the other.

5. Whenever I think of it, I shall always speak of mental and vocal prayer together, my daughters, that you may not be troubled at the idea of mental prayer. I know how these things work, for I have had difficulties of this sort myself and I do not want you to be made uneasy by anyone; it is very harmful to walk in fear along the road of prayer. It is most important for you to understand that you are on the right path. If you tell a traveler that he has made a false turn and has lost his way, it makes him go round and round seeking the right way, tiring himself out, wasting his time and reaching his destination later than he should.

6. Now suppose that before you begin your office or the rosary, you stop to consider who it is you will speak to and who you yourselves are, that you may know how to act—can anyone say there is anything wrong with that? Well, I assure you, my sisters, that if you are careful to do all that is implied in undertsanding these two points before

you begin your vocal prayer, such as your office or rosary, you will have spent many hours in mental prayer.

7. Obviously, we are not going to speak to a prince in the careless fashion we may use toward a peasant or a poor nun like ourselves. It does not matter what form of address is used in speaking to us; anything is acceptable. It is true that our King is so humble that He will not refuse to hear me or let me draw near Him because I am too ignorant to know how to speak to Him. Neither will His guards dismiss me, for the angels who attend Him know what their King is like and that He is more pleased by the rude simplicity of a humble shepherd who, He knows, would say more if he knew how, than by the most elaborate language of the greatest scholars if they are not also humble. But we must not be rude just because our King is good. Were it only to express my gratitude that He allow someone like myself to be near Him, I should seek to understand His purity and who He is. We do, in truth, understand this when we draw near Him, even as we get to know the great ones of the world by ascertaining who their parents were, what income they have, and what their title is. With them, however, we need know no more, for in the world people are not honored according to their merit, no matter how deserving they may be, but by what they possess. O despicable world! Thank God sincerely, my daughters, that you have left so evil a place, where people are esteemed, not for their personal worth, but according to their estates. If they lose these, they lose their title to honor. Here you have, my daughters, an amusing topic for your recreation time, for it is an excellent thing to consider the stupid way in which the worldly-wise spend their time.

8. O my Sovereign! Thou who art the Supreme Power, the Sovereign Good, and Wisdom itself, thou who art without beginning or end, whose works have no term; whose perfections are infinite and beyond our faintest comprehension; thou who art that Beauty which contains all beauties, who are Strength itself! Thou shalt ever reign! O my God! would that I had now all the wisdom and eloquence of men that I might make known—so far as can be known here on earth, where all knowledge is as nothing—some little of the many things we might consider in order to understand the nature of Him who is our Lord and our God!

9. So stop to think and to understand, as you pray, who the Person is with whom you are going to speak or are already speaking. A thousand of our lifetimes are not enough to make you understand how this Lord, before whom the angels tremble, deserves to be treated. He commands everything and can do all things; for Him to will is to act.

10. Rightly, then, my daughters, should we seek our joy in these perfections of our Spouse, and try to understand Him whose brides we are and undertsand too what our lives should be. Here in this life, my God, when a person marries, her first concern is to know who it is she is marrying, what kind of person he is, and what are his means.

We are already promised, as all souls are by baptism. Shall we not, then, think of our Spouse before the nuptials, when He will lead us to His house? When those who are espoused on earth may have such thoughts, shall we be forbidden to know who this Spouse is, who His Father is, what the country is to which He will take us, what possessions He promises to give us, what His character is, and how we can best make Him happy, or give Him pleasure, and conform our wills to His?

11. This is the advice people give a woman who wishes to make her marriage happy, even though her husband is a person of no importance. O my Spouse! art thou then to be less esteemed than men? If the world does not agree with what I say, let it at least leave thee thy brides, to spend their lives with thee. It is truly a happy life when a husband is so jealous that he does not want his wife to leave his house or have anything to do with others, and an extraordinary thing if she does not seek to give him this pleasure. Her reason for obeying him and for leaving all other creatures is simply that he is capable of giving her all she can desire.

12. Now, my daughters, this is mental prayer: to understand these truths. If you wish to join this understanding to vocal prayer, well and good. But do not go talking to God and thinking of other things, which is what people do who do not understand the meaning of mental prayer. I believe I have made it clear to you; do not let anyone frighten you.

13. Praise God, who is more powerful than all creatures and whom no one can force you to abandon. If any of you cannot pray vocally with this attention, she should know that she is not fulfilling her obligation; and, if she would pray perfectly, she is obliged to try with all her strength to pray thus, else she will not be doing the duty of the spouse of a great King. Beseech Him, my daughters, to give me the grace to do as I counsel you, for I am still a long way from it.

14. May His Majesty, in His mercy, supply for the lack!

St. John of the Cross on the Communion of the Divine Persons

The following verses give some insight into the glowing poetry of St. John of the Cross (1542-1591), cofounder of the Discalced Carmelites, whose mystical doctrine stems from personal experience fed by Scripture, Thomistic, philosophy, and keen psychological intuition.[1]

Out of the love immense and bright
That from the two had thus begun,
Words of ineffable delight
The Father spoke unto the Son:

Words of so infinite a rapture
Their drift by none could be explained:
Only the Son their sense could capture
That only to Himself pertained.

●

[1] Translated by Roy Campbell, *The Poems of St. John of the Cross* (New York: Pantheon, 1951) pp. 53, 55.

What of them we can sense the clearest
Was in this manner said and thought:
Out of Your company, my Dearest,
I can be satisfied by nought.

But if aught please me, I as duly
In You, Yourself, the cause construe.
The one who satisfies Me truly
Is him who most resembles You.

He who in naught resembles You
Shall find of Me no trace or sign,
Life of My Life for only through
Your own can I rejoice in Mine.

You are the brilliance of My light
My wisdom and My power divine,
The figure of My substance bright
In whom I am well pleased to shine!

The man who loves You, O my Son,
To him Myself I will belong.
The love that in Yourself I won
I'll plant in him and root it strong,
Because he loved the very one
I loved so deeply and so long.

St. Francis de Sales
on Christian Devotion

St. Francis de Sales (1567-1622) was one of the leaders of the Counter Reformation and a remarkable spiritual director and writer. The following extracts are taken from Part 1 of his celebrated Introduction to the Devout Life, *whose purpose is to foster a life of genuine Christian devotion in the midst of the world's distractions.*[1]

THE DESCRIPTION OF TRUE DEVOTION

You aspire to devotion, dearest Philothea, because, being a Christian, you know it to be a virtue extremely pleasing to the Divine Majesty. Since small faults, committed in the beginning of any undertaking, grow in the progress infinitely greater and become in the end almost irreparable, you must above all else know what the virtue of devotion

●

[1] Translated by John K. Ryan, *Introduction to the Devout Life by St. Francis de Sales* (Image Books; Garden City, N.Y.: Doubleday, 1955) pp. 35-37, 39-40.

is. There is but one true devotion, and there are many that are false and deceitful. Hence, if you cannot distinguish that which is true, you may easily deceive and distract yourself in following one that is offensive and superstitious.

As Arelius painted all the faces in his pictures in the manner and likeness of the woman he loved, so everyone paints devotion according to his own love and fancy. The man who is addicted to fasting thinks himself very devout if he fasts, though his heart be at the same time filled with rancor. He scruples to moisten his tongue with wine, or even with water, because of his sobriety, but he makes no difficulty of drinking deep of his neighbor's blood by detraction and calumny. Another considers himself devout because he recites daily a multiplicity of prayers, although immediately afterward he utters the most disagreeable, arrogant, and injurious words in his home and among his neighbors. Another cheerfully draws an alms out of his purse to give to the poor, but he cannot draw meekness out of his heart to forgive his enemies. Another readily forgives his enemies, but he never satisfies his creditors except when compelled by the sharp power of the law. All these are commonly esteemed devout, while in reality they are by no means so. Saul's servants sought David in his house, but Michol laid a statue in his bed, covered it over with clothes, and made them believe that it was David himself. In the same manner, many persons by covering themselves with certain external actions belonging to holy devotion make the world believe that they are truly devout, whereas they are in truth nothing but images and phantoms of devotion.

True, living devotion, Philothea, presupposes the love of God, and hence it is nothing else than the love of God. But it is not always love as such. Inasmuch as divine love adorns the soul, it is called grace, which makes us pleasing to His Divine Majesty. Inasmuch as it gives us the strength to do good, it is called charity. When it has arrived at that degree of perfection by which it not only makes us do well but also do this diligently, frequently, and readily, then it is called devotion. Ostriches never fly; hens fly close to the ground, clumsily, and only occasionally; but eagles, doves, and swallows fly aloft, swiftly, and frequently. In like manner, sinners fly not at all toward God, but make their whole course upon the earth and for the earth. Good people who have not as yet attained to devotion fly toward God by their good works, but infrequently, slowly, and clumsily. Devout souls ascend to Him by more frequent, prompt, and lofty flights. In short, devotion is nothing else than that spiritual agility and vivacity by which charity works in us, or we work by her aid, with alacrity and affection. As it is the function of charity to make us observe all of God's commandments in general and without exception, so it is the part of devotion to make us observe them more quickly and with diligence. Wherefore, the man who does not observe all the commandments of God cannot be esteemed either good or devout. For to be good he must be possessed of charity, and to be devout, in addition to charity, he must show a cheerfulness and alacrity in the performance of charitable actions.

As devotion consists in a certain degree of eminent charity, it not only makes us active and diligent in the observance of God's commandments, but beyond this it arouses us to do quickly and lovingly as many good works as we can, both those commanded and those that are merely counseled and inspired. Just as a man newly recovered from an illness walks only as much as is necessary for him, but yet slowly and with difficulty, so a sinner, just healed of his iniquity, walks as far as God commands him, but slowly and with difficulty, until such time as he attains to devotion. Then, like a man in sound health, he not only walks but runs and leaps forward in the way of God's commandments. Moreover, he moves and runs in the paths of His heavenly counsels and inspirations. To conclude, charity and devotion differ no more from each other than does the flame from the fire, for charity is a spiritual fire, which, when inflamed, is called devotion. Hence, it appears that devotion adds nothing to the fire of charity but the flame that makes it ready, active, and diligent, not only in the observance of the commandments of God, but also in the execution of His heavenly counsels and inspirations.

THAT DEVOTION IS COMPATIBLE
WITH EVERY VOCATION AND PROFESSION

In the creation God commanded the plants to bring forth their fruits, each one after its kind. So does He command all Christians, who are the living plants of His Church, to bring forth the fruits of devotion, each according to his character and vocation. Devotion must be exercised in different ways by the gentleman, the workman, the servant, the prince, the widow, the maid, and the married woman. Not only this, but the practice of devotion must be also adapted to the strength, the employment, and the duties of each one in particular. I ask you, Philothea, is it fit that a bishop should lead the solitary life of a Carthusian? Or that married people should lay up no greater store of goods than the Capuchin? If a tradesman were to remain the whole day in church, like a member of a religious order, or were a religious continually exposed to encounter difficulties in the service of his neighbor, as a bishop is, would not such devotion be ridiculous, unorganized, and insupportable? Nevertheless, this fault is very common. Hence, the world, which does not distinguish, or does not wish to distinguish, between real devotion and the indiscretion of those who imagine themselves to be devout, murmurs at devotion and censures it, as if it were unable to prevent these disorders.

No, Philothea, true devotion does no harm whatever, but rather gives perfection to all things. But when it goes contrary to our lawful vocation, then without doubt it is false. "The bee," says Aristotle, "extracts honey from flowers without injuring them," and leaves them as whole and fresh as she found them. True devotion does still better. It not only does no injury to any vocation or employment, but on the contrary it adorns and beautifies it. Every kind of precious stone receives a greater luster when cast into honey, each according to its color. So also every vocation becomes more agreeable when united with devotion. The care of the family is rendered more peaceable, the love of the husband and wife more sincere, the service of the prince more faithful, and every type of employment more pleasant and agreeable.

It is an error, or rather a heresy, to try to banish the devout life from the regiment of soldiers, the shop of the mechanic, the court of princes, or the home of married folk. It is true, Philothea, that a purely contemplative, monastic, and religious devotion cannot be exercised in such ways of life. But besides these three kinds of devotion, there are several others adapted to bring to perfection those who live in the secular state. Abraham, Isaac, and Jacob, David, Job, Tobias, Sarah, Rebecca, and Judith bear witness of this in the Old Testament. As for the New Testament, St. Joseph, Lydia, and St. Crispin were perfectly devout in their workshops; St. Anne, St. Martha, St. Monica, Aquila, and Priscilla in their families; Cornelius, St. Sebastian, and St. Maurice in the army; Constantine, Helena, St. Louis, Blessed Amatus, and St. Edward on the throne. It has even happened that many have lost perfection in solitude, which is nonetheless so desirable for perfection, and have preserved it among the multitude, which seems so little favorable to it. "Lot," says St. Gregory, "who was so chaste in the city, defiled himself in the wilderness." Wheresoever we are, we can and should aspire to a perfect life.

St. Theresa of Lisieux: The Story of a Soul

St. Theresa's Story of a Soul *is her remarkable autobiography—actually a collection of three letters of unequal length written at different times to different people. What follows here is the opening chapter of the first letter, entitled by Theresa "The Story of a Little White Flower." This letter, dedicated to Reverend Mother Agnes of Jesus (her sister Pauline), was written between the beginning of January, 1895, and January 20, 1896.*[1]

Dearest Mother, it is to you, who are my mother twice over, that I am going to tell the history of my soul. When you first asked me to do it, I was frightened: it looked as if it meant wasting my spiritual energies on introspection. But, since then, our Lord has made it clear to me that all He wanted of me was plain obedience. And in any case, what I shall be doing is only what will be my task in eternity—telling over and over again the story of God's mercies to me.

●

[1] Translated by Ronald Knox, *Autobiography of St. Thérèse of Lisieux* (New York: Kenedy, 1958) pp. 33-37.

Before taking up my pen, I knelt down before our Lady's statue; the one which has so often assured us that the Queen of Heaven looks on our community with special favor. My prayer was that she would guide my hand, and never let my pen write a single line which wasn't as she wanted it to be. After that, I opened the Gospels at random, and the words my eyes fell on were these: "Then He went up on to the mountainside and called to Him those whom it pleased Him to call; so these came to Him" (Mk 3:13). There it all was, the history of my life, of my whole vocation; above all, of the special claims Jesus makes on my soul. He doesn't call the people who are worthy of it; no, just the people it pleases Him to call; as St. Paul says, God shows pity on those He pities, shows mercy where He is merciful; the effect comes from God's mercy, not from man's will or man's alacrity.

I had always wondered why it was that God has His preferences, instead of giving each soul an equal degree of grace. Why does He shower such extraordinary favors on the saints who at one time have been His enemies, people like St. Paul and St. Augustine, compelling them (you might say) to accept the graces He sends them? Why do you find, in reading the lives of the saints, that there are some of them our Lord sees fit to hold in His arms, all the way from the cradle to the grave? Never an obstacle in their path, as they make their way up to Him; grace still heading them off, so that they never manage to soil the robe of baptismal innocence! And again, I used to wonder about the poor savages and people like that, who die, such numbers of them, without ever so much as hearing the name of God mentioned. But Jesus has been gracious enough to teach me a lesson about this mystery, simply by holding up to my eyes the book of nature. I realized, then, that all the flowers He has made are beautiful; the rose in its glory, the lily in its whiteness, don't rob the tiny violet of its sweet smell, or the daisy of its charming simplicity. I saw that if all these lesser blooms wanted to be roses instead, nature would lose the gaiety of her springtide dress—there would be no little flowers to make a pattern over the countryside. And so it is with the world of souls, which is His garden. He wanted to have great saints, to be His lilies and roses, but He has made lesser saints as well; and these lesser ones must be content to rank as daisies and violets, lying at His feet and giving pleasure to His eye like that. Perfection consists simply in doing His will, and being just what He wants us to be.

This, too, was made clear to me—that our Lord's love makes itself seen quite as much in the simplest of souls as in the most highly gifted, as long as there is no resistance offered to His grace. After all, the whole point of love is making yourself small; and if we were all like the great doctors who have shed luster on the Church by their brilliant teaching, there wouldn't be much condescension on God's part, would there, about coming into hearts like these? But no, He has created little children, who have no idea what's going on and can only express themselves by helpless crying: He has made the poor savages, with nothing better than the natural law to live by; and He is content to forget His dignity and come into their hearts too—these are the wild flowers that delight Him by their simplicity. It is by such condescension that God shows His infinite greatness. The sun's light, that plays on the cedar trees, plays on each tiny flower as if it were the only one in existence; and in the same way our Lord takes a special interest in each soul, as if there were no other like it. Everything conspires for the good of each individual soul, just as the march of the seasons is designed to make the most insignificant daisy unfold its petals on the day appointed for it.

Dear Mother, you must be wondering by now what all this is leading up to; not a word yet to suggest that I am telling the story of my life! But, you see, you told me to write down, without reserve, all the thoughts which came into my mind, and it isn't exactly an account of my life that I mean to write; these are the thoughts which occur to me about the graces which God in His mercy has seen fit to grant me. I am now at a moment of my life when I can afford to look back at the past. The fire of sufferings, outward and inward, has brought me to maturity; I am like a flower that can lift its head, refreshed, after the storm has passed by. I can read my own experience in the words of the twenty-second Psalm: "The Lord is my shepherd; how can I lack anything? He gives me a resting place where there is green pasture, leads me out to the cool water's brink, refreshed and content. As in honor pledged, by sure paths He leads me: dark be the valley about my path, hurt I fear none while thou, Lord, art with me." To me, the Lord has always been "pitying and gracious, patient and rich in mercy" (Ps 102:8).

What happiness, Mother, to "put the Lord's mercies on record" with you at my side! It's for you only that I mean to write down the story of the little flower Jesus has picked, so I can talk to you quite freely, without any qualms about my style, or about wandering away from the point so often. A mother's instinct can always understand, even when her child can only talk baby language; and you, Mother, who had the shaping of my heart and gave it to Jesus, surely you will be able to understand, and to guess what I mean.

If a wild flower could talk, I imagine it would tell us quite candidly about all God has done for it; there would be no point in hushing up His gifts to it, out of mock humility, and pretending that it was ugly, that it had no smell, that the sun had robbed it of its bloom, or the wind broken its stem, knowing that all that wasn't true. Anyhow, this isn't going to be the autobiography of a flower like that. On the contrary, I'm delighted to be able to put them on record, the favors our Lord has shown me, all quite undeserved. I fully realize that there was nothing about me which could have claimed His divine attention; anything which is good in me is the effect of His mercy—that and nothing else.

It was He that chose the soil I was to grow in—holy ground, all steeped (you might say) in the scent of purity. He saw to it that eight lilies of dazzling whitness should grow up there before me. Even so, His little flower must be lovingly protected from the pestilential airs of worldliness; He would transplant it, when its petals were only just beginning to open, to Mount Carmel—a place already perfumed by the scent of two lilies that had blessed her springtide with their gentle companionship. It is seven years now since that flower took root in the garden where the Lover of Souls had planted it; and now there are *three* lilies to lift their heads close by; a fourth is unfolding, still under the watchful care of Jesus, not far away. And what of our parents, the blessed stock from which we all sprang? They have been reunited, for all eternity, in their heavenly country, and found there, waiting for them, those other four lilies that never unfolded to earthly eyes. May Jesus be merciful to us, who are still exiles here, and not leave us long on this alien shore; soon, soon may the lily plant be complete in heaven!

So far, Mother, I've just been giving a brief summary of the blessings God has granted me; now I must talk about my childhood in detail. Anybody else would find it a dull story, but you, with your mother's heart, will find something there that appeals to you. Besides, the memories I'm going to conjure up are your memories as well as mine; my childhood was passed in your near neighborhood, and I had the happiness to claim the same parents—parents you couldn't have matched anywhere; the same loving care surrounded both of us. May they have a blessing to spare for the youngest of their children, and help her to set on record the story of the divine mercies.

Modern Papal Pronouncements

PREFACE

To understand the Catholic Church, one must know more than the essential dogmas which constitute her faith. For the Church exists in the world of time, and faith is always seeking further understanding, always meeting new demands for action. This aspect of the Church, her fresh insights and her adaptation to changing social conditions, is manifested in every age in the teaching of her bishops—especially in the pronouncements of their primate, the Bishop of Rome.

The selections which follow do not exhaust modern papal teaching; they rather suggest the extraordinary range of papal concern, which extends from the scientific study of Scripture to the field of entertainment. Most of these excerpts are from encyclicals, that is, from letters written by the Pope to his brother bishops and their flocks throughout the world. Several are statements made to specialized audiences in Rome. One is an example of the Church's solemn and infallible teaching: the declaration that Mary's bodily Assumption is an article of Catholic faith.

These documents are evidence of both the ancient faith and the modern problems of the Church. Those who share that faith and face those problems read these documents not as facile solutions to complicated issues, but as authoritative guidance and sympathetic encouragement in their effort to reach a more mature understanding of Catholicism and its exigencies.

Christian Marriage

What was decreed and constituted in respect to marriage by the authority of God, has been more fully and more clearly handed down to us, by tradition and the written Word, through the apostles, those heralds of the laws of God. To the apostles, indeed, as our masters, are to be referred the doctrines which "our holy Fathers, the councils, and the tradition of the Universal Church have always taught" (Trent), namely, that Christ our Lord raised marriage to the dignity of a sacrament; that to husband and wife, guarded and strengthened by the heavenly grace which His merits gained for them, He gave power to attain holiness in the married state; and that, in a wondrous way, making marriage an example of the mystical union between Himself and His Church, He not only perfected that love which is according to nature, but also made the natural union of one man with one woman far more perfect through the bond of heavenly love. Paul says to the Ephesians: "Husbands, love your wives, as Christ also loved the Church and delivered Himself up for it, that He might sanctify it. . . .

So also ought men to love their wives as their own bodies. . . . For no man ever hated his own flesh, but nourisheth and cherisheth it, as also Christ doth the Church; because we are members of His body, of His flesh, and of His bones. For this cause shall a man leave His father and mother, and shall cleave to his wife, and they shall be two in one flesh. This is a great sacrament; but I speak in Christ and in the Church" (Eph 5:25-32). In like manner from the teaching of the apostles we learn that the unity of marriage and its perpetual indissolubility, the indispensable conditions of its very origin, must, according to the command of Christ, be holy and inviolable without exception. Paul says again: "To them that are married, not I but the Lord commandeth that the wife depart not from her husband; and if she depart, that she remain unmarried or be reconciled to her husband" (1 Cor 7:10-11). And again: "A woman is bound by the law as long as her husband liveth; but if her husband die, she is at liberty" (1 Cor 7:39). It is for these reasons that marriage "is a great sacrament"; "honorable in all" (Heb 13:14); holy, pure, and to be reverenced as a type and symbol of most high mysteries.

Furthermore, the Christian perfection and completeness of marriage are not comprised in those points only which have been mentioned. For, first, there has been vouchsafed to the marriage union a higher and nobler purpose than was ever previously given to it. By the command of Christ, it not only looks to the propagation of the human race, but to the bringing forth of children for the Church, "fellow citizens with the saints, and the domestics of God" (Eph 2:19), so that "a people might be born and brought up for the worship and religion of the true God and our Saviour Jesus Christ" (Roman Catechism).

Secondly, the mutual duties of husband and wife have been defined, and their several rights accurately established. They are bound, namely, to have such feelings for one another as to cherish always very great mutual love, to be ever faithful to their marriage vow, and to give one another an unfailing and unselfish help. The husband is the chief of the family and the head of the wife. The woman, because she is flesh of his flesh, and bone of his bone, must be subject to her husband and obey him; not, indeed, as a servant, but as a companion, so that her obedience shall be wanting in neither honor nor dignity. Since the husband represents Christ, and since the wife represents the Church, let there always be, both in him who commands and in her who obeys, a heaven-born love guiding in their respective duties. For "the husband is the head of the wife; as Christ is the head of the Church. . . . Therefore, as the Church is subject to Christ, so also let wives be to their husbands in all things" (Eph 5:23-24). . . .[1]

●

[1] From the Encyclical Letter of Pope Leo XIII, *Arcanum divinae sapientiae,* on Christian Marriage, Feb. 10, 1880; authorized English translation from Paulist Press edition (New York: Paulist Press, 1942) pp. 7-9.

The Church and Education

The proper and immediate end of Christian education is to co-operate with divine grace in forming the true and perfect Christian, that is, to form Christ Himself in those regenerated by baptism, according to the emphatic expression of the Apostle: "My little children, of whom I am in labor again, until Christ be formed in you" (Gal 4:19). For the true Christian must live a supernatural life in Christ: "Christ who is your life" (Col 3:4) and display it in all his actions: "That the life also of Jesus may be made manifest in our mortal flesh" (2 Cor 4:11).

For precisely this reason, Christian education takes in the whole aggregate of human life, physical and spiritual, intellectual and moral, individual, domestic, and social, not with a view of reducing it in any way, but in order to elevate, regulate, and perfect it, in accordance with the example and teaching of Christ.

Hence the true Christian, product of Christian education, is the supernatural man who thinks, judges, and acts constantly and consistently in accordance with right reason illumined by the supernatural light of the example and teaching of Christ; in other words, to use the current term, the true and finished man of character. For it is not every kind of consistency and firmness of conduct based on subjective principles that makes true character, but only constancy in following the eternal principles of justice, as is admitted even by the pagan poet when he praises as one and the same "the man who is just and firm of purpose" (Horace). And on the other hand, there cannot be full justice except in giving to God what is due to God, as the true Christian does.

The scope and aim of Christian education as here described appears to the worldly as an abstraction, or rather as something that cannot be attained without the suppression or dwarfing of the natural faculties, and without a renunciation of the activities of the present life, and hence inimical to social life and temporal prosperity, and contrary to all progress in letters, arts, and sciences, and all the other elements of civilization. To a like objection raised by the ignorance and the prejudice of even cultured pagans of a former day, and repeated with greater frequency and insistence in modern times, Tertullian has replied as follows: "We are not strangers to life. We are fully aware of the gratitude we owe to God, our Lord and Creator. We reject none of the fruits of His handiwork; we only abstain from their immoderate or unlawful use. We are living in the world with you; we do not shun your forum, your markets, your baths, your shops, your factories, your stables, your places of business and traffic. We take ship with you and we serve in your armies, we are farmers and merchants with you; we interchange skilled labor and display our works in public for your service. How we can seem unprofitable to you with whom we live and of whom we are, I know not."

The true Christian does not renounce the activities of this life, he does not stunt his natural faculties; but he develops and perfects them, by co-ordinating them with the supernatural. He thus ennobles what is merely natural in life and secures for it new strength in the material and temporal order, no less than in the spiritual and eternal. . . .

And first of all, education belongs pre-eminently to the Church, by reason of a double title in the supernatural order, conferred exclusively upon her by God Himself; absolutely superior therefore to any other title in the natural order.

The first title is founded upon the express mission and supreme authority to teach given her by her divine Founder: "All power is given to me in heaven and in earth. Going, therefore, teach ye all nations, baptizing them in the name of the Father, and of the Son, and of the Holy Ghost, teaching them to observe all things whatsoever I have commanded you, and behold I am with you all days, even to the consummation of the world" (Mt 18:18-20). Upon this magisterial office Christ conferred infallibility, together with the command to teach His doctrine. Hence the Church "was set by her divine Author as the pillar and ground of truth, in order to teach the divine faith to men, and keep whole and inviolate the deposit confided to her; to direct and fashion men, in all their actions individually and socially, to purity of morals and integrity of life, in accordance with revealed doctrine" (Pius IX).

The second title is the supernatural motherhood in virtue of which the Church, spotless spouse of Christ, generates, nurtures, and educates souls in the divine life of grace, with her sacraments and her doctrine. With good reason then does St. Augustine maintain: "He has not God for father who refuses to have the Church as mother."

Hence it is that in this proper object of her mission, that is, "in faith and morals, God Himself has made the Church sharer in the divine magisterium and, by a special privilege, granted her immunity from error; hence she is the mistress of men, supreme and absolutely sure, and she has inherent in herself an inviolable right to freedom in teaching" (Leo XIII). By necessary consequence the Church is independent of any sort of earthly power as well in the origin as in the exercise of her mission as educator, not merely in regard to her proper end and object, but also in regard to the means necessary and suitable to attain that end. Hence with regard to every other kind of human learning and instruction, which is the common patrimony of individuals and society, the Church has an independent right to make use of it, and above all to decide what may help or harm Christian education. And this must be so, because the Church as a perfect society has an independent right to the means conducive to its end, and because every form of instruction, no less than every human action, has a necessary connection with man's last end, and therefore cannot be withdrawn from the dictates of the divine law, of which the Church is guardian, interpreter, and infallible mistress.

This truth is clearly set forth by Pius X of saintly memory: "Whatever a Christian does even in the order of things of earth, he may not overlook the supernatural; indeed, he must, according to the teaching of Christian wisdom, direct all things towards the supreme good as to his last end; all his actions, besides, in so far as good or evil in the order of morality, that is, in keeping or not with natural and divine law, fall under the judgment and jurisdiction of the Church."

It is worthy of note how a layman, an excellent writer and at the same time a profound and conscientious thinker, has been able to understand well and express exactly this fundamental Catholic doctrine! "The Church does not say that morality belongs purely, in the sense of exclusively, to her; but that it belongs wholly to her. She has never maintained that outside her fold and apart from her teaching, man cannot arrive at any moral truth; she has on the contrary more than once condemned this opinion because it has appeared under more forms than one. She does however say, has said, and will ever say that because of her institution by Jesus Christ, because of the Holy Ghost sent her in His name by the Father, she alone possesses what she has had immediately from God and can never lose, the whole of moral truth, *omnem veritatem,* in which all individual moral truths are included, as well those which man may learn by the help of reason, as those which form part of revelation or which may be deduced from it."

Therefore with full right the Church promotes letters, science, art, in so far as necessary or helpful to Christian education, in addition to her work for the salvation of souls; founding and maintaining schools and institutions adapted to every branch of learning and degree of culture. Nor may even physical culture, as it is called, be considered outside the range of her maternal supervision, for the reason that it also is a means which may help or harm Christian education.

And this work of the Church in every branch of culture is of immense benefit to families and nations which without Christ are lost, as St. Hilary points out correctly: "What can be more fraught with danger for the world than the rejection of Christ?" Nor does it interfere in the least with the regulations of the state, because the Church in her motherly prudence is not unwilling that her schools and institutions for the education of the laity be in keeping with the legitimate dispositions of civil authority; she is in every way ready to cooperate with this authority and to make provision for a mutual understanding, should difficulties arise.

Again it is the inalienable right as well as the indispensable duty of the Church to watch over the entire education of her children, in all institutions, public or private, not merely in regard to the religious instruction there given, but in regard to every other branch of learning and every regulation in so far as religion and morality are concerned.

Nor should the exercise of this right be considered undue interference, but rather maternal care on the part of the Church in protecting her children from the grave danger of all kinds of doctrinal and moral evil. Moreover this watchfulness of the Church not merely can create no real inconvenience, but must on the contrary confer valuable assistance in the right ordering and well-being of families and of civil society; for it keeps far away from youth the moral poison which at that inexperienced and changeable age more easily penetrates the mind and more rapidly spreads its baneful effects. For it is true, as Leo XIII has wisely pointed out, that without proper religious and moral instruction "every form of intellectual culture will be injurious; for young people, not accustomed to respect God, will be unable to bear the restraint of a virtuous life, and never having learned to deny themselves anything, they will easily be incited to disturb the public order. . . ." [1]

[1] From the Encyclical Letter of Pope Pius XI, *Divini illius magistri*, on Christian Education of Youth, Dec. 31, 1929; authorized English translation from Paulist Press edition (New York: Paulist Press, n.d.) pp. 35-37, 7-10.

The Worker and His Wage

Not every kind of distribution of wealth and property among men is such that it can at all, and still less can adequately, attain the end intended by God. *Wealth, therefore, which is constantly being augmented by social and economic progress, must be so distributed amongst the various individuals and classes of society that the common good of all, of which Leo XIII spoke, is thereby promoted. In other words, the good of the whole community must be safeguarded. By these principles of social justice one class is forbidden to exclude the other from a share in the profits.* This sacred law is violated by a wealthy class who, as it were, carefree in their possessions, deem it a just state of things that they should receive everything and the laborer nothing. It is violated also by a propertyless wage-earning class who demand for themselves all the fruits of production, as being the product of their hands. Such men, vehemently incensed against the violation of justice by capitalists, go too far in wrongly vindicating the one right of which they are conscious. They attack and seek to abolish all forms of ownership and all income not obtained by labor, whatever be their naure or whatever function these represent in human society, for the sole reason that they are not acquired by toil. In this connection it must be noted that the appeal made by some to the words of the Apostle: "If any man will not work, neither let him eat" (2 Th 3:10), is as inept as it is unfounded. The Apostle is here passing judgment on those who refuse to work though they could and ought to do so; he admonishes us to use diligently our time and our powers of body and mind, and not to become burdensome to others as long as we are able to provide for ourselves. In no sense does he teach that labor is the sole title to a living or to an income.

Each one, then, must receive his due share, and the distribution of created goods must be brought into conformity with the demands of the common good, that is, of social justice. For every sincere observer is conscious that the vast differences between the few who hold excessive wealth and the many who live in destitution constitute a grave evil in modern society.

This is the aim which Our predecessor urged as the necessary object of our efforts: the uplifting of propertyless, insecure working people. It calls for more emphatic assertion and more insistent repetition on the present occasion because these salutary injunctions of the Pontiff have not infrequently been forgotten, deliberately ignored, or deemed impracticable, though they were both feasible and imperative. They have lost none of their force or wisdom for our own age, even though the horrible "pauperism" of the days of Leo XIII is less prevalent today. The condition of the workingman has indeed been improved and rendered more equitable, particularly in the larger and more civilized states, where the laboring class can no longer be said to be universally in misery and want. But after modern machinery and modern industry had progressed with astonishing speed and taken possession of many newly colonized countries no less than of the ancient civilizations of the Far East, the number of the dispossessed laboring masses, whose groans mount to heaven from these lands, increased beyond all measure.

Moreover, there is the immense army of hired rural laborers, whose condition is depressed in the extreme and who have no hope of ever obtaining "a share in the land." These, too, unless proper and efficacious remedies be applied, will remain perpetually sunk in the proletarian condition.

It is true that there is a formal difference between paupers and propertyless, insecure workers. *Nevertheless, the immense number of propertyless wage earners on the one hand, and the enormous wealth of the fortunate few on the other, are an unanswerable argument that the earthly goods so abundantly produced in this age of industrialism are far from rightly distributed and equitably shared among the various classes of men.*

Every effort, therefore, must be made that at least in future a just share only of the fruits of production be permitted to accumulate in the hands of the wealthy, and that an ample sufficiency be supplied to the workingmen. The purpose is not that these become slack at their work, for man is born to labor as the bird to fly, but that by thrift they may increase their possessions and by the prudent management of the same may be enabled to bear the family burden with greater ease and security, being freed from that hand-to-mouth uncertainty which is the lot of the propertyless and insecure worker. Thus they will not only be in a position to support life's changing fortunes, but will also have the reassuring confidence that when their lives are ended some little provision will remain for those whom they leave behind them.

These ideas were not merely suggested, but stated in frank and open terms by Our predecessor. We emphasize them with renewed insistence in this present encyclical; for unless serious attempts be made, with all energy and without delay, to put them into practice, let nobody persuade himself that the peace and tranquility of human society can be effectively defended against the forces of revolution.

This program cannot, however, be realized unless the propertyless wage earner be placed in such circumstances that by skill and thrift he can acquire a certain moderate ownership, as was already declared by Us, following the footsteps of Our predecessor. But how can he ever save money, except from his wages and by living sparingly, who has nothing but his labor by which to obtain food and the necessities of life? Let us turn, therefore, to the question of wages, which Leo XIII held to be "of very great importance," stating and explaining where necessary its principles and precepts.

And first of all, *those who hold that the wage contract is essentially unjust,* and that in its place must be introduced the contract of partnership, *are certainly in error.* They do a grave injury to Our predecessor, whose encyclical not only admits the "wage contract," but devotes much space to its determination according to the principles of justice.

In the present state of human society, however, *We deem it advisable that the wage contract should, when possible, be modified somewhat by a contract of partnership,* as is already being tried in various ways to the no small gain of wage earners and employers. *In this way wage-earning workers and salaried officials are made sharers in the ownership or the management, or in some way participants in the profits.*

In estimating a just wage, not one consideration alone but many must be taken into account. According to the wise words of Leo XIII: "Before we can decide whether wages are equitable, many things have to be considered." In this way he refuted the irresponsible view of certain writers who declare that this momentous question can easily be solved by the application of a single principle, and that one quite untrue.

For entirely false is the principle, widely propagated today, that the worth of labor and therefore the equitable return to be made for it, should equal the entire value of the product, and that therefore hired labor has a right to demand all that is produced through its work. How erroneous this is appears from what We have written above concerning capital and labor.

The obvious truth is that in labor, especially hired labor, as in ownership, there is a social as well as a personal or individual aspect to be considered. For unless there exists a truly social and organic body; unless labor be protected in the social and juridical order; unless the various occupations, dependent one upon the other, co-operate with and complete each other; unless, above all, *brains, capital, and labor* combine together for common effort, man's toil cannot produce due fruit. Hence, if the social and individual character of labor be overlooked, it can be neither justly appraised nor equitably recompensed.

From this double aspect, growing out of the very notion of human labor, follow important conclusions for the regulation and fixing of wages.

In the first place, the wage paid to the workingman must be sufficient for the support of himself and of his family. It is right, indeed, that the rest of the family contribute according to their power toward the common maintenance, as in the rural home or in the families of many artisans and small shopkeepers. But it is wrong to abuse the tender years of children or the weakness of woman. Mothers should do their work principally at home or near the home, giving their time to domestic cares. Intolerable, and to be opposed with all our strength, is the abuse whereby mothers of families, because of the insufficiency of the father's salary, are forced to engage in gainful occupations outside the domestic walls, to the neglect of their own proper cares and duties, particularly the education of their children.

Every effort must therefore be made that fathers of families receive a wage sufficient to meet adequately ordinary domestic needs. If in the present state of society this is not always feasible, social justice demands that reforms be introduced without delay which will guarantee every adult workingman just such a wage. In this connection We might utter a word of praise for various systems devised and attempted in practice by which an increased wage is paid in view of increased family burdens, or special provision is made for special needs.

The condition of any particular business and of its owner must also come into question in settling the scale of wages; for it is unjust to demand wages so high that an employer cannot pay them without ruin, and without consequent distress among the working people themselves. Should the business make smaller profit on account of bad management, want of enterprise, or out-of-date methods, this is not a just reason for reducing the workingmen's wages. If, however, the business does not make enough money to pay the workman a just wage, either because it is overwhelmed with unjust burdens, or because it is compelled to sell its products at an unjustly low price, those who thus injure it are guilty of grievous wrong; for it is they who deprive the workingmen of the just wage and force them to accept lower terms.

Let employers and employed, therefore, unite in their plans and efforts to overcome all difficulties and obstacles, and let them be aided in this wholesome endeavor by wise measures of the public authority. If the businessman has been reduced to extremes, counsel must be taken whether the business can continue, or whether some other provision should be made for the workers. The guiding spirit in this crucial decision should be one of mutual understanding and Christian harmony between employers and workers.

Finally, the wage scale must be regulated with a view to the economic welfare of the whole people. We have already shown how conducive it is to the common welfare that wage earners of all kinds, by saving that portion of their wages which remains after necessary expenses have been met, attain to the possession of a certain modest fortune. Another point, however, of no less importance must not be overlooked, in these days especially, namely, *that opportunities for work be provided for those who are willing and able to work. This depends in large measure upon the scale of wages,* which multiplies opportunities for work as long as it remains within proper limits, and reduces them if allowed to pass these limits. *All are aware that a rate of wages too low, no less than a rate excessively high, causes unemployment.* Now unemployment, particularly if widespread and of long duration, as We have been forced to witness it during Our pontificate, is a dreadful scourge; it causes misery and temptation to the laborer, ruins the prosperity of nations, and endangers public order, peace, and tranquillity the world over. *To lower or raise wages unduly, with a view to private profit, and with no consideration for the common good, is contrary to social justice,* which demands that by voluntary agreement such a scale of wages be set up, if possible, as to offer to the greatest number opportunities of employment and of securing for themselves suitable means of livelihood.

A right proportion between different wages is also of moment. Intimately connected with this is a reasonable proportion between the prices obtained for the products of the various economic groups, agrarian, industrial, and others. Where this harmonious proportion is kept, the various branches of industry combine and unite into one single organism, and as members of a common body lend one another help and service. For *then only will the economic and social order be soundly established and attain its end, when it secures for all and each those goods which the wealth and resources of nature, technical achievement, and social organization of economic affairs can give.* These goods should be sufficient to supply all needs and an honest livelihood, and to uplift men to that higher level of prosperity and culture which, provided it be used with prudence, is not only no hindrance but is of singular help to virtue. . . .[1]

●

[1] From the Encyclical Letter of Pope Pius XI, *Quadragesimo anno,* on the Reconstruction of the Social Order, May 15, 1931; America Press translation (New York: America Press, n.d.) pp. 19-25.

Pius xi

The Catholic Priesthood

The priest, according to the magnificent definition given by St. Paul, is indeed a man "taken from amongst men," yet "ordained for men in the things that appertain to God" (Heb 5:1): his office is not for human things that pass away, however lofty and valuable these may seem, but for things divine and enduring. These eternal things may, perhaps, through ignorance, be scorned and contemned, or even attacked with diabolical fury and malice, as sad experience has often proved and proves even today; but they always continue to hold the first place in the aspirations, individual and social, of humanity, because the human heart feels irresistibly it is made for God and is restless till it rests in Him. . . .

The Apostle of the Gentiles thus perfectly sums up what may be said of the greatness, the dignity, and the duty of the Christian priesthood: "Let a man so account of us as of the ministers of Christ and the dispensers of the mysteries of God" (1 Cor 4:1). The priest is the minister of Christ, an instrument, that is to say, in the hands of the divine Redeemer. He continues the work of the redemption in all its world-embracing universality and divine efficacy, that work that wrought so marvelous a transformation in the world. Thus the priest, as is said with good reason, is indeed "another Christ"; for, in some way, he is himself a continuation of Christ. "As the Father hath sent me, I also send you" (Jn 20:21) is spoken to the priest, and hence the priest, like Christ, continues to give "glory to God in the highest; and on earth peace to men of good will" (Lk 2:14). . . .

Now a priest is the appointed "dispenser of the mysteries of God" for the benefit of the members of the Mystical Body of Christ, since he is the ordinary minister of nearly all the sacraments—those channels through which the grace of the Saviour flows for the good of humanity. The Christian, at almost every important stage of his mortal career, finds at his side the priest with power received from God, in the act of communicating that grace which is the supernatural life of his soul. Scarcely is he born before the priest, baptizing him, brings him a new birth to a more noble and precious life, a supernatural life, and makes him a son of God and of the Church of Jesus Christ. To strengthen him to fight bravely in spiritual combats, a priest invested with special dignity makes him a soldier of Christ by holy chrism. Then, as soon as he is able to recognize and value the Bread of Angels, the priest gives It to him, the living and life-giving Food come down from heaven. If he fall, the priest raises him up again in the name of God and reconciles him to God with the sacrament of penance. Again, if he is called by God to found a family and to collaborate with Him in the transmission of human life throughout the world, thus increasing the number of the faithful on earth and thereafter the ranks of the elect in heaven, the priest is there to bless his espousals and unblemished love; and when, finally, arrived at the portals of eternity, the Christian feels the need of strength and courage before presenting himself at the tribunal of the divine Judge, the priest with the holy oils anoints the failing members of the sick or dying Christian, and reconsecrates and comforts him. Thus the priest accompanies the Christian throughout the pilgrimage of this life to the gates of heaven. He accompanies the body to its resting place in the grave with rites and prayers of immortal hope. And even beyond the threshold of eternity he follows the soul to aid it with Christian suffrages, if need there be of further purification and alleviation. Thus, from the cradle to the grave the priest is ever beside the faithful, a guide, a solace, a minister of salvation, and a dispenser of grace and blessing.[1]

●

[1] From the Encyclical Letter of Pope Pius XI, *Ad catholici sacerdotii,* on the Catholic Priesthood, Dec. 20, 1935; authorized English translation from NCWC edition (Washington, D.C.: National Catholic Welfare Conference, 1936) pp. 7-9, 11-13.

Contemporary Biblical Study

There is no one who cannot easily perceive that the conditions of biblical studies and their subsidiary sciences have greatly changed within the last fifty years. For, apart from anything else, when Our predecessor published the Encyclical Letter *Providentissimus Deus*, hardly a single place in Palestine had begun to be explored by means of relevant excavations. Now, however, this kind of investigation is much more frequent and, since precise methods and technical skill have been developed in the course of actual experience, it gives us information at once more abundant and more accurate. How much light has been derived from these explorations for the more correct and fuller understanding of the Sacred Books all experts know, as well as all those who devote themselves to these studies. The value of these excavations is enhanced by the discovery from time to time of written documents, which help much towards the knowledge of the languages, letters, events, customs, and forms of worship of most ancient times. And of no less importance is the discovery and investigation, so frequent in our times of papyri which have contributed so much to the knowledge of letters and institutions, both public and private, especially of the time of our Saviour.

Moreover, ancient codices of the Sacred Books have been found and edited with discerning thoroughness; the exegesis of the Fathers of the Church has been more widely and thoroughly examined; in fine, the manner of speaking, relating, and writing in use among the ancients is made clear by innumerable examples. All these advantages which, not without a special design of divine Providence, our age has acquired, are as it were an invitation and inducement to interpreters of the Sacred Literature to make diligent use of this light, so abundantly given, to penetrate more deeply, explain more clearly, and expound more lucidly the divine oracles. . . .

What is the literal sense of a passage is not always as obvious in the speeches and writings of the ancient authors of the East as it is in the works of the writers of our own time. For what they wished to express is not to be determined by the rules of grammar and philology alone, nor solely by the context; the interpreter must, as it were, go back wholly in spirit to those remote centuries of the East and with the aid of history, archeology, ethnology, and other sciences, accurately determine what modes of writing, so to speak, the authors of that ancient period would be likely to use, and in fact did use.

For the ancient peoples of the East, in order to express their ideas, did not always employ those forms or kinds of speech which we use today, but rather those used by the men of their times and countries. What those exactly were, the commentator cannot determine as it were in advance, but only after a careful examination of the ancient literature of the East. The investigation carried out on this point during the past forty or fifty years with greater care and diligence than ever before, has more clearly shown what forms of expression were used in those far-off times, whether in poetic description or in the formulation of laws and rules of life or in recording the facts and events of history. The same inquiry has also clearly shown the special pre-eminence of the people of Israel among all the other ancient nations of the East in their mode of compiling history, both by reason of its antiquity and by reason of the faithful record of the events—qualities which may well be attributed to the gift of divine inspiration and to the peculiar religious purpose of biblical history.

Nevertheless, no one who has a correct idea of biblical inspiration will be surprised to find, even in the sacred writers, as in other ancient authors, certain fixed ways of expounding and narrating, certain definite idioms, especially of a kind peculiar to the Semitic tongues, so-called approximations, and certain hyperbolical modes of expression, nay, at times, even paradoxical, which help to impress the ideas more deeply on the mind. For of the modes of expression which among ancient peoples, and especially those of the East, human language used to express its thought, none is excluded from the Sacred Books, provided the way of speaking adopted in no wise contradicts the holiness and truth of God, as, with his customary wisdom, the Angelic Doctor already observed in these words: "In Scripture divine things are presented to us in the manner which is in common use amongst men."[1] For as the substantial Word of God became like to men in all things "except sin" (Heb 4:15), so the words of God, expressed in human language, are made like to human speech in every respect except error. In this consists that "condescension" of the God of providence which St. John Chrysostom extolled with the highest praise and repeatedly declared to be found in the Sacred Books.

Hence, the Catholic commentator, in order to comply with the present needs of biblical studies, in explaining the Sacred Scripture and in demonstrating and proving its immunity from all error, should also make a prudent use of this means, determine, that is, to what extent the manner of expression or the literary mode adopted by the sacred writer may lead to a correct and genuine interpretation; and let him be convinced that this part of his office cannot be neglected without serious detriment to Catholic exegesis. Not infrequently—to mention only one instance—when some persons reproachfully charge the sacred writers with some historical error or inaccuracy in the recording of facts, on closer examination it turns out to be nothing else than those customary modes of expression and narration peculiar to the ancients which used to be employed in the mutual dealings of social life and which in fact were sanctioned by common usage.

When, then, such modes of expression are met with in the sacred text, which, being meant for men, is couched in human language, justice demands that they be no more taxed with error than when they occur in the ordinary intercourse of daily life. By this knowledge and exact appreciation of the modes of speaking and writing in use among the ancients can be solved many difficulties which are raised against the veracity and historical value of the divine Scriptures, and no less efficaciously does this study contribute to a fuller and more luminous understanding of the mind of the sacred writer.

Let those who cultivate biblical studies turn their attention with all due diligence towards this point and let them neglect none of those discoveries, whether in the domain of archeology or in ancient history or literature, which serve to make better known the mentality of the ancient writers, as well as their manner and art of reasoning, narrating, and writing. In this connection Catholic laymen also should consider that they will not only further profane science, but moreover will render a conspicuous service to the Christian cause, if they devote themselves with all due diligence and application to the exploration and investigation of the monuments of antiquity and contribute, according to their abilities, to the solution of questions hitherto obscure.

For all human knowledge, even the nonsacred, has indeed its own

●

[1] St. Thomas Aquinas, *Comm. in Heb.* 1, 4.

proper dignity and excellence, being a finite participation of the infinite knowledge of God, but it acquires a new and higher dignity and, as it were, a consecration when it is employed to cast a brighter light upon the things of God.[2]

[2] From the Encyclical Letter of Pope Pius XII, *Divino afflante Spiritu,* on the Most Opportune Way to Promote Biblical Studies, Sept. 30, 1943; authorized English translation from NCWC edition (Washington, D.C.: National Catholic Welfare Conference, n.d.) pp. 10, 18-20.

Democracy

To express his own views of the duties and sacrifices that are imposed on him; not to be compelled to obey without being heard: these are two rights of the citizen which find in democracy, as its name implies, their expression.

From the solidity, harmony, and good results produced by this between the citizens and the government one may decide which democracy is really healthy and well balanced, and what is its life energy and power of expansion.

If, then, we consider the extent and nature of the sacrifices demanded of all citizens, especially in our day when the activity of the state is so vast and decisive, the democratic form of government appears to many as a postulate of nature imposed by reason itself.

When, however, people call for "democracy and better democracy," such a demand cannot have any other meaning than to place the citizen ever more in the position to hold his own personal opinion, to express it, and to make it prevail in a fashion conducive to common good.

Hence follows a first conclusion with its practical consequence. The state does not contain in itself and does not mechanically bring together in a given territory a shapeless mass of individuals.

It is and should be in practice the organic and organizing unity of a real people. The people and a shapeless multitude (or, as it is called, "the masses") are two distinct concepts.

The people lives and moves by its own life energy; the masses are inert of themselves and can only be moved from outside. The people lives by the fulness of life in the men that compose it, each of whom—at his proper place and in his own way—is a person conscious of his own responsibility and of his own views.

The masses, on the contrary, wait for the impulse from outside, an easy plaything in the hands of anyone who exploits their instincts and impressions; ready to follow, in turn, today this flag, tomorrow another.

From the exuberant life of a true people, an abundant rich life is diffused in the state and all its organs, instilling into them, with a vigor that is always renewing itself, the consciousness of their own responsibility, the true instinct for the common good.

The elementary power of the masses, deftly managed and employed, the state also can utilize. In the ambitious hands of one or of several who have been artificially brought together for selfish aims, the state itself, with the support of the masses, reduced to the minimum status of a mere machine, can impose its whims on the better part of the real people, the common interest remains seriously and for a long time injured by this process, and the injury is very often hard to heal.

Hence follows clearly another conclusion: the masses—as we have just defined them—are the capital enemy of true democracy and of its ideal of liberty and equality.

In a people worthy of the name the citizen feels within him the consciousness of his personality, of his duties and rights, of his own freedom joined to respect for the freedom and dignity of others.

In a people worthy of the name all inequalities based not on whim but on the nature of things, inequalities of culture, possessions, social standing—without, of course, prejudice to justice and mutual charity—do not constitute any obstacle to the existence and the prevalence of a true spirit of union and brotherhood.

On the contrary, so far from impairing civil equality in any way, they give it its true meaning, namely, that before the state everyone has the right to live honorably his own personal life in the place and under the conditions in which the designs and dispositions of Providence have placed him.

As against this picture of the democratic ideal of liberty and equality in a people's government by honest and farseeing men, what a spectacle is that of a democratic state left to the whims of the masses:

Liberty, from being a moral duty of the individual, becomes a tyrannous claim to give free rein to a man's impulses and appetites to the detriment of others.

Equality degenerates to a mechanical level, a colorless uniformity; the sense of true honor, of personal activity, of respect for tradition, of dignity—in a word, all that gives life its worth—gradually fades away and disappears.

And the only survivors are, on the one hand, the victims deluded by the specious mirage of democracy, naively taken for the genuine spirit of democracy with its liberty and equality; and on the other, the more or less numerous exploiters who have known how to use the power of money and of organization in order to secure a privileged position above the others, and have gained power.[1]

●

[1] From the Christmas Message of Pope Pius XII to the whole world, Dec. 24, 1944; authorized English translation from *Catholic Mind* 43 (1945) 67-69.

Lay Participation
in the Liturgy

We deem it necessary to recall that the priest acts for the people only because he represents Jesus Christ, who is Head of all His members and offers Himself in their stead. Hence, he goes to the altar as the minister of Christ, inferior to Christ but superior to the people. The people, on the other hand, since they in no sense represent the divine Redeemer and are not mediator between themselves and God, can in no way possess the sacerdotal power.

All this has the certitude of faith. However, it must also be said that the faithful do offer the divine Victim, though in a different sense.

This has already been stated in the clearest terms by some of Our predecessors and some Doctors of the Church. "Not only," says Innocent III of immortal memory, "do the priests offer the sacrifice, but also all the faithful: for what the priest does personally by virtue of his ministry, the faithful do collectively by virtue of their intention." [1] We are happy to recall one of St. Robert Bellarmine's many statements on this subject. "The sacrifice," he says, "is principally offered in the person of Christ. Thus the oblation that follows the consecration is

●

[1] *De sacro altaris mysterio* 3, 6.

a sort of attestation that the whole Church consents in the oblation
made by Christ, and offers it along with Him." [2]

Moreover, the rites and prayers of the Eucharistic Sacrifice signify
and show no less clearly that the oblation of the Victim is made by
the priests in company with the people. For not only does the sacred
minister, after the oblation of the bread and wine when he turns to
the people, say the significant prayer: "Pray, brethren, that my sacrifice
and yours may be acceptable to God the Father almighty"; but also the
prayers by which the divine Victim is offered to God are generally expressed in the plural number, and in these it is indicated more than
once that the people also participate in this august Sacrifice inasmuch
as they offer the same. The following words, for example, are used:
"For whom we offer, or who offer up to thee. . . . We therefore beseech thee, O Lord, to be appeased and to receive this offering of our
bounden duty, as also of thy whole household. . . . We thy servants,
as also thy whole people . . . do offer unto thy most excellent majesty,
of thine own gifts bestowed upon us, a pure victim, a holy victim, a
spotless victim."

Nor is it to be wondered at, that the faithful should be raised to
this dignity. By the waters of baptism, as by common right, Christians
are made members of the Mystical Body of Christ the Priest, and by
the "character" which is imprinted on their souls they are appointed
to give worship to God. Thus they participate, according to their
condition, in the priesthood of Christ.

In every age of the Church's history, the mind of man, enlightened
by faith, has aimed at the greatest possible knowledge of things divine.
It is fitting, then, that the Christian people should also desire to know
in what sense they are said in the Canon of the Mass to offer up the
sacrifice. To satisfy such a pious desire, then, We shall here explain
the matter briefly and concisely.

First of all, the more extrinsic explanations are these: it frequently
happens that the faithful assisting at Mass join their prayers alternately
with those of the priest, and sometimes—a more frequent occurrence
in ancient times—they offer to the ministers at the altar bread and wine
to be changed into the body and blood of Christ, and, finally, by their
alms they get the priest to offer the divine Victim for their intentions.

But there is also a more profound reason why all Christians, especially those who are present at Mass, are said to offer the sacrifice.

In this most important subject it is necessary, in order to avoid giving
rise to a dangerous error, that we define the exact meaning of the word
"offer." The unbloody immolation at the words of consecration, when
Christ is made present upon the altar in the state of a Victim, is performed by the priest and by him alone, as the representative of Christ
and not as the representative of the faithful. But it is because the
priest places the divine Victim upon the altar that he offers it to God
the Father as an oblation for the glory of the Blessed Trinity and for

●

[2] *De missa* 1, 27.

the good of the whole Church. Now the faithful participate in the oblation, understood in this limited sense, after their own fashion and in a twofold manner, namely, because they not only offer the sacrifice by the hands of the priest, but also, to a certain extent, in union with him. It is by reason of this participation that the offering made by the people is also included in liturgical worship.

Now it is clear that the faithful offer the sacrifice by the hands of the priest from the fact that the minister at the altar, in offering a sacrifice in the name of all His members, represents Christ, the Head of the Mystical Body. Hence the whole Church can rightly be said to offer up the Victim through Christ. But the conclusion that the people offer the sacrifice with the priest himself is not based on the fact that, being members of the Church no less than the priest himself, they perform a visible liturgical rite; for this is the privilege only of the minister who has been divinely appointed to this office; rather it is based on the fact that the people unite their hearts in praise, impetration, expiation, and thanksgiving with the prayers or intention of the priest, even of the High Priest Himself, so that in the one and same offering of the Victim and according to a visible sacerdotal rite they may be presented to God the Father. It is obviously necessary that the external sacrificial rite should, of its very nature, signify the internal worship of the heart. Now the Sacrifice of the New Law signifies that supreme worship by which the principal Offerer Himself, who is Christ, and, in union with Him and through Him, all the members of the Mystical Body pay God the honor and reverence that are due to Him. . . .

Therefore, they are to be praised who, with the idea of getting the Christian people to take part more easily and more fruitfully in the Mass, strive to make them familiar with the Roman Missal, so that the faithful, united with the priest, may pray together in the very words and sentiments of the Church. They also are to be commended who strive to make the liturgy even in an external way a sacred act in which all who are present may share. This can be done in more than one way, when, for instance, the whole congregation, in accordance with the rules of the liturgy, either answer the priest in an orderly and fitting manner, or sing hymns suitable to the different parts of the Mass, or do both, or finally in high Masses when they answer the prayers of the minister of Jesus Christ and also sing the liturgical chant.

These methods of participation in the Mass are to be approved and commended when they are in complete agreement with the precepts of the Church and the rubrics of the liturgy. Their chief aim is to foster and promote the people's piety and intimate union with Christ and His visible minister and to arouse those internal sentiments and dispositions which should make our hearts become like to that of the High Priest of the New Testament.[3]

●

[3] From the Encyclical Letter of Pope Pius XII, *Mediator Dei*, on the Sacred Liturgy, Nov. 20, 1947; authorized English translation from America Press edition (New York: America Press, 1948) pp. 43-46, 49-50.

The Dogma of the Assumption

The Sacred Writings . . . set the revered Mother of God as it were before our very eyes as most intimately joined to her divine Son and as always sharing His lot. Consequently it seems impossible to think of her, the one who conceived Christ, brought Him forth, gave Him milk, held Him in her arms, and fondled Him at her breast, as being apart from Him in body, even though not in soul. Since our Redeemer is the Son of Mary, He could not do otherwise, as the perfect observer of God's law, than to honor, not only His eternal Father, but also His most beloved Mother. And, since it was within His power to grant her this great honor, to preserve her from the corruption of the tomb, we must believe that He really acted in this way.

We must remember especially that, since the second century, the Virgin Mary has been designated by the holy Fathers as the New Eve, who, although subject to the New Adam, is most intimately associated with Him in that struggle against the infernal foe which, as foretold in the protevangelium, finally resulted in that most complete victory over the sin and death which are always mentioned together in the writings of the Apostle of the Gentiles. Consequently, just as the glorious resurrection of Christ was an essential part and the final sign of this victory, so that struggle which was common to the Blessed Virgin and her divine Son should be brought to a close by the glorification of her virginal body, for the same Apostle says: "when this mortal thing hath put on immortality, then shall come to pass the saying that is written: Death is swallowed up in victory" (1 Cor 15:54).

Hence the revered Mother of God, from all eternity joined in a hidden way with Jesus Christ in one and the same decree of predestination, immaculate in her conception, a most perfect virgin in her divine motherhood, the noble associate of the divine Redeemer who has won a complete triumph over sin and its consequences, was finally granted, as the supreme culmination of her privileges, that she should be preserved free from the corruption of the tomb and that, like her own Son, having overcome death, she might be taken up body and soul to the glory of heaven where, as Queen, she sits in splendor at the right hand of her Son, the immortal King of the ages. . . .

For which reason, after We have poured forth prayers of supplication again and again to God, and have called upon the Spirit of truth, for the glory of Almighty God who has lavished His special affection upon the Virgin Mary, for the honor of her Son, the immortal King of the ages and the victor over sin and death, for the increase of the glory of that same august Mother, and for the joy and exultation of the entire Church; by the authority of our Lord Jesus Christ, of the blessed Apostles Peter and Paul, and by Our own authority, We pronounce, declare, and define it to be a divinely revealed dogma: that the Immaculate Mother of God, the ever-virgin Mary, having completed the course of her earthly life, was assumed body and soul into heavenly glory.

Hence if anyone, which God forbid, should dare willfully to deny or to call into doubt that which We have defined, let him know that he has fallen away completely from the divine and Catholic faith.[1]

●

[1] From the Bull of Pope Pius XII, *Munificentissimus Deus*, proclaiming the dogma of the Assumption, Nov. 1, 1950; authorized English translation from Paulist Press edition (New York: Paulist Press, 1951) pp. 19, 20, 22.

Foreign Missions

Catholic missionaries toiling in a vast field of labor "that the word of the Lord may run its course triumphantly" (2 Th 3:1) are in Our thoughts in a special way on the occasion of the twenty-fifth anniversary of the Encyclical Letter, *Rerum ecclesiae* of Our predecessor of immortal memory, Pius XI, wherein he laid down wise norms for the greater development of Catholic missions. The consideration of the progress this holy cause has made in the intervening years has brought Us no small consolation. As We remarked in an audience on June 24, 1944, to the directors of the Pontifical Missionary Work: "The Catholic missionary movement both in Christian and pagan lands has gained such force and momentum and is of such proportions as perhaps was never witnessed before in the annals of Catholic missions."

In view of the upheavals and dangers of the present time, when not a few peoples are divided by conflicting interests, We consider it very opportune on the present occasion to reiterate Our approval of this work. For missionaries preach to all men the practice of natural and Christian virtues and that brotherly and common fellowship which transcends racial conflicts and national frontiers.

On that occasion when We addressed the directors of the above-mentioned Work, We made the following observations among others: ". . . It is in keeping with your apostolate not to be hampered by any national frontiers; for your work, which unites you in fraternal co-operation, clearly manifests to all that note of the Catholic Church which rejects discord, flees division, and abhors all disputes which agitate nations and sometimes bring them to utter ruin. We refer to that Christian faith and universal Christian charity which transcend all opposing camps and national boundaries and reach out to the ends of the earth. They are the motives that spur each one of you on to reach your goal, which is the establishment of the kingdom of God throughout the whole world." . . .

The object of missionary activity, as all know, is to bring the light of the gospel to new races and to form new Christians. However, the ultimate goal of missionary endeavor, which should never be lost sight of, is to establish the Church on sound foundations among non-Christian peoples and place it under its own native hierarchy.

In a letter which we wrote on August 9 last year to Our beloved son, Cardinal Fumasoni Biondi, Prefect of the S. Congregation of Propaganda Fide, We mentioned the following points among others: "The Church's aim is not the domination of peoples or the gaining of temporal dominions; she is eager only to bring the supernatural light of faith to all peoples, and to promote the interests of civilization and culture and fraternal concord among nations."

In the Apostolic Letter, *Maximum illud,* of Our predecessor of immortal memory, Benedict XV, given in the year 1919, and in the Encyclical Letter, *Rerum ecclesiae,* of Our immediate predecessor of happy memory, Pius XI, it was laid down that the missions should have as the final goal of their activities the establishment of the Church in new territories. And We Ourselves when, as We have said, We received in audience the directors of mission activities in 1944, made the following statement: "The magnanimous and noble purpose which missionaries have is the propagation of the faith in new lands in such a way that the Church may ever become more firmly established in them and as soon as possible reach such a stage of development that it can continue to exist and flourish without the aid of missionary organizations. These missionary organizations do not serve their own ends, but it is their task to use every endeavor to realize the lofty purpose We have already mentioned. When that has been attained, then let them be happy to turn to other fields.

"Wherefore let the missionary take up no permanent abode in those places where the work of the apostolate has reached full development, since it is up to him to evangelize and sanctify the whole world. The missionary's appointed task is to promote Christ's kingdom ever more rapidly in district after district till the last man in the most remote corner of the earth has been reached, and the kingdom of the divine Redeemer who rose triumphant from the dead and to whom is given all power in heaven and on earth is established." . . .

Another end remains to be achieved, and We desire that all should fully understand it. The Church from the beginning down to our own time has always followed this wise practice: let not the gospel on being introduced into any new land destroy or extinguish whatever its people possess that is naturally good, just, or beautiful. For the Church, when she calls people to a higher culture and a better way of life under the inspiration of the Christian religion, does not act like one who recklessly cuts down and uproots a thriving forest. No, she grafts a good scion upon the wild stock that it may bear a crop of more delicious fruit.

Human nature, though owing to Adam's fall it is tainted with original sin, has in itself something that is naturally Christian; and this, if illumined by divine light and nourished by God's grace, can eventually be changed into true and supernatural virtue.

This is the reason why the Catholic Church has neither scorned nor rejected the pagan philosophies. Instead, after freeing them from error and all contamination, she has perfected and completed them by Christian revelation. So likewise the Church has graciously made her own the native art and culture which in some countries is so highly developed. She has carefully encouraged them and has brought them to a point of aesthetic perfection that of themselves they probably would never have attained. By no means has she repressed native customs and traditions but has given them a certain religious significance; she has even transformed their feast days and made them serve to commemorate the martyrs and to celebrate mysteries of the faith.[1]

●

[1] From the Encyclical Letter of Pope Pius XII, *Evangelii praecones* ("Heralds of the Gospel"), June 2, 1951; authorized English translation from Paulist Press edition (New York: Paulist Press, 1951) pp. 3-4, 12-13, 25-26.

The Spirit of Research

That which especially strikes one who gazes at this picture of the universe, so imposing even in this present brief outline, and which is the fruit of long and laborious researches not of just one individual, but rather of entire generations of scholars belonging to the most diverse nations, is not only the gigantic mass of the whole and of its parts, nor merely the harmony of their movements in space, but also the wonders accomplished by the human spirit in unveiling this vast cosmic panorama.

Though man is essentially bound within the narrow limits of bodily conditions, he has exceeded every expectation that the limited power of the human senses at first sight could promise him, and with his intelligence has succeeded in mastering the immense universe.

Truly extraordinary has man's labor been if one considers the starting point of his wonderful climb to the heavens; for the senses, from whose data man necessarily has to start, dispose of a very limited power of knowing, generally restricted to their immediate neighborhood in space and time.

The first accomplishment of the human spirit, therefore, consists in having broken down the narrow enclosure imposed on the senses by the conditions of their very nature. It has done this by inventing means and constructing ingenious instruments which increase beyond all limits both the amplitude and the precision of sense perceptions: the telescope which almost annihilates the enormous distances between the human eye and the remote stars, allowing us, as it were, to reach out and touch them; and the photographic plate which accumulates and preserves the faint light coming to us from the most inaccessible galaxies.

While the human spirit thus gradually increases the power of the senses, it uses these heightened potentialities in order to deepen its researches on nature, thinking up a thousand devices for revealing the most subtle and abstruse phenomena.

In this way it accumulates the tiny defects that are being constantly repeated and builds them up to a perceptible whole and, conversely, it invents instruments like the photoelectric cell and the Wilson cloud chamber for investigating the extremely delicate individual processes involved in radioactive materials and cosmic rays.

The human spirit, by ever more careful scrutiny, finds the laws which rule over energy processes and thus succeeds in converting energy forms which are impervious to the senses, such as electric waves and infrared and ultraviolet rays, into other forms which are directly accessible to precise sense perception.

The human spirit of research questions nature in laboratory experiments and deduces there laws that are valid for the restricted experimental conditions. Not yet satisfied, it then tests these laws and extends their range of application by means of astrophysical observations.

Observational and theoretical knowledge of molecular spectra enables it to venture out into the dense atmosphere of the outer planets and to determine the composition, temperature, and density of these gases.

Taking advantage of the facts and theories of spectroscopic science, it scrutinizes the fixed stars and gathers together an exact body of knowledge concerning the composition, temperature, density, and ionization of their mysterious atmosphere.

With the aid of modern quantum theory, the mind of man reads the script of the spectral lines and is able to state to which elements the lines belong and to explain how they arise, even before it is possible to excite them in the laboratory.

Not even the deep interior of the solar orb escapes the penetrating gaze of the human mind equipped with astrophysical theories; the intelligence of man thus succeeds in following the transformation of matter itself, practically witnessing the nuclear processes which take place in the center of the sun and which compensate for the energy losses due to the escape of solar radiation during billions of years.

Bold and unafraid, the human spirit does not hesitate even before the tremendous cataclysms occurring in a nova or supernova, but measures the immense velocities of the exploding gases and tries to discover the causes of the observed phenomena.

It even retraces the path of the fleeing galaxies back through the billions of years of past time, in order to witness the mighty cosmic processes that took place in the first morning of the creation of the world.

What thing is, then, this spirit of infinitesimal man, physically lost on the ocean of the universe but daring to ask his extremely limited senses to discover the countenance and the history of the boundless universe, and then succeeding in revealing both of them?

Only one answer, strikingly evident, can be given, and that is: The spirit of man belongs to an order of being essentially different from, and superior to, that of matter, even though that matter be of immeasurable mass.

Finally, this question spontaneously presents itself: Will this path, begun by the spirit of man with undisputed honor to himself, be open indefinitely to him in the future, and will it be trod by him unceasingly until he is able to reveal the very last mystery of the universe? Or, on the contrary, is the mystery of nature so stupendous and so hidden that the human spirit, through its own intrinsic limitations and inadequacies, will never succeed in fathoming it completely?

The answer of vigorous minds who have penetrated most deeply into the secrets of the cosmos is quite modest and reserved: We are, they think, at the very beginning; there is a long way still to go and the path will be tirelessly followed; however, it is completely improbable that even the most gifted investigator will ever succeed in recognizing, and much less in solving, the mysteries locked up in the physical universe.

Such mysteries, therefore, postulate and point to the existence of one Spirit who is infinitely superior: the divine creative Spirit who created everything that exists, conserves it in being and governs it, and meanwhile with supreme insight knows and scrutinizes His handiwork, now just as He did at the dawn of the first day of creation. "The spirit of God moved over the waters" (Gn 1:2).

Both happy and transcendent is this meeting of the human spirit and the Spirit of the Creator. We mean a spirit truly divine and not a world soul to be confounded with the universe, as pantheism dreamed of. The universe itself, as perceived by our own experience, rebels against this error, declaring itself to be a composite whole in spite of its dynamic unity, and manifesting, in addition to its undeniable harmonies and beauties, also evident imperfections that are irreconcilable with the divine plenitude of Being.

This divine Spirit is distinct and different from the world but not outside of the world, nor secluded as it were in disdainful isolation and abandoning His own handiworks to themselves, as the deistic theories would have it. Rather, this divine Spirit is present in the world which

He omnipotently creates, conserves, and governs; to Him an essential dependence binds the world in its intimate being and operation.

Moreover, to the mind of the scientist who knows how to find a meaning in the totality of existing reality, this divine Spirit reveals Himself not as the cold cosmos, but as the breath of goodness and love which pervades all and explains all, and which in a particular way concentrates itself and reveals itself in the human creature made to His own image and likeness. Hence it is that this divine Spirit does not disdain to make man the constant object of His ineffable loving operation, such as the redemption by means of the mystery of His Incarnation.

The subsequent development of man's concepts of the universe—which has rightly overturned the ancient geocentric and anthropocentric ideas, has contracted our planet to the dimensions of microscopic stardust, and has shrunk man to the size of an atom on this bit of dust, confining both in a corner of the universe—does not constitute an obstacle, as some have claimed, in discussing the mystery of the Incarnation, either for the love or the omnipotence of Him who is pure spirit and as such possesses an infinite superiority to matter, whatever be its cosmic dimensions in space, time, mass, and energy.

And so, besides the profound esteem which We cherish for your science and for all other sciences, a further motive, looking toward higher and universal horizons, incites Us to formulate these good wishes for you.

May the modern conception of astronomical science, which has been the goal of so many great scholars of the past, like Copernicus, Galileo, Kepler, and Newton, remain still fruitful of further marvelous progress in modern astrophysics; and, thanks to the peaceful collaboration of which the International Astronomical Union is a shining example, may the astronomical picture of the universe become ever more and more perfect.

And in order that the eternal light of God may guide and illuminate your studies, which are directed toward revealing the traces of His perfection and toward hearing the echoes of His harmonies, We invoke on all here present the celestial favors, in pledge of which may there descend upon you Our Apostolic Benediction.[1]

●

[1] From an address of Pope Pius XII, *The Progress of Astronomy*, to the World Astronomical Congress, Sept. 7, 1952; authorized English translation from *Catholic Mind* 50 (1952) 745-48.

War and Peace

If unpleasant realities force Us to set forth the terms of the struggle in clear language, no one can properly accuse Us of favoring the stiffening of opposing blocks and still less of having in some fashion abandoned that mission of peace which flows from our Apostolic office. Rather, if We kept silence, We would have to fear the judgment of God. We remain closely allied to the cause of peace, and God alone knows how much We yearn to be able to announce it in full and happy tones with the angels of Christmas. But precisely in order to protect it from the present threats, We must point out where the danger lies, the tactics of its enemies, and what marks them as such. Not otherwise did the newborn Son of God, Himself infinite goodness, unhesitatingly draw clear lines of demarcation and face death on behalf of the truth.

We are convinced that today too, in the face of an enemy determined to impose on all peoples, in one way or another, a special and intolerable way of life, only the unanimous and courageous behavior of all who live the truth and the good can preserve peace and will preserve it. It would be a fatal error to repeat what, in similar circumstances, happened during the years preceding the Second

World War, when all the threatened nations, and not merely the smallest, sought their safety at the expense of others, using them as shields, so to speak, and even seeking very questionable economic and political advantages from their neighbors' suffering. In the end all were together overwhelmed in the holocaust.

Hence, a definite need of this period—a means of insuring the whole world's peace and a fruitful share of its goods, a force which embraces, too, the peoples of Asia, Africa, and the Near East, including Palestine with its Holy Places—is the restoring of European solidarity. But this unity is not assured until all the associated nations realize that the political and economic defeats of one can nowhere in the long run result in true gains for the others. This unity is not strong, as far as the forming of public opinion is concerned, if in the hour of common peril criticism, even though justified, of one nation's actions is expressed by the other with such onesidedness as to cause doubt that any bond of union at all remains. A good course of action can never be had through mere sentiment. Much less can a true political course for today be maintained with the sentiments of yesterday and the day before. Under such influence it would be impossible to judge correctly certain important questions, such as military service, weapons, and war.

Present-day conditions, which find no counterparts in the past, should be clear to everyone. There is no longer room for doubt concerning aims and methods which rely on tanks, when these latter noisily crash over borders and sow death in order to force civilian people into a pattern of life they explicitly detest, when, destroying as it were the stages of possible negotiation and mediation, the threat is made of using atomic weapons to gain certain demands, be they justified or not. It is clear that in the present circumstances there can be verified in a nation the situation wherein, every effort to avoid war being expended in vain, war—for effective self-defense and with the hope of a favorable outcome against unjust attack—could not be considered unlawful.

If, therefore, a body representative of the people and a government —both having been chosen by free elections—in a moment of extreme danger decides, by legitimate instruments of internal and external policy, on defensive precautions, and carries out the plans which they consider necessary, it does not act immorally. Therefore, a Catholic citizen cannot invoke his own conscience in order to refuse to serve and fulfil those duties the law imposes. On this matter we feel that We are in perfect harmony with Our predecessors, Leo XIII and Benedict XV, who never denied that obligation, but lamented the headlong armaments-race and the moral dangers accompanying barracks life, and urged, as We do likewise, general disarmament as an effective remedy.

There are, then, occasions and times in the life of nations in which only recourse to higher principles can establish clearly the boundaries between right and wrong, between what is lawful and what is immoral, and bring peace to consciences faced with grave decisions. It is, therefore, consoling that in some countries, amid today's debates, men are talking about conscience and its demands.

This shows that they have not forgotten that social life is saved from chaos only insofar as it permits itself to be supported by absolute norms and an absolute end. It shows that they implicitly condemn those who believe that they can resolve the questions of human coexistence on the basis of good external appearances and with a practical view, aiming to act according to where interest and power may be found in individual cases.

Although the program which is at the foundation of the United Nations aims at the realization of absolute values in the coexistence of peoples, the recent past has shown that false realism is succeeding in prevailing in not a few of its members, even when it is a question of restoring respect for these same values of human society, openly trampled upon. The unilateral view which tends to work in the various circumstances only according to personal interest and power is succeeding in bringing it about that accusations of destroying the peace are treated very differently, and thus the different degree of gravity which in these cases, taken individually, should be judged in the light of absolute values, is forthwith completely perverted.

No one expects or demands the impossible, not even from the United Nations. But one should have a right to expect that their authority should have had its weight, at least through observers, in the places in which the essential values of man are in extreme danger.

Although the United Nations' condemnation of the grave violations of the rights of men and entire nations is worthy of recognition, one can nevertheless wish that, in similar cases, the exercise of their rights, as members of this organization, be denied to states which refuse even the admission of observers—thus showing that their concept of state sovereignty threatens the very foundations of the United Nations. This organization ought also to have the right and the power of forestalling all military intervention of one state in another, whatever the pretext under which it is effected, and also the right and power of assuming, by means of a sufficient police force, the safeguarding of order in the state which is threatened.

If We allude to these defects, it is because We desire to see strengthened the authority of the United Nations, especially for effecting general disarmament which We have so much at heart and on which We have already spoken in other discourses. In fact, only in the ambit of an institution like the United Nations can the promise of individual nations to reduce armament, especially to abandon the production and use of certain arms, be mutually exchanged under the strict obligation of international law. Likewise, only the United Nations is at present in a position to exact the observance of this obligation by assuming effective control of the armaments of all nations without exception. Its exercise of aerial observation will assure certain and effective knowledge of production and military preparedness for war with relative ease, while avoiding the disadvantages which the presence of foreign troops in a country can give rise to.[1]

●

[1] From the Christmas Message of Pope Pius XII to the whole world, Dec. 23, 1956; authorized English translation from *Catholic Mind* 55 (1957) 177-80.

Communication Arts

The marvelous technical inventions which are the boast of the men of our generation, though they spring from human intelligence and industry, are nevertheless the gifts of God, our Creator, from whom are all good gifts: "for He has not only brought forth creatures, but sustains and fosters them once created" (St. John Chrysostom).

Of these inventions, some increase and multiply the strength and power of men. Others improve their conditions of life. Others still— and these particularly concern the mind—reach the mass of the people themselves, either directly or through the pictures and sounds they produce, conveying to them, in a form easily understood, news, thoughts, and instruction of all kinds; and by these means they provide, as it were, food for the mind, especially during the hours of rest and recreation.

With regard to this last type of invention, in our own age the greatest progress has been achieved in the arts connected with motion pictures, radio and television.

From the time when these arts first came into use, the Church welcomed them, not only with great joy but also with a motherly care and watchfulness, having in mind to protect her children from every danger as they set out on this new path of progress.

This watchful care springs from the mission she has received from the divine Saviour Himself; for, as is clear to all, these new forms of art have a very great influence on the manner of thinking and acting of individuals and of society.

There is, in addition, another reason why the Church considers a matter of this kind to be particularly her concern; she has the duty of announcing to all men a message which is more urgent than any other. This is the message of eternal salvation; a message unrivaled in its richness and power; a message, in fine, which all men of every race and every age must accept and embrace, according to the saying of the Apostle of the Gentiles: "To me, the least of all the saints, is given this grace, to preach among the Gentiles the unsearchable riches of Christ, and to enlighten all men that they may see what is the dispensation of the mystery which hath been hidden from eternity in God, who created all things" (Eph 3:8-9). . . .

Since the Church is the teacher of the doctrine which leads to salvation and has all that is necessary for the attainment of holiness, she is exercising an inviolable right when she teaches what has been committed to her by divine command. It ought, therefore, to be the duty of all public officials to recognize this sacred right, so that the Church should have ready access to those arts by which she may spread truth and virtue. Indeed, all true and active sons of the Church, since they recognize the priceless gift of the redemption, are bidden to ensure, to the extent of their power, that the Church may be free to use these technical discoveries in so far as they may assist the sanctification of souls.

In asserting and claiming these rights for the Church, it is not, of course, Our desire to deny to the state the right of spreading by the same means the news and teachings that are necessary or useful for the common good of human society.

And further, let it be permitted even to individual citizens—due regard being paid to actual circumstances and the safeguarding of principles which promote the common good—to contribute according to their capacity to the enriching and development of their own and others' intellectual and spiritual culture.

Contrary, however, to Christian teaching and the principal end of these arts is the will and intention of those who desire to use these inventions exclusively for the advancement and propagation of political measures or to achieve economic ends, and who treat this noble calling as if it were a mere trade or business. In like manner, approval cannot be given to the false principles of those who assert and claim freedom to depict and propagate anything and everything, even though in these past years both the kind and the extent of the damage to bodies and souls which is rooted in these principles have become very evident.

There is no question here of the true liberty of which We have spoken above, but rather of an uncontrolled license, disregarding all precaution, of communicating with others anything at all, even though it be contrary to sound morals and can result in serious danger to souls.

The Church encourages and supports everything which truly concerns a fuller enrichment of the mind—for she is the patron and foster mother of human knowledge and the noble arts. Therefore she cannot permit the violation of those principles and laws which direct and govern man in his path to God, his final end.

Let no one, then, be surprised if in this matter, where many reservations are necessary, the Church acts with due forethought and discretion, according to that saying of the Apostle: "But prove all things: hold fast that which is good. From all appearance of evil refrain yourselves" (1 Th 5:21-22).

Those, therefore, are certainly to be blamed who openly declare that the public communication even of matters which impede, or are directly opposed to, principles of morality should be encouraged and carried out so long as the presentation is in accord with the laws of the liberal or technical arts.

In a short discourse, on the occasion of the fifth centenary of the death of Fra Angelico, We recalled to the minds of Our hearers that "it is true that an explicitly moral or religious function is not demanded of art as art." But "if artistic expression, whether of words, music, or images, is cast in false, empty, and confused forms not in harmony with the Creator's design; if, rather than lifting mind and heart to noble sentiments, it stirs the baser passions, it might perhaps find welcome among some people, but only by nature of its novelty, a quality not always of value, or because of that slight measure of truth which will be found in anything. But such an art would degrade itself, denying its primary and essential element: it would not be universal and perennial as is the human spirit to which it is addressed." [1] . . .

What we have written has doubtless more force when it is a question of imparting instruction. Documentary films, radio broadcasts, and television for schools provide ideas and open up new possibilities here, not only with regard to the young, but also for those of mature years. Yet every care must be taken that the lessons taught are in no way contrary to the Church's doctrine and its sacred rights, or impede or frustrate the due education of the young within the home circle. Similarly, it is to be hoped that these new communications arts, whether exercised by private citizens or controlled by rulers of states, will not spread doctrines that contain no mention of God's name and take no account of His divine law.

We are fully aware, alas, that in some nations, where atheistic com-

●

[1] Address on the occasion of the fifth centenary of the death of Fra Angelico, Apr. 20, 1955; *Acta apostolicae sedis* 47 (1955) 291-92.

munism reigns, these methods of telecommunication are used in the schools to root out all religious ideas from the mind. One who considers this situation calmly and without prejudice cannot fail to see that the consciences of children and youths, deprived of divine truth, are being oppressed in a new and subtle way, since they are unable to learn the truth revealed by God, which, as our Redeemer declared, makes us free. This constitutes a new and cunning attack on religion.

But we earnestly desire, Venerable Brethren, that these technical instruments, by which eyes and ears are easily and pleasantly attracted to events happening far away, should be employed to a particular end, namely, to provide men with a broader cultural background, with the knowledge necessary for the fulfilment of their duties, and above all with Christian principles. For if these principles are neglected, there can be no progress worthy of the name, even in merely human matters.

We desire therefore, to pay due tribute of praise to all those teachers and educators who, whether by films or radio broadcasting or television, direct their efforts toward this most honorable goal.

Further, it must be noted that apart from the published news and the instructions delivered, these new arts can contribute considerably towards the true good of men by shows as well. For the programs usually offer not only entertainment and news, but also something that contributes to mental culture.

With complete justice, then, Our predecessor of happy memory, Pius XI, called film theaters the "schools of events." [2] For they can be called schools in this sense, that to spectacle is added dramatic action in which vivid pictures are synchronized with dialog and music in a fascinating manner, with the result that they reach not only the intelligence and other faculties, but the whole man, and, in some way, link him to themselves and seem to sweep him into a participation in the plot presented.

Though the arts of the motion pictures, radio, and television include in some fashion various types of spectacle already long in use, yet each employs a new technique, and thus a new kind of spectacle is produced, aimed, not at a small and select audience, but at vast throngs of men differing in age, way of life, and culture.

In order, then, that under these conditions shows may be able to achieve their proper purpose, it is essential that the minds and inclinations of the spectators be rightly trained and educated, so that they may not only understand the form proper to each of the arts, but especially that they may be guided in this matter by a right conscience. Thus they will be enabled to weigh and pass mature judgment on the various items which the film or television or radio puts before them and not, as frequently happens, be lured and arbitrarily swept away by their power and attractiveness.

●

[2] Encyclical Letter, *Vigilanti cura*, June 29, 1936; *Acta apostolicae sedis* 28 (1936) 255.

If there is lacking this mental training and formation, enlightened by Christian teaching, then neither reasonable pleasures, which "everyone readily admits are necessary for all who are involved in the business and troubles of life," [3] nor the progress of mental development can be kept safe.

The sound policy of those Catholics who, especially in recent years, have understood the need to educate the spectators in this way is most praiseworthy. And several plans have been launched which aim at stimulating both youths and grownups to examine adequately and competently the benefits and the dangers of these shows, and to arrive at a balanced judgment on them.

This, however, should not provide an excuse for attending shows which are contrary to right morals. Rather, it should lead to pointing out and choosing only those which in regard to religion and the moral law are in accord with the Church's teaching and which conform to the instructions issued by the ecclesiastical offices in this matter.

If such plans, as We trust will be the case, follow pedagogical principles and right rules of mental development, We not only give them Our approval, but also heartily commend them; and hence We desire them to be introduced into schools of every type, Catholic Action groups, and parish societies.

Right training and education of the spectators in this fashion will ensure, on the one hand, a lessening of the dangers which can threaten harm to morals, and, on the other hand, enable Christians through the new knowledge they acquire, to raise their minds to a contemplation of heavenly truths.

While We are on this point, We should like particularly to praise those preachers of the divine word who make a wise use of motion pictures, radio, and television to assist them in fulfilling their duty of preserving the moral integrity of those to whom they minister and leading toward the path of truth. Thus they share with them the genuinely salutary benefits of the inventions which our times have introduced. We therefore desire that those who wield authority either in Church or state should in a special way support the activity and enterprise of these preachers.[4]

●

[3] *Ibid.*, p. 254.
[4] From the Encyclical Letter of Pope Pius XII, *Miranda prorsus*, on Films, Radio, and TV, Sept. 8, 1957; authorized English translation from *Catholic Mind* 55 (1957) 539-40, 545-46, 549-51.

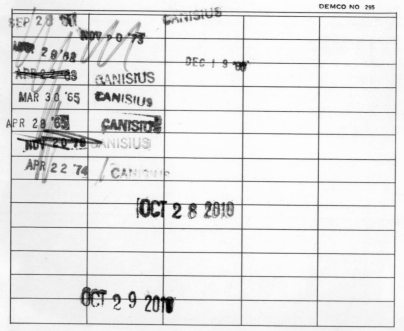

Date Due

DEMCO NO 295